KU-053-006

Mini & Me

Michael Cooper

Ziji

Copyright © Michael Cooper 2013

The right of Michael Cooper to be identified as the author of this work
has been asserted in accordance with sections 77 and 78 of the Copyright,
Designs and Patents Act 1988.

All rights reserved. No part of this publication may be reproduced, stored
in a retrieval sytem, or transmitted in any form or by any means, electronic,
mechanical, photocopying, recording, or otherwise, without the prior
permission of both the copyright owner and the above publisher of this book.

Published by Ziji Publishing Ltd.
www.zijipublishing.com

Distributed by Turnaround Distribution Services Ltd.
www.turnaround-uk.com
Telephone 020 8829 3000

ISBN 978-1-908628-06-0

Printed and bound in Great Britain by CPI Group (UK) Ltd, Croydon, CR0 4YY

Your children are not your children.
They are the sons and daughters of Life's longing for itself.
They come through you but not from you,
And though they are with you yet they belong not to you.

Khalil Gibran

North Ayrshire Libraries	
10035453 X	
Askews & Holts	01-Aug-2019
364.164	£11.99
	SK

CANCELLED

PROLOGUE

There was only one temptation and I was fighting every urge to indulge it, whilst never taking my eyes off that box. It was quite simply impossible to walk away for there was nothing, nothing in my thinking that had space for it. I was oblivious to everything. My mum could have returned at any moment yet I hadn't given it a second's thought; my dad could have returned from work, an even scarier thought, but I simply couldn't find the time to locate such fears.

That house had to go. Ugliness seeped from every crack in the walls, and each flake of paint bore witness to the cowardly betrayal that prevented growth through a brutal and vengeful coalition.

I stepped out of the pantry and picked up a chair, which I dragged back inside. I hurriedly climbed up and grabbed the matches, then climbed back down again. My hands were a little shaky but I opened the box, it was full.

I returned to the lounge, not bothering to bring the chair, it wasn't even a consideration, my thoughts too deeply embedded inside that box. Having taken the decision, there was no room for hesitation.

My mind raced; I wanted it finished, wanted to be out of there. The act itself held no joy, no fascination, it was merely protection, a statement of intent that allowed me, at least in the moment, to bully the bullies. Their games were institutionally contrived and uniformly administered and my parents had their backing for they read from the same manual. There was no escape unless I attempted to manufacture one. Something had to give, someone had to bend and I was damned sure it wasn't going to be me. I ran frantically from room to room looking for something combustible.

I found a cupboard that housed a huge pile of old newspapers, perfect! I began stuffing them down the sides of the sofa and the armchairs and without any hesitation, lit them. Such was my haste, I became more and more disorganised, standing there with smoke billowing around me as I tried to decide what to do. The curtains were next as I became more haphazard and chaotic. As they blazed away, I stood watching, satisfied that I would never see that place again. I climbed the stairs in order to make my exit.

Once inside my bedroom, or rather my cell, I stopped, not giving any thought to the fire raging downstairs. It didn't even occur to me to leave via the backdoor, which could be opened from the inside. I had no capacity to think beyond what I was doing, consumed by a sense of control that made me a giant.

It was a dangerous addiction and as such I wasn't ready to immediately bail out, instead I set fire to the beds that had so often been the instruments of torture, keeping me warm as I dried my tears, listening to my cries but largely ignoring them, their impartiality colluding with my parents and keeping them safe.

As the room filled with smoke it concentrated my mind sufficiently to remind me that it was time to get the hell out of there. I opened the window and went out the same way I came in. As I crawled along the wall I almost fell off, hanging there by my fingertips. I dropped down into the neighbours' yard before making my way out into the street. As I stood leaning against the wall of our own yard I suddenly heard someone coughing and spluttering directly above me. I hugged the wall, afraid of being seen, whilst trying to figure out who could be on the roof.

It was my father, naked and struggling with the effects of smoke inhalation. What the fuck was he doing in the house? He was supposed to be at work, this was totally fucked up and definitely not part of the plan!

A group of women over the street were huddled together, pointing and laughing. I remember thinking that he looked like a hairy gorilla and that must be what they were laughing at. Then pretty soon everyone started spilling into the street. I was relatively inconspicuous for a while but that wouldn't last; in fact, it was just getting started.

I was nine years old.

PART ONE
(0-10)

Am
by a famil
quired
r's

CHAPTER ONE

'Michael! I won't tell you again, put that on the fire, it's dirty and full of germs.'

The name of my birth, two syllables that jabbed at me with the power and precision of a world heavyweight boxer. There was no defence; I was already punch drunk.

Mum was once again busying herself in the tiny alcove that served as a kitchen. There was always some job that needed her attention, some job that kept her busy enough to ignore the things she didn't want to have to deal with; husband, kids and her fragile state of mind. She had arrived with three young children and heavily pregnant with the fourth, six of us living in a tiny two-bedroom apartment with no bathroom and an outside toilet. This wasn't 1869 it was 1969 in the North East of England and I was six years old.

'But Mum, I'm playing with it.'

'Just do as I ask, I'm sick and tired of you causing trouble all the time. Now for the last time, put it on the fire.'

Raising a family of her own didn't help fill the void, it merely added to the pain and resentment. Hers had been a fractured existence that some mythical figure beyond the skies was now expected to repair.

'You know little boys who don't do as they're told won't go to Heaven. God doesn't like naughty children.'

I guess the celestial kindergarten is pretty empty, then.

After the death of her parents my mother, along with her sisters, were raised by a family friend, Jenny, an austere woman. My mother being the youngest was required to perform a number of menial tasks, including getting up on a freezing winter's morning and lighting the fire, before having to walk to school in the snow.

She still feels the cold.

Now, in the time of her greatest need, it was Jenny she once again turned to.

My father had been a paratrooper serving in Aden (Now Yemen). He had been part of a special ops unit whose mission was to stop the gunrunners from getting their deadly supplies to the guerrilla forces. This would often require them to spend weeks, sometimes months, in the mountains, unwashed and unshaven. On returning to base camp, high on a mixture of adrenalin and hostility, with something of a superiority complex, he and his men would pick a fight with another regiment purely for sport. On returning to the UK, he was given low-key tasks as part of the de-briefing process, but he simply couldn't handle the mundane, or his resentment towards colleagues who had never seen active service. He craved a return to the action-packed assaults that allowed you to kill in the dark; by sunrise the dead were just names carved into stone.

My father instantly requested a transfer back to his playground but this was flatly refused. He then sought to buy himself out of his contract, but this too was denied. Disillusioned and dejected, he went AWOL from his camp in North Yorkshire by stealing a Land Rover. Unfortunately, he was completely unaware that it contained emergency blood supplies. He was eventually captured and sentenced to fifty-six days in Colchester military prison before being dishonourably discharged. Although he had indeed served honourably, there would be no record of this.

Jobless and homeless, the family returned to the North East where my parents had grown up. We took an apartment above Jenny's own property; she, of course, owned them both. I shared a bedroom with my brother who was two years older than me and the eldest of my two sisters had a makeshift bed in the lounge, whilst my parents shared a room with my newly arrived baby sister. It was stifling and claustrophobic with very few escape routes. Sometimes I would chase litter around the streets just to see where it came to rest. I quickly developed a liking for things that couldn't talk.

My favourite place was the local tip just behind the row of terraced houses that served as our street. It was an adventure playground and on this day I had found some plasticine, perfectly innocuous, or so I thought. I was sat at the dining table trying to create a world I could safely inhabit but I guess it was unrealistic to expect so much in a single day.

I didn't really pay too much attention to the eruption as they had become commonplace with very little to separate them. The shriek, though, was a different matter, it held little disguise and at its height could have brought a small house down. I saw the knife flying angrily through the air towards me but actually did little to prevent it hitting me until the very last moment when I instinctively raised my hand to prevent it striking my face. It would have been far wiser, and indeed safer, to have ducked, but sheer astonishment fixed me solidly to the chair.

The knife struck the back of my hand and I grimaced before crying out in pain.

'You've made my hand bleed!'

'Well, if you'd just done as I asked in the first place none of this would have happened. Now go and run it under a cold tap.'

'No, I don't like you anymore!'

I ran out of the apartment and bumped into my dad as he was coming in from work, having secured a job as a lorry driver.

'What's gannin on, like?' my father demanded in the old-fashioned, almost Biblical, Durham style of speaking he had retained.

I managed to wriggle free and ran down the stairs as fast as I could. In the yard I could still hear my dad.

'Kathleen, what's gannin on? And why is his hand bleeding?'

'Don't you blame me! You're at work all day. I'm the one that has to deal with it.'

Once in the street I ran as fast as six-year-old legs could go, my heart pumping and my head pounding. It was perhaps the first time I'd really experienced how brutal some adults could be and how they were allowed to abuse their power.

I ran to the bottom of the street and hid around the corner just waiting, I wanted to see if they cared enough to come after me. Although blood continued to drip off the end of my hand, I gave it little consideration. I wanted them to chase me through the streets and fields, I wanted them to pant, not because they were out of shape but because they were out of touch. I wanted them to feel as scared as I had when that knife struck.

It's a child's instinct to run away from danger, but when it comes from within the family it's difficult to know when it's safe to stop. An ancient treaty had been left blood-stained and hidden as I held onto my sleeve and allowed the other children in the streets to continue laughing and playing, on what for them was an ordinary day. I felt nauseous and dizzy and totally detached from the frivolity that surrounded me. I was trapped inside an adult's world where the rules changed according to whim, and like the seasons, didn't always deliver what you wanted.

Or hoped for.

In order to change those rules I would have to change the shape of my imagination and perhaps even sacrifice the things that made me smile.

Back at home, within a few minutes of my leaving the apartment, a posse had been formed and the hunt was on: uncles, cousins, even my own brother, so afraid of his own shadow but even more afraid of my father. I, on the other hand, was so consumed by my bloodletting I was in danger of wanting to drink it. I taunted them, even laughed at them from afar. I don't really know if they heard what I was calling out to them and at the time I don't suppose I really cared that much, but it was fun dragging them around the village, watching them look in all the wrong places.

I covered a lot of ground that evening, trying to stop my bloodstained sleeve from sticking to my arm whilst also attempting to hide the injury from the whispers. How sad it is that we sometimes protect those we need protecting from.

I don't know if I really wanted to die but tired, hungry and homeless, I lay down in the undergrowth and took a chance. The voices that woke me spoke like a pack of baying hounds but looked like family; they were trespassing.

'Why didn't yer stop when we called yer? We've been all over this village chasin' thee.'

My father was panting, desperately searching for a breath of humanity.

'Well I'm not carrying yer, yer've run aroond long enough, yer can fuckin' walk.'

'He needs the hospital. Look at the blood, he probably needs stitches.'

My uncle Trevor ran a barber's shop at the bottom of the village and provided free haircuts for me, my brother and my father, military style. He was probably the least histrionic, he could sometimes appear a little dour but he was by no means an unpleasant man.

'Of course he doesn't need fuckin' stitches, it's just a scratch, man.'

'She's gone too far this time, Rob, it's obvious the lad needs the hospital.'

'Look, Trevor man, I know thee's always wanted a son but thee can't have mine, so try keeping yer own fuckin' hoos in order.'

'Aye, I'll do that, but if anything comes of this, I'll say what I saw, don't expect me to keep quiet.'

'I expect nothing from thee.'

Everyone departed and took with them the landscape. My father scurried off, followed by my brother, who glanced over his shoulder and saw that I had remained static.

'He's not coming, dad.'

'Come on, thee, stop dawdling! As if thee hasn't caused enough trouble for one day, and if anyone asks aboot yer arm, just tell them a dog bit yer.'

Each step grew heavier than the last, each moment of inevitability broader. I wonder if that's how it feels for a condemned man as he slowly makes his way towards the execution chamber. At least for him, once it's over, it's over.

When we entered the apartment mum was laying the table.

'It's probably cold by now but I'm not cooking anything else.'

'Well, why couldn't yer have waited until we got back? I've been at work all day, I want a hot meal.'

'Don't you go blaming me again, you always do that when it's your fault!'

'How the bloody hell is any of this my fault? I didn't do that to him! Michael, go and run your hand under the cold tap and wipe all that blood off.'

My siblings were sat at the table staring at me, even the baby with the big eyes that wept more than they shone. As the evidence swiftly disappeared down the plughole, a chance had gone, along with my childhood. Stitches or not, the scar aged a boy not yet equipped to be a man.

'And what are we goin' ter tell the flamin' social worker? He'll be here in a couple of days.'

'Oh, tell them what yer like.'

My time was already beginning to run out, having gone in search of a quieter existence since I was aged three. That was the first time I ran away from home, the first time I chose to distance myself from the shouting, but it stops the path to play, and you learn a language you can't share, not even with yourself.

CHAPTER TWO

Whilst my father was driving his lorry up and down the country, alone in his cab and away from the inconvenience of family, the rest of us would march downstairs to Jenny's. She loved it, thrived on the conflict that was omnipresent in a family already showing all the signs of decay. She unashamedly exploited my mother's weakness and inability to cope, knowing of course that my mother was heavily dependant on her for both financial and emotional support. Jenny provided a bolthole and in return she got to play her poisonous game, a game whose rules were largely dependant on the Catholic Church being able to hide the wounds. Her spanners were thrown through a blindfold yet always managed to find their target.

I would often be banished to the backyard whilst this medieval treaty was being drawn up, my mother being coerced into accepting that a candle never bleeds whilst it glows in remembrance, the wrath of God bringing driftwood back to the vessel.

I was kicking a piece of coal around the yard, it was the FA Cup final and I was making my debut for Manchester United. With the scores level and only a minute remaining on the clock, a sublime pass from George Best had put me through one on one with their keeper. The crowd went silent in anticipation, such was the hold Liverpool had over United, they were scared to death of distracting me, mindful that this would be a monumental victory. All I could hear was my heart beating faster and faster, and I was desperately in need of the toilet. I could hear the photographers snapping away and the United dugout were on their feet. I rounded the goalkeeper with ease, never doubting the outcome and with the goal at my mercy… disaster!

'Michael, I need you to run to the shops for me.'

'I need the toilet, mum.'

'You can go when you get back.'

'But, mum, I'm bursting.'

'I'm sure you can hold it in for a couple of minutes. Now hurry on, and just do as you're told for once.'

I hated shopping for my mother at the best of times, as she often expected more change than she would actually receive. I would then be accused of stealing and have to face the wrath of my father. The fact that I had, on occasion, been guilty

16

lent little weight to my protestations when I wasn't. He also had a 'winner takes all' philosophy.

'If I hit yer for something yer didn't do, it makes up for all the things I didn't catch yer for.'

My stomach began cramping, such was the strain on my entire body to keep in what was desperate to escape. I managed to complete the shopping and was only a few yards from the house when my world fell apart, along with my bowels. Hot stinking shit ran down my leg in a triumphant salute to the wisdom of nature and its immovability. In a final derisory 'fuck you!' it began escaping from the bottom of my trousers, seeping onto my shoes and then the pavement. People going past screwed up their faces at me.

Shaken and upset, I rang the doorbell.

'Mum, I've pooed my pants.'

'I'm sick of this, Michael, anything for attention! Well, there's more than you in this family.'

She grabbed me and dragged me into the house, cursing me for messing up the carpet. When we reached the lounge, Jenny was sat on her throne with her arms folded tightly across her chest.

'What's goin' on, Kathleen?'

'He's up to his antics again and I don't know if I can cope with it much longer. Rob doesn't help, he just says he'll grow out of it.'

'Well, that's Rob all over. I've never understood why you married him, first sign of a problem and he's out the door, anywhere not to be near it. His father was just the same, would rather go down his allotment, than go to work when he had a family to feed. Michael, stop hanging around! Go to the toilet and get those filthy things off.'

Jenny pointed out of the window towards the toilet, her finger like a missile. I obeyed, not to be unduly compliant, I just wanted to get my clothes off, they fucking stank! Outside in the yard, I emerged from the toilet to be faced with her, hate disguised as love, the kind of love that makes you bleed because it's good for you in the long run.

'Give them here.'

My soiled underwear was hanging from my index finger and I was only too pleased to hand it over, however no sooner had I unburdened myself when she had me in a virtual headlock. She rubbed the pants violently across my face, allowing some of their contents to fall into my mouth.

'That's what little boys deserve when they're too lazy to go to the toilet! Let's hope it puts an end to these wicked ways.'

She released me, smiling for my mum, probably believing she had performed a truly groundbreaking feat. I guess she had. Like the rest of us, I have taken my fair share of shit over the years, but that's the only time I ever had to taste it.

* * * *

'It wasn't me!'

'Don't lie to me boy, I saw you chewing gum. Now, for the last time, this isn't a gymnasium or dining room or in fact anything else. When we give thanks to the Lord, this is His house and it will be respected.'

I had been at St. Mary's Catholic School for around eighteen months and although it was a junior school the regime was pretty brutal, corporal punishment being administered by means of a leather strap. From the very first day I became resistant to their methods and their ideology. I often absconded, spending entire days wandering the streets, penniless and bereft of any meaningful ideas.

'Spit it out, this instant!'

I had, of course, swallowed it the moment he went into his rant. Well, if God can see everything, then I'm sure he'll find a way of communicating my indiscretion to these arbiters of truth.

He yanked my hair back yet it was strangely comfortable, being smug in the knowledge that he wouldn't find what he was looking for. Nevertheless he had a good poke around inside my mouth. His fingers were nicotine-stained and tasted of cigarettes and it was nauseating. He grabbed me by the ear and marched me out of the room, another space trampled on for the good of creation.

'This is becoming something of a regular occurrence, wouldn't you agree?'

'Dunno.'

'You don't know? Well, I suggest you try and find out. Christmas is over, lad, this isn't playtime and I will not have you disrespect the Lord, do I make myself perfectly clear?'

'I don't like praying.'

'Well, fortunately this school isn't run in accordance with your likes and dislikes. How old are you now?'

'Nearly eight.'

'Well, from now on I'm going to be watching every move you make so if you want to reach eight I suggest you buckle down immediately. It's time to put an end to this nonsense once and for all, you're the most problematic pupil I've ever taught.'

'You can't make me say prayers if I don't want to.'

I was pushed hard against the wall and the force of the impact winded me and I began to wheeze a little. His eyes were almost bulging and his face was so red it could have lit up the entire school.

'I seriously advise that you do not try testing my patience, boy, I've been around the block a few more times than you, and I simply won't have you try and disrupt this school, do you hear me? Now get back in that hall, get down on your knees and pray for forgiveness.'

'No!'

It seems this is the one word teachers and other authority figures don't have a dictionary for. Eloquent, erudite individuals suddenly lose the power of speech but not the ability to grunt their way through a syntax rebellion.

I was dragged into a classroom and thrown onto a chair, the force of which sent both myself and the chair crashing to the floor.

'Pick it up.'

I stared up at him, his chest heaving, sweat dripping down the side of his temple and his suit as crumpled as his ideology, but he was determined to stay and see this thing through, despite his inability to balance the books.

'I said, pick it up!'

I picked it up in absence, placed it down right in front of him and sat there cross- legged.

'I'll deal with you later.'

He left the classroom, locking the door behind him. The silence that followed was incredibly enticing, an open invitation. The classroom belonged to the deputy headmistress, Mrs Connelly, and her bag was hibernating under the desk. Just standing, staring at it, filled me with the kind of excitement that strikes back. I walked over and sat at her desk, staring at the locked door. Outside in the corridor, children's footsteps could be heard but there was no laughter, no frivolity. They would be here soon, bringing with them a storm. I reached under the desk and picked up the bag; inside was a purse containing five pounds and some cigarettes and matches. Well, Jesus wouldn't be needing those.

I pocketed the money and cigarettes but toyed with the matches in my hand. I shook the box to hear the seductive comfort of equality. The more I stared at those matches, the more temptation flooded my senses and like a great man once said, 'I can resist everything except temptation.' I wanted to strike each one of them, then swallow each match one by one until the fire raged within me, but no one would see it, no one would feel it and more importantly, no one would fear it. The classroom had become a great expanse but I still felt tiny and breakable. I had experimented with fire for a while now so I was no virgin, but a waste bin in a park or the bristles of a yard brush outside a derelict house had no name on them, as I would disappear within seconds of igniting them.

The decision was taken with considerable anxiety and some confusion for I was so very young, yet wanted to scream like an adult, wanted that power and strength but I couldn't articulate any of this without the matches. Striking that first match and holding it in my hand like it was a friend, took away my innocence and catapulted me into the future before I was due. Several matches later and the plastic model aircraft that had sat so invitingly on a small cluttered table was ablaze. Both my father and my brother had an interest in building these models so it was an obvious choice, my first lesson in separation. I used to sit and watch them build these things, often spending weeks at it, but I had no real practical skills so I was only ever allowed to be a spectator and mostly a bored one.

I spun around and around as bits of melting plastic cascaded to the floor in a fantasy show that choreographed itself, whilst still retaining all the characteristics of a flawless performance. So absorbed was I in this mythical kingdom of which I was ruler, I almost didn't hear the door open or the pandemonium that followed. Young girls running screaming in all directions along with most of the boys, teachers trying desperately not to panic and suddenly, without any meaningful voice, stammering their way through incoherent instructions.

Eventually some semblance of calm was restored, the children having been guided towards a place of safety. Nicotine fingers returned, breathless and doing a great impersonation of a calm, responsible adult as my burning aircraft continued to cast its spell.

'Now, don't do anything silly, Michael, this can all be sorted out but we must remain calm. I want you to go over there and drop that into the sink then turn on the taps.'

As soon as the fire was extinguished, I was grabbed by the shoulder and shaken like a rag doll.

'You wicked, wicked boy! Have you any idea how dangerous that was? But I don't suppose you give a fig, do you?'

His words were lost on me for I was too busy rewinding the tape. I had stood in the coliseum whilst terror engulfed all around me, the peasants fled but more significantly, the lions whimpered. It was a defining moment, I had rolled the dice and got a six, perhaps it was the only number visible. It had all been frighteningly easy, a few tiny specks of phosphorous sulphate, yet the impact had been devastating in a way my young mind could never have envisaged or hoped for. The fall-out would come later for I quickly learnt that adults were myopic in their denial of their failures, and those adults who taught from the pages of an antiquated script didn't know how to read. Their world was a labyrinth of cunning, deceit and duplicity, backed up with a violent intent that marched through time and was passed down like a precious family heirloom. I didn't want what they wanted but I was being denied that choice, for whilst I had not yet painted my landscape, the colours were already being prepared and they didn't match theirs.

'I'll have the matches, please.'

I resented having to hand them over, knowing they would be returned to darkness, having previously shone.

'And would it be too foolish a question to ask how you got these?'

'Found them.'

'Really? Well, I think the police might have something to say about that! I seriously hope they lock you away for good. You've been nothing but trouble from the day you walked through those school gates, you're un-teachable and I for one will be glad to see the back of you.'

Once again the lock went on the door and he scurried off to call the police, as excited as a child on Christmas morning. This time there was nothing comforting about the silence as its slow strangulation shrank the room and emptied my mind. I wasn't willing to walk myself to the slaughter. Having put my name to the deed I may well have closed off my escape routes, but surrender simply wasn't an option, not when I had a fiver in my pocket that I would rather give away than give back. I quickly scanned the room, my senses becoming livelier by the second, but it didn't take a lot of figuring out, indeed the decision was the least taxing of the day. I climbed onto the window ledge and opened it. The air was fresh and intoxicating, made all the more so by sheer defiance, the thrill of which was highly addictive, but only when measured.

'You, boy, stop right where you are and don't you dare move a muscle!'

I glanced over my shoulder to find that nicotine fingers, along with the headmistress and the deputy headmistress, had stormed into the classroom, a trio of child catchers. The headmistress was holding the leather strap she had previously used on me for being caught whistling in the corridor during my first week at the school. The sight of it once again made me recoil.

'Close that window and step down off that ledge immediately.'

Now that would have been plain fucking stupid!

'No.'

'Don't you dare defy me, you impudent devil! Get down, right now!'

I disappeared through the window and laughed my way past the beautiful little pond that was full of life that no one got to see because we weren't allowed near it, like a flower hidden in a rock. The chase was on, for as I headed across the sports field, I was being pursued by both nicotine fingers and the caretaker. Danger outweighed excitement but nevertheless it allowed me to step outside, a game of significant consequences being played by a novice, a child who learnt to steal before he could read.

'Michael, this is silly, come back to the school. Your mum and dad will be worried about you, you'll just cause more trouble for yourself by running away.'

Perhaps the caretaker should have been the teacher. It's not always easy to comprehend common sense when it comes from an unusual quarter, but I did at least stop for a moment, perhaps wanting to believe him, not wanting to believe myself.

'The police have been called, they'll be here any minute. You can't get away, so there's no point in trying. I have a class who want to be taught but I'm out here with you.'

This from nicotine fingers, who never spoke, just spat like a cobra, intelligence fuelled by hatred and a mindset slowly being eroded by self-contamination.

'If you come back now, of your own accord, it's bound to look better for you in the long run. If the police have to search all over for you it will be worse, I promise you.'

I noticed that they had both tried surreptitiously to creep a little further forward. I wonder what they really saw beyond the mist? They knew my name but on their lips it was nothing more than a bar code.

I knew I couldn't out-run them, but I figured they would probably be reluctant to get their feet wet (an irony in itself), so I headed straight for the stream and waded through it until I came to the entrance to a tunnel. I stopped to catch my breath. I couldn't swim and was knee high in water, but it never occurred to me to go back.

'Michael? I'm PC Collins, I think it's time we got you home, kidda, don't you?'

I quickly spun around to see where the voice was coming from. The roof of the tunnel was very low, even for someone of my limited inches, and in my haste I managed to crack my head and lost my balance. I fell into the water and in my panic began thrashing about furiously. The policeman waded into the water to save me from a potential drowning but dry land wasn't altogether less hazardous. I felt something wet trickle down my face and I assumed it was water, but it turned out to be blood.

* * * *

'I'm going to have to take statements from you all but obviously that can wait until the morning. In the meantime, I'll take him to the hospital and get him patched up.'

Once inside the hospital I was fast-tracked through the accident and emergency department and within minutes I was indeed patched up. I emerged looking like Geronimo, with a huge bandage wrapped around my head. For the second time, my wound did not require stitches. How much longer could I hope to push that particular boundary?

'So, Michael, what's next, the Houses of Parliament?'

'Dunno.'

'You don't know? Well, there are going to be people who will want to know. Running away is one thing but trying to set fire to your school is very serious, do you understand that?'

I didn't.

'The teachers seem to think you did, now why would they say that if it wasn't true?'

'They're liars.'

'And you tell the truth all the time, I suppose?'

I didn't always understand the truth as it became more and more elusive, I just didn't want to fish their waters and be left empty-handed.

'Am I going to jail?'

'No, I'm taking you home, but how long you stay there is down to you.'

Once at home, the cop explained things to my parents as I stood there, a spectator wishing I was somewhere else, anywhere.

'Right, thee, get ter yer room! Divin't think coz thee's wounded yer've got away with it, coz yer haven't. I'll deal with thee in the morning. In the meantime yer can forget yer tea.'

I lay on my bed, closed my eyes and saw it all again. I wondered why no one had mentioned the fiver, and so once I reached the hospital I reached into my pocket, and it was gone, having floated off down the river. I guess it just wasn't for spending, not by me at least, and I guess you're only allowed to be silent when you're told to because like most things in this crazy world of the adult child, anything self-imposed creates paranoia, suspicion and confusion. They lock you in a room for a week and you ask for another, they can't handle it: they hit you and you say it doesn't hurt, they can't handle it, but when they bark, growl and insist you answer them and you don't, they can't handle themselves.

'This isn't over, believe me! I want answers and I'll get them whatever it takes, this isn't yer mother! in the meantime, yer can stay in here until the social worker arrives and there'll be nowt until yay start talking.'

During my father's army career, he once trained alongside the SAS, that specialised brand of psychopathic legitimacy with the motto, 'Who Dares, Wins.' Part of the training was trying to resist torture, and to do this my father said you had to view your interrogator as a weak man who hid behind authority.

By the third day my silence was broken by another of my mother's blood-curdling shrieks. I snuck out of the room and into the lounge to find my mother all over my sister, hugging, kissing and crying.

'I'm so sorry, darling, I'm so sorry, mummy is so sorry, I didn't mean it.'

My mother had thrown another knife, this time at my sister, the handle striking her on the side of the head. She looked up and saw me standing there.

'And you, get to your room and don't come out!'

I skulked off back to my room, wondering why it was better to be a girl. Due to a dire shortage of storage space, my sister's clothes were kept in my room, so I put them on and stood staring out of the window. I wanted all the people in the street to see me wearing a dress, but no one was looking, no one saw the change, so I took them off and knew it would always be this way.

Tomorrow the social worker would be here to sort out a new school.

CHAPTER THREE

REDWORTH HALL SCHOOL
FOR MALADJUSTED CHILDREN

That's what the sign proudly read at the entrance to the driveway, hardly an invitation, more a warning to anyone passing by to look the other way. The social worker had pulled out a glossy brochure and sold my parents a bum timeshare. In exchange for a signature they got to retreat behind professional protocol and tick the box with the smiling face. My parents had courted these people but they never had an invite to the ball, their Sunday clothes were reserved for church and court and their brusque language was sometimes smiled at, often nodded at, but never heard.

'Why do I have to go to school that's a long way away?'

'Because it's a special school, that's all yer need to nah.'

It had taken three buses to get here. The walk up the driveway was certainly long enough, tree-lined with lawns either side, but my steps had become leaden. I was instinctively suspicious, of what I wasn't exactly sure, I just knew this wasn't okay and therefore neither was I.

'Yer've got scrambled brains so now yer have ter live at this school. Yer should have thought about that when yer were setting fire ter things.'

'It's really lovely, pet. If yer just give it a chance, yer could do really well here.'

'Aye, maybe I should have set the fuckin' class aleet myself! Now, listen, when yer get in there, don't try sounding clever coz these people won't stand for it, they'll see right through thee.'

We entered the reception area with its wood-panelled walls and insipid paintings hanging everywhere. I was about to be housed in a fucking museum!

Everyone seemed nervous, my father was fidgeting and my mother had become withdrawn. I received a slap because apparently I was planning to steal the clock. I had no intention of stealing it, I stared at it because I was desperate to wind it back.

'New boy, headmaster wants to see you. Come on, I won't hurt you.'

I stood with as much grace as I could muster which was probably none, but it's nicer to remember it differently. I was about to go walking into the unknown yet it felt familiar.

'So what's yer name?'

'Michael.'

'I'm Billy.'

He ruffled my hair and I hate having my hair ruffled. He was also overly familiar and friendly which I didn't care for either, but I just put it down to not being used to it.

'Now, listen, the old man can seem a bit strict but he's okay once yer get ter know him.'

I had no intention of getting to know him because at the end of the day it was just a different body attached to the same head. His office was huge and rather impressive with a plush carpet, what looked like an antique desk and by the window, two large leather armchairs and a coffee table. This little lot probably cost more than my father earned in a year; mthat's education for you.

'Ah, master Cooper, please have a seat.'

I sat down but was determined not to speak unless it was absolutely necessary, having very quickly learned that they can't hear what's in your head and no amount of prodding will reveal it unless you choose to. Right then, I wasn't ready.

'For one so young, quite a lot has been written about you already. Now, you're going to be with us for quite some time and it's up to you how you utilize it. This could be a wonderful opportunity to put behind you some of your more unfortunate escapades and concentrate on personal development.'

I thought I already was, despite the dichotomy of being expected to flourish within a society that discourages any form of individuality or self-expression; speak when spoken to, respect your elders' corrupt brutality and know you are wrong if they say you are. Well, fuck you, because there's none more dangerous than a happy slave!

'So, the running away has to stop immediately.'

Running away isn't a pastime that you opt for when there's nothing better to do. You're left friendless, peerless and homeless. You learn skills you shouldn't know as a child and the bitterly cold nights harden your heart more than your bones.

Having nodded my phoney agreement, I was dismissed. Billy was waiting outside to escort me to my house-block, which was run by 'Uncle' Charlie and 'Aunty' Kath. I thought it was an odd way for a child to address adults who were essentially strangers. On the way up to the house, I felt increasingly lonely and miserable, and the cold merely added to that sense of isolation. I turned to Billy.

'How long have you been here?'

'Five years.'

'Five years!'

'Time flies, so it's not so bad.'

I wanted to fly with it, wanted to be as invisible as the wind and have no name or memory.

Once at the house, I was immediately shown to my custodians and had an instant introduction to what the future held. I was already beginning to feel instinctively resistant to it.

'So, you're the young runaway everyone's been talking about? Well, if you run from me, you'll never run again.'

This was 'Uncle' Charlie. He ordered me to follow him up the stairs where he showed me into a dormitory. I had never slept in one before and it was a pretty scary prospect. He grabbed my bag and threw it onto an empty bed. I sat next to it while he lit a cigarette and blew a huge cloud of smoke in my face, before ordering me to unpack my bag and place the contents in a bedside cabinet. I felt like I was under siege from his barked instructions. I picked up the bag and nursed it in my lap, at which point he became abusive with a disturbing anger that was disproportionate to any perceived infraction on my part. He waved his hands about, shouting and spitting, as I fought back tears, not of sadness or loss, but of sheer frustration and hopelessness. I just wanted him to shut the fuck up and give me a chance to breathe!

I never heard Kath enter the dorm, perhaps her spite wrapped a protective layer of invisibility around her. There she stood, hands on hips, hate seeping out of her like puss from an open wound.

'Well, is there any wonder your mother off-loaded yer onto us if this is the way you carry on?'

This was their very own propaganda term, a phrase used to describe any act of defiance. Even when refusing to acquiesce to their abusive demands, it was a verbal punch designed to knock you off balance, but it was a big mistake. My mother might not have been perfect, but she's still my mum, and she battled daily against her own fragility, lack of money and inadequate housing, without seeking refuge in a rural closet.

My resolve had quickly returned and I was really pissed. It was time to step up to the plate, a little sooner than I had hoped but at least it was clean. I threw down my bag and flatly refused to pick it up, just as Charlie walked back in. He stood over me, breathing heavily and looking like he wanted to beat the living crap out of me, but in the end he just bent down and picked up my bag.

'I'll lock these in the cupboard and you can have them back when your behaviour warrants it.'

'Don't care.'

'And early to bed, no supper.'

In a futile act of defiance, I decided not to eat my tea either and I was simply dispatched to bed earlier than expected, the other boys being instructed not to speak to me. I lay there for hours, pretending to be asleep, burying myself deep into the covers for added protection and comfort. In that moment, I both missed and resented my parents, though I'm not sure which was the more dominant. I was divorced from family, my place at the table given up to occasional visitation rights. It seemed I no longer had anyone to answer to, no one I was sufficiently attached to that would make any kind of difference. My decisions were my own but my rationale was imported. I was a child without the usual repertoire therefore other children didn't always understand me, and the playground became my pavilion. They slept comfortably in their beds, hugging teddies or sucking thumbs, never experiencing the night, never having to walk through it in order to find a different kind of day. It was neither a playground nor a battlefield, neither school nor home, it was just a place to stare at without compromise, and no one came calling.

* * * *

'Well done young Cooper, another dry night, no need for these ter go in the wash. Seems we're beginning ter make progress at last.'

I had started to wet the bed about a year or so earlier, infrequently at first and then on a more consistent basis, however in recent months it had all but been eradicated, until now that is.

His progress not mine, dry or wet, it was still a bed only occasionally slept in. Sleep was my progress, but I never kept a chart, it came and went without specific meaning and never wrapped itself in plaudits.

So it continued, that on any given night I would sneak out of the house and hope to return unnoticed to my bed before the sun came up. On this particular night, I found some roast beef sandwiches neatly wrapped in cling film sitting invitingly in the bottom of the fridge. Progress deserves a proper reward! With my booty in my pocket I left the house. I had developed animal cunning and instincts, constantly on the alert, seeking to identify any possible danger, using the cover of darkness to watch without being watched.

There were a number of tunnels running under the main building, all of which were strictly out of bounds, each one secured by a heavy metal gate and heavily padlocked. They were a throwback to a time when the incumbents of the house might have had to make a quick and safe getaway to flee from religious or political persecution, the house having once belonged to local landed gentry, The Surtees family, a couple of hundred years ago. I found all the tunnels, but preferred the open fields, running unseen and giggling my way across miles of countryside. Thoughts of taking off were never far from my mind, often dominating them and overwhelming me.

I hadn't long been at the school and had no real idea of where I was, but was working on it. I knew I was a fair distance from home as it had taken us three buses to get here. Despite being contained the daily routine was pretty much as it would have been in a mainstream school, with one or two fundamental differences. We all ate breakfast in a huge dining hall that was quite intimidating, not to mention noisy, and during lessons I lost count of how many times a desk was tipped over or chairs went flying through the air. Occasionally, a lesson was aborted because of some violent eruption. They were hugely stressful days with tensions often running high. During evenings and weekends, extra curricular activities were offered, model making, chess clubs etc, but these required me to engage with the very people I feared.

Instead, I preferred to wander the grounds, alone and undisturbed, but I sometimes struggled with an illusionary world of beauty combined with waste. It was the worst kind of prison imaginable, surrounded by jaw-dropping magnificence, yet unable to view it from the correct angle. But at least, for now, this was perfect, I could enjoy all the benefits of having absconded without the downside.

Having walked the open grounds, I retired to the woods to enjoy a well-deserved snack. I sat on a tree stump that was sticking out of the ground and unwrapped my sandwiches. I took one and bit into it; there was some kind of sauce on it and it tasted spicy. Whist trying to decide whether I liked it or not I heard a rustling noise coming from a nearby bush and seconds later something emerged from it.

I tried to adjust my eyes as it was obviously dark, and there it was, standing right in front of me. I didn't know whether to just stare in wonderment or run as fast as I could, it was a compelling sight, which made it impossible to do anything but simply honour its presence and remain still. An adult fox, bright eyed and standing as still as a statue, perhaps having similar thoughts to myself, perhaps he too was scared. I don't know whose heart was beating the fastest or who needed to pee the most, but of one thing I was certain: he needed the sandwiches more than I did, so I tried desperately to slow my breathing and when I couldn't hear it anymore, I rose from my seat.

As soon as I stood up the fox lowered his head and, for the first time in my life, I experienced a different kind of fear; not fear of attack, but the fear that he or she might run off, afraid of what I might do. Ultimately we weren't all that different, each seeking nourishment in dangerous places, hunting in the dark and sometimes meeting those that can hurt or heal.

'It's okay, I'm not going to hurt you.'

The words had a resonance, as if I had just invented them, and he was still there wanting it to be true and I needing it to be, but on his terms. Everything that was suddenly so beautiful and bright was wholly dependant on my next move. On the one hand its importance made me sick with nerves; on the other, I was already his brother. I slowly took a couple of steps forward and he took a couple of steps backwards, never taking his eyes off me, but he was still there. I placed the food on the ground and backed off sufficiently so as not to pose any kind of a threat. Having nervously looked around, he slowly came forward and devoured the first sandwich. I was right about that. He then picked up the rest and trotted off with them firmly clamped in his jaws.

It was the ultimate shared experience, we simply offered what we had, there was no other expectation, except to want more of it. We were both hunter and hunted, both afraid of daylight.

I began secreting food from the dining hall and returned each night and waited, it became my main focus as I spent the day clock-watching, knowing I had nothing else to wait for, nothing worthy of my dinner. I sat for hours, waiting for my friend, but he didn't show, nor did he the next night or the one after that. I began to experience emotions I didn't previously know existed, profound sadness and loss. He was free to roam wherever he chose and I guess he didn't need what I was offering as much as I did. My days became heavy with little cohesion and purpose, I was simply filling them out, and even my midnight wandering had stopped. I couldn't chase his freedom, no matter how fast I ran, but run I would.

One gloomy day, both in terms of landscape and mood, a teacher stopped me.

'Bloody hell, Cooper, you look like you've lost a quid and found a shilling! Buck up, lad.'

'Where's the fox gone?'

'What fox?'

'The one that lives in the woods.'

'Oh, I don't know, there was a hunt in the village a few days ago, the hounds probably got him.'

His words were like bullets I couldn't dodge and I was a child who had experienced a wrongful death in the name of sport. Was there any wonder we only met at night?

CHAPTER FOUR

'I hate this place! We'll never clean all these shoes, they're not even ours. It's not fair, I'm missing Top of the Pops!'

Music was my newly discovered way of filling the void left by the death of the fox, having had to return momentarily at least, to the dog pound. I needed colour restoring to my eyes and Glam Rock provided it once a week, and my newfound ability to shut off from my surroundings did the rest.

'We'll have to clean them all otherwise Uncle Charlie will make us clean the toilets as well.'

'Well, I'm not scared of him.'

'You should be 'coz he can do what he likes and there's nowt nee one can dee aboot it. He made my nose bleed once.'

'Did you tell your dad?'

'Me dad ran off when I was a baby.'

'So what's your name?'

'Mickey Reardon.'

Mickey was taller than I was, but then most people were and still are. He was also slightly older, and he came from Jarrow, deep in the heart of the North East, once famous for a march on parliament during the depression of the nineteen twenties.

'Mine's Michael Cooper. What did you do to have to clean all these shoes?'

'I didn't eat all of my tea. Uncle Charlie said I asked for it so I should have eaten it as there's starving Africans could have had it. What did you do?'

'Wee'd the bed last night. Charlie said I did it on purpose 'coz he'd already cured me, said I did it just to be bad so it would annoy him. First chance I get, I'm doin' a bunk. I've thought about it for ages but now I'm going to do it.'

'Yer don't want ter dee that, man. The last kid that ran away ended up crying all the time 'coz Uncle Charlie was so horrible to him.'

'Well, he won't make me cry. You can come with me, if you like, it'll be brilliant.'

'I dunno, it's not so bad here really, if yer stay out of his way.'

'Well, I'm going.'

A few days later, having cleaned out the fish tank, almost killing the fish into the bargain, more punishments followed. Our psychopathic guardians had clearly targeted Mickey and me. It was time to hand back an empty dinner plate.

It seems to me that Bibles are never very far away from misery. At times they have made me wish I was illiterate, but I will always remember the day the Gideons arrived and helped put the smile back on my face, if only for a few precious moments. I was due to mow the lawn manually and the only way to get out of it was to agree to attend the class which the Gideons were leading. Charlie was almost beside himself, delighted that I was seeking spiritual enrichment in an attempt to 'mend my ways.' I, too, was delighted at being able to spoon-feed him his own stupidity. On my way back to the house block, a familiar voice put Charlie to bed for a while.

'Michael, hang on, man.'

'Mickey, what's in the bag?'

'Bibles, we could sell them and dee a bunk with the money.'

'Okay, whoever wakes up first gets the other one up, but you better not change your mind.'

We slept in separate dormitories so it was a fairly risky enterprise but by sunrise I was awake, Mickey was already dressed and sat on the edge of his bed, clutching the bag like a last goodbye. I, however, was having second thoughts. I'd never been on a joint venture before, yet here I was, almost a veteran, taking along a novice. We spoke in whispers; what couldn't be heard, couldn't be proved.

Every Saturday the minibus would take a group of lads into Shildon, the nearest town, about a mile from the school. I had never been allowed on one of these trips as Charlie maintained I had yet to earn one. Mickey, on the other hand, had been on several and, like it or not, I needed his compass. We crept downstairs and climbed out through the lounge window. I was back at work again and there's nothing more fulfilling than being awake whilst everyone else sleeps. We made our way across the fields until we came to town. The previous night we'd hidden ourselves away in a toilet cubicle, and tore out the page that proudly declared that the Bibles had been donated. It was a work of consummate planning

'Look, Mickey man, you hold the bag and let me do all the talking.'

'Aye, okay.'

We knocked on several doors without reply and were beginning to get fed up with having to drag the bag about, when a young lady answered the door.

'Good morning, madam, me and my friend are raising money for St. Bartholomew's church and we have to sell these Bibles before we go to school.'

We had passed the church on our way into town.

'How much are they?'

'Twenty five pence or five for a pound.'

Perfect delivery! I turned to Mickey, confident of a sale, only to find him trying to light a cigarette in the wind, total bummer.

'I'll just get my husband.'

I was so pissed with Mickey, it didn't instantly register that we were in danger. I just wanted to take that cigarette and shove it up his arse, lit end first. He was making me think and act in a way I was unaccustomed to, and in the mêlée I had forgotten the rules, safety first. It was fucking basic!

I eventually came to my senses and told him to make a run for it, but he was too preoccupied with the money. The woman's husband suddenly appeared and he was one big bruiser, he probably ate a couple of kids as a mid-morning snack. Well, he wasn't having me. Normality was quickly restored as I fled through the gate and down a back alley, heart pumping, mind racing. I no longer had a plan other than to get away, to survive the odds with the hounds gathering for their feast.

Running away from home was a far more intimate exercise, a personalized, 'fuck you!' Now, here I was, taking on the might of the machine with no money and no direction home. I had only my will to invest in, so I put everything into it in a single breath and was gone. Mickey, on the other hand, had frozen with fear and fell at the first hurdle. He was now a captive of a different sort. He lacked the commitment and intensity to fight for the right to express his qualities and not theirs, and now the sharks had already begun to circle him and there was nothing I could do.

I wandered streets with names I didn't recognise, looking for a signpost to Durham, but there were none and I needed a cigarette. I came upon a small corner shop but with no money, I most certainly did need a plan. I pulled out a scrap of paper from my pocket and entered the shop, hoping to convince the shop owner that I was reading from a shopping list. Inside was a little old guy not a whole lot bigger than me, but his shelves were tall, perfect.

'Alright, young 'un, how come yer not at school today?'

'Me mum's taking me to the doctors but she asked me to go to the shops first.'

'What can I get yer?'

'Can I have a loaf of bread, please?'

He placed the bread down on the counter and continued to place each item requested, including a pack of cigarettes and a box of matches.

'I hope these aren't for thee.'

'No, I don't smoke, they're for me mum.'

'Aye, I expect she needs them.'

'Can I have a box of cornflakes, and that's it?'

The cornflakes were on the top shelf and it required him to stand on a small set of step-ladders in order to reach them. As soon as he reached up for them, I grabbed the cigarettes and ran like my fucking life depended on it.

I didn't expect the old guy to come after me and whilst he wasn't a great mover he had healthy lungs and began wailing. Initially I panicked, but the fear of capture gave me a speed and strength I didn't know I possessed. I just wanted a cigarette without the adrenalin. I needed somewhere to hide and enjoy the fruits of my somewhat contemptible labour. There was no pleasure in what I did, he simply belonged to a world I didn't recognise and lived by rules I couldn't apply. Nowadays kids as old as I was then, openly walk down the street smoking and drinking alcohol with impunity, but back then there was no such luxury, there was always someone itching to report you to those responsible for apprehending you. Whilst smoking was still viewed by some as rebellious, it had to be enjoyed in private when you were just eight years old. All the glorious pleasures do.

I found a park and sat on a swing, a childish act I was unable to enjoy without the innocence and laughter that accompanied it. I lit up a cigarette, ostensibly an adult act, but the fag wasn't the way home, just a way of acknowledging the crisis. For a kid not too familiar with play, a park held no special attraction in terms of the rides etc., it was simply a retreat where I could seek comfort and rest. For an hour or so I smoked and thought, I even managed the occasional smile, but then it was time to move on.

No sooner had I left the park, lost in my own wilderness, when a police car pulled up alongside of me, and a cop jumped out.

'Right, you, turn out your pockets, now.'

'Why?'

'Because I'm asking you to and when a policeman asks you to do something, you do it, understood?'

I reluctantly took the cigarettes from my pocket and handed them over. There was a certain amount of acceptance matched with resentment, for not only had I lost the cigarettes I had also lost time. But for a couple of hours it had all been mine.

'The shopkeeper said you looked like butter wouldn't melt in your mouth. Well, you might look like an angel but you don't flaming act like one. Right, in you go, you thieving little git!'

He pulled the back of his seat forward and I climbed into the back of the car without uttering a word, the disappointment having robbed me of speech.

'You know, you won't always get away with pulling stunts like this, one day you'll be old enough to be charged so you might like to think about that. I didn't join the police force to ferry kids back and forth, you know. First, your mate and now you.'

I wasn't really listening, I had become gripped by fear, worried about what awaited me back at the school. Having some violent fantasy acted out on me by some inadequate kind of upset the balance but not my determination. I was walking a tightrope between two sides, without a doubt the thought of a beating would scare the shit out of me but allowing it to silence me into submission would have been a far greater pain.

I was dropped of at reception, which was situated in the main house, and within minutes ushered into the headmaster's office, where I immediately sat down.

'Stand up, boy, I didn't tell you to sit. Stand up!'

I rose a little nervously to my feet. He wanted me to explain my actions but I couldn't. I couldn't always explain them to myself, but generally I had a better debate.

'So, what have you got to say for yourself?'

'Nothing.'

'Nothing what?'

'Just nothing.'

He wanted me to call him sir, yet he calls me boy.

'Do not test my patience. I can be very rewarding when I want to be, but I will also come down like a ton of bricks on any boy who does not follow the rules and procedures of this school. Do I make myself absolutely clear?'

'Yeah.'

'You're here because you need the correct guidance and that's what we will give you. All boys have problems when they first arrive here but they're soon corrected so they can leave more adjusted.'

I just wanted to leave intact.

'Now, this morning's indiscretion obviously can't go unpunished, as I'm sure you will agree. Weekend leave suspended for one month, along with pocket money. Right, off you go to the dining room and get your lunch and remember, Cooper, there is to be no repeat of this behaviour, understood?'

'Yeah.'

'Do I have your word on that?'

'Yeah.'

'Excellent.'

I made my way to the dining room already feeling different, for as well as doing the things I had done, I was learning what not to do. Indeed, it was as if it really was that simple, tell them what they wanted to hear and allow them to pretend it wasn't their egos they were listening to.

Once inside the dining room, I headed towards my table. Each one had a head boy at the helm who naturally got the lion's share of any meal and left the rats to fight over the scraps. They were also responsible for maintaining discipline at the table and used all the means at their disposal including bullying. It was a system guaranteed to maintain its structure, both within the school and in the wider world.

Later that day, at Charlie's behest, I was banished from the dining room and deprived of my tea, and then dispatched to bed early without any supper. I was absolutely starving and couldn't sleep, so I crept downstairs to the kitchen to see what was in the fridge. As soon as I opened it and the light came on I thought I was going to faint.

'Well, well, I can read yer like a book.'

At the far end of the kitchen was a door leading to Charlie's quarters and the bastard must have been hiding behind it. A classic ambush and I had just walked right into it. I was so angry I could hardly speak, and I was still fucking hungry.

'I'm hungry.'

'You don't know what it's like to be hungry, but you thought you could just sneak down here and nick some food?'

'No.'

'Oh yer were gonna pay for it, were yer?'

'Dunno.'

'Well I do, hands on the table.'

I pulled down my pyjama bottoms and placed my hands on the table. My legs were shaking and I closed my eyes. He administered six strokes of a leather slipper across my bare buttocks while I gritted my teeth and tried not to cry but it was impossible. The physical pain was intense but the humiliation, as droplets of piss ran down my leg, spoke only of retribution. No amount of hurting could prevent the anger and frustration from raging within, he had set this up purely so he could do this, it wasn't punishment, it was a corrupt form of entertainment. I could not afford to compromise, I had far more to lose than a night without sleep.

CHAPTER FIVE

'Well, your temperature's normal but I'll keep you in the sick bay overnight just to keep an eye on you. You've probably just picked up a bug.'

I had felt utterly wretched and miserable since my failed bid for freedom, made all the more unpalatable by its amateurish execution. I needed a respite from Charlie's continued war of attrition; I was beginning to taste defeat. I couldn't, however, afford another catastrophe, it would have been terminal so an entirely different plan was born.

I feigned illness.

One morning on my way to classes I headed for the medical room and told the nurse I had spent the night throwing up. Now I had time, and in my own way had rubbed shit in his face. The sick bay was situated at the top of the main house and wonderfully isolated. I was taken there by the nurse and told to sit on the bed and wait.

'I'll ring your house block and get someone to fetch your pyjamas and toothbrush. In the meantime, try and rest. There's books and magazines over there if you want to read.'

Books, magazines and a fucking television all to myself! It was more choice than I was used to and more decisions than I usually had to make, and the silence, which I had often craved, now felt disturbing in its novelty and made me restless. I wanted to pace the room but was afraid that if I was seen I would be returned to my house block, so I sat still trying to look as sorry for myself as possible.

It was a look I had cultivated before.

I don't know how long I sat there, enjoying the rare luxury of basking in my own thoughts. I was even able to enjoy the odd exchange with myself and the occasional giggle, knowing that guile had rubbed salt into the aggressor's wounds. It mattered intensely. When the door opened and Charlie walked in, I wasn't afraid, I was protected by quarantine.

'Does thee think I've nowt better ter dee than chase around after yay?'

He threw my pyjamas onto the bed like something he was desperate to be rid of. It was not a relationship he relished, just one on which his foundation was built.

'Well, enjoy the rest 'coz there's toilets need cleaning when thee gets back.'

'Not doin' them.'

His face was so close to mine I could feel his spit spraying my face. His features were so screwed up, his face looked crumpled and old and beat.

'You'll do whatever I tell yer ter do.'

'I won't, you're not my dad!'

There are only so many threats that can be issued and so many rebuttals before a stalemate is reached. On my part, sheer pig-headedness was at work. I like to think that as he turned and left he knew for certain that he could never bully me again, that I was willing to say no unless it was reasonable or justified. The truth, however, was that it probably didn't matter as much to him as it did to me, there would be others to make him feel fertile again.

The days were long but without pain and meals came and went without being eaten. It was a kind of hunger strike without the politics. One afternoon, hungry and bored, I opened the window and looked out across the manicured lawns. Billy, who shared a room in the main house with a guy called Chris, was also looking out of his window, smoking a cigarette.

'Want some?'

'Yeah.'

'Come on then.'

I walked down the corridor to his room, quite excited by the prospect of a smoke. When I reached the door, he was already holding it open. I walked in and stood in the middle of his large room with two single beds and a high ceiling.

'Come over to the window. If the head walks past, he'll smell it.'

It felt like I was a member of an exclusive club, an older boy being willing to share his cigarette and his time, Normally this would have been unheard of. I stood by the window and he stood behind me, while he put his arm around my neck and fed the cigarette into my mouth. I took a drag and didn't cough which made him laugh. He placed his hands on the windowsill and I could feel his breath on the back of my neck.

'Do yer want ter toss me off?'

This was completely outside of my vocabulary. I simply had no idea what he was referring to, yet instinctively knew it was something I didn't want to do.

'No.'

'It's okay, we won't get caught. I'll lock the door.'

'I don't want to.'

'You're gonna do it one day, everyone does. If yer do it with me, I'll make yer my special friend.'

It was a language that fell to the ground yet kept you standing there through a combination of fear and confusion.

'Chris will be back in a bit. We could get into bed and play with each other and be done before he gets here.'

I no longer had the words for no, I simply brushed past him, leaving his own sentences intact.

'If yer really didn't want to, yer'd have run off by now.'

Fucking difficult when he was stood directly behind me pinning me up against the windowsill! Then he started to thrust and though fully clothed I could feel his erect penis thrusting against my arse.

'Bet yer like that, don't yer?'

I neither liked nor disliked it, I just wanted to get out of there with my arse intact.

'Go on then, fuck off! But don't come ter me next time yer want a fag, and if yer tell anyone I'll kick yer fuckin' head in.'

Outside in the corridor I was almost hyperventilating. I was also so disorientated I struggled to find my way back to the sick bay.

I spent the remainder of the day in a daze, locked in a tunnel, hardly able to breathe or form a sentence that could make sense of all this. By evening, I had begun to formulate a plan. Whilst weekend leave could be suspended or withdrawn, school holidays couldn't, it was a statutory obligation. Besides, the school shut down completely. Easter holidays were only a week away and I would not be returning when required to.

I lay there thinking about my parents but it upset my stomach and unsettled my mind. I couldn't explain my feelings to myself, couldn't adjust myself to how I was thinking, it seemed like mind and heart were locked in combat, strangers to themselves and to me. And now there was an entirely new danger I had no previous experience of, a cock-hungry paedophile! Well, the bastard starved that night but not before a final flourish. I was lost in my own thoughts when the door suddenly flew open.

A stark naked Billy ran into the room, laughing like a maniac and sporting a huge erection. He stood in the middle of the room facing me and proceeded to masturbate while Chris held the door open. After a while, he walked towards me, still holding his erection like a proud owner.

'Yer can suck it if yer like, it's clean.'

Before I could offer a reply, he ran out of the room, giggling hysterically and it was left to me to close the door, which I promptly did. I was on unfamiliar territory and it began to manifest itself in anger that was boiling at such a rapid rate I was in danger of combusting. I wanted my dad but he wasn't there, and that's when it hit me. As I looked around the room at the dog-eared magazines and the dust on the walls, there was only me; I would have to be mother, father, friend and foe. I was the only weapon I had.

And in that moment the anger dissipated.

After a night spent pacing the room with the television providing background noise and with the tray on wheels ready to be sent crashing into any naked person foolish enough to come through the door, morning arrived. I gobbled up my breakfast as if my life depended on it, my appetite having miraculously returned. Nurse was suitably impressed.

'My word, we are hungry today! Very encouraging, I must say.'

'I don't feel poorly anymore.'

'Well, you've certainly got a bit more colour in your cheeks. Okay, I'll ring your house and let them know you're being discharged.'

I fell over myself in an attempt to get dressed as quickly as possible, terrified that she might change her mind. I walked down the corridor and when I walked past Billy's room, I stuck two fingers up at the door.

On my way back to my house, I noticed a boy getting into a car with a man and a woman, they seemed in an awful hurry to get away. I stood and stared after the car as it sped down the drive and was gone. Mr Edmondson, the games master, was coming towards me. I liked him because he smiled a lot.

'Mr Edmondson, what was that boy doing in that car?'

'Goin' home, kidda.'

'But it's not Easter yet.'

'He's not gone on leave, he's left.'

'Left?'

'Aye, his parents have taken him home.'

'Can mine take me home?'

'Aye, any time they like. Why, is it that bad here?'

'You're not but I still don't like it.'

'Well, running off isn't goin' to do you any favours now, is it?'

'Dunno.'

'Go on, get to where you're goin'.'

I didn't know whether to fly or crawl, the thought of not having to remain trapped inside Charlie's ideological desolation made me want to burst open and scatter myself on the wind. But a way out of there was really only that I'd be returning home like it was new, but everything old would still remain. I was lost in a mixture of confusion and excitement. Unusually and perhaps even rather staggeringly, I didn't opt for the instant remedy that had so far been so irresistible it had mostly blinded me to other options, instead I chose to stay and bide my time. In doing so I had unwittingly invested in two of the virtues that had so far eluded me: patience and trust, patience providing the discipline to stay and trust in my parents to invoke their parental control

One evening, I was walking past the concrete playground where during a break in lessons a group of us would play a game of British Bulldog. I really enjoyed this game as it allowed me to employ cunning against the primitive brawn of the older, stronger boys and thus allow me to evade capture for longer than most. Mr Edmondson was supervising cricket practice between two boys who, having reached their sixteenth birthday, were on the verge of leaving the school. I watched as the ball was hoisted so high into the sky, I expected it to come down covered in snow. Immediately the cry of, 'Catch it!' rang out, and without a moment's hesitation, I was off.

'I'll catch it!'

I didn't have time to look around and gauge their reaction as my eyes were fixed firmly on the ball. I quickly positioned myself directly under it and waited. As it dropped from the sky I had no other thought than to catch it, nothing else mattered and nothing else seemed to be happening. It stuck like glue and I was so scared to open my hands in case it had somehow managed to escape that I clasped them together with all my might.

'Bloody hell, young Cooper! Where the hell did you learn to catch a cricket ball like that?'

'Nowhere.'

'Hands stinging?'

'A bit.'

'Well, there's football practice tomorrow evening, I suggest you come along, lad, show them what you're made of.'

'Okay.'

I had only once before played in an organised game and it was quite farcical to say the least. My brother was a gifted footballer and played for the school team, and whilst I was attending the same school I was determined to also shine at football. Once, during practice, I took a shot but slipped and fell over. When I got to my feet, all of my team mates were celebrating. I had scored, but knew nothing about it, the goalkeeper clearly being as hapless as I was.

Nevertheless, I was excited at being given this chance in somewhat more difficult circumstances. By becoming a valued member of the team I would gain access to the inner circle, perhaps I might find a home there. I obviously wasn't as skilled or as strong as the older boys but I was fitter than most. What I lacked in ability I made up for with enthusiasm.

The following day, I turned up at the football pitch and, as directed, joined in. I ran around the pitch like a headless chicken, a dog trying to catch a gazelle. Each time I got the ball I ran and ran, then would fall under some vengeful tackle that often involved more than one player. None of it mattered, I was making my mark in the only way I knew how: sheer defiance. Bruises heal, submission doesn't and size doesn't matter.

'Bloody hell! Look at him running all over the place like a little Mini Cooper!'

It stuck and followed me wherever I went. I now had an identity that was entirely my own, something to protect, nurture and refuse to relinquish.

CHAPTER SIX

A holiday is a holiday, wherever it takes you, but it can be kind of like moving an empty box from one room to another, then moving it back again. The sun had yet to shine on a place that would make me want to stay and I still didn't know what it looked like, just that it would be a place where the light wouldn't stop following you, not even when you were sleeping. I wanted my room back and a school that taught rather than dismissed. I wanted to be heard and my siblings not to treat me like the next-door neighbours' kid. I had already had enough of each day being a constant battle to breathe, and the rules being changed to suit the bullies who control who eats, who sleeps and who bleeds.

I have my rules too.

So the Easter holiday arrived, and although it kind of came down to a toss of a coin, I decided to talk to my mother about having me back home. Talking to my father would be like swallowing live maggots.

The first day of holidays offered no real structure, there was only a skeleton staff supervising departures, everyone else just hung around. After a hearty breakfast the next port of call was the staff room where we were each handed a small brown envelope containing our pocket money. Since arriving here the only money I ever saw was that which my mother sometimes sent in a letter. Money from the state, on the other hand, with the size of their pockets, felt far more hedonistic in its level of joy and satisfaction. Eighteen pence, the equivalent of ten cigarettes; who knows, perhaps it's moments such as these, when put together, that make up a life?

By lunchtime, every one else had departed so I had the pick of the sandwiches. I grabbed the first that came to hand. I didn't really want it, just an excuse to sit outside. The staff amused themselves by playing cards in the staff room and occasionally opened the window to call out to me.

'Any sign of them yet?'

I would shake my head, tired of hearing the same question, tired of giving the same answer, so I walked over to the woods and fed my sandwich to the birds. When I returned to the main house I was met by Charlie, cards in hand, fag in mouth.

'Where the hell have yay been?'

'I was bored.'

'You'd be bored in a toyshop, lad. Anyway, your father's here to take you home.'

My father emerged alone from the staff room, unshaven and his hair windswept. He had an immense presence and I often felt tiny stood next to him, and nervous. We walked in silence down to the village, although his mouth continuously twitched as if he wanted to say something but couldn't quite decide what it was and I was in no hurry to prompt him. However, no sooner had we reached the bus stop, he decided to open proceedings, this being the man who could hold court in a telephone kiosk.

'Uncle Charlie says you ran off a bit back, is that right?

'He's not my uncle.'

'Never mind that, is he right?'

'Yeah.'

'Keep goin' like that and they'll lock you up.'

I had completely shut off from him as we stood in the village waiting for a bus. I was looking for a way out, not a way in. I didn't want to stand in a village that chased foxes.

'Now, listen, when it's time to bring yer back, I'll be at work so yer mum will have ter bring yer and divin't think yer can giver her the run around, do yer hear me?'

Well, I certainly owed her one and I was licking my lips with anticipation as I stared down at the scar she cut through my skin. I simply wanted to get under hers.

'Right then, the bus is coming. How much pocket money do yer have?'

'Eighteen pence.'

'Yer can pay yer own bus fare, then.'

I noticed that the front of the bus read, 'Bishop Auckland.' On arrival I tried desperately to survey my surroundings but the old man quickly bundled me onto another bus. I settled into my seat and concentrated like never before. When I listened, mine was the only voice I heard, swirling around my head every other noise was just that.

'I've something ter tell yay, I've got a job at the pit and they've given us a house.'

When he worked the lorries, he would often set off for work long before I was up and return home long after I had gone to bed, so this was good news wrapped in shit, but the house was a bonus.

As soon as we reached Durham, my father took off as if he had forgotten that I was there, and I had to break into a trot just to keep him in my sights.

'Come on, no dawdling, we need ter get there before they close.'

I had no idea what was making him so determined and so animated, but if it took this amount of effort then surely it would be worth it.

The sight of the river could breathe stillness into the busiest mind, and its enchanting view always made me want to taste the air on my tongue. We crossed the market square and then off down a side street until we came to a small sports shop.

'Wait here and divin't move.'

He went inside and, unusually, left me unattended. This must be something really special, I figured. When he emerged from the shop, he held two small cardboard boxes cupped in his hand. His pride was disconcerting, his smile reaching each passing father, son, daughter and wife, but to me it was like a discarded photograph.

'Here, look at these.'

He was like a child in his enthusiasm but I wasn't expected to recognise that, it was a game adults played and children obeyed.

'What are they?'

'What do yer think they are, they're medals! Look, I've even had your name engraved on the back.'

'Why?'

'Yer want yer mum ter be proud of yer, don't yer? We'll just tell her yer won them playing football, so keep thee mouth shut and let me dee the talking. Look, after all the worry you've caused her, it's not a lot to ask now, is it?'

'Suppose.'

'Here, put them in yer pocket til we get home.'

I didn't want to go home because it was no different to school. The hypocrisy was just as claustrophobic, along with rules that didn't make sense, being told to lie by people who hit you when you lie to them, and not wanting to speak so that no one can know what you're thinking. We boarded our third and final bus and some twenty minutes later arrived in the village of Craghead, this time my dawdling was quite deliberate. Our house once again had an outside toilet and no bathroom, not even a cooker, the oven was built into the wall next to the fire and, of course, there was no central heating.

When we entered the house there was no greeting. I hadn't seen my mum in months and it seemed longer, but it was as if she couldn't bear to look at me for despite several attempts on my part, she refused me eye contact and spoke only to my father. My siblings were locked in play and as I had never been part of these games they didn't feel compelled to invite me in either.

'You'll have to make do with sandwiches 'coz the fire's gone out.'

'I'm cold.'

'Well, I don't know what you want me to do about it. If you'd gotten here earlier you could have had a hot meal.'

There was so much tension I was scared to breathe out in case I ignited it. I watched everyone trying not to watch me and just stood waiting and waiting and waiting and only one plate arrived, my father having eaten in the kitchen.

'Michael, show yer mum what you've won.'

'Can't I have me tea first? I'm hungry.'

'Yer can have yer tea in a minute. Go and fetch them.'

'What's he want to show me?'

'Some football medals he's won.'

'I'll look at them later, I want to watch Crossroads now.'

After finishing my meal, such as it was, I stared at the plate and played with the crumbs, although doing little more than chasing them around the edge of the plate.

'Stop playing with thee food! If yer finished, I'll show yer where yer room is.'

We climbed the stairs again in silence, which made me even more nervous, because as a general rule it means I'm not about to like what I'm being shown. The room had no carpet, but I could live with that, it was the plastic bucket that gained my undivided attention.

'That's for yer ter wee in.'

He took me outside the room to show me that he had attached a sneck to the door, which is basically a small hook that slots into a bracket to secure a door. Traditionally, they are used to secure garden gates or barn doors, but not on this occasion.

'I've had to put it on because if yer run off when yer on home leave then they'll stop yer coming home.'

'I don't want to be locked in my room, it's like Colditz.'

'Colditz? I'll give thee Colditz.'

The force of the blow sent me flying backwards into the door and I cracked my head. Dazed, I wet myself a little in shock, and in that moment I hated him and didn't recognise him as my father, just another brutal stranger.

That night I didn't sleep through the claustrophobia, trapped with my brother, unable to walk away from him should I feel the need. I just lay there until morning bursting for a piss.

* * * *

'Right, youse two, get yer kit on, we're goin' down the field.'

'I don't want to play football, it's pouring with rain.'

I'd spent several fine days under virtual house arrest, not being allowed out unless it was to run an errand for my mother, then as soon as it starts pissing down with rain he wants to play fucking football!

'Yer won't melt.'

I couldn't afford to fucking shrink either.

We crossed the road and there it was: child-sized goal posts and a scrap of land that didn't know why it was there.

'Michael, you get in goal. Right, same as always, we'll play up ter three goals but if yer let the last one in on purpose, we'll start from scratch.'

The first shot flew past me into the goal because the rain got in my eyes.

'Howay man, yer didn't even try!'

'I couldn't see.'

I saved the second with my legs and got knocked off my feet, and the third hit me full in the face and came back off the post. As I got back on my feet, my father ran in and smacked the rebound straight into my midriff, doubling me up, and my brother took full advantage by kicking the ball into an empty goal.

It's shit being an eight-year old, pint-sized goalkeeper.

CHAPTER SEVEN

On the eve of being returned to school, my father had gone out and my sisters were in bed. My brother was in the next room building a model aircraft, a passion he continued to share with my father. It was dark outside and the glow from the fire was encouraging, it felt like I had a friend in the room, an ally, a confidante that couldn't be broken. My mother sat in her favourite armchair by the fire drinking coffee. I knelt by its warm, seductive ambition and lost myself in it for a moment, thinking about my father and about what I was going to say.

'Mum, you know my new school?'

'What about it?'

'Well, if mums and dads don't want you to stay there anymore, you can come back home.'

'You have to go to that school, Michael, because you're naughty and they'll help you to stop running away and setting fires.'

'I'm not called Michael anymore, I'm called Mini.'

'Who told you that?'

'The teacher.'

'Well, I'll have words with him. You were christened Michael and that's what you'll be called.'

She held onto it like a stranglehold, perhaps it was all she had left of me.

'Anyway, tomorrow I could stay here.'

'I've already told you, you're going back to school and that's the end of the matter.'

'But horrible things happen.'

'Oh, Michael, you'll say anything to get your own way. Well, it's not going to work, it's not up to us what happens to you, it's up to the police and the social workers, so you'll just have to get used to it.'

If she truly believed in that crudely manufactured denial she did so because it was easier, an abdication that allowed both her and my father to play their roles of the aggrieved parents, swallowed up by the system. A space had opened, a viewpoint, allowing me to see each from the other and not wanting either. I began my recovery by retrieving the medals from my coat and throwing them down at my mother's feet.

'I don't want them, they're rubbish!'

'Well, throw them away, see if I care.'

'I didn't win them, Dad bought them in a shop.'

'You know, Michael, a mother loves her children no matter what, you don't have to pretend you've won things when you haven't.'

I think she amended her script minute by minute and it was becoming increasingly frustrating. The more she spoke, the less I understood, or wanted to.

'I didn't pretend, Dad did.'

'Just be yourself, don't try and be someone you're not.'

Fucking incredible! I could have cried, such was the overwhelming need to articulate what I couldn't. There was nothing behind the eyes and her mouth twitched at the corners like she was trying to smile but had forgotten how, such was her fabrication. Perhaps she had just borrowed his mask.

The following morning my father was at work and so my mother, along with my younger sister, provided the escort. Against all the odds, I had decided not to do a runner. I had been deeply wounded by their refusal to have me back home, an energy sapping wound that left me feeling unmotivated. I felt like I was bouncing between two walls, unable to break through, not yet knowing how to make a difference.

On arrival at Durham, I needed the toilet and told my mum. To my absolute shock and surprise, she told me to go off and find the toilet whilst she waited for me at the bus station. It gave me a lift, not being marshalled, a real sense of being in control, of having choices and for once having the freedom to exercise the right one, without regret but not out of a growing sense of maturity or responsibility, more an inverted form of rebellion, preferring to go back.

Having duly relieved myself I made my way back to the bus station only to find both mother and sister had quite simply vanished. I scoured every inch of the place but they were nowhere to be seen. It's one thing to choose this but no one likes a copycat, especially if they do it better than you. I set off in the hope they had simply stopped off at a shop, but there were an awful lot to choose from. However, I had only travelled twenty or thirty yards when my mother leapt out of a shop doorway and grabbed me forcibly by the arm.

'Right, I've got you! You must think I'm daft, I knew you would try something like this.'

'I haven't done anything, I was looking for you.'

'You're not a very good liar. I'm telling the school what you've done.'

'But I haven't done anything! When I came back from the toilet you weren't there.'

She marched me back towards the bus station and quite frankly I was both mentally and physically depleted. It wasn't so much a grave sense of injustice I was feeling, though it was present, it was more the madness of it all.

When we arrived at the school, I waited in reception whilst my mother went into the headmaster's office and presumably manufactured a scenario specifically designed to make life even more complicated. When she emerged she left, unable to look at me and without saying goodbye. I, of course, got the usual suspension of weekend leave, a reminder of the conduct expected of me, and a personal reminder of how right turned wrong.

On returning to my house Charlie was his usual, predictable self.

'Yer must be losing yer touch, Cooper, fancy getting nabbed by yer mam?'

Abandoned and then nabbed, putting the two together drew me no closer to understanding what had motivated her.

'Anyway, normal service has resumed. You're swimming tomorrow.'

'I'm not allowed to go, I nearly drowned last time, they said I didn't have to go.'

'Well, I've been told yer goin'. And anyway, if yer nearly drowned it's time yer learnt ter swim. I mean, it's not like yer've learnt 'owt else.'

He chuckled his way out of the dorm, but there would definitely be one less for swimming. I had no money and not much of a clue, just a vague idea. I decided to travel with the rest of the party to Shildon, on the premise that any free travel would further my cause without unnecessary explanation or worry. Once there the eye contact and banter meant that I was invisible which was perfect for comfort, camouflage and eventually pity.

'Sir, I don't feel well, I feel sick.'

'Better sit this one out, then, but you'll have to stay here in the changing rooms, there's nowhere to sit by the pool.'

Sitting wasn't an option. It was fucking cold, freezing in fact, and I had no coat, but I didn't need one, everything now was left to chance. Only two teachers had travelled with us and whilst they were busy supervising the rest, I simply slipped out the back door. It was an open invitation, so easy it would have been a crime to refuse.

I managed to make my way on foot to Bishop Auckland, without encountering anyone on the way. It was a journey of only a couple of miles, but had nevertheless felt challenging for it was the furthest I had gone to date. It bred confidence and allowed for a little creativity, as the next stage of the journey was going to be extremely tricky and the whole thing could unravel in an instant and set me back even further. This level of fear and the disappointment of failure increasingly helped to concentrate my mind, raising my level of consciousness. I was small, angelic and apparently cherubic; well, there's no point in possessing such attributes if they can't get you the occasional free ride! I strode purposefully onto a double-decker bus and headed straight for the top deck. I sat, nervously fidgeting, crossing and uncrossing my legs and was about to correct myself, insisting that I try and get a grip, when it occurred to me that my demeanour actually helped, rather than hindered my cause. It was method acting before the fashion became more important than the method.

'Fares, please.'

I was instantly relieved that the conductor was a middle aged woman who looked like she might invite you around on a Sunday afternoon for cake and a glass of homemade lemonade. I looked down at my shoes whilst sitting on my hands, gently rocking back and forth, and in a whisper that was barely audible announced that I didn't have it. She assumed that I'd spent it on sweets but after I'd fabricated a story about two older boys stealing my coat and my money, she gave me a ticket.

There is no obvious pleasure in manipulating someone in that way, no glee in receiving their sympathy or pity, it was just a tool, bereft of ego or vanity.

On arrival at Durham I stepped off the bus and having spotted a policeman, ran with breath that was on fire, burning my lungs even though they were young and resilient. The city was busy and claustrophobic, and far from being a place to hide, I stood out like a pair of bulldog's bollocks. I was just passing through, there was nothing but beauty here, remaining still and impervious, except for the river, whose journey could never be thwarted or abandoned. I hadn't a coat or a sweater so I was clearly ill prepared for whatever the elements threw at me, but fear was the initial motivating factor in jumping on that bus. Then there was another bus to catch and another lie. I simply pretended I had lost my fare, whilst frantically searching through my pockets. To my absolute surprise I was handed a ticket with a knowing wink. I wasn't as good as I thought I was. I travelled through Craghead and on to Hustle Down, home of my former Catholic school and across the road, the church.

'I'll say I saw you, next time I see your dad.'

I was too busy looking out for him to be worried about some future rebuke. In order to earn a little extra money he sometimes drove for the same bus company at weekends, and he obviously knew a number of the drivers. He was forever telling people that I was attending a 'special school' like it was a badge of honour. This particular driver obviously suspected that I was on the run, yet he allowed me to continue with my journey.

Now, as I stood outside the entrance to the school, I was even more alert. My old man often went to watch my brother's football matches; should he be there, the game was up for me, but it was a risk I decided to take. It had been a while since I was last here and the thought of my brother being inside, selling his soul, made me chuckle rather than recoil. They couldn't touch me now.

Armed with the fake football medals, I brazenly strode into the school with more purpose than I had ever mustered during my brief attendance, unshackled but still feeling all the old contempt rising like bile. I had ignored my mother's instruction to throw them in the bin, and I now had them in my pocket, fully intent on invading some lesson to proudly show them off. However, it's too simplistic to suggest I was there solely to show off, I think the truth probably lies somewhere between wanting to proclaim, 'Do you really think you got the better of me by sending me off to boot camp? Look at these fuckers!' Or, 'Hey! I'm still here in spite of you.'

The door to the headmistress' office was slightly ajar so I knocked and waited. There was no answer, so I knocked again, still no answer.

Perfect.

I entered the office and immediately noticed her bag sitting invitingly on a chair. As I approached it, I felt like there were eyes everywhere, even in the silence. All I could see was the bag and an opportunity to extend my sabbatical by obtaining the necessary means; at their expense, it would be worth more than gold. I reached in and found an envelope containing twelve pounds and fifty pence.

It had been so breathtakingly easy! I was in no rush to leave and go spend my compensation, rather I wanted to capitalize on the unexpected friendliness of these walls. I quietly floated up the stairs towards the staff room, the sense of danger omnipresent and the penalties increased with every step, but so did the desire to repel them.

The room was empty in every sense, except for the odd reminder: a tattered old briefcase, a dog-eared religious text and more cigarette butts than there were empty coffee cups. I opened the briefcase, mainly because it was the only thing to open and offered the only possibility of something hidden. Amongst some papers I didn't even bother to read, was a set of car keys. As I held them in my hand, I remembered how my father had taught me to steer his lorry some time earlier, so I rather foolishly believed that I could drive. The whole expedition began shaping itself into a major coup, bringing with it an excitement that was too thick to swallow.

I almost ran out of there, such was my inability to saunter. I wanted things to happen faster than I could think of them, I had a ticket to the unknown and though I didn't know how to get there, I wouldn't be asking anyone for directions. There was only one car located in the car park, directly across the road from the school and right next to the church. I nervously fumbled with the keys, aware of my limitations but not recognizing the need for caution. Once inside, I immediately locked all the doors. There's recklessness and there's downright stupidity, and although guilty of both, I was not willing to surrender and whimper my way through a series of lame excuses. I eagerly slotted the key into the ignition and turned it. Much to my surprise, the engine roared into life and so did mine. It felt powerful, sitting there in my capsule, observing the unforgiving stare of the church whose reach had begun to shrink. I pressed the accelerator to the floor and the whole car felt like it was vibrating, but it never moved an inch. I tried again and again but each time it sent out its battle cry and gave away my position.

I never saw the crack from which she crawled, nor did I notice her creeping towards me in an attempt to take me by surprise. Sadly she did, banging on the window so loud I pissed a little.

'Turn that off right now! Go on, turn it off!'

I stared back at her, silenced by hate, blood pressure red. The deputy headmistress, who by then probably thought I was deliberately targeting her. The truth was, I didn't know whose fucking car it was, just that it probably stank of piety.

'I won't tell you again, turn that off, you're coming with me!'

I don't fucking think so! I haven't completely lost my mind, nor the ability to resist infiltration.

'Right, I'm fetching the police.'

I watched her disappear across the car park and having fleetingly glanced over her shoulder to check that I was still there, was gone. I waited a moment or two, expecting some kind of ambush, but it soon became clear that her need to dial that number was more important than personal heroics. I climbed out of the car and locked it, placing the keys on the roof. They were redundant now, as was the car itself, and despite an overwhelming feeling of disappointment, I was back on foot with reduced options, but surrendering wasn't one of them. I stood and stared at the church with an incredibly mischievous urge to take refuge there, but common sense prevailed; it was the first place the police would search, such was its close proximity to the vehicle.

Adjacent to the church was some woodland that backed onto a sprawling housing estate, perfect for a rabbit seeking to avoid capture by a four-wheeled predator who prefers the main road. I headed for Stanley. Under normal circumstances, I wouldn't have considered it to be the smartest move, given that the police station that covered a large part of the district was housed there. Nevertheless, need transcended risk; I was cold and hungry and it was the nearest town where I could provide myself with food and warmth.

First stop was a clothes shop where I purchased a duffle coat for approximately eight pounds. Then I needed something to eat. The Roma café was run by an Italian family. I had been there so the proprietors knew me. I ordered a simple meal and sat alone at a vacant table but I struggled to eat, convinced that the police would walk in at any moment and cart me off to their factory, more questions and probably more lies, because to conform would have been the biggest lie of them all.

I hit the high street and felt totally exposed, like a wild animal afraid of humans, afraid of their potential to harm. Every time a man walked towards me I expected him to reach out and try to grab me; the women, too, for I was the only child not at school.

I made it to the bus station without a police escort, but still couldn't relax, that would have been terminal. My eyes never fixed on a target for more than a second or two, constantly on the move, hoping to spot danger before it spotted me. I needed the bus to transport me away from the immediate area and put some distance between myself and the crime scene. I figured my parents would have already received a visit from the cops, so where better to hide? The problem was, I didn't want the same conductor so when the bus pulled in I hid behind a group of people and checked it out.

Relief.

I paid my fare and travelled unhindered. When I got off at Craghead, I once again kept my eyes on the move. There was a large expanse of woodland around the village and several fields, so this is where I headed and at last my heart rate returned to something like normal and my eyes stopped moving so frenetically. I was in what was fast becoming my natural habitat and I was still hungry. The village was small and other than at weekends when the pubs were chucking out it didn't generally have large throngs of people parading down the streets, therefore it would be easy to spot a potential captor in plenty of time

As dusk fell on a tired village and my reasons for being there began to diminish, it was time to leave my hideout. I had no real idea of the time; unlike the Native American Indians or the Aborigines of Australia, I hadn't learned to read the sun, but I could see it had gone down. I had earlier built a small camp fire which had provided comfort, but soon it would be visible to every chancer in the village, including an ex-paratrooper for a father, so I bade farewell to the party. It made no real sense to be wandering around the village without a single idea as to what to do or where to sleep. I was inviting trouble by boxing myself in. I guess I was just seeking some kind of familiarity, no matter how desolate. Perhaps that's why, when needing the toilet, I marched up the street and into our back yard where I took a piss.

I was about to pull the flush when I heard a car pull up directly outside the house.

My senses were so finely tuned I could have heard a gnat taking a piss in the next street. The latch went on the gate and it was pushed open. I slowed my breathing, almost stopping it altogether, afraid of being heard. I was so paranoid, I was convinced the steam from my piss would escape through a crack in the door and expose me.

Then there was a knock at the door and my father answered it.

'Mr Cooper, we're here about Michael.'

'Well, we've already had a visit earlier, they said if he shows up ter contact yay lot, but he's not been here.'

'Well, it's not just about him running away. Do you mind if we come in?'

'Aye, come in we've nowt ter hide.'

My father stood aside and allowed the cops to sully his doorstep. Once inside, he closed the door and I hesitated, still paranoid. After a few seconds peering through the tiniest gap in the door, it seemed fairly obvious there was to be no ambush. I left the toilet door open with a smile and a sideways glance towards the window. I did the same with the gate, then once outside, I fled towards the unlit wasteland that had become my secret tunnel.

I don't really know why I took such a huge risk for scraps, maybe I just wanted to feel that tingling sensation again. I knew they would be looking for me, so I took refuge in a derelict building that allowed me to observe with relish the two roads the cops would have to access. If my father arrived on foot I had him covered, too, and my smile grew broader as I grew taller. Eventually I did give in to hunger and broke cover. The fish and chip shop was on the one main road that ran through the village so the risks were pretty obvious. If I was to be captured going in search of a meal, it would at least have been more bearable than being captured through day-dreaming, to which I was prone.

Having arrived unimpeded at the chip shop I didn't hesitate, I quickly purchased a fish cake and a bag of chips, and didn't hang around. It had started to rain but I was unable to take shelter in a shop doorway, so I moved behind the shops where there were some garages, most of which were never locked, neither did they house any cars. I walked in and could instantly smell shit, but there was nothing I could do, except leave the door slightly ajar and try gulping down my dinner as quickly as was humanly possible, trying not to breathe through my nose.

I was absolutely stuffed and began to suffer from trapped wind, and I needed a cigarette. I had managed to purchase these from the local pub, saying they were for my father. I don't know if the barman believed me, but he sold them to me anyway. Hard to imagine that back then a packet of twenty cigarettes cost around thirty pence.

The rain had severely limited my options, for even had it stopped the ground would still be wet. So I walked and walked, through woods and across fields, getting wetter and wetter, heavier and heavier, both in mood and in movement. Sadness left its calling card, no number, no address, but I knew where to find it, unlike sleep. The night was a reluctant guardian but it's all I had, watching without comment, stretching the time and silencing my words. It felt like I was now on the run from myself.

Strangely I made a conscious decision to go to the church. I knew it would be open and of course shield me from the elements. I stared at the pictures depicting the various stages of Christ's crucifixion and then at the stained glass windows; a window that can't be seen out of, keeps everything trapped inside. I guess maybe I wanted to be there on my own terms, and sitting there smoking a cigarette stripped the place of its camp paraphernalia, leaving nothing to replace it; ultimately, it was just an old building, a house that hid secrets. Coercion bought your life for a penance; my penance was a slap in the face for the glory of God, an assault perpetrated by a man in a frock. My crime? Failing to attend confession, preferring instead to spend the bus fare on sweets. It was a while ago now, but I could still see his yellow teeth and nicotine-stained fingers. Without the frock, he would have looked no different to the men my father drank with, but he preferred to drink alone and eat alone, for the secret must remain in the vault.

My presence there began as a kind of fuck you, being able to shelter from the rain in a place that would have me drown, but it quickly turned to the same old resentments, the same old sense of futility, corrupt in origin and interpretation. I guess ultimately I was seeking my own.

I made my way to the front and sat facing the cart that housed the cheap candles. People who had less money than sense were persuaded to light one of these and leave a donation that was invariably of a higher value than the candle itself. They did this, believing that the bigger the donation, the more healing they would receive. I didn't want to be nervous, I just wanted it to be over, wanted the derelict soundtrack to be engulfed in smoke and sent coughing and spluttering through one of those cartoon windows. Just a boy, nerves coursing through his veins, unable to sit still, unable to stop fidgeting and ultimately, unable to dispatch the matches back into his pocket or the thought from his mind.

It has to happen.

The words of others had caused me to hesitate for a while, but once the decision was taken and I rose to my feet, I was alone in a unilateral state of mind that heard only itself. I lit a candle and held it upside down, watching as the wax dripped relentlessly onto the wooden floor and not a coin in sight. The momentum gathered pace almost faster than I could keep up with it, and I was breathing heavier than if I'd run a marathon.

Candle after candle was lit until the whole cart was liberated. I then wheeled it over to the pew, the very one that had made my arse sore and my heart burdened. Wax spilled everywhere, I even dipped my fingers in it, the warmth settling the silence into something more accommodating, but the anger hadn't quite cried itself out. I found a handful of bibles and one by one I lit them, placing them ceremoniously on the cart, then I lit a fag from one. On the way out I dropped it into the font containing the holy water.

I made for the woods and smoked another cigarette. Everything was different now, I wasn't just a runaway searching for some esoteric truth, I had begun to attack theirs, the church, the state, all brutal in their own way, making decisions in ignorance and expecting the recipients to be grateful.

I made my way back to Craghead, not a particularly smart move, but I didn't know what else to do, or where else to go. I was trying to decide when a passing police car caught me unawares.

'Michael, don't make me run after you, I'm a lot fitter and faster.'

I stopped, thinking that if he chased and caught me things would get rough. I turned dejectedly, and with head bowed, walked back to his car.

'I've been looking all over for you. I think you've got some explaining to do, don't you?'

'Dunno.'

'You don't know? Well, I think you do. Come on, we'd better let your parents know you're safe at last.'

We walked through the gate and approached the door. The cop knocked and we waited, and when the door opened, my mother was stood there; it could have been worse.

'Hello, Mrs Cooper, just thought you might like to know, we found Michael.'

'Where was he?'

'Well, actually, he was coming out of the yard as I was coming up the street to tell you that there have been a couple of allegations made against him. Were you aware he was here?'

'No, I had no idea. What kind of allegations?'

Was I fucking invisible?

'Theft and arson.'

'What did he set fire to?'

'The Catholic church opposite the school. I'm taking him to the station now and obviously because of his age he's going to need an adult present when he's being questioned.'

'Well, I can't come, I've got three other children to look after.'

'What about your husband?'

'He's at work.'

'Okay, we'll contact social services. In the meantime, if you have any concerns, you know how to contact us.'

And that was that. I was put in the back of the police car and driven to Stanley police station, all the time reminding myself that I had brazenly walked through the town only the day before. None of it mattered, it was just a way of passing the journey. I wasn't placed in a cell, I sat in reception on a swivel chair which was great fun, although the desk sergeant didn't agree and kept telling me off, but I was bored.

* * * *

'Hello, Michael, I'm the duty social worker. Is there anything you want to tell me before we go into interview?'

'No.'

She was cold and static and wore glasses on the end of her nose; she was indeed the child snatcher.

'Well, you've been accused of some pretty serious things, perhaps I can help?'

I didn't need her help, it couldn't be offered without a price I couldn't afford or a sincerity I couldn't expect.

'I'm okay.'

All around me the machine was oiling its wheels, a provincial militia plus supporting cast. It was me against them with only one roll of the dice.

'Right, Michael, we need to talk about what happened today. This officer is going to write everything down and at the end if you agree that it's a true account of what's been said, I'm going to ask you and your social worker to sign it, okay?'

'Yeah.'

'We know you went into the school, Michael, you were spotted by one of the teachers, and it just so happens that around the same time some money went missing from an office, and you were identified as being behind the wheel of a car…'

I remained silent.

'Look, Michael, we can prove you were in the school and we can prove you tried to steal the car so this silent routine isn't going to help at all… You were also seen running from the church as it went up in smoke. I think it's time you talked to us, don't you? I know you had some problems at the school but what have you got against the church?'

'I don't like the priest.'

'I don't like my wife's mother but I don't plan on setting her house on fire! So, what is it about the priest that you don't like?'

'He hits me.'

'That's a pretty serious allegation. You do know it's wrong to make these things up, don't you?... Do you want to know what I think? I think you've just thought that up to shift the blame onto someone else.'

'No, I haven't, you're making it up.'

'Excuse me, officer, can I have a quick word with him, please?'

'No problem.'

Fuck me! For a minute, I thought there were three cops in the room. Perhaps her vocal chords simply needed a little waxing, or she was bored.

'Michael, are you saying the priest assaulted you?'

'Yeah.'

'Well, why didn't you report it?'

'Because everyone does the same. I get hit at school just for not saying their stupid prayers, I get hit at my new school for nothing and I get hit off my dad because he says I'm a girl.'

'You could have reported all this to us.'

'You just write things down and take no notice.'

'I think that's very unfair, we took notice before and got you a nice new school.'

Fucking unbelievable!

'Well, if we could press on. Michael, did you steal that money? Did you attempt to steal a car and did you commit an act of arson on the Catholic church of St. Mary?'

'Yes.'

'Why, son? Why does such a young boy want to do these things? What do you get out of it?'

They were asking me to try to describe air or attempt to teach Shakespeare to an illiterate, they wanted answers to questions they didn't hear themselves ask, just like they never heard me, therefore a shrug of the shoulders was all I could muster.

'You're going to have to do better than that at some point, Michael. I don't think this is just going to go away. Anyway, read the statement and if you agree with it sign the bottom.'

I took the statement and began reading, not an easy task given the style of handwriting, which also contained the odd spelling mistake. I signed it, then passed it to the social worker who changed her glasses, then signed it without bothering to read it first.

'You didn't read it.'

'I've been sat here listening to everything, haven't I?'

The cops left the room and within minutes had returned.

'We're done here, he's all yours.

I was too young to be prosecuted so I was to be returned to Redworth. She grabbed me very forcibly by the arm and marched me out of the station towards her car.

'I'm sorry if that hurts but we can't have you running away, I'll never catch you in these shoes.'

On arrival at the school I was ordered into the headmaster's office where I duly sat facing his desk. He looked like he was ready to leap over it.

'Stand up, boy, I didn't tell you to sit. Stand up!'

I slowly rose to my feet. I hated being barked at like I was some kind of wild animal that needed taming.

'I understand you've made a number of scurrilous allegations against members of my staff, am I right?'

It was pretty clear from his tone that this wasn't going to be a frank examination of the truth, rather a pernicious attempt to extract an immediate retraction which would not only put the matter to bed, but would discredit me against any future claim, allowing future abusers impunity to act.

'It's the truth.'

'You don't know the meaning of the word! You steal, you set fires, you run away, do you seriously expect an intelligent person to fall for this malicious clap trap which, I hasten to add, ties in very conveniently with your own indiscretions?'

'Dunno.'

'I have a duty to have these claims independently investigated but mark my words, Cooper, if they prove to be false, your position at the school will come under serious review. If I had my way you'd be gone already, but it seems your age has come to your rescue. Well, you won't be able to rely on that for very much longer.'

I had stopped listening for he was mostly talking to himself. I had hoped that the severity of my actions would have had a somewhat different impact; how naïve could one be, to expect the anger to dissipate when it was their only form of control?

'Now get to your house block and I assure you, Cooper, you are going to be very carefully monitored from now on. If you so much as sneeze without permission, I will come down on you like a ton of bricks.'

I very slowly made my way up the drive. The bollocking I had just received, whilst aggressive in tone and content, was just words, whereas Charlie had his own brand of retribution. As I entered the house, I saw my bag flying through the air towards me. Unable to catch it, it fell to the floor.

'Pick it up!'

I did as instructed, trying not to take my eyes off him. I was nervous and expecting some kind of physical punishment.

'House block two. As I seem to be the ogre, you can no longer stay here. Now, get out of my sight.'

I didn't hesitate, house block two was run by Cyril and Betty. Cyril was a bear of a man, and whilst Betty was small and timid, anyone attempting to take advantage of that fact would usually be sent flying across the room. I was shown to a dorm and unpacked my things in the usual way. Cyril suddenly appeared, carrying a plate full of sandwiches and a glass of orange juice.

'I thought you might be hungry. If you can't eat them all, don't worry, I'll give them to the dog.'

'I'm starving.'

The fish and chips they had provided for me at the police station had looked like they belonged there so I hadn't eaten them.

'Now listen, kidda, I know all about thee, but I always believe in starting with a clean slate, so you do right by me and I'll do right by thee.'

If this was all meant to be some kind of punishment, then like everything else, they got it badly wrong.

CHAPTER EIGHT

My claims were investigated and inevitably found to be unproven or, in school parlance, 'malicious', so weekend leave, along with all other privileges, was suspended indefinitely. Presumably such a punishment was designed to help concentrate my mind; well, it did, but not in the way they intended or hoped for.

I was conspicuous whilst they could hide behind authority, an authority that would, if necessary, lie on their behalf, not to protect them, but in order to protect the apparatus that constantly needed feeding, this was somehow more important than a child's life. I had only myself now, and quickly had to learn to adapt to a changing environment, one where the boundaries were being stretched and then, when convenient, put back for the purposes of retribution and on occasions, sadistic pleasure. I became increasingly subdued and withdrawn, living in a fantasy world of my own creation, impersonating various animals I had encountered in the woods, feeling a deep connection with them. By the time the summer holidays came around, I had only managed one weekend at home, which was largely spent watching my father playing football for a local team he had joined, or being trained to do the same if and when I reached adulthood. The prospect of spending six weeks doing more of the same did not exactly fill me with glee. In fact, I would rather have spent it in the woods.

'Cooper, who's supposed to be picking you up?'

'Dunno, my Dad, I suppose.'

'Well, he needs to hurry up, we're not running a bleeding taxi service, you know.'

It was late afternoon and everyone else had already left. When I was eventually collected sometime later, it was not at all what I expected.

'Hello, Michael, do you remember me? Your normal social worker is on leave this week, so they sent me as we've already met.'

How could I forget the sanctimonious cow? What I wanted to know was, what the fuck was she doing there? And she was fucking late!'

'Where's my Dad?'

'We can talk about it in the car, I think they're keen to get us out of here.'

A conspiratorial whisper in my ear, I'm surprised she didn't try and twist my arm up my back at the same time. We walked to her car and I walked purposefully to the passenger side. Once we had set off I was desperate for information. I instinctively knew something was wrong and I didn't like it.

'Why isn't my Dad taking me?'

'The thing is, Michael, things are pretty tough at home at the moment. Your parents have three other children to look after, it's not just about you. Anyway, it's been decided you'd be better off spending your summer holidays somewhere else, that's all.'

What a fucking knife in the back!

Great Lumley is a small place just outside of Chester-le-Street in the North East. I was taken to a children's home which housed around ten kids of varying ages. The middle-aged lady who ran it, and whom I'd been assured was looking forward to meeting me, clearly wasn't. No sooner had I stepped inside, than she began growling out a whole series of 'don't's'. Some of the other kids who were hanging around even began issuing their own house rules which I completely ignored, and rather enjoyed their feeble attempts at enforcement. During dinner I was largely ignored and by bedtime had to share with a fourteen year old, an arrangement that suited neither of us.

By first light he was sleeping blissfully alone. The surge of energy instantly released, as I stepped through the door and into the garden, was overwhelming. At the bottom of the garden lay a shed, curiously unlocked given that it housed a number of bicycles. I chose one the right size and peddled away on a sea of adrenalin, excitement more tangible than ever. I had the freedom of the land for a couple of hours then the police, social services and even my family would seek to evict me and have me returned to my pig pen, to once again be ostracised by the pigs ready for slaughter. All that mattered was to keep peddling, it's all I had, and it was stolen.

I found my way to Chester-le-Street pretty quickly and then headed towards Craghead, already knowing the way. I guess the familiarity was comforting, as was the feeling of being so close to the family domain and still wanting to be a part of it, but not knowing how to articulate it in the normal way. Just a kid still wanting his mum and dad and wanting them to want him. So I ran away that day, and the day after that and the day after that.

* * * *

'They'll stop yer coming home, yer know, if yer carry on like this. Is that what thee wants?'

And that's what they did, at least in the interim. Fed up with spending their holidays in police stations or having to chauffer me back to the holding pen, the social services decided that the only way to guarantee my presence was to lock me up.

'It's for your own good, Michael, you'll see that in the end. Anything could happen to you when you're wandering about at night and think of the worry you've caused your mum and dad. Anyway if you give it a chance, I think you'll like Penshaw.'

My parents were in the back of the car, very depressing with Mum struggling with her own fragility and completely wrapped up in herself, and the old man competing with the social worker, the pair of them fighting over banalities.

'Now listen, son, the best thing thee can dee noo is just dee as yer told and don't think thee's cleverer than everyone else coz thee's not.'

'Your dad's right, Michael, you need to start obeying the rules then you'll find that you won't be in trouble so much. Surely that's got to be better than being told off all the time?'

Being told off had been my entire experience and perhaps I would have felt lonely without it, unnerved even. I'd never really had a substantive conversation that didn't have anger and hostility as its core elements. I'd never really had a peer group and now I was being given one I couldn't walk away from, far more terrifying than a locked door.

Penshaw House was in Houghton-le-Spring, a few miles from Sunderland on the North East coast. It housed a number of boys, from the very young to teenagers of school leaving age, and it was completely secure. The windows, whilst made of glass, came in the form of narrow slats and only opened a matter of inches and every door that led outside was secured with a heavy-duty lock that a master criminal would struggle to open. The main door had an entry alarm and we had to be buzzed in. It was daunting and intimidating, and I was struggling to keep myself together, but it had to be done and I ended up gritting my teeth so tightly I couldn't speak. We were shown into a small cramped office that simply couldn't cope with the numbers and it was quite amusing, seeing everybody trying not to trip over each other.

'Right, then, I don't suppose this is enjoyable for anyone, so why don't we say our goodbyes now so as not to make it any more difficult?'

At that moment I was struggling to fight the surge of emotion that was threatening to engulf me and render me useless, but I knew what to do, knew the quiet signalled departure and that boys didn't cry. Instead, I stood rigid as my mum promised to write and my father shook hands without even looking. Once they had left, taking the social worker with them, normal service was resumed. This was my reality and anything wished for would have to wait until it couldn't be heard or interrupted.

'I'm the deputy head, Michael. I hear you also like being called Mini, am I right?'

'Yeah.'

'So would you rather we call you Michael or Mini?'

The question, if genuine, offered choice and caused a moment's hesitation as I eyed him suspiciously. I had no experience of being completely on the level and it required a shift in attitude and, more significantly, a belief in my own ability to show discernment and know who to trust.

'Mini.'

'I'll make a note of it.'

I pretty quickly guessed I'd be making a few of my own. I never imagined that a gentle, ostensibly warm and friendly manner could disturb my mind far more effectively than the violent, aggressive machinations that continued to be rolled off the production line.

'How long will I have to stay here?'

'Just for the holidays, then you'll be returned to your normal school. It's not all bad here, you know. Obviously we're not your mum and dad, and it is a locked unit and we try to remain mindful of that, but the staff are a pretty friendly lot and the other lads are fairly easy to get along with.'

And then came the smile again, perhaps unable to contain his amusement at a system that prevents someone from absconding for the duration of the summer holidays, then gives carte blanche to do just that, knowing full well that he will. It was ridiculous beyond all reasonable comprehension, and I wasn't laughing. As we spoke, the door flew open and in strolled a pair of boxer dogs, one fairly old and one much younger.

'Sorry about that, the older one has learned how to open doors, I'll get rid of them.'

I was hoping he knew how to pick locks, too. I allowed them to stay and fed them the chocolate my mum had left.

'They seem to like you, are you fond of dogs?'

'Yeah.'

Dogs never asked for anything I couldn't deliver or wasn't willing to give freely, they had simple needs and didn't aspire to be anything other than what they already were; it's all they knew and it was enough.

Once the formalities were over I was escorted through the unit and shown to my room, which was on the top floor. Although the unit was secure, the smell of fear and despondency was strangely absent. The walls were brimming with artwork, some displaying genuine talent, whilst others were clearly an exercise in time management and sleep deprivation. Walking through the various study groups and play areas, being introduced as Mini Cooper, made me instantly recognizable by arousing curiosity. My own had also been aroused, but not in the same way. Everyone was so fucking happy! Laughter, fooling around and even the odd attempt at mocking my name seemed to be the staple diet in this strange, rather experimental, diversion. Perhaps the locks were designed to keep people from getting in, for the ones already there seemed happy to stay.

I had a single room, which was perfect. I sensed I would need the space to be able to think on my own terms, be angry when I needed to be and in weaker moments indulge myself, and then regroup. It was my own private existence.

That night, as the door locked behind me and the lights went out, I buried my head in the pillow and crumpled. Tears of anger, growls of despair, frustration, making noises I couldn't silence. I was here because I shouldn't have been there, and so I ran away, it was the only logical thing to do. When people try to fuck you, you can either bend over or stand up straight. If I'd stayed and played at being a happy slave, that pillow would have been my only friend and the darkness my only confidante, and if I broke out and found my way home, I'd be even more lost; some choice.

Chance arrived in unexpected form. I had spent several days examining every tiny crack of that building, looking for a potential blind spot. One lunchtime I was chasing a gooseberry around my bowl, much more fun than screwing up my face at the taste, when I was summoned to the office.

'Min, come in, have a seat.'

I sat, hands clasped together, knees knocking, figuring I had been rumbled just when I was on the verge of getting out of here.

'So, how do you think you've settled in?'

I couldn't determine whether his smile was smug satisfaction or just a mask he always wore. Even during the pauses, it never left his face as the colour must have surely been leaving mine, my guilty mind filling in the gaps and trying to figure out what it was that had alerted them to my intentions. I hadn't told anyone or written anything down, nor did I make it obvious that I had noticed one of the windows in the dining room appeared to open a fraction wider than the others. I had needed an opportunity to investigate this more fully, but now my heart was in my bowels.

'Okay, I suppose.'

'Just okay?'

'Dunno really.'

'Well, I'm pleased to say the reports coming in from staff have so far been nothing short of glowing. No incidents of bad behaviour, no attempts to abscond, polite and courteous at all times and basically complying with all requirements.'

I had just been taught another way, quite by mistake: the art of manipulation, that until now hadn't been deliberate, yet had nevertheless turned a watchful eye into a sleepy one. The initial assessment, with its warm pages based around the fact that by doing the complete opposite to what was expected, rather than baffle it, simply fed their vanity.

'So, how do you fancy taking the dogs for a little walk around the field at the back?'

'Take the dogs for a walk?'

'We try and reward good behaviour, Mini, and I personally like to teach responsibility to those I feel are capable of taking up the challenge. I suppose that's what I'm doing with you, taking up the challenge, because once out there, there's no locked doors or indeed any other impediment. Should you choose to take off there's nothing to stop you.'

Christmas in summertime! Now, that doesn't very often happen. Thankfully, my giddiness was misinterpreted as over-excitement at the prospect of a little freedom in the company of the dogs. Thankfully, he didn't panic and change his mind.

'You'll probably need this.'

He reached into his desk drawer and removed a bar of chocolate that he threw at me. I caught it, hopefully a sign of my regained composure.

'If they try and wander off, just show them the chocolate, they'll soon come back.'

Even the dogs had been psychologically evaluated, but what inducement would stop me from wandering off? As I was escorted to the back door, I fell silent in an attempt to give nothing away. The closer I got to that door, the more irregular my breathing became, so I fussed the dogs.

After he let me out onto the huge playing field, he just as quickly disappeared back inside. For the first time in days, there were no voices and I could laugh, cry, or take a piss without being observed. Or could I? It had all been so incredibly easy, too easy, or reckless beyond comprehension. Could a massaged ego really bend so badly out of shape?

I ignored the dogs for a while, they weren't a concern as this field was theirs and I was the one who stood out. I scoured the trees, searching for a possible vantage point, convinced I was being watched. I searched every window, unaware that it's virtually impossible to view the inside from the out, especially from a distance. Such was my paranoia and general disturbance of mind, I was unable to move from the spot. I'd been frozen by things I couldn't see, and disturbed by words I wasn't used to hearing. Now I searched for something else, a place to saunter towards under the pretence of walking the dogs, a place that would hide me at least long enough to bring out the reinforcements, should there be any, and having not wandered off campus the only explanation would be theirs. Having found a spot the dogs were willing to occupy, I simply had to wait, and the waiting talks to you, making you more eager than is sometimes wise, but caution can be equally unwise, for should they arrive, I get the brownie point as the key turns in the lock.

I was perfectly placed and still had the chocolate, and though it had probably melted, I shouldn't think the dogs would mind. In fact, the more they licked, engrossed in their simple pleasure, the more they wouldn't notice me as I slipped away. It was simple and uncomplicated, our respective needs immersed in what was available and what we chose from that. I showed them their delights and they sat in front of me obediently, no tails wagging for they didn't have any, but their paws waved at the air in a gesture of longing and I couldn't deny them. I unwrapped the chocolate and placed it on the ground, taking one final look around me as I did so, and then I walked away, taking quicker and quicker steps until I was away from the building and the dogs were out of sight.

Having reached the side of the road, I simply had to cross, avoiding the traffic as I did, then I would be gone, out of sight and out of reach. But I couldn't stop myself from looking back. The dogs were wandering aimlessly, sniffing at the ground and looking for where I might be, so I crossed the road in order to throw them off the scent, along with anyone else who might want to pick up the trail. It was perfect, now all I had to do was disappear amongst the maze of streets and houses, keeping away from busy roads. It was so easy, I couldn't believe it was happening. It was time to go, the clock was ticking, vanity has its limits and temptation had to be measured. I guess delirium must have set in, for my mind was being pulled in all directions and taking me to places I didn't want to go.

I had only ever had myself to consider, allowing the decision-making process to be fast, efficient and generally without doubts or hesitation. Now I was in danger of being apprehended at the side of the road through a combination of thought processes that had somehow contaminated me. They weren't my dogs but they had been entrusted to me, their welfare had become my concern, preventing my legs from moving in the direction they so wanted to. My greatest fear was if they had and the dogs had seen me, they might have attempted to cross the road themselves.

So, with a gap in the traffic, I crossed back over onto the field, although the road still called out to me, screaming in my head. I once again hesitated, but my legs were still being controlled by unfamiliar conditions. When the dogs saw me, they quickly came running over, no howls of derision, no questions I didn't want to answer, just unconditional affection, something of a novelty in itself.

Walking back towards the unit was the hardest thing I'd ever had to do, not so much because an opportunity had slipped so unceremoniously through my fingers, but because their egos would be bristling with conceit. I consoled myself with the thought that there would be other opportunities, but for the moment a just cause wasn't worth a dog's life, or a motorist's. I walked them back to the unit and pressed the bell. When the deputy head came to the door, his smile couldn't have been more fucking smug and it irritated the hell out of me.

'I'm not generally wrong about people.'

Or dogs it would seem. For once I did the right thing for the right reasons, because it was right for me, and that helped me to ignore their smugness. The dog walking became a regular feature of my time there, I guess they quickly figured that it was the only way to guarantee my return, and for me it was a guaranteed friendship on acceptable terms.

A number of other psychological evaluations were conducted during my stay, one of my favourites involving a group of us being taken into a room and, despite our tender years, each of us was given a cigarette which would be lit by a member of staff. The rules were simple: holding the cigarette between our fingers, we simply had to let it burn down naturally and the person whose cigarette took the longest to burn won the prize. It was fascinating, watching people stare longingly at their cigarette. Some would last a third of the way before starting to puff furiously, some would get halfway and some managed to hold out until the last couple of drags. I stayed the distance but was beaten quite arbitrarily by a boy whose cigarette just happened to burn slower and he won a prize of a single cigarette. I therefore quickly learned that as the prize was what I already had, better to just get on and smoke it. Hence, I didn't get any future invites to the game.

Shortly before I was due to leave the home, we were invited to put ourselves forward as contestants for a beauty pageant that one member of staff decided to call, 'Miss Lovely Legs.' I had stick legs and was pigeon-toed, so I didn't really fancy my chances but I was a big fan of Glam Rock, therefore having the chance to dress up was just too compelling an invitation to ignore. I didn't think of winning, I didn't even think of it in terms of a competition, it was a chance to do something without explanation, in the full knowledge that my old man would never know because he wasn't there. Such freedom could not be held back, so I found myself at the front of the queue, more talkative than ever, mainly trying to talk myself into a dress that I could wear whenever I closed my eyes. I wonder what he saw when he closed his? I had a curtain wrapped around me to form an evening gown, a real off-the-shoulder little number complete with sandal type shoes. Then came make-up and hair, and when it was finished, I actually felt different.

I stood looking in the mirror, no hint of embarrassment or self-consciousness. I was the antithesis of everything my father represented, that was my victory, the only one worth hanging onto. Had he been in the audience, I don't think I would have ever stopped smiling. Better still to smile and him not know, such a secret is a friend that never betrays.

We were paraded across the stage and asked a couple of dumb questions before the judges announced their decision. Remarkably, I won and was awarded a rosette and a couple of chocolate bars.

A few days later, the holidays were over and I was delivered back to Redworth Hall. It seemed strange that something as simple as the passage of time could turn things upside down as it so patently had. The previous night I had slept behind a locked door, now there wasn't one in sight and no one seemed concerned. I had my regular social worker with me but I was in no mood to talk, so I didn't. He quickly figured this, so he too shut the fuck up! As I climbed into the car, I wasn't even sure that I wanted to leave. I knew only too well where I was going and equally well what I would be facing, whereas the place I was leaving was still a mystery to me and strangely enchanting. A different approach had been used, non-violent and non-threatening.

When we arrived back at the school, I quickly made my way up to my house block. I was in no mood to discuss the holidays with anyone, was in no mood to see anyone and wished I had run away from Penshaw, maybe then they would have kept me. Cyril was nowhere to be found, instead there was a strange-looking man, pacing up and down in the lounge.

'Where's Cyril?'

He stopped pacing and looked down at the floor for a second or two, then slowly raised his head until he was looking me directly in the eye.

'Uncle Cyril to you.'

'He lets me call him Cyril.'

I was nervous, for in the space of something like a forty-minute car journey, normal service had been resumed, only I hadn't yet had the chance to readjust.

'Well, I'm Don, but you won't be calling me Don, you can call me Uncle or sir.'

And you can fuck right off, and don't think by standing a millimetre from my face it's going to change a damn thing! I was nervous because I was out of practice, but now being back brought with it everything. It was game on again.

'So where is he?'

'He's sick, so you're just going to have to put up with me for a month or so.'

I was utterly sad and despondent and it took several days for me to adjust to being back, then just as soon as I did, I wanted to take off again. Sometimes I was gone a couple of hours, sometimes a couple of days. On one occasion, I had crossed the fields into Shildon only to find, on climbing through the hedge, that Don was standing there with the car doors open. Six stokes of the slipper awaited my safe return.

A similar pattern saw me through that autumn, but things had changed in a way that I didn't expect and struggled to comprehend. I had become largely invisible, sometimes approaching a member of staff to speak, just to see if he would talk back. The constant berating had ceased and if I asked a question, I would sometimes be ignored. Each time I absconded, I would receive the slipper but once the punishment had been administered, they went their way and I went mine, pocket money intact along with all other privileges, including weekend leave. Even the boys in the dorm walked around me, neither speaking nor prodding or even blaming. I couldn't seem to piss anyone off anymore.

CHAPTER NINE

My parents would always sign up to some peace treaty that generally held out from Christmas Day until teatime on Boxing Day. You took what you could get. Everything was different, the sky seemed so full of stars and the things you couldn't see sometimes offered the most excitement, for they had to be invented. It was the only time I felt like a child.

Since the summer, I had spent several weekends at home, locked in my room, receiving bed, breakfast and evening meal. Would there be room at the inn this yuletide?

On the day I was due to depart I had eventually ventured indoors, having spent several hours wandering the grounds in the cold, dragging my bag and my feet. I sat in reception, wondering why no one had come to pick me up when everyone else had already gone, including most of the staff. Those remaining seemed irritated by my presence like I was suddenly on their time. I didn't like being noticed in this way, I had no immediate defence with which to resist. The sadness had slowed my mind and not knowing where I was supposed to be left me feeling like a stranger who shouldn't be approached.

'Come on, kidda, let's get you out of here.'

Cyril was standing in reception, holding a piece of paper in one hand and his car keys in the other.

'Where are we going?'

'Where would you like to go?'

'Dunno.'

'Well, I'm taking you home. I've got the directions here, let's hope they're right or we might be spending Christmas in Scotland.'

I hesitated in picking up my bag, wanting desperately to ask if I could stay with him, only I knew I couldn't, and hearing that from him would have hurt far more than the predictably long wait.

'What's up?'

'Nothing.'

'Come on, then, grab your bag and we'll get you out of here.'

As we set off I had the same feelings as I'd often had coming the other way;

I hoped we'd get lost. But we didn't, we pulled up outside my parents' house and it looked the way it always did when I stood in the yard without them knowing I was there. Cyril knocked on the door and within a few moments my father answered, chewing a mouthful of food.

'Bliddy hell, he hasn't run off again has he?'

'No, Mr. Cooper, it's the start of the Christmas holidays today.'

'And who are yay, like?'

'I'm Mini's housemaster.'

'His name's Michael, but yer'd better come in.'

Cyril put his hand on my back and gently pushed me forwards. I stepped through the door and was followed into the lounge by Cyril and my father. All eyes were on me, as I stood motionless, not knowing where to look.

'Did yay nah aboot the holidays starting today, luv?'

'Well no, I thought they started next week.'

She was lying. Christmas Day fell one day the following week so if they were genuinely mistaken they were using subterfuge in place of contrition.

'Well, we did send out letters to all the parents, outlining the dates.'

'Well, we've not seen a letter like, have yay, luv?'

'No, I haven't seen one.'

I was just stood there, I had no part to play in the way I entered the house and wasn't even sure if I was staying. I hadn't put my bag down or removed my coat, I was waiting for instructions.

'Well, I'd better be getting off. Enjoy your Christmas, Min, and I'll see you in the new year.'

'Thanks for bringing me.'

My father walked him to the door and I still didn't know if I was staying or even if I wanted to. It certainly didn't feel festive, nor did it feel like home. My siblings no longer expected me to be there as we had, quite naturally, lost an affinity to one another; all that remained was the colour of blood.

'Don't stand so close to the fire, Michael, you're blocking the heat for everyone else.'

Perhaps if I had erected a tent in the garden, that would have satisfied everyone else's needs, too.

'Where should I stand, then?'

Without waiting for her reply, which seemed a long time in coming, I walked out of the lounge towards the stairs.

'Now where are yer goin'?'

'To my room to put my bag away.'

'Well, don't be up there all night.'

A decade wouldn't have been long enough. I looked out of the bedroom window and into the street. Chimneys were smoking and Christmas lights shone from every window of every house, ringing out the same message, 'Merry Christmas'.

* * * *

Christmas Eve, and the wait was almost over! Some weeks earlier, I had requested a transistor radio, despite my father's protests and attempts at persuading me to ask for a leather football. It's all I could think of, I'd made my own choice. A football wouldn't fit in my pocket or under my pillow, it wasn't company and it couldn't tell the time.

Nor, it seemed could we. The agreement was, first awake woke the others. This fell to me as I hadn't slept at all, lying there for what seemed like an age, then convinced it must have been four or five in the morning. I woke my brother, then we tiptoed into my sisters' room and woke them, the youngest being the hardest to rouse. The stairs were our greatest hazard, but thankfully the few drinks my parents had shared before going to bed allowed us free passage. When we reached the lounge and turned on the lights, it was like entering Santa's Grotto. We stood there absolutely dumbstruck, our excitement silenced by the sight of four huge piles of presents.

'God, it's only two o'clock!'

Well, something had to break the silence otherwise we'd have stood there all night until our parents rose, breaking the silence in an entirely different way. We found our respective piles and on the count of three, attacked.

My sisters wasted no time in separating their gifts from their bondage whilst my brother couldn't decide which to open first.

'Which one do you think's the Subbuteo?'

'One that looks like it's a big box.'

He picked one up, opened it and his face dropped.

'I didn't ask for Monopoly.'

I picked up the wrapping and read the tag.

'It's off Nan and Granddad, it's for both of us.'

He carried on, happy in the knowledge that his football game was still buried in there, somewhere between the tangerine and the tin of toffees. I searched for something round and didn't find it; now I, too, could allow myself a little unfettered excitement as I ripped furiously at the paper until I came to it, my own box of delights. I made room to sit down and removed the lid from the box, slowly, almost too afraid to look. There it sat in its red plastic casing, my hands trembling so much I almost dropped it. I switched it on, nothing. I switched it off and then back on again, still nothing.

'It won't work.'

My brother, always the practical one, checked it out for me and concluded that the battery, having probably been attached to the radio for several weeks, was dead. I continued to unwrap the remaining presents but kept glancing down at the box on the floor, wishing it would burst into life.

Time was lost in excitement, my sisters were almost deliriously happy whilst my brother spent the remainder of the night trying out various tactical formations, growing more and more animated. I enjoyed the room being full of us, no adult interruption, but it couldn't last, not even on a day of giving. My parents eventually emerged, my mother heading straight for the kitchen whilst my father took over the sofa and lit a cigarette.

'So, is everyone happy?'

'Aye, do yer want a game of Subbuteo, Dad?'

'Aye, son, once we've had breakfast I'll play thee. Michael, you can play the winner.'

'Not bothered.'

'Now listen, don't start, it's Christmas Day, thee's playing, whether thee wants to or not.'

Perhaps I should have asked for a tape recorder instead. After initially being accused of trying to spoil everyone's Christmas, he did relent and put the battery in the oven in the hope I might get a couple of hours out of it. I spent most of the rest of the day watching him and my brother trying their best to cheat without being caught and when my father was, he simply changed the rules. When finally I was allowed a game, I broke one of the figures and was not only banished from the pitch, I was sent from the room. By bedtime, none of us needed asking twice, so we made our way, utterly exhausted.

Shortly after Christmas, my sisters both went down with chicken pox within a couple of days of one another, followed soon after by my brother and then, of course, yours truly. As the last to get it, I was obviously the last out of quarantine. My brother and sisters had returned to school and nursery whilst I remained at home, social services having already been informed. With my dad at work and my mum busy around the house, my radio was my best friend, singing away the hours between meals. I was completely housebound, not even allowed into the yard for fresh air.

'Michael, come down I need you.'

I went downstairs to see what she wanted. We had managed so far to avoid each other's radar, she controlled downstairs, whilst I remained in my room. At least whilst the old man was at work.

'What?'

'Put yer coat on, we're going to Aunt Jenny's.'

'I don't want to.'

'Never mind what you want, we're going.'

'You said I'm not allowed out.'

'Look, I haven't got time for this, now do as you're told.'

I sat down and folded my arms, whilst trying to look as indignant as possible.

'You wouldn't cheek your father like this! Now, for the last time, put your coat on.'

For the last few syllables she increased the decibels and boy did it shake the house, but not my resolve.

'No.'

'Right then, get to your room.'

She marched me up the stairs. I didn't understand why it was necessary to follow me until we got there and she snatched the radio off the bed.

'I'll take that. Little boys who don't do what they're told don't deserve nice things.'

'It's mine.'

'And who paid for it? Now, you can stay in here until your dad gets in from work and he can deal with you then.'

On her way out she locked the door and I shouted through the gap as she went down the stairs.

'I hate this house.'

'Then you'll be pleased to go back.'

I chewed what was left of my fingernails, something I often did when my mind was on fire and needed settling down.

I went over to the window and without a plan or a moment's hesitation, I opened it and climbed out. I carefully dropped onto the kitchen roof, closing the window until it was almost shut, then crawled along the exterior wall that separated our house from the next, climbed onto the roof of the toilet and dropped onto the street. I took a quick look around and, satisfied I hadn't been seen, ran up the street and across wasteland until I reached the other side of the village. I didn't really want to be there, it was cold, with nothing to do and nothing to do it with, just an angry mind on the loose. I wandered around aimlessly for a couple of hours, no longer taking care to hide myself, not bothered if the cops, or even people who knew my parents, saw me.

That radio belonged to me and I intended to get it back, even if it hurt and it probably would, for it was no longer a gift, it had to be fought over and won.

I marched down the street with real purpose, determined not to give in, knowing I couldn't really afford to, for it wasn't the radio that mattered the most. I didn't bother to knock, not wanting to break my concentration and not wanting the wait to facilitate a change of heart and a return to the cold, damp allotment from where I had come. I turned the handle to open the door except it wouldn't. I pushed a little harder and still it wouldn't open, it seemed I was locked out. I was confused and somewhat frustrated at being faced with a locked door, so I peered through the window in the hope of seeing some sign of life, desperate not to lose the momentum, but there was nothing.

I marched up the street and around to the front of the house but that door, too, was locked and again there was no sign of life. Clearly the lure of Jenny had proven too much. My spirits were low and my options severely reduced when I remembered my window was left partially open. I desperately hoped it hadn't been spotted by my Mum before she went out, so I rushed once again to the back of the house. From the yard, I couldn't tell whether it was open or closed, so using the toilet door I climbed onto the roof, once again crawled along the wall and then onto the kitchen roof.

Christmas wasn't quite over as I stood staring at a gap about an inch wide; it was enough and I wasted no time in opening it wide enough to climb through. Such was my determination, I completely overlooked the fact that I may have been spotted by the neighbours. I crawled through head first, hoping to fall onto the bed but somehow managed to get my feet stuck against the windowsill, forcing me to wriggle free. Once fully inside and on my feet, I closed the window and instantly felt a rush of adrenalin and excitement that made me forget all about the radio. I sat down, and bounced up and down on the bed. It was knowing I was there without them knowing that gave the house a brand new perspective and me a reason, at last, to be there.

I checked my bedroom door and it was open. Clearly my mother had been to check on me and discovered I was gone before she herself took flight. I walked down the stairs, no longer needing to listen intently to gauge what kind of reception awaited me. Everything was so quiet, everything looked so different, as if it had just been put there and I didn't know why. The glow of the fire welcomed me, it was the only thing that did as I stood in its glare, warming my exterior.

I was hungry and searched the kitchen, looking for something readily available to eat but there was nothing. I would have to prepare something and whilst I had never done this before, I had seen my mother do it and figured it was fairly straightforward. I filled a bowl with water and took it over to the dining table, I then grabbed a handful of potatoes and dropped them into the bowl and, potato peeler in hand, began to peel the spuds.

What a fucking nightmare! Lumps flew off in all directions, on the table, on the floor, I'm surprised I didn't manage to stick a couple to the ceiling! I completely lost interest but unfortunately couldn't shake off my hunger. Having decimated the potatoes, I went in search of something simpler. I wandered into the pantry in the hope of finding a tin of soup, or indeed anything that didn't require a fucking degree to work out. But it wasn't food that I found, or at least that wasn't what transfixed me and rooted me to the spot: there, on the top shelf and temporarily out of reach, sat a virgin box of matches. All thoughts of food vanished, I wasn't even looking at any of it, there was only one temptation and I was fighting every urge to indulge it, whilst never taking my eyes off that box. It was, quite simply, impossible to walk away for there was nothing in that, nothing in my thinking had a space for it.

I was oblivious to everything. My Mum could have returned at any moment yet I hadn't given it a second's thought; my Dad could return from work, an even scarier prospect, but I simply didn't have the time to locate such fears. I stepped out of the pantry and returned to the table to pick up a chair, which I dragged back in. I hurriedly climbed up, grabbed the matches and climbed back down, my hands shaking a little, but I opened the box. It was full.

I walked back into the lounge, not bothering to take the chair with me, my mind too deeply embedded inside that box. It wasn't a friend, nor was it an abuser, it was an occasional tonic that carried with it some serious side effects. Having taken the decision, there was no room for hesitation. A change of heart now and it might have been changed forever, the lights would have permanently gone out. It's all I knew and I was good at it, had to be, because everything was invested in it.

My mind was racing, I wanted it finished, wanted to be out of there. There was no joy, no fascination in the act itself, it wasn't fun, it was protection, a statement of intent that allowed me to bully the bullies. Something had to give, someone had to bend and it wasn't going to be me. I ran frantically around the house, searching for anything combustible. I found a cupboard that housed a huge pile of old newspapers, perfect! I began stuffing them down the side of the sofa and the armchairs and without any hesitation, lit them.

Such was my haste, I became more and more disorganised, standing in the middle of the lounge with smoke billowing all around me whilst deciding what to do next. I was panting a little, such was the enormity of my actions, both in terms of the impact it would have on my family and on me. That house had to go, ugliness seeped from every crack in every wall, and each tiny flake of paint was witness to the cowardly betrayal that prevented growth through a brutal and vengeful coalition. The curtains were next, blazing away as I became more haphazard and chaotic. Satisfied I would never see this place again, I made my way up the stairs to make my exit.

Once inside my bedroom, or rather my cell, I stopped, not giving any thought to the fire raging downstairs. It didn't even occur to me to exit via the door that could have been opened from the inside. I had no capacity to think beyond what I was doing, it was absolutely everything, consuming me, controlling me, through the control that I felt that made me a giant.

It was a dangerous addiction.

I wasn't ready to immediately bail out, so I set fire to the beds that had so often been the instruments of torture, keeping me warm whilst drying my tears, listening to my cries but largely ignoring them, their impartiality colluding with my parents and keeping them safe. As the room filled with smoke and the flames rose, it concentrated my mind sufficiently to know it was time to leave. I opened the window and went out the way I came in, and as I crawled along the wall I almost fell off. Hanging there by my fingertips, I dropped down into the neighbours' yard and made my way onto the street. As I stood against the wall of our yard, trying to collect myself, I suddenly heard someone coughing and spluttering directly above me. I hugged the wall, afraid of being seen whilst trying to work out who the hell was on the roof.

It was my father, naked and suffering the effects of smoke inhalation. What the fuck was he doing in the house, he was supposed to be at work!

This was totally fucked up and not part of the plan. I stood there afraid to move, but knowing if I stayed too long I was sure to be spotted and my arse would be toast, as people started spilling into the street. I felt totally exposed, so hugging the wall I began to slowly make my way up the street and out of sight. No one seemed to pay me much attention, concentrating on my father's plight, with someone throwing him a blanket to cover himself up. A group of women had appeared and were laughing at him, and I remember thinking it must have been because he looked like a hairy gorilla. But I didn't want him dead, I just wanted to reduce him in size. To a small boy he was enormous and powerful, and had gotten away with so much because he was part of the machine that protected those who kept it rolling, and not those who opposed it.

I hid behind the garages at the top of the street but soon heard the sirens. Curiosity got the better of me and brought me back. A couple of fire engines, an ambulance and a police car were in attendance and I figured that pretty soon someone would be attending to me, yet still I remained.

My father had climbed down off the roof and with the blanket still wrapped around him, was busy receiving condolences from people whose names he didn't even know, nor, I suspect, did he care, as someone handed him a hot cup of tea. There was concern all round that the emergency services would quell the fire before it spread to other houses in the street, a concern that sadly I hadn't even considered. None of them were on the radar, nor did I want them to be, but lighting that first match could have changed their lives forever. Thankfully, through luck or the gods, it didn't.

'It's Michael, isn't it?'

'Mini.'

'Is that your nickname?'

'Yeah.'

'Well, my name's Derek and I'm a police officer.'

He had a gentle voice and a friendly face that looked like it would break into a smile at any moment.

'So what happened in the house, son?'

'Dunno.'

I'm not at all sure that's what I wanted to say but the rubberneck population of the street were showing an unprecedented interest in me, with eyes that listened to more than they saw.

'Mrs Lee saw you leave moments before the fire took hold.'

'A piece of coal fell off the fire and burnt the carpet.'

'No it didn't, son.'

I looked at him and looked at my father, and then at my mother who was marching up the street with my youngest sister in tow. I wanted to be away from there but I couldn't just leave it behind.

'I did it, I lit the fire.'

'Why son?'

'Because people are horrible all the time and that house is horrible.'

'Well, I'm going to have to take you to the police station and ask a few more questions, then we'll get the social worker to take you back to the school.'

I was put into the back of a panda car and I could see Derek and my father deep in conversation, my father becoming more and more animated. At one point he made an angry move towards the car and had to be restrained. For once, I was protected but it couldn't last, nor did the radio.

* * * *

I arrived at Stanley police station and once again sat in reception rather than a cell, though a cell would have been more familiar and the solitude it provided more comforting.

I was ushered into an interview room for the formalities, which was all that it was; the truth couldn't be heard, it was protected by law. Once they had established how I got into the house and set the fire, the social worker who had sat quietly through my interrogation drove me back to the school. My parents were offered financial assistance through social services and the Coal Board provided alternative accommodation almost directly across the street from the burnt out house.

Back at school, nothing changed. My days were spent the same, talking to people who didn't listen and listening to people who didn't say anything. Although I was too young to be prosecuted, I still expected a tougher, sterner response but it never came, leaving me confused, but unafraid.

A couple of months after returning, I had once again taken off. It was all I had to kill the tedium and it had become habit-forming, the alternative being to play their game, by their rules, and become someone I couldn't look at.

I returned to my village and by nightfall I was stood by the front of the house. Although somewhat darkened by the fire and in a state of dereliction, it was still standing as a reminder of the prison it once was, still towering over me, making me small again. It had to go, it was my only chance, so I climbed through a window that had been blown out and not yet boarded up. It was dark and cold in a house that had never really known warmth, with some partially burnt furniture still remaining. I didn't want to risk the stairs so I remained on the ground floor, then lit it again, without the same intensity as before. It was still in the way, still a monument to betrayal.

I quickly left as the fire just as quickly took hold. I looked around, but there was nobody about on this dark night in Craghead. I found a good vantage point that also afforded me protection and waited; how quickly they gathered, flocking around each other. Then, of course, came the emergency services. I decided to test the water by taking a stroll over to where they were all stood. I was pushing my luck in the extreme, yet strangely driven to do just that, I both recognised and dismissed the risks. Getting caught was no longer failure, not on this occasion, when it was more important to be recognised, yet still the idea of coming clean wasn't an option.

It was incredible, I was standing there amongst the very neighbours who, only a couple of months ago, watched as my father staggered onto the roof, and I took a trip to the police station. Yet no one seemed to recognise that I was stood amongst them, and I kept looking around, as the firemen were busy trying to extinguish the flames. On one occasion, I got a little too close to the building and one of the firemen, unaware of my presence, spun around and squirted me full in the face with his hose, almost knocking me clean off my feet. It was pure vaudeville and the audience loved it, but I was now wet and cold and in need of a blanket.

'Is this more of your handiwork, Michael?'

I was startled to find that the voice belonged to a cop who moments earlier had walked past me as if I wasn't there, but had now readjusted his sights. Standing there as each head turned towards me, however, wasn't about to make me confess.

'No.'

It was a very lonely patch of ground on which I stood, for all eyes were on me. I'd seen these eyes before, they were the same as my father's and my mother's. Their children ate from the same bowl and never got to dance unless they set the rhythm.

The cop walked towards me and sniffed at my clothes.

'Your clothes stink of smoke, how do you explain that?'

'I've been standing here watching.'

'So, how come you're not at your school? Holidays are over.'

'I ran away.'

'Empty out your pockets, Michael.'

'Why?'

'Because I've just told you to and I'm a police officer.'

I didn't want to do it because all I had was a box of matches and whilst that was normally enough, I didn't like sharing them. There were gasps and groans and whispers I didn't hear, but had probably heard before.

'So, why do you need these?'

'In case it gets cold and I need to light a little camp fire.'

'He needs locking up before he ends up killing some poor sod!'

'Okay, sir, leave it to us, we're dealing with it.'

'Aye, yer say yer are but he'll be back here again tomorrow.'

The cop gripped my arm and marched me to the top of the street where his vehicle was parked.

'You know the drill, Michael, in the back.'

I climbed into the back of the car, relieved to be away from the mob and relieved at being in the warmth.

'How old are you now, Michael?'

'Nearly ten.'

'Well, you won't keep getting away with this. Once you reach ten you can be charged, then you'll have to go to court and it will be up to them to decide what to do with you, is that what you want?'

I wanted what no one was offering: I wanted to be a child, with only a child's expectations.

PART TWO
(10-20)

CHAPTER TEN

Shortly after my tenth birthday, on a beautiful sunny day, I decided to act on an idea stemming from the 'Miss Lovely Legs' competition. I simply hadn't been able to shake off the notion that I really had looked like a girl. I had become increasingly frustrated by my efforts to separate myself from those who only ever spoke at you, and each return to school made the wall a higher one to climb. If I could just look like a girl while they were searching for a boy, I could be lost forever. With this in mind, I entered a store in Durham, in an attempt to steal make-up and a dress. Not being a particularly gifted thief, however, I was caught.

I was transferred to Durham police station and charged with theft, ironic that when they finally got me into court it was for stealing lipstick and mascara. The social worker was once again summoned but on this occasion I wasn't returned to school, I went straight back to Penshaw House.

'I don't know what the court will decide, Michael, but obviously we can't go on like this, can we? With people being called out in the middle of the night and you setting fires left, right and centre.'

I sat in silence.

'Your mum and dad are really worried about you, they don't want you wandering the streets in the middle of the night.'

'I like Penshaw House, the staff are really nice and kind, and we play nice games.'

Ironically, Penshaw was secure whereas Redworth wasn't. I guess I had now become so accustomed to being away from home and having decisions made on my behalf, that I began to make assessments of my own, and Penshaw scored higher than Redworth because whilst it locked me up, I was treated fairer than when I wasn't.

'Well, obviously I can't guarantee that you'll be staying there, but it's the one place you haven't run away from.'

'No.'

In a little over two years I had absconded twenty six times from Redworth Hall, a disappointing tally for it meant they had more of my time than they deserved, and now someone else was about to lay claim to it.

* * * *

'Mr Cooper, could you remove yourself from the courtroom please, and only return after you've gotten rid of the gum?'

The preliminaries were under way for stage two of the tour and not even my father was exempt; his crime, chewing gum, for which he was temporarily banished and embarrassed. The proceedings were over before they had really started, the outcome clearly having already been decided. I admitted to two counts of theft, at which point and with a minimum of fuss, the court imposed a care order to subsist until I was eighteen years old. It took less than a minute, less time than it took me to steal, but I was now ten years old, and whilst ostensibly it was for the theft of make-up it seemed a harsh punishment for a misdemeanour.

'What does a care order mean?'

The social worker broke off from the conversation he was having with my parents and came and sat down next to me. After a moment's consideration, he spoke to the floor.

'Well, basically, all it really means is that until you're eighteen, you'll be in the care of the local authority, that's all.'

That's fucking all!

I didn't understand what any of it meant and my father was too busy nursing a bruised ego to explain. He hadn't been allowed to take to the stage and for him it was an opportunity lost. Instead, he simply had to sit and watch as the myopic machine beneath a huge coat of arms gave the social services the freedom of the city. I wasn't asked to explain my actions, that would have been too dangerous. I wasn't asked anything that might have altered the prescription, I was simply ushered into the waiting area whilst the next doll was rolled off the conveyor belt.

'We need to put a stop to all this, Michael, we can't have you running around doing what you've been doing.'

'Does that mean I don't have a mum and dad anymore?'

'Of course you do, it's just that any decisions about your future will now be taken by the authorities instead.'

Well, that kind of changed everything. I mean, my parents might not have always met the job description but now that's all it was. I was a child of the state but they would only own the clothes I wore.

Once in the car, I noticed we seemed to be taking a different route. I had taught myself to memorise landmarks, not being so good at remembering street names.

'Where are we going?'

'We've found you a new school which isn't far from your old one, it's just a bit different.'

Different was simply a euphemism for secure, a fact quickly established by the fact that on arrival he grabbed me tightly by the arm and marched me towards my new quarters.

Aycliffe School was on the edge of Newton Aycliffe, one of a number of new towns that sprang up during the sixties. It comprised an assessment centre, which was little more than a transit camp, and a training school, which had neglected to train the staff. Each campus could be seen from the other and stood on the same land, along with an educational block that also housed the psychology department. Only one house in the entire school was secure and that's where I was headed.

Royston House was the assessment centre's 'specialist' unit with only half the incumbents deserving to be there. On the face of it, I was there because I had stolen some make-up that was worth less than the petrol it cost to deliver me there. I arrived without luggage or any personal effects, my pockets were empty and my clothes belonged to someone else, but not my mind, and that's what they wanted to take and never give back.

The house was small and all on one level, making it hugely claustrophobic, stifling, a perfectly designed fish tank. Once inside, I was ushered into the office where the paperwork was handed over in order to minimize the guesswork. I sat there waiting for someone to say something.

'Right then, Michael, I need to be getting off. I'll let your mum and dad know you've arrived here safely.'

Well, that should put their minds at rest! They worried when I ran off, whereas I worried when I didn't. He held out his hand like a serpent's tongue, but I kept mine in my pockets.

'Okay.'

He left without any further need for textbook goodbyes, better to just go when you don't want to stay, it worked for me.

'Right then, Michael, or should it be Mini? It says here you like being called Mini.'

'Yeah, I do.'

'Mini it is, then. Okay, well let's get the dreaded formalities out of the way then we can get you settled in. You've not got any personal belongings but I need you to empty your pockets out onto this desk.'

'They're empty.'

'Well, you don't mind if I just have a quick check?'

It wouldn't have fucking mattered if I did!

'Do you understand why you're here?'

'Yeah.'

'Okay, well basically what's going to happen now is, you'll undergo a period of assessment and hopefully it will help us to decide what's best for you.'

They wouldn't have known what was best for me if I wrote it down on paper for them and I wasn't about to do that, that really would have spoilt the fun when I'd only just got there.

'Well, obviously this isn't the first time you've been in secure accommodation, Mini, so I guess you're a bit of an old hand at it and shouldn't have too many problems settling in. I'll take you down to the clothing store and get you kitted out but I must warn you, I can run a lot faster than you.'

His papers had clearly misled him, for such an attempt would have lacked class, but much more importantly, would have severely limited my chances of success and made me look like a shit.

'I wasn't going to run away.'

'Pleased to hear it, we can't help you if you're not here.'

I wasn't.

I was kitted out in '70's chic at its most disabling, and made to look what I was, a fucking refugee in my own country! I was shown to a dormitory which housed four single beds with a wooden locker standing next to each one. The room was spacious and sterile with everything hidden.

'The doors are not usually locked during the day but obviously they are at night. If you need the toilet or anything you just press the bell here on the wall.'

We proceeded to the lounge where one or two people were watching television. They were sat on plastic chairs or beanbags and even the windows were made of reinforced plastic and only opened to a few inches. In the games room, there was a gathering of people engaged in blow painting.

'Listen up everyone, this is Mini Cooper. He's just joined us today so I hope you're all going to make him feel welcome. Remember how it felt on your first day.'

'Mini? That's a lass's name, sir.'

'Come on now, give him a chance.'

They did indeed give me a chance but it was all of little consequence. We lived, ate and played together but not as a team, for one by one our travel documents were being prepared.

* * * *

I settled into the routine fairly quickly, one institution is pretty much like any other, besides this life had already begun to feel more familiar than the nuclear family. The day-to-day routine consisted of play along with some fairly basic educational classes, and if you were lucky you got to go outside.

A week or two later, I was lying on my bed when the door opened and I was suddenly jumped by a young girl who had become friendly with me. I was so startled by both her presence and boldness that I rolled off the bed, taking her with me. She was giggling, which was partly a relief, as I hadn't wanted her to be injured in the fall, but there was something in her eyes that knew too much.

'Do you want to feel my tits or my fanny?'

A shocking invitation for a ten-year-old boy who didn't have a sexual bone in his body. I had no tools for dealing with this, it was a terrifying moment that I struggled to articulate, particularly as I was fighting for breath and every part of me was trying not to tremble.

'No.'

'Have you never had sexual intercourse?'

'No.'

'I have! My mum caught me in bed with my boyfriend.'

'Is that why you got sent here?'

As her demeanour changed from brassy to contemplative, the door opened once again and a female member of staff entered the room.

'Come on, you two, you know girls shouldn't be in the boys' dorm. Anyway, we're going out soon so you'll need to get ready.'

Going out wasn't a phrase I was expecting to hear anytime soon but as I was beginning to develop cabin fever, I didn't want to miss out either, so before I could give any more thought to what had just happened, I jumped to my feet and obeyed the command. Once we were all assembled, we were packed into a mini bus and driven to the coast where we spent a couple of hours doing nothing much, but it was enough, because it was just done.

I, however, was becoming deeply suspicious and sceptical, believing all this was nothing more than a cynical attempt at creating fraudulent relationships between prisoners and custodians. I struggled to accept it as just a fun day out and an opportunity to do normal things amongst normal people, because I'd never really had the experience. I only had my instincts to inform me and I figured this was just another game, but one played in the mind and not with fists. Perhaps they wanted information, whereas the others had wanted blood. But a child needs to laugh and get excited about things, especially those not normally offered by adults, and that was the danger, wanting it to be real.

'Do you smoke, tiger?'

This wasn't a reference to the brand of cigarette he was offering, it was his pet name for all the boys, but there was nothing sinister in it.

'Yeah, I do.'

I answered routinely, expecting the usual diatribe about it being a filthy habit, how it would stunt my growth and of course, use up all my money.

'Here, share this with him.'

He handed me a cigarette in the same manner he would have handed me a tissue if I had needed to blow my nose. Naturally, I took it. The 'him' he referred to was the boy walking alongside me, slightly older than me, that's all I knew.

'I'll have the first half, I don't want you giving me a duck's arse.'

He snatched the cigarette away from me as I was about to put it in my mouth. I didn't mind, as I had shared cigarettes before and the second half was always stronger, and therefore left you feeling like you'd had more than you had. After finishing the cigarette I felt a little dizzy, having not had one for a while, or perhaps I just wasn't used to the things that were bad for me tasting so good. It never crossed my mind to attempt to slip away unnoticed, I guess some basic humanity was at work, or maybe I just hadn't seen so many people smile at once. It was fun to act without having to pre-empt why you shouldn't.

The following days were spent pretty much moping about, generally feeling very sorry for myself. The initial flavour had become stale and the claustrophobia was beginning to shrink me. I felt in dire need of some clean air.

'Min, come with me, kidda, the principal wants to see you.'

'What for?'

'You'll soon find out, come on.'

I was ushered into his office and sat opposite his desk in a large leather armchair. It felt important being here so I tried to look serious.

'So, Michael, you've been here a few weeks now, how are you finding it?'

'It's better than Redworth, I suppose.'

'You didn't like that place very much, did you?'

'No.'

'But here is much better, I hope.'

He was Persian and had a wonderful accent and a soft, gentle, kind voice that hid a mind of steel. It was a well-cultivated persona that would get the best and the worst out of me.

'It's okay, except we're locked in.'

'Yes, I know, and I know you're not very happy about it but there's not very much we can do about that. Besides, think of it as helping to keep the bad people out.'

Even at ten I knew that was a complete crock.

'How are your parents? Are they still coming here at weekends and taking you out for the day?'

'Yeah, but they just argue all the time over nothing, I don't even know why they bothered getting married because they're just miserable all the time.'

He had inserted the batteries and switched me on and I had let him, for it was time to come down off the shelf; it was getting dusty and I needed to breathe.

'I spoke to your parents recently, in fact I have spoken to a lot of people about you. That must make you feel quite important.'

A shrug of the shoulders.

'I have been talking to some people who make television programmes, and they want to make one about you. How do you feel about that?'

Far from jumping up and down with glee, however, I sat there tight-lipped and gritting my teeth so hard I'm surprised they didn't break. I was ready to burst and that's what I was afraid of, wanting something so badly only to have it snatched away in an instant just because they could.

'So, do you think it might be something you would be interested in doing?'

'Dunno.'

'Well, it's a big decision. Perhaps you'd like to think about it for a few days.'

I couldn't think of anything else, I was thinking so hard I was in danger of driving myself insane, but if madness were the price for finally being heard, then I would have traded everything for it. When I returned to the house I was immediately ushered into the office. Everything seemed different, like I was suddenly a different person but I wasn't, I was the same person; they hadn't noticed.

'So, we might be asking you for autographs soon, I hope you're not going to charge us.'

Having that amount of attention heaped upon me was both alien in concept and in practise. In an hour I had become everybody's best friend, all of them hoping to canvass the yes vote. But the decision had to be mine to own outright and I resented their attempts to credit themselves with having a pivotal role in the process.

I was finally going on the television and the script had already been written. By parents, social workers and anyone else with a vested interest or a reputation to protect, but when the cameras started to roll it would just be me, and a performance I could never have imagined for I forgot it all and just remembered myself.

CHAPTER ELEVEN

'Hi, Mini, I'm Franc. I'm going to be directing this film.'

He had long hair and a moustache, and a voice I could have listened to all day, rich with the confidence of a man who knew himself well. I already began to feel that he knew me too, or at least understood that part of me that made this film a real event. He was the antithesis to everyone I had so far encountered in my young life, demonstrating qualities that had so far eluded me: sincerity, kindness and honesty. He never promised what he couldn't deliver, and whilst he was there essentially to make an interesting and dramatic film, he didn't direct me that much either. He simply pointed a camera at me and gave me licence to just be myself.

It was the best fucking feeling I'd ever had and I wanted it to last forever, but would have settled for a day because it was exclusively mine, and worth far more than what had so far been on offer!

'What do I have to do?'

'You don't have to do anything, just be who you already are. I mean, there's an awful lot of people who think it would be fabulous to make this film about you.'

'But they said it was your idea.'

'Well, when the idea was first presented it was about the school and then we were told about you.'

I was feeling a little edgy, there were people coming and going, the crew were hovering and everyone wanted a piece of the action, even the staff had dressed for the occasion. I couldn't talk like this, couldn't expose the lie and be comfortable, at least not until the camera was switched on. Franc sensed my edginess and summoned a member of staff.

'Is there somewhere myself and Mini can have a quick word in private, just to talk through a few details?'

'Sure, I can let you into the isolation room. I'll have to lock you in, mind, but just knock on the door when you want to come out.'

It was probably also the first time he'd ever been locked in a room. Franc had an air of authority; he didn't care for their protocol, for their rules, he didn't pander to them. Perhaps he understood his own power.

'So, Mini, I guess this thing hasn't been properly explained to you?'

'No.'

'Well, we had a lot of discussions with the authorities. I wanted to do a film for a series called 'Inside Story'. The public don't have any real insight as to what goes on in places like this, so we thought we'd make a film that showed the entire process.'

Strangely, I felt I could have said anything to him and there would have been space to rethink it, or the freedom to defend it. His manner invited you in, rather than kept you at a distance. It was strange having an opinion at last.

'I don't like doing things just because they want me to.'

'So, Mini, have you had time to think about it, because really this is about what you want?'

'Dunno.'

'You know, Mini, you're only eleven years old, and already people have been making decisions about you, mostly behind closed doors, without any discussion with you and without you ever knowing the full story.'

'I know.'

'These decisions are going to shape your future. This film could be an opportunity to show people who you really are and let them decide whether the authorities are right or wrong in their treatment of you.'

'But they lie, Franc, and say I'm wrong all the time.'

'Look, Mini, what really matters is you. I'd love to make this film with you but I don't want it to hurt you. I want it to be special and but only if you want to do it.'

'I do want to do it, Franc, I really do, I'm just mad that they lie all the time and nothing ever happens! They don't get sent to bed early or get stopped from going home at the weekends but it happens to me and sometimes it's for nothing.'

'You know, they want to show that their assessment procedures work and the way they treat people like you is right.'

'They'll just say what they want anyway.'

'But so can you, buddy, maybe for the first time in your life, without having to guard yourself against punishment.'

'Don't worry, as soon as you go they'll take it out on me if they don't like it. But I don't really care because that's what they do anyway and I can't hit them back, so I'll just have to do this.'

And there was the rub: they had punished me so many times needlessly and would do so again if they didn't like what I was saying on film. The difference being that once it was in the can it had an audience.

'Well, listen, I need to set up and speak to a few people but I'll come back and we'll talk again soon.'

'Yeah.'

* * * *

'So, Mini, a few questions and just be yourself.'

'I keep getting asked the same questions all the time, Franc.'

'We'll try not to keep you in there too long and we'll take a break in the middle. Let's get you wired for sound and then start.'

By the time the mike was attached to me and the sound check was complete, I was already flagging from the heat and my interest was waning too. I struggled to find a comfortable position and shifted uneasily in my seat, my whole body language was a mess.

'What are the things you've been accused of? Let's write them down.'

Yes, please do, then we can play with the list, you know what you want me to say and so do I, but I said it yesterday.

'Stealing and doin' a bunk and that's it.'

'Stealing and running away and that's it?'

'Yeah, no setting fires.'

I sat right back in my seat as if to say, 'there you have it, parcel it up and let's go because I am fucking bored!'

'Right, let's examine the list. We've got stealing, running away and setting fires, is that the order you would put them in? Stealing first and setting fires last?'

'Yeah.'

'Do you want to know which order I would put them in?'

'Fires first.'

'You've noticed that before with people, why do you think we concentrate on that one?'

'Because fire is very dangerous if you don't use it properly.'

Spoken in a manner that suggested I did, and would take umbrage at any suggestion that I was nothing more than a wild reckless pyromaniac.

'Presumably you do know how to use it?'

'Yeah.'

'Do you do anything special with these fires?'

Clearly they were attempting to build a complete picture and part of that process was to try to discover how much thought and preparation went into each fire. Equally, I wanted to share it with them, share my expertise for sadly it was the only talent I had, and I was good at it.

'Depends what kind of fire I'm having.'

'There are different kinds, are there?'

'Well, I could be having a little stick fire or setting fire to a shed.'

'So what's the difference?'

'Well, with sticks you just need paper but with a shed, you need to squirt oil or something to make the wood burn.'

'What kind of oil do you use?'

'Do you know 3 in 1 oil?'

'I didn't know that burnt.'

'It does, it's very good stuff.'

An emphatic reply, reinforcing a point already made: believe in what I'm saying because it's true.

'Now, you've worked out 3 in 1 oil and firelighters all by yourself because, well, presumably you're interested in doing it.

'Yeah.'

'Now, that's what you do, but what do you think about as you're doing it? Do you think it's a good thing to do?'

It took a while to get there, but then again it took a while for me to get here. No one, it seemed, was in a rush.

'To me it is, but to other people it's not.'

'To you it is, but to other people it's not. Do you understand their point of view when you say that?'

'Because people don't like fires being set all over the place.'

'And do you not agree with them?'

'I don't agree with them. If I want to set a fire, I should be allowed to.'

'If you want to do it, you think you should be allowed to?'

'Yeah, and if they want to stop it, wait 'til the fire's going, then put it out.'

I was so rigid in my views, so deeply entrenched in pyrotechnical warfare that the voice of the battlefield was the only one I had, the only one that had ever been heard and I didn't know how to switch to the diplomatic corps.

'What about setting fire to someone's house, though, do you think you should be allowed to do that?'

'Nah, I wouldn't set fire to someone else's house.'

'Am I right in thinking that at your house, when you saw the smoke coming from the bedroom window, you thought, oh God, if there was a person left in there?'

'God help them.'

'And it just so happens that there was and that person was your Dad, is that right?'

'Yeah.'

'I see. Tell me about the church you set fire to, did it all burn down?'

'Half of it did.'

'Were you disappointed at that?'

'Uh-huh.'

'Would you have liked it all to burn down?'

'Uh-huh.'

The truth didn't faze me because it was all I had, I just wish I'd known how to bend it a little.

'You know you didn't like the school you were in, had you never thought of burning it or the headmistress?'

'No, too many kids about.'

'You don't like to do it when there's people about?'

'I don't want to be involved in, you know, a murder.'

'Are you careful about that?'

'Well, if I did, it would just be a murder.'

'That's too bad, is it?'

'Uh-huh.'

'What do you do if you don't agree with someone?'

'If I don't agree with them I say I'm not doing it, I don't agree with it.'

'You say I'm not going to do it?'

'I'm not having people telling me we're sticking with this or we're sticking with that. If I don't agree with it, I say I don't agree with it.'

'You have your own opinions strongly, whereas people who don't, get into trouble...?'

'Don't have their opinions strongly.'

'What's better, that's what I'm trying to get at? Do you think it's better to be like you?'

'Yes, it's getting me into trouble but still, I'm not just going to let everyone say this or say that.'

'It's getting you into trouble but you don't mind?'

'No.'

It was never in question. I would rather have spent the rest of my days like this, than spend a single minute on my knees. It was a lonely place but lonelier for them, trapped in their revolving door, spinning guesswork into theory just to start again.

When the camera stopped rolling there was uncertainty and a little hesitancy floating around the room but rather than wait and be told what to do, I simply got up walked to the next room and waited to be escorted back.

'Wow, Mini, that was pretty powerful stuff, how are you feeling now?'

'I'm tired.'

'Well, I guess you've earned a rest, buddy.'

He threw open his arms and I stood up, not really sure what to do.

'Give me a hug, man.'

I stepped forward and he hugged me. At first I was a little stiff, but quickly relaxed into it. I had never been hugged by a man before, but far from feeling strange, it was the warmest sensation I had ever experienced and I didn't want to let go. I had never felt anything before that had allowed me to step forward.

* * * *

Saturday morning quickly came and I was anxious to pick up where we'd left off. The last couple of days had been restful but also restless, the entire structure to my day had been removed and replaced with counting numbers on a dial.

Since arriving here, I had been out with my family several times, and also spent a couple of weekends at home, so there was nothing novel about it. Rather bizarrely, though, we remained in the same village, almost directly adjacent to the old house, which still stood, burnt out and derelict, and could be seen from my bedroom window.

I was sat in the office receiving the obligatory last-minute instructions from the housemaster, when there was a knock at the door.

'Hello, Mr. Cooper, have you just got off work again?'

'Aye, I've just come to take Michael home for the weekend and I'll bring him back Sunday night.'

'Right, off you go, Min, and behave yourself.'

'I will.'

I stepped through the door, straight into a personality blockade. With each step I could feel my character becoming more and more frozen, I needed the protection of the camera to speak to him, but I'd still need to learn how. Franc was outside the building waiting for us and as soon as we approached, he explained the situation in detail.

'Bob, we're going to follow behind in our car but the camera will be on you both at all times. Now, we're going to put a mike on you so we can pick up your conversation and then we'll get going.'

'What do you want me to say, like?'

'Anything you like, talk about the assessment, the school, stuff like that.'

My father stood rigid as the microphone was attached to his tie. He wasn't comfortable with the process but why should he be, he wasn't accustomed to being probed. I wasn't entirely comfortable with the crew following behind, being alone with my father was something I had spent most of my lifetime trying to avoid.

'You see, what you don't seem to realize is that by getting you put in that school we were trying to help you, not go against you.'

This, to date, was without question the most help he had ever proffered. My understanding at the time was limited but not withdrawn or subdued. In a desperate attempt to claw back control, he did what he did best; he lied. It was the court's decision and theirs alone, but I wasn't about to contradict him, I didn't need to, better to let him speak.

'I know you are.'

'Of course we are, but you don't seem to realise, because sometimes when you're at the school you just up and off for no apparent reason and when we ask you why you've run away, you say you don't know.'

His reaction was one of surprise and he was pretty good at maintaining it.

'So what can we do to help you? We're doing our best by sending you to school. I mean, we didn't lock you away, we don't hate you.'

I never thought he did, but I never thought he liked me that much either, he wanted someone he could understand in straightforward terms, someone who was more like him than I was.

'Now you know, when I take you back I have to report anything you do wrong, that's not me going against you, that's me trying to help you.'

Perhaps it was a duty, but he didn't have to sound so fucking delighted, so eager to have something to report in order to have a role.

'I know you are.'

We pulled up outside the house and I was greeted by Kim, the dog my parents had acquired some months earlier. Given how rarely I saw him, we had developed a very strong bond.

Once the initial introductions were over and we started filming, the conversation soon turned to God, but it was going to take more than Him to save me. In such debates my father would normally take the leading role but on this occasion it was my mother and her favourite anorak.

'Think about it, He was crucified for no reason.'

'He shouldn't say He was the king of all kings.'

'But He was the king of all kings.'

'Well, He shouldn't go around telling everyone.'

It was wonderfully stage-managed, with my parents kneeling on the floor (very symbolic) and me sat on the edge of a chair. My youngest sister sat by my mother having her hair brushed, my other siblings were nowhere to be seen lest they crowd the space.

'Yes, but He said His Kingdom was not of this world, it was of a much higher place.'

'That's why they crucified Him.'

'Yes, but the people back then wouldn't have understood that.'

'Get that out of your mouth.'

The first words my father spoke and it wasn't a request, perhaps he was fulfilling his own stereotype by ordering me to remove a plastic toy I had been chewing on.

'Don't you want to follow it?'

He had found his voice but it didn't reveal anything new.

'I don't want to follow it.'

'You know, if you wanted to, you could understand it.'

'I don't want to understand it.'

'Why? Give me a proper reason.'

'Why?'

My father had returned to offer my mother some solidarity. Strangely, though, on this particular subject at least, hers was the more dominant voice.

'Because I don't like it.'

'You don't like it, why don't you like it?'

'Because I haven't seen Him and you can't believe in someone if you've never seen them.'

'Oh, but you can.'

Followed by a chorus of, 'we've never seen Him and we still believe it', then my mother went straight for the bull's eye.

'Look what he said to doubting Thomas.'

'Who?'

'Thomas the disciple, the Lord said to him, blessed are those who haven't seen or believed.'

She probably believed in what she was saying because it was easier than believing in her own will. Personally, I think it's the most irrational belief system I have ever encountered outside of a psychiatric institution.

'Think of it, think of the birth of the baby and what a marvellous thing it was. It takes a better brain than ours, God can see into your mind and know why people do things.'

'I know what's in my mind.'

'I know you do, pet, but you're not the only one who does, God can see into your mind. Well, I believe that because there's too much happened that we can't understand, there has to be a better person than what we are.'

'He's not worked any miracles for me.'

'Pardon?'

'He's not worked one miracle for me yet.'

CHAPTER TWELVE

'So, Mini, it's your case conference today, all those people trying to decide what's best for you.'

Franc had walked into the dormitory as ebullient as ever, but I wasn't really thinking about the case conference. Whatever was to be decided, was done without any participation from me. After today he would be gone, back to London, and I wanted to go with him, not just to get out of this place, I could do that just for fun. I wanted to remain by his side and not have to pretend, it was a new experience for me to hand myself over so willingly and I didn't want to say goodbye, I was afraid to. So I did what I always did, I shut down and prepared myself for the inevitable. I was missing him already instead of making the most of what time was left, thinking more of what I might be losing than what I had already gained; an ally, a friend and an emotional investment I was still learning to understand.

'Yeah.'

'So, what would you like to happen, has anyone asked you that?'

'No.'

'Have you thought about it?'

'Don't want to. If I say what I want then something different will happen, then they'll know they got their own way.'

'Well, if you let them decide for you then they will have, anyway.'

'But they won't know what's in my mind.'

That's the one thing they can't transport or take from you, it has to be offered freely and those who did never recovered.

'Well listen, after it's over we're going to be leaving, but I'll come by and say goodbye properly.'

I had obviously known that this was to be the moment but hearing it drift from his own lips made him already further away.

'Yeah.'

I was barely audible and couldn't look at him. If I had, I would have been totally exposed through the tears that would have made me a child again in a place where children get eaten. Although the entire case conference was filmed, very little of it was actually shown and it was left to the principal, Masoud Houghougi, to summarize its findings.

'It is clear from the reports and the various assessments that we cannot allow Michael to roam about freely doing the things he's been doing. It's not fair on the public and it's not fair on him. It is imperative that he be housed in conditions of physical security. I will make the necessary referral and let you know as soon as I hear anything. Thank you all for your time.'

Then I was wheeled in for the pronouncement, only this time the escort was far less relaxed. I instinctively knew the prognosis wasn't good, perhaps I always had. I was told that I needed specialist care and was to be sent to a secure unit in Essex and that my forthcoming home leave had been cancelled. This time the tears did flow and I was so wrapped up in my emotional swamp, I was oblivious to my tears being seen by the nation. Houghougi, too, was oblivious to my pain and made no attempt at offering comfort. It was left to Franc to provide me with a tissue, once again coming to my aid. In three weeks, I had gone from walking on the moon to being trapped in ice.

When I returned to the house I was almost catatonic, my condition compounded by the girls also being in floods of tears as the glamour of a television crew had helped them to forget, but now their own fate was in the balance.

Franc was as good as his word and did come by, despite obviously wanting to start the long journey home where his family awaited him. He arrived with a huge hamper containing fruit, chocolate and other hedonistic delights. I felt like a spare part as everyone started devouring the food and the excitement reached unprecedented levels, even amongst the staff. I watched Franc playing the perfect host, saying his goodbyes, wishing people luck and whilst it was perfectly proper, I deeply resented it. I wanted my time with him, he would be gone soon and I would go back to talking to myself, and even I didn't always listen. I skulked off and went and sat in the dormitory, chewing my fingernails furiously.

Franc did eventually locate me, completely unaware of how long I'd been sat there or why I had chosen to sit alone.

'So Mini, we've had a pretty wild time?'

'Yeah.'

I was battling with myself, trying to convince myself that this wasn't the final goodbye, because I wasn't ready for closure, wasn't ready to accept it.

'You know, you've worked really hard and we can't pay you but I'd like to get you a little gift, so is there anything you'd really like?'

'A tape recorder.'

Why I wanted it, I don't know, except maybe I wanted to record music off the radio and the television during the weekly edition of 'Top of the Pops'.

'Okay. Well, this is from the crew, they really liked you and they wanted you to have something.'

He handed me a gift-wrapped package and I nervously unwrapped it. Part of me didn't want to know what was inside, part of me wanted to keep everything locked inside, just as it was, with no prospect of change. But unwrap it I did and there, sitting in my lap, was a brand new Manchester United football strip. I had never owned one and for a moment words failed me.

I came to support Manchester United purely by chance. My father had taken both myself and my brother to St James Park, home of Newcastle United. The team in red were winning and, quite irrationally and with absolutely no evidence, I convinced myself they were Manchester United, and they were going to be my team. They won 2-1 and I waited until we got home to proudly announce my allegiance. It was a quite awesome feeling, to be a part of something that I couldn't control and to hope for something that would occasionally happen, though rarely in the manner I had conceived it. Except they were really Derby County, as my father would often remind me; all that really mattered was that they weren't Newcastle. After all these years I have never once swapped my allegiance, nor would I. They have even been relegated in my lifetime, yet still I would rather be dead than wear anything other than their red.

'Would you say thank you for me?'

I sounded like a condemned man saying goodbye to family and friends before being murdered by the state.

'Sure. Well, big hug, my friend.'

I walked over to him and hugged him like I belonged. It was natural and felt like I'd never done anything else, nor was meant to and that's why the tears didn't flow. They came later.

'Be brave and you'll make it.'

He stood back and put his hands on my shoulders, looked at me, then left. I just stood there, hoping he would change his mind and come back, but of course he couldn't. That night, I lay in bed and cried savagely whilst somehow remaining silent. My pain was not a public exhibit.

* * * *

'You've got a letter, Min. Open it, in case there's any money in it that needs to go into your account.'

I'd rather it went straight into my pocket! Opening a letter whilst someone was stood over you was a disturbing exercise, made all the more so by their complete inability to show embarrassment at such an intrusion. There was no money in it and he left, but not before checking for himself. I'm surprised he didn't rip off the stamp to check that there was no contraband hidden behind it.

The letter was from Franc and my spirits were given an instant lift, especially as I now had an address that would allow me to correspond with him. This was hugely important, for since he had left, he had taken with him the only tool that made them listen. I read the letter, thought about it, then read it again. Apart from it being the only stimulation made available to me, it offered hope, because there was nothing disingenuous about his questions and if I could have seen him smile, I just knew it wouldn't have been lopsided.

I hit the buzzer and stood by the door with my eyes closed, not because I was afraid, but because I wanted to hear those words again with my own visual commentary that I didn't want contaminating.

'What's up, Mini?'

'I need a pen and a piece of writing paper.'

'You can't have a pen while you're in seclusion.'

I was in seclusion because after Franc left, I had taken off again, getting as far as Nottingham before being apprehended and returned.

'Why not?'

'You can't have anything you can hurt yourself with, those are the rules.'

'I don't want to hurt myself, I want to write a letter.'

'Well, you can have the paper but not the pen.'

'What good's the paper without a pen?'

'Well, you could always make a paper aeroplane out of it.'

I think I was more frustrated than angry. I had no history of self-harm, though by their definition my recent actions clearly fell into that category. Much more disconcerting was the fact that as soon as you walked into that room there was a blanket policy that didn't cater for individual need. Such rules were introduced to protect those who favoured placing the end of a biro into their penis or using the ink in a futile attempt at poisoning themselves, I wanted to do neither. I was full of resentment aimed at a system that could only affect change in a docile mind, by damaging it even further until submission was inevitable, but that's all they got and that's all they wanted, compliance at no cost to themselves.

For now, I was still the majority shareholder of my mind and I wanted to continue maintaining that position. The table and chair had been placed rather recklessly by the far wall, directly beneath a light fitting. The lights themselves came in the form of a Perspex panel that could be slid back and removed, and once inside there was a false ceiling to crawl along and make good your escape.

I figured all I needed to do was slowly crawl along in a straight line, avoiding the obvious hazards such as live wires, and then drop down into the interview room, which was only locked when in use. I could feel my breathing becoming more and more erratic as pure adrenalin coursed through my veins faster than a junkie's fix, my mind in danger of going into overload as a monumental 'fuck you' was fast approaching and had I been older, I'm sure it would have felt orgasmic. I lay on the bed and waited as every part of me was urging me on, wanting already to be flying down those stairs and across the car park and not give a flying fuck what happened next, for if I was bored, lonely, hungry and cold, then I'd know I had gotten out. It was paradoxically euphoric, whilst remaining a sadness that still hadn't found a cure, but it's all I had, an addiction that regularly needed feeding in order to mask the putrid smell of their dishonesty.

There were security checks every thirty minutes, and by lying on the bed and staring at the peephole, a tiny dot of light could be seen, then blocked out as soon as someone's eye peeped through it, and there it was. I now had no time to waste in making my move and once again getting the blood flowing freely and rapidly, along with a mind fresh out of hibernation. I climbed onto the table and whilst I was able to reach the light panel, it was going to be something of a struggle to pull myself up and into the ceiling, but I was not deterred, the added challenge providing a greater incentive to succeed.

'Mini, it's Sandra again, come to the door.'

I had quite literally just slid back the panel and was about to remove it, when there was a thunderous bang on the door that startled me so much that I almost fell of the table. I quickly regained my composure but was nevertheless seething inside.

'What do you want?'

'I want to tell you something.'

'I'm busy.'

'Busy? There's nowt to do in there, how can you be busy?'

'I'm thinking, go away.'

'But I've got something right good to tell you.'

'Tell me later.'

'It will be too late then.'

It was absolutely impossible. She wasn't going to shift, she clearly didn't understand what her feet were for, or why mine needed pointing in a different direction. I slid back the panel and walked to the door.

'What do you want to tell me?'

'They're letting you out today.'

'Letting me out, when?'

'After their meeting. They've been in there ages already, so it shouldn't be long. It's brilliant isn't it?'

Fucking wonderful! Good news just turned bad, they get to gloat without ever knowing how close I had come to the greatest illusion never seen. I don't recall how long I'd spent isolated in that room, a week, ten days maybe, time has no presence in a capsule, or much relevance either. However when I did finally emerge I noticed a new girl had arrived. She was quiet but that wasn't unusual during the first few days of incarceration. One morning she was standing by the sink, washing the cups that the staff drank out of. Unlike Sandra, who was slim, pretty and bubbly, but could also at times be extremely irritating, the new girl was a little plain and chubby and, I figured, was probably less demanding, so I strode up to the sink.

'Do you need any help?'

'You can dry them if you like.'

We didn't say a lot because we didn't need to, it was simply a distraction that allowed us to think, whilst seemingly subdued by the banality of the task.

After having dried all the cups, I requested and received pen and paper and attempted to write a letter to Franc. Inexplicably, I began to sob uncontrollably, tears cascading down onto the paper and soiling my desperate attempts to speak to someone with an unfettered heart that didn't need to hide.

The letter was posted, but if he ever managed to read it I would love to know how. The writing of it, however, gave me back what he had helped to preserve: the will to continue asserting my identity, an unassailable right that I could not and would not betray.

CHAPTER THIRTEEN

'So, do you prefer Michael or Mini?'

'Mini.'

'Well, we're from St Charles and we've been asked to come up here and assess you.'

A man and a woman with poker faces my granddad would have been proud of, they sat stiffly, as if they'd been nailed to the seats. Quite frankly, I was hearing monotone in fucking stereo!

'Will I have my own room then?'

'Yes, all our clients have their own rooms.'

'So, Mini, what is it you want from us? How do you feel you would benefit from coming to St Charles?'

'Wouldn't benefit from any of those kind of places and it's miles away.'

They exchanged a sly glance but by then it didn't really matter. Whilst I hadn't gone in there to sabotage the meeting, I equally didn't counterfeit my thoughts. From there the conversation became surprisingly light-hearted, we spoke about music, joked about football and occasionally even agreed.

'Well, we're going to discuss this meeting with the rest of the team, then you'll be informed of our decision.'

Days rolled into weeks and I soon began to forget all about St Charles, when I was once again summoned to the principal's office.

'Sit down, Michael. You saw some people from St Charles a little while ago, am I right?'

'Yeah.'

'Well, they've been in touch with me and they shared a number of concerns. They think the distance between home and school would be too great and should you run off, it would place you at great risk.'

I had no real concept of how far it was, just that I would be somewhere that didn't share an identity with me. I could forget what I wanted to and retain only the parts of me that I would need.

'Also, your father has been canvassing many people, arguing that your contact with the family would be less and therefore damaging to you.'

I was stunned into silence. I couldn't really make much sense out of what he was saying because it was constantly changing and I no longer knew what I was supposed to get excited about. Or what to run away from; the map had been spoilt.

'Yesterday, there was a meeting with a lot of people who all wanted to do what was best for you and also for your family, so we've decided not to send you there.'

'Where am I going then?'

'We thought it would be best if you remained here.'

'In Royston?'

I really didn't know how to feel and no one was about to tell me. Royston was only a tiny part of the institution, one small house that would become increasingly claustrophobic should I be expected to spend any length of time there. I began to wonder if Essex was indeed the better option.

'No, not Royston, you're going to be placed in a house called Frankland. It's bigger than Royston but it only houses a few boys, it has a relaxed regime and is a little bit of an experiment. You can see it from Royston if you look out of the games room window.'

'Is it locked up?'

'No, there are no locks. This is a very big opportunity for you, Michael, to show everyone that you can work hard and live by the rules.'

He was making it my responsibility when once again I had no part to play in the decision-making process, nor I suspected did he, it was simple expedience dressed up as opportunity. I could have suffocated on the hypocrisy. I guess my old man felt he was doing me a huge favour, keeping me in the North East, but as always he never sought my counsel nor did anyone else. I hadn't entirely written off St Charles in my mind, but now I would never know.

'You've been here long enough, son, you must be ready for a move by now.'

An involuntary shrug of the shoulders, it was hardly a move when only the width of a football pitch separated the two houses. I was bored and in need of something entirely different, but now I would just have to wait and see. I wasn't ready to make a decision before I could make a choice.

'How long is it since you went home for a week-end?'

'Dunno, weeks.'

'It's not fair to keep you locked up when soon you will be able to come and go quite freely. I will arrange it.'

I returned to the house under escort and spent a day or two walking around in a daze, struggling to comprehend the enormity of this particular u-turn. Within a couple of hours, Essex had been shredded and a new set of papers had been drawn up, even home leave had been restored. I was struggling to keep up and it left me feeling uncertain and on edge, not sure where the next surprise was coming from, and whether or not I would have to decode it.

* * * *

'Michael, are you awake?'

'Yeah, what do you want?'

My brother shook me.

'Mini! You know when Franc went back to London, did he tell you where he lived?'

'Aye, I've got his address and his phone number.'

'Do you fancy gannin' doon to see him?'

I was thrown by the boldness of his approach and even a little suspicious, believing my father might have set him up to catch me out. Nevertheless, since receiving the letter it had often been on my mind, so it would have been wasteful to dismiss him without first hearing his plan.

'When?'

'Tomorrow.'

'Tomorrow?'

'Aye, listen, you know mum borrows money off Aunt Jenny? Well, we'll pretend we've been sent by her and if we get the money we'll go on the train.'

It was risky, mainly because it was his plan and not mine. If anything went wrong, I wasn't sure I could rely on him and I was the one with the price on my head. Still, I willingly agreed for the sake of myself.

'Aye, okay but if anything goes wrong it's every man for himself.'

'Aye, I nah.'

I slept poorly, reminded of why I was going and why I would have gladly taken the money and thrown it to the wind. As soon as it was light, I was up and dressed and woke my brother. As he was dressing, I overturned the plastic bucket and stood on it and, using a butter knife I had secreted some months earlier, I undid the sneck and we made our way downstairs. My legs were a little shaky going down the stairs, as part of me still half expected my father to jump out and praise my brother for his sterling work, whilst systematically bouncing me off the walls. But all I could hear was his snoring. Once in the lounge, we wasted no time in exiting the house and bouncing into the street, where the sun poured down its approval. I was stunned that my brother appeared to be showing such a distinct lack of nerves, indeed, he was more impatient than anything else, barking at me to hurry up. I was in no rush, this was the easy bit, the bit to be savoured.

'Now, listen, when we get to the hoos I'll knock on the front door you gan roond the back, 'coz if she sees yay, she'll get suspicious.'

I was impressed with his attention to detail and it took a weight off me, as I didn't find myself constantly having to question his judgment. It was approximately a mile and a half to her house and we walked but I never relaxed. What's important needs achieving, and that's why I was here, not for a day trip. Once we reached the house we did as planned, he rang the doorbell as I slowly made my way around the back.

The street smelled the same and looked as I remembered it, each wooden gate needing a lick of paint and most of the cars needing a tax disc. Her gate was as I remembered it too, immaculate, the perfect disguise, I pulled down the latch and slowly opened the gate to within a few inches. The yard had been brushed and was orderly, containing only what needed to be there, including me, but this time I was collecting without squirming. That money, should we get it in the manner that we planned, would make shit taste a whole lot better! I just hoped that when she discovered what we had done, she'd be choking on mine.

'What yer doin'? If she sees yer, we've had it!'

He pushed me to one side and closed the gate, then took off down the street counting the money. He'd gotten exactly what he wanted but I would have to wait, it was becoming a habit that needed breaking, otherwise by the time satisfaction came it would no longer be that important.

'Howay, then, hurry on!'

He had briefly looked up to see if I was in tow then pocketed the money almost with a flourish as I struggled to keep up with him. He was clearly on a mission, though to what end I had absolutely no idea. He had little to do with the making of the film and therefore had enjoyed very little contact with Franc, but he was not about to be dissuaded.

We took a bus to Durham and made our way up the hill to the station. I figured by now the alarm may have been raised, so once again I was unable to relax, whilst he appeared completely impervious to the potential dangers. He only had one thought in his head, London and a utopian meeting with Mr Roddam, clearly unaware of the many ways in which our intentions could be thwarted. It was a lot for him to handle and I hoped for his sake he could.

'Right, wait here and I'll go and get the tickets.'

I began to feel like a novice as he constantly took charge, making unilateral decisions, but I didn't allow complacency to creep in. Adrenalin alone wouldn't keep us out of the police station, my role was to keep him away from himself.

'We've not got enough for the tickets.'

'We'll just have to get on without paying, then.'

I assumed he knew how much the tickets would cost and just took it for granted that he'd gone in there and asked for the actual amount we needed. He seemed to have a plan, a strategy, but it was hung together with thread. I was also suspicious that the guy in the ticket kiosk didn't question why a young boy would be travelling to London without an adult. I felt we were being observed and wanted to get on the train, rather than ride in the back of a patrol car.

'How are we going to get all the way to London without paying?'

'It's dead easy, man, I went all the way to Nottingham a while ago.'

'Aye, but what if we get caught?'

'We'll get caught anyway because of that money. I'm getting on the train whether you want to or not.'

'Ahlreet, I'll get on but don't forget this was my idea.'

We got on the train and he was a complete bundle of nervous energy, twitching and ticking his way through several carriages until I found the one we needed, the fullest one. I found two seats and sat down, but he wasn't having it, he wanted to decide where we were sitting, which of course was the empty one. Why not just have us drive the fucking train! Better still, wave a white flag!

'Look man, you're getting on me nerves, you're gonna get us caught.'

'Well, what if all these people tell on us?'

'They don't know unless you tell them and you're attracting attention to yourself! If you don't sit down I'm getting off and you can go on your own and see how far you get.'

He slumped in the seat and sulked. I could have cheered, I only agreed to his fucked up enterprise because I thought he had a plan, not an agenda scribbled on the bedroom wall.

'We wouldn't be here now if it wasn't for me.'

And so it went on.

As the train sped towards London, so my heart tried to compete with it, the excitement increasing with every passing mile. For a small boy raised in a North Eastern mining village, London represented an escape from the village mentality and claustrophobic family dynamics that squeezed rather than caressed. Franc fed my dreams and he fed them well, but not without caution. He wasn't reckless with my heart nor did he stretch my mind beyond its limits, but he didn't try and shrink it either. I wanted to immerse myself in the warmth of this mood, but I couldn't. I couldn't forget how we got on the train, nor could I forget that I wasn't just keeping an eye out for the conductor, he had become the least of my worries, for I already knew him, or at least knew how to evade him. My brother wanted an adventure, knowing full well it would be me who would foot the bill. I knew it too, that's how crazy family ties can be.

As we hit the outskirts of London, there still hadn't been any sign of the conductor and I knew we had made it. Excitement soared and the approach to Kings Cross was almost unbearable, increasing my giddiness at the expense of awareness. People began retrieving their bags, putting away their books and magazines, and the reality of the journey's end immediately concentrated my mind. My brother's restlessness also reminded me of what was at stake and how quickly it could all be lost, and then it hit me. I hadn't got a fucking clue how to get to Franc's place near Paddington and had nothing to rely on, except a determination that refused to wilt, and a brother still in search of bragging rights! For once I hadn't considered the impact my actions may have had on my captors. I wasn't doing this for them, wasn't trying to show them a raised stake, I needed this just to keep going and then come back when I needed a top up.

'Do you know the way to his house?'

'No, I've never been but we can ask at the enquiries desk.'

When we disembarked, we were immediately confronted by our own inexperience and naivety, which threatened to swallow us up. The length of the platform stretched as far as the eye could see and it was only one of many, the place was absolutely huge and bustling with human traffic. We hadn't walked a few yards before someone had barged past, almost knocking me over in the process, and my brother was completely overwhelmed by the sheer size and volume. The fucking concourse was bigger than Durham's two standard platforms, which didn't even have a buffet bar! My mind was racing, trying desperately to keep pace with the constant movement and jostling for position. We were invisible, passing unnoticed by all these blinkered adults who saw only the gap that helped them to breathe.

What I saw next threatened my breath and temporarily rooted me to the spot, an unexpected obstacle and an adrenalin-fuelled challenge that wouldn't have merited such recognition had I been alone.

'What's up?'

'There's a conductor by the gate up there, checking everyone's tickets.'

'What we ganna dee?'

'Follow these two men in front and when we reach the gate sneak past them and run as fast as you can.'

'What if he runs after us?'

'He won't, man, he's too busy checking the tickets. All you've got to concentrate on is making sure we don't get separated.'

I wanted to walk faster than I was being allowed to, wanted to execute the plan immediately for the longer it took, I could be running on my own and he would be lost. We were seconds away from a race to the unknown when suddenly he strode purposefully up to the conductor before I had a chance to grab him. I could have run but I hesitated, waiting to see what he was doing and growing angrier by the second, betrayed by a sense of responsibility that was both shocking and surprising.

'We haven't got any tickets, we've run away.'

I couldn't fucking believe it, couldn't believe I shared his genes! Four and a half hours on a train, almost two hundred miles travelled and the smallest of all the potential obstacles got his arse twitching and his mind on rewind.

'Where have you come from?'

'Durham, we've come to see Franc Roddam.'

'And who might he be?'

'Our uncle.'

I had to jump in before his tongue got stuck on fast forward and couldn't be switched off.

'Well, stand here while I check those who have got tickets.'

There were plenty of opportunities to run, as he was busy checking tickets and every strand of rational thought, every vessel that carried blood to my heart and oxygen to my mind implored me and fought with me, but I stayed. The simple truth was, I couldn't abandon him to himself.

'Right you two, you'd better come with me and see if we can get this sorted out.'

He walked us across the concourse and out through a side exit towards a Portakabin that was clearly marked, 'British Transport Police.' Whilst it was fully expected, it didn't get better with practise. Within minutes of arriving, the police had more information than they needed or indeed wanted. My brother had run away from home whilst I, of course, had run off from a 'special school.' He wanted out of there so badly, he would have donned a uniform and arrested me just to show whose side he was really on, his own. Yet only hours earlier, he had tried to walk in my shoes like it was a fucking gift, because he thought it was a game without consequences.

But that's what made it real.

I had to try to stop him, so intent was he on finding a safe passage home at the expense of myself and possibly even Franc, so when asked if our 'uncle' knew we were coming, I said no whilst he said yes.

'So which is it, yes or no?'

'No.'

I shot my brother a glance to say, shut the fuck up!

'We ran away to come and see him, but he didn't know we were coming. He just lies, it's the first time he's run away.'

I handed over the letter to the police as requested, and they duly called Franc. Within an hour he had arrived and it was a precious moment with so much resting on a simple word that could trickle or spill. He strode up to the desk, confident and full of smiles. I wanted him to be everything I needed him to be.

'Hi, I'm Franc Roddam.'

'Ah, yes sir, you're the uncle of these two boys.'

'Well, not really…'

Franc sat in his reserved seat, the one that allows you to walk out before or after any decisions are made. He could have walked without further explanation but he didn't, he waited.

'Okay, sir, the social services have been informed and they're sending someone down to collect them. If you're happy to take them for a few hours, it would make our life a lot easier. There's no provision for holding anyone here so we'd have to transfer them to a nearby police station.'

'Sure, I can take them for something to eat, then drop them back here.'

It was a truly Messianic moment that could never have happened today and what a fucking loss that would have been! I danced out of that Portakabin believing that everything he touched turned to smiles. Or maybe it was just as it should have been. His car was parked around the back and I dashed forward to claim the front seat, there would be no negotiation, it was mine. My brother climbed into the back and sat there strangely subdued, his time had passed, he was just a passenger, grateful for a ride in Franc's car instead of one of theirs.

'So, Mini, this is pretty wild?'

'Yeah.'

'I guess you guys didn't have a ticket and ended up with the police. But you travelled all that way.'

'Aye, and we'd have gotten away if he hadn't told the conductor we'd run off.'

'Well, you know Mini, perhaps it was good that he did. I mean, what would you have done?'

'I would have asked someone.'

'Well, London is a huge place, it's not like Craghead.'

He was right of course, and had I been alone with him, I would have acknowledged that, but not on this day.

'It was my idea, Franc, not his.'

He'd found his voice in the usual way and I began to wish he wasn't there. I didn't want my voice to sound like his.

Franc drove us to his apartment in Paddington and I began taking in the landscape along the way. The streets were full of people in brightly coloured clothes that reflected the light rather than masking it. They were busy and the buildings were tall, and everyone was in a rush to get there, everyone except me. I wanted to stretch the time, I wanted to be old enough to be here and never have to go back, except for the funerals.

We arrived at Franc's apartment and were met by his wife who was very sweet to us. We cleaned up and were taken to some friends of his, a nice couple, with whom I immediately felt at ease because they didn't talk behind barriers. Afterwards, we went for food at a place called The Great American Disaster, and never was there a more aptly named restaurant. The food was late, then when it finally arrived we'd been given someone else's order, which prompted them to enquire as to where their food was. Finally, some nourishment arrived at our table that we had actually ordered and it was fucking burnt! My brother and I weren't accustomed to eating burgers but we both instantly identified the food as being burnt. My illusions had been shattered and had it not been for the fabulous milkshakes, I'm not sure if I would have recovered.

'You know, Mini, I've been busy editing our little film and I think you'll be proud of it.'

'I want to be a journalist, Franc, I just know it's what I want to do.'

Actually, I probably just wanted a sense of what he had, wanted him to know that I wanted it, wanted him to know that he had the same dreams once.

'Well, that's great. I mean, it's not going to be easy but you know, if you were to write every day and get your mind working in that way, I don't see why it couldn't happen.'

That's all I needed.

Franc spent the remainder of the meal engaging with my brother. It was right and proper, he had to some extent been excluded, not by design but by a need that wasn't shared. On the way back to the station, Franc bought me a shorthand notebook and a pen, a testament that allowed me to believe, yet again. We were handed over to the police, not coldly as was the usual way, but because it was necessary. He couldn't re-invent the rules, nor could I expect him to break them, much as I wished he would. We shared a hug but words were superfluous, then some time later my brother and I boarded a train, accompanied by the social worker, and headed north. I wrote whatever I could, just to write. As long as the ink flowed, I wasn't thinking about tomorrow. When we arrived in Durham we were driven back to the school where I was handed over with a minimum of fuss, then my brother was driven back home.

CHAPTER FOURTEEN

'You know I only hurt the boys I care about.'

He was standing over me, panting, having just administered some examples of his care, which included bouncing my head off virtually every wall of the tiny cockpit he called an office. Despite the loud crashing sounds as I was thrown against the furniture, no one came to investigate. I was absolutely terrified and to make matters worse, I had pissed my pants.

Several days after returning from London I was, as expected, transferred to Frankland House. The house had no real structure and no basic routine, it seemed that no one had any real idea of what was expected of them. They were aimless days, spent trying to keep the staff from boredom. It was far more spacious than Royston, which simply heightened my feelings of abandonment. This place was nothing more than an overflow and that just wouldn't do. At the helm and weighing in at a modest twenty stones, was Roger Gibson. A more frightening figure I have yet to meet, he could disorientate just by being there, and he often was. He clearly disliked me from the moment I arrived and I disliked his irrationality in arriving arbitrarily at such a bleak judgment. I equally disliked the manner in which he often tried to undermine me in front of my fellow housemates. I despised even more the smug infallibility he felt his position afforded him; not even the other staff members challenged him, he was the supreme leader and I was the dissident who refused to accept his authority, for it was usually delivered on a bed of shit.

In order to escape the smell and to feel safe, I ran off, not a difficult task, given that there was no security and I certainly wasn't going to walk to the abattoir. Instead, I once again made my way to London. It was a moment to savour, so much so, that lying in bed alone in my single room I couldn't sleep just thinking of it. I had made it to Franc's and he had fed me and generally lifted the gloom for a few hours, but now I was back and pinned up against the wall. The foul warmth of Gibson's breath pounded my senses and distorted my ability to think.

'Do you think I enjoy this?'

Well, I didn't! My father had been playing peek-a-boo compared to this fucking heavyweight! Ultimately, I guess, he was far smaller than I was. I wasn't trying to terrify him, I didn't need to roar to feel like a lion.

'Well, I don't, but I care enough to want to stop you hurting yourself.'

There was one final crack to the side of my head, which knocked me off balance and one final friction burn from the carpet.

'Oh, pick yourself up and stop playing for sympathy. Go and clean yourself up, you're a disgrace to this house.'

Essex didn't seem so far away as I went about the task of cleaning him off me. The violence and the terror of it had me thinking about St Charles again and if I could have walked barefoot, I would have, because there was no fear quite like this. Finally, I sat on my bed and wept myself dry.

The following lunchtime, I was sat eating when he unexpectedly walked into the dining room. My hands began to tremble and I lost control of both my utensils and my appetite.

'Cooper, follow me.'

I slowly rose to my feet, partly out of fear and partly due to some physical withdrawal that seemed to be taking place.

'Where to?'

'Don't question me, boy, just follow.'

I reluctantly followed him out of the dining room and into the corridor. Everything seemed to fall silent including my mind, which had gone into hiding. He suddenly grabbed me by the hair and dragged me up the corridor, throwing me against the walls. The unexpectedness of the attack once again disorientated me and traumatised my entire body. I was aware that people could hear and see what was going on, but no one ventured into that corridor, no one wanted to swap places. By the time he had finished, I had once again pissed my pants and he was left holding huge clumps of hair in his hands.

'Get back in there and finish off your lunch!'

Those were the only words he spoke throughout the entire physical tirade. His appetite, it seemed, was insatiable and his needs were hungry once again, for whilst the earlier beating was a warped form of punishment for absconding, this was even more twisted in its randomness, and of even greater concern was the fact I never witnessed him assaulting any of the other boys.

'My trousers are wet.'

'Well, whose fault is that? Get back in there, you can sort out your trousers later.'

I didn't finish my lunch, nor did I ignore the looks I was receiving but in hindsight would I have swapped places with one of them? It was never an issue; what I was afraid of, made me afraid of fearing it, made me afraid of answering to it and begging it not to hurt me. If it chose my words, it would all be over and I would be nothing I could speak to. In the end I chose language, and I even had a word for the bruises that were the closest I ever came to wearing a medal. They bore his name but it was my passion that wore them best.

Several weeks into my stay and I was informed that the 'Inside Story' programme was soon to be aired but I was **not** allowed to watch it, nor indeed were any of my housemates. This seemed hugely unjust, given the way everyone was fawning over me to get me to make it.

In order to make sure that the television remained off during the crucial period, a trip to the cinema was arranged for the entire house to see 'Tommy', with a fish and chip supper included. Back then, to see such a film you had to be fourteen years old, yet I wasn't quite twelve. I was given strict instructions to hide behind Gibson (not a difficult task), and I would be sneaked in. Except I didn't want to watch fucking Tommy, I wanted to watch Mini! So I kept peering out from behind him and pretty soon the game was up. Gibson was furious at having to drive me back to school, nevertheless he invited me into his quarters and offered to let me watch the first few minutes of the programme, providing I kept my mouth shut. Naturally I agreed.

His mother was staying with him and wondered why I didn't have fish and chips just because I'd been excluded from the cinema. She argued quite forcefully that it wasn't my fault that I was too young and that those responsible should have known better. Gibson tried in vain to stand his ground, but it was a no contest and he was dispatched to the chip shop.

As the credits rolled, I sat transfixed to the television. It was an astonishing experience, watching myself battle with officials, almost oblivious to the camera when those around me weren't. There was a scene just before I was ordered back to bed, between myself and a psychiatrist, in which we were discussing a pretty explosive row between my parents, and he asked:

'In situations like this, whose side are you on?'

'My own.'

'The side you are on is your own?'

My response didn't fit the model and despite the question being asked in isolation, it was decided that by ignoring the plight of my mother in favour of survival, I had presented the hallmark of a classic psychopath.

An enormous amount of media coverage followed the broadcast. Gibson had read several of the articles and went out of his way to try and knock me off my perch. His language was brutal and so was the manner in which he manipulated and coerced the other boys into launching their own verbal attacks. He wrote the script and they delivered it word perfect, without an ounce of understanding. Over the following weeks, he also took great delight in informing me that a substantial amount of mail had been sent to the BBC, but that I wouldn't receive it because the decision had been taken by the authorities to destroy it. They had unleashed a beast and were now looking to tame it.

* * * *

As Christmas approached, we were in the grip of a typical North Eastern winter, temperatures were low and a thick blanket of snow covered the grounds. Gibson, though, still managed to find his way to the local shops to stuff himself full of the deadly snacks that were his hourly fix. He kept a bag of silver in the desk drawer of his office and I presumed this to be his candy kitty. The temptation grew and grew until I could hardly breathe, or indeed think of anything other than depriving him of that vital link to his disgustingly large gut, nature's own devil. I gritted my teeth so hard I almost crunched them and without any hesitation, I snuck into his office and grabbed the bag. After satisfying myself that no one was outside, I quickly left and headed straight for my room.

Once inside, I was palpitating and in danger of hyperventilating. I looked inside the bag and there must have been ten or twenty pounds, all in fifty pence coins. I had to get out of there before it was missed, so I grabbed my coat and took off through the window, cutting through some side buildings, and headed for the hedge that separated the school from a nearby field. It would have been suicide to cross our own field and head for the local housing estate as I was wearing a black coat against a backdrop of pure white. If he wanted me, or rather his money, he'd have to find me.

My journey towards possible safety was, as a result, somewhat convoluted and tiresome. As I trudged through the snow, the constant threat of capture contributed to the energy-sapping effect. I reached a bus stop a safe enough distance from the school and was hugely relieved when I didn't have to wait long before one arrived. I entered the warmth and could have fallen asleep in its womb. I was even able to pay the fare.

'Excuse me, pet, aren't you the little lad that was on the telly a while ago?'

Great! I was stunned into silence as my mind worked at grand prix speed to come up with a suitable reply but ultimately I just wanted her to fuck off and mind someone else's business!

'No, it's not me, I've never been on telly in me life.'

'You look a lot like him. You don't have to be shy with me, have they let you out of that school then?'

I hadn't been expecting anything like this and was totally unprepared for it, or the feeling of being completely exposed, and at the mercy of those who thought they knew me because they had seen me. But their naivety was dangerous.

'Okay, it is me, but you don't have to tell everyone on the bus.'

'So have you left that school now?'

'No, I'm going home for the Christmas holidays, that's all.'

'Well, I hope you're not running away, pet, because it's freezing outside.'

'I wouldn't run away in the freezing cold, I'm not that stupid.'

Wasn't I? Exposing myself to temperatures that would probably plummet into the minuses by nightfall, with nowhere to sleep, and no guarantee of finding anywhere that would provide the necessary shelter and warmth. Whilst the desire to strike at the heart of Gibson had been slowly building for several weeks, the decision on the day had been an impulsive one. I had been blinkered by a desperate need to hurt him and at the same time show him that he could never hurt me enough to make me his. It overrode everything, including any thoughts regarding my own personal safety. It wasn't even a consideration, there was no safety, just survival, and the satisfaction it gave.

As I stepped off the bus at Durham station - or could it have been the North Pole? - the cold instantly reminded me of how desperate my situation had become, and the lengths it took to try and abate it, but I couldn't go back. The woman I had been talking to on the bus began making her way to the far end of the station where a policeman was stood talking to some shoppers. I disappeared quickly, and without slipping or sliding. I didn't know Durham particularly well but I had an innate talent for hide and seek.

I hung around the city for a while. People were busy shopping for gifts, the lights framed the old city streets beautifully and there was laughter and joy, all of which jabbed at my heart. I stood there like the ghost of Christmas past, seeing without being seen, witnessing but not participating. I knew how to steal from these people and I knew how to hide from them, I just didn't know how to walk amongst them and with them. What I'd learned had made me old but I could still weep like a child, I just couldn't play like one. I walked the streets despondently, trying not to hear the carols booming out from loudspeakers. The words never made much sense to me anyway, a baby born in a manger, destined to save the world from itself. Well, that was a couple of thousand years ago now. I was trying to save myself from the world and it wasn't about to give up. My feet were numb, my eyes streaming and my joints were close to withdrawing their labour. But I was still breathing. The cold had helped my appetite return, but I was still in conflict and initially reluctant to spend any of the booty. The theft wasn't motivated by greed and therefore I was in no great rush to be splashing the cash just because I could and because it wasn't mine. The prize was having taken it right from under his nose; nevertheless, I was extremely hungry and he owed me much more than a dinner.

But that's all I got.

Along with a bus ride back to my village, because I wanted to feel close to home, whatever that was. No one knew I was there except me, and I was there just to be there, wanting something that wasn't really mine. It could have been any village on the map, any house on any street. I walked passed it but I didn't stop to look, it would have just made the cold seem colder and I was already starting to feel pretty sorry for myself, angry that common sense had deserted me when I needed it most. I wanted to drop that fat bastard to his knees so badly, I lost patience, and rather than enjoy the fruits of my labour, albeit with a bruise or two nursed within warm bed linen, I was standing there freezing my nuts off, getting closer and closer to madness and possibly even death.

At the top of the street was a row of garages and parked at the side of them, was an old mini van. All the windows were missing apart from the windscreen, but at least it had a roof and the doors were locked. I climbed through one of the windows and sat in the front passenger seat. It was instantly comforting to be sat in a leather seat and to at least feel like I had a place and the search was over. I quickly became bored, however, just sat there, watching the stars and the odd person going by with a dog on a leash. Strangely, though, I wasn't afraid of how cold I was feeling, even though my hands and feet were almost numb and my breath steamed up the windscreen. I wasn't afraid because it wasn't a danger I'd ever had to face and its insidious nature was the perfect bluff, for it never announced its intent before delivering it.

If only I had a cigarette, at least it would keep my hands warm as I cupped them around the warm glow. In my haste to get through the window, I slipped and fell straight into the snow. I stood up, looking like a snowman.

* * * *

The take-out counter of the Punch Bowl pub was always busy, usually with kids who had been sent by their parents to buy booze and crisps, and as this was the seventies, no one really questioned it. I was hoping for a long queue that would allow me to hug the warmth then take it with me when I left, but there was no one except me.

I dithered, pretending that I couldn't remember what I'd been sent to collect, a pitiful attempt at buying time, and I eventually left with a packet of cigarettes, a box of matches and a bottle of cider. Someone had once told me it kept you warm in the cold, well, I couldn't afford a fur coat. There I sat, drinking like a wino in the front seat of a car with locked doors. I looked like a monk engaged in some extreme form of meditation, with my hood up and my hands tucked into my sleeves, and then I fell asleep, intoxicated from the liquor even though I'd only drank a small amount. It was still dark when I opened my eyes and they appeared to be the only things that were moving; my jaw was locked and my limbs were stiff, and I was convinced I had frozen during the night. I took out the matches and after dropping a few into my lap, managed to strike one and then another, placing them in my mouth then cupping my hands around the lit end. Just feeling the heat was comfort in itself, but it wasn't sustainable.

I climbed out into the street, shivering so badly I could almost feel the back of my throat rattling and I began to hum, the vibration gave me something to listen to, a distraction. The mind isn't so easily fooled, however, and as soon as I tried to walk, the illusion was exposed. My legs were in complete opposition to one another and I looked like the latest recruit to the ministry of funny walks. I simply couldn't coordinate them and at one point cried out in frustration and even nearly cried.

The situation was hopeless and not being able to do anything about it confused and angered me. I wasn't used to being at the mercy of events I couldn't change. I struggled as I made my way down the street, hitting the deck and turning the air blue on more than one occasion. It was starting to get light, so I decided to head to the bus stop and take a bus to Stanley, where I could find a café and sit nursing a cup of coffee until I'd thawed out. It came quicker than expected, but not the way I wanted, a passing police car saw me and pulled over.

'Get in, Michael, if you try and run in this, you'll probably slip and break your leg.'

My legs already felt broken, along with my spirit. I couldn't run if I wanted to and sadly I didn't, I crossed the road and climbed into his car. It was over but I hoped I'd done enough. Hoped I'd shown the fat bastard that he could never scare me enough to make me acquiesce, that would have been the real crime.

'So, Michael, where did you stay last night?'

'I slept in an old Mini van at the top of the street.'

'You're going to get yourself killed one of these days, do you know that? It was freezing last night, why didn't you just knock on your mum and dad's door?'

'Dunno.'

It was easier not to, easier not to have to answer questions instead of telling the truth in a straight line.

I was driven to Stanley police station with the usual commentary of how my parents were fretting about me and how I basically didn't give a fig about anyone other than myself. I was the only one who recognised my self, was trying to preserve it and occasionally promote it, but the rules didn't allow it, so I broke them before they broke me.

Later that morning, a social worker returned me to Frankland House. I was nervous, scared even, but not undeterred. I would take the beating but that's all it would be, he would never have my eyes look his way. When it came, it was brutal and much the same as it had always been. He couldn't hurt me as much as he wanted to because he couldn't adapt, he did what had already been done and he wasn't my father.

Later that day, he called a house meeting where I was the star attraction. Apparently the money I stole wasn't his snack fund but instead was going to be used to buy Christmas gifts for the entire house. I didn't feel good about myself but that would have to wait. He opened the meeting in grandiose style, he was a consummate actor and was flawless in presenting me as the cog that wouldn't grind. He put me over his knee, pulled down my trousers and pants and spanked my bare buttocks, then threw me to the floor. He stood up, walked to the door, then with a smile that I knew well, turned to the house.

'It's your Christmas he's spoiled, you deal with him.'

No sooner had I pulled up my pants and fixed my trousers, than a couple of older and much stronger boys had grabbed me. They marched me to a chair and held me there whilst the other boys took it in turns to punch me in the face.

I was even spat at.

All for his pleasure, for it was a complete charade; presents were subsequently delivered, there was even one for me, and the festivities continued as originally planned.

The house closed down over the holiday period and as I had forfeited my leave I was returned to spend Christmas at Royston. I'm convinced I cheated death out there in the snow, perhaps it just wasn't my time, but it should have been, because desperation led to stupidity and those weren't the rules.

CHAPTER FIFTEEN

Summer had arrived, bringing with it an abundance of sunshine and warm weather and I was now a teenager, having celebrated my thirteenth birthday. The conditions were perfect for my needs and I took full advantage, indeed on one occasion it was so humid I slept out in a field without a blanket or any other form of covering, and the memory of the previous winter wasn't far from my mind.

The summer holidays were split into three periods: two weeks at home, two weeks at camp and two weeks on campus, engaging in various leisure activities. Despite having absconded on numerous occasions, I hadn't forfeited my home leave, primarily because they didn't know what the fuck to do with me! They had tried everything imaginable to keep me there, they bribed me with tobacco, then having discovered that I had a passion for Manchester United, they bribed me with posters. On being returned from one particular unofficial day trip, I discovered Gibson had destroyed them all, tearing them into pieces and scattering them across my bed. Two days later, whilst I was having my lunch, he threw two sew-on patches onto the table with such contempt I left them there. None of his bullying persuaded me to pick them up.

During the two weeks on campus, we often visited the local roller-skating rink, which was directly across the road from the school. On one outing, I got talking to a couple of girls, with one of the other boys who was much more confident than I was, and I was somewhat in awe of him. One of the girls, Caroline, didn't seem to mind too much that I wasn't brash and full of the usual bollocks, and she was gentle and unassuming, and quite witty, too. I enjoyed being around her but had no thoughts of wanting to be in her.

I had no emotional identity and no shared experience, I acted alone to protect what was mine and it couldn't be halved. Nevertheless, by the end of the afternoon my gregarious friend and myself had started to date the girls and we began to see quite a lot of them. We even invited them to our youth club that took place every Wednesday night on the school grounds and it was there I discovered that Caroline was a fantastic dancer. I, on the other hand, danced as if I had wooden legs, so I would just sit back and enjoy the show, and the adulation I received from the other boys on learning that she was my girlfriend. I had never been so popular and never had anything they had wanted before, I wasn't sure if that made me normal or just greedy, but I didn't particularly care.

Then when she kissed me, she took me away from this world and as priceless as that was, she then issued me with an ultimatum.

'If you don't stop running away, I'll have to finish with you.'

I went to London, a long way to go to get dumped, but if I'd stayed, the concession would have been intolerable and more painful than the beating I received upon my return. Caroline eventually took up with my friend, who had been dumped himself because of his demands.

By now, I must have already made around a dozen trips to London since the film had been shown and quite naturally, had grown in confidence, although it didn't bode well in the beginning when a conductor nabbed me, having recognised me from the television. I began to wonder what Franc had done. Cursed him, even.

Initially, I still had some problems shaking off the village mentality. When I asked a newsvendor outside Kings Cross station the way to Cleveland Square and he didn't know, I thought he was an imbecile, having no real concept of the size of the capital. On another occasion, I took a tube to Paddington but still didn't know the way to Franc's apartment, so I asked a policeman; it was weeks before I could wipe the smile off my face.

For months, my only point of contact with my sanity had been these trips, plus the letters and phone calls I'd received, but they always made me want more because they kept offering a glimpse of a world I could belong to and contribute to, instead of the one that didn't fit. Franc had moved from his apartment to a house nearby but I still managed to find it, thanks to the local post office.

'Mini, wow, you've made it again. Come in and give me a hug.'

When he hugged it always felt like he was squeezing a little goodness into my soul, a little light. Perhaps that's where hope comes from; either way, I never wanted to let go in case it wore off.

'So Mini, here you are again, fearless as always.'

Little did he know that fear was one of the elements that drove me, the fear of being too afraid to seek an alternative, too afraid to hear my own voice and instead have to listen to theirs, never really knowing the difference.

'Yeah.'

'Well, you keep making these tough journeys, as you know. I guess you're hungry, right?'

'Starving.'

'How about some Perrier water then I'll get you something to eat?'

'What's that?'

'Perrier water? It's French, it's kind of a fizzy mineral water and it's a bit of an acquired taste.'

I might as well have been in fucking France! My local shops had never even heard of Perrier, let alone sold any of it. I so desperately wanted to like it, to show that I had the necessary sophistication to appreciate such an acquired taste, but who was I kidding? I simply hadn't got the palate for it and try as I did, it was futile.

'It's not to everyone's liking.'

The water found its natural home down the sink and we set off in search of some food. He took me to a place close to his home but I still enjoyed being driven there; the streets, the people, the apparent opulence, it was like walking through a dream you had stumbled upon by accident. Franc was clearly well known to the owners and chatted away to them as I ate in silence. Despite my hunger, I was in no hurry to finish the meal, I would have left some for the following day if I could.

When the plate was finally empty I stared at it, afraid to look up in case the party was over. Franc strode across the room and joined me at the table. We were alone as the owners had kept the place open as a favour to Franc, but it felt like a favour to me too.

'So Mini, this is pretty wild, don't you think? Travelling free on the train and even getting a free lunch? There are people in my industry would kill to have that.'

He smiled and I wanted to smile with him but I couldn't. He made it sound like fun, like it was something worth having, something others might be envious of, but it was just another borrowed moment that I could take back with me, but couldn't keep.

'You know, Mini, I always love seeing you. You know that, don't you?'

'Yeah.'

'Well, wouldn't it be fantastic if you could come down for, like, a week at a time, with your fare paid so you don't have to jump the train and hide from the conductor or worry about the police?'

'It'd be absolutely brilliant but ....'

'But what, Min?'

'They'll never let me, Franc, they only like it when I do what they want, not when I do what I want. They don't like it when I come to see you.'

'Well, maybe they don't like you running away to see me because there's so many risks attached to it, but if you didn't run away for a while, we'd be in a position to negotiate with the authorities. What do you think?'

I wanted to travel with him but I had inside information. His intellect and rationale couldn't be argued with, if dealing with reasonable people, and that's why I couldn't safely allow myself to believe, so I just shrugged my shoulders.

'Well, you know Min, at the moment we've had a little lunch, then I hand you over to the police, they contact the authorities in Durham and then they send someone down to take you back. That's going to piss a lot of people off.'

I had become a little introverted as the internal battle raged on. I couldn't say what I wanted, without saying what I didn't.

'I think what would enhance your position with the authorities would be, instead of taking you to the police station, I take you to the train station and put you on a train back to the North East.'

I was stunned into complete silence and for a moment or two was even plotting how to get away from him. It was an alien concept and in part it saddened me for having even thought of it, but he was asking me to adopt a different position and I wasn't ready. Wasn't ready to surrender the truth to the game.

'If you walk back into that school on your own and say, okay, I ran away and I know it was a mistake and so I've come back to accept my punishment, that's going to take everybody by surprise. This could be huge for you, if all these people who wanted to lock you up suddenly turn around and say, sure, go to London for a week, we think you can handle it.'

It was hard to resist his energy because it took me away from where I was and extended the possibilities beyond what I normally expected, but it was all just space in the mind. I wanted him to be right and for them to be wrong, I believed that to be the case anyway, morally and intellectually, but what he hoped for came directly from his experience of where I lived, and he'd never met Gibson. I did, however, agree to return, mainly because I didn't know how to say no and I wanted to make him happy.

When Franc dropped me at the station and saw me onto the train, I knew I'd be back, I just didn't expect it to be so soon. I had my ticket in my pocket and a few quid that Franc gave me to cover any additional expenses. As he waved his goodbyes and walked away from the platform, I felt like he was walking away from me and I instantly began to feel helpless and trapped, my head spinning. It felt like there was nothing because away from here, there was just the way back. It had kept the matches out of my pocket, the shit out of my hair and the blood out of my clothes. I stepped off the train and hurriedly made my way along the platform, checking to see if Franc was still there. I was breathing heavily and in a state of panic because this was different to anything I'd ever done.

I really didn't have a fucking clue, I was chasing adult themes on a child's budget! It had always been this way, living more in their world than mine, for mine merely counted the time. That's why I got off the train before it left, and even knowing Franc was going to be seriously pissed off, couldn't persuade me to get back on. His wrath was the least of my worries, we'd both get over it. Nevertheless, I wasn't ready to immediately go banging on his door. I had the heart and desire for the fight but no real way of articulating it. Without that, it would have looked like I was sticking two fingers up at him as well as everybody else, so I tried to buy a little time riding the tube.

Eventually, as darkness fell, I plucked up the courage to ring the doorbell. Everything seems to take longer in the dark, but finally his wife answered the door.

'Franc, it's Mini.'

'Mini!'

Franc appeared in the doorway and I felt smaller than I had done for quite a while. I think initially, he was more flabbergasted than anything else and I was already regretting my decision.

'So, Mini, I guess you fucked up!'

'Yeah.'

What else was there to say? I walked past him into the house and sat down. I was fidgety but I knew it was okay to sit, knew I didn't have to ask to do something without thinking.

'So, I thought we had a deal? You were going to go back on your own, win some favour and improve your situation, yet here you are, less than a few hours after I left you sitting on the train.'

'I know.'

I'd lost the ability to expand beyond more than a couple of syllables. His disappointment was palpable but so was mine. We'd both lost what was never there to be gained, but I'd lost my charm, too.

'Well, you've left me no choice, now I'm going to have to take you to the police station.'

I didn't want him to be unhappy or upset with me, but mostly I didn't want him to think he was wrong about me, and that they were right, as I doubt a lonelier place has ever existed.

'It's impossible for me to allow you to stay here, you know that, don't you? You do understand that, don't you?'

Even when you accept it's an unalienable truth, there's a tiny part of your brain wishes it wasn't. I just nodded and wanted it over with. He drove me to the police station, talking all the while, words of encouragement, mainly, but they drifted past me for they'd already found a home and had no time for guests. In the yard of the station, Franc turned off the engine, but was in no rush to get out of the car, and I certainly wasn't going to hurry him along.

'Listen, Min, I know it's not always easy to talk when other people are around. When it's just you and me, we don't have a problem with what we're saying.'

'Yeah.'

'When we made the film, I deliberately edited it and presented it in a way where just as the authorities were deciding that you should be locked up, the audience, hopefully, were deciding that you shouldn't be, and judging by the public response, I think we pulled it off.'

I wanted to believe that it had made a difference, that the authorities were nervous and circumspect but the evidence contradicted that. The media captured the moment and the public went along with it for a while, a free ride, a forty minute journey that only really started after they got off. At least Franc cashed in his ticket and stayed awhile. He wasn't a messiah, he was just a man, but he spoke my language more eloquently than I did.

'You know, Mini, I've always had faith in your ability to turn this situation around.'

I don't know if I cried because of what he said or because it made me feel like a complete shit, having earlier betrayed his trust. I just know I didn't fight it because I didn't have to. Paradoxically, I walked into the police station with the man who had the potential to help set me free. It was bizarre because I could have run and under any other circumstances I would have. Instinctively, I trusted his judgment and I didn't want to let go of it.

I spent the night in the cells and the following day I was returned in silence, not a word spoken throughout the entire journey.

* * * *

Within a few days, I was off to summer camp, another part of the school holidays.

Halfway through the first week, we were ordered to sit in a circle on the grass. Gibson appeared, and in floods of tears began explaining that his wife had died. Although we later discovered she had committed suicide, such was the man's fucked up mentality, he travelled approximately forty miles just to perform that particular floor show. Unbelievably, some of the boys also started crying and I was surrounded by a chorus of sobs and sniffles. I would have been bigger had I been able to show him a little empathy, but I didn't have it in me and I wasn't prepared to stomach his narcissistic indulgence any longer, so I got up and walked off.

'Cooper, where the bloody hell do you think you're going?'

I was stopped by Sanderson, who had led these camps for years. I ignored him and walked into the dining room. No sooner had I sat down, than he followed me in, seething.

'What are you playing at, lad?'

'Don't want to listen to him.'

'Well, this may surprise you but I don't care what you want. Now, get back out there and rejoin the group!'

'I don't want to.'

I knew where it was heading but I couldn't turn back, I was angrier than he was, only mine was justified and that's what kept it from dying.

'I won't ask you again.'

'Don't want to, he doesn't cry when he hits me and makes me wee my pants. He's not bothered and neither are you, nobody is.'

I spat those lines out and was still catching my breath when he cracked me so hard it knocked me off the chair. The side of my face felt like it was on fire but I still refused to budge.

I spent the rest of the camp emptying the portable lavatories, the smell made me want to vomit and one boy did. I wasn't willing to continually be punished because it was easier to hide the truth this way. When I was allowed home, I told my father all about Gibson and he erupted. He turned up at the school, incandescent with rage, and had to be physically restrained. He eventually calmed down and was persuaded that I had invented the whole thing. I was now in a hopeless position and completely at Gibson's mercy for if my father could be so easily persuaded, he would use that to persuade others of a higher authority. It would never be mentioned again.

Collingwood House was next door to Frankland and could be accessed via the main entrance or through the kitchen that linked the two together. In every other way it belonged to an entirely different culture and one I wasn't willing to embrace. This was to be my new home, punishment for having made a 'malicious' allegation against an experienced and highly respected member of staff, and I was given several reminders of how I could have destroyed the career of a decent and dedicated housemaster.

I was marked, so I was unable to form any meaningful relationships with any of the staff and their hostility transferred to the other boys, who clearly felt they could act with impunity. I was housed in an upstairs dormitory with four other boys, all of them older than me and considerably bigger. They were instructed that should

I run away, they would be held responsible so it wouldn't just be me swimming up the effluent canal; oh, what fun! Within minutes of the edict being passed, the other members of the dorm rounded on me. Whilst expected, it was no less frightening.

'If thee fucks off and drops us in the shit, thee'll get thee face smashed in, yer little runt!'

'Aye, I'm not taking the blame for thee.'

A few days later, I woke in the early hours of the morning needing the toilet. I made my way down the corridor and was confronted with the same two boys, standing in front of the urinals, masturbating each other. I was totally fascinated as I had never seen this before and didn't really know what it was, or that a penis could grow so big. Eventually, one of the boys caught me watching them.

'What the fuck's thee deein'? Standing there watching, yer dirty bastard!'

'Dunno.'

'Well, fuck off then!'

'I need a wee.'

'Well, gan in there and shut the door.'

They weren't at all fazed and carried on as if I wasn't there.

'If thee tells anyone, yer dead!'

Later that night I was woken by someone urinating over my bedclothes. It was dark and I could only make out a silhouette of someone, but I was utterly convinced it was one of those boys. There was nothing I could do at that time of night so I went back to sleep. By the morning, I stank of piss and so did my bedclothes, and I felt like I'd been the victim of some kind of sexual assault. I'd been stripped of my dignity in the dark by some piece of shit who thought he was a tough guy. I hated the way he made me feel because he thought I couldn't hurt him, but within a couple of hours, the inevitable happened and I was off on my travels again, partly out of revenge, but most importantly to empower myself. It was the only way to stop it, the only way to stop feeling so fucking helpless!

Of course, on my return the beating was vicious and severe, but I did get my own room downstairs and those boys never laid a hand on me again, nor did I have to witness their sexual habits.

* * * *

A few days later I received a wonderful letter from Franc, on beautiful headed notepaper, saying he had been commissioned to co-write and then direct a film called 'Quadrophenia', based on a Who album. Indeed, it was their company that were to produce the movie. It was very exciting news and caused me to be more animated than I had been for several months. I felt privileged to be sharing this moment because it allowed me to feel more than my circumstances usually allowed. A couple of days later, whilst still on a high, I was summoned to the principal's office, where I was taken by a two man escort. Once at the office, one came in, the other stood outside the door; I was tempted to go out through the window, but I was curious.

'Michael, there are quite a few people expressing concerns about you, do you understand how this might be?'

'No.'

'You've run away quite a lot to London recently and this is not good for you. London can be a very dangerous place for a young boy.'

'I'm not scared, I know what I'm doing and I know where I'm going.'

'Well, you've been at Aycliffe a couple of years now and in that time you've absconded an awful lot, and we just don't think it's working for you anymore. So you're going to be with us until a bed becomes available somewhere else, somewhere more suited to your needs.'

'St Charles?'

'No, it's a place called Redbank, I think it's near Manchester.'

Every week I listened to the football results following Manchester United's progress, or lack of it, but I had no idea where Manchester was. It felt strangely comforting to think I might be close to Old Trafford.

'Is it locked up?'

'Well, yes it is, but it's only for your own safety.'

I took care of my own safety, it was the only way to remain safe. If there was no way to hit back then the hitting would never stop, nor would the lies that should lock up the liars.

'Your parents have written to me about your relationship with Mr Roddam and they're not very happy about it. They don't think it's good for you and neither do we, and it's our job to protect you.'

'You said I should make the programme, now you've changed your mind.'

The contradictions stank the room out but the smell lingered and hovered over his head.

'We don't want you to have any more contact with Franc Roddam, Michael, it's not good for you.'

'I don't care! I'm not listening! If I want to go and see him you can't stop me, you just see if you can!'

'You're going to Redbank tomorrow, Michael. They, as well as Franc, have been informed of the decision, there will be no more contact with him, not even by letter.'

I was stunned into silence because that's all that was left. A face that was once kind couldn't have gloated any more, and a face so angelic couldn't have looked at him with more contempt than I did, knowing it was goodbye. But I never got to say goodbye to Franc nor he to me, they left it like it had never happened, but they couldn't take what I already had because they couldn't assess its nature, so they locked it up and hoped to dilute it.

In a little over two years I had absconded probably twenty times or more, mostly to London, and they just didn't get it or refused to, because it exposed them to danger more than it did me.

CHAPTER SIXTEEN

'So, Min, I guess we won't be seeing you again. This is a new opportunity for you, you should grab it, and who knows what the future may hold?'

I stood by the door, waiting to embark on the next leg of the tour. Grantham, my newly appointed social worker, tried smiling too but clearly hadn't been trained in the art, whereas the young trainee who was also along for the ride never stopped smiling, even when there was nothing to smile about which was pretty much all of it. They talk about the future like it can be bought with a book of green shield stamps and then swapped for something more alluring when the rust rots the base and masks the aesthetic. My future was going over the wall because it was the only way of keeping score with opponents who were vastly experienced cheats and, if allowed, would grind time to a halt just to remind you they owned the freehold to your life. Which was currently being held in a brown Manila envelope that was thrown dismissively onto the dashboard of the car I was travelling in.

I didn't know when I would see the North East again, didn't know that I wanted to, it had never really been home, just a series of arguments that were never resolved. Even my accent was something I often disagreed with. I was heading to the North West, approximately one hundred miles away and home of Manchester United. I would be needing them in the months to come, needing something to feel passionate about and to have a relationship with that could only hurt through disappointment, but would occasionally allow me to walk tall amongst my peers. As we approached a town called Brighouse in West Yorkshire, once famous for its brass band, we pulled into a service station for refreshments and a toilet break. The young trainee climbed out of the car, smiling once again, and challenged me.

'Come on, I'll race you to the entrance.'

He ran at full speed, his jacket flapping in the wind whilst I held back and only ran as fast as I wanted to. It was clearly a test but I too observed what was going on. I couldn't outrun him; in an even contest it would require guile, but I was curious and that's what made me stay. I couldn't run from what I hadn't yet seen or experienced, it always had to happen first then I would punch on the counter. I finally caught up with him as he was bent double trying to catch his breath. He was fast but clearly not very fit.

'You're not as fast as I expected you to be. I'm quite disappointed, really, I'd heard so much about you.'

I guess I ought to have been flattered that my reputation could cause so much disappointment but I wasn't. Not only did he not matter, nor did the information he relied on.

When we arrived at Redbank, there was a huge wall circling the place and I won't pretend that it wasn't a frightening sight. Whatever I was expecting, it wasn't this, I had no idea such a place could exist and wondered if anyone really knew I was here. To enter, we had to go through an air lock by pressing a buzzer. A member of staff unlocked the main door then came through and unlocked the gate we were standing beside. It was a regimented process, designed to immediately disarm and intimidate, control through uncertainty, never revealing what might come next. This was a new set of standards and I would have to adapt just to remain in the game.

I was ushered into the office and the envelope handed over. They didn't look at it, or at me. I was merely there to be processed, an administrative function that only knew the numbers. The social workers were clearly more overwhelmed than I was and couldn't wait to get away. As soon as the preliminaries were out of the way, they beat a hasty retreat.

'Michael, I'll let your parents know you've been delivered safely and no doubt they'll arrange to come and visit you.'

I'm not a fucking parcel! Except I was, and though torn at the edges I was always delivered on time and to the right address. It had only been a couple of years since the film had been broadcast and therefore it was still fresh in some people's minds, but it didn't win me any favours, it merely helped them to confirm why I was there.

'I heard you were coming today. I saw the programme with you on the television, you were such a cute little boy but look at you now, locked up here! I don't know what to make of it. Well, you must deserve to be here otherwise you wouldn't be.'

A cleaning lady from Northern Ireland and a proclamation that meant little to me other than to serve as a reminder to remain concentrated. Preliminaries over, I was shown to the common room where all the other boys were assembled. I was introduced to Hewitt, who was running proceedings.

'Have you just got here today?'

'Yes.'

'Yes, what?'

'Yes, I just got here today.'

'Are you trying to be funny with me because I'm warning you now, that's not a good idea, especially not on your first day.'

'I'm not trying to be funny.'

'Good. Well, I don't know where you've just come from but here we address members of staff as sir.'

I'd sooner eat my own shit.

'You're not my dad, you can't tell me what to do.'

'I can see we're going to have fun with you but that's okay. Ask any of this lot, and they'll tell you there's plenty of lads come here thinking they know it all but they soon learn that they don't.'

Some of the others were listening intently to what was going on. On the one hand it was intimidating because I didn't know any of them, on the other it was a moment to be seized, because I wanted them to back off already. I was the new boy but not the new toy.

'I'm not calling you sir, no way. You can hit me if you want but I still won't call you sir.'

'Have it your way, follow me.'

I followed him out of the common room to an area just outside of the main office known as the square, because that's precisely what it was, a square-shaped piece of flooring.

'Right, stand on there.'

'What do I have to do?'

'Stand on it.'

'Just stand here?'

'Just stand there.'

At that he walked off whistling. I couldn't have felt more exposed had I been naked; there was a constant flow of traffic, some giggled, some whispered and some didn't even notice me, they were the ones to watch.

'Are you Cooper?'

'Yes.'

'I'm Mr McKenna and I guarantee that by the end of the week you **will** be calling me sir or you'll wish we'd never met.'

I was already wishing that as I stood there surrounded by all their artillery.

'I'm not scared of you. I won't call you sir, why should I?'

He stepped forward and glared at me. In my experience, when someone looks at you that way, they either want to kill you or fuck you.

'We'll see, in the meantime the headmaster wants to see you.'

The headmaster delivered the usual speech about good behaviour being rewarded and everything else being punished severely. He clearly hadn't delivered the same speech to his troops. I was informed that as there were only two weeks to go before Christmas it would not be possible for me to go on leave as I needed to settle in first and let the staff get to know me. They already thought they did.

I wept at receiving the news about Christmas and at the prospect of having to spend it in a place I didn't yet know, surrounded by people I didn't want to.

Meals were served in the dining room and there were no set places, you just grabbed any available chair and claimed it. On arriving for my first meal I was a little fazed by the rush and just stood there.

'Cooper, you're with me!'

A member of staff would sit at the head of each table and McKenna wasted no time in reacquainting himself.

'Sit there, he's one of your lot.'

By one of 'my lot' he meant a native of the North East, and he was addressing a mixed race kid who was subject to a section fifty-three order. These were Home Office sanctions drawn up to cater for young people convicted of serious crimes but too young to be sent to prison. Some would spend a period of time in a place such as this and were then released. Others, on reaching eighteen, would be transferred to prison. Back then there were very few places to house such people and as a consequence, a once notorious child-killer, who was only a child herself, was housed here, the only girl amongst a unit full of boys. But this lad, along with two others, had broken into an old man's house whilst he was still inside. They tied him to a chair and ransacked the place, looking for money and valuables. Once they had gotten all they came for, they prepared themselves a fry-up, then on leaving, said to the poor bastard, still tied to his chair:

'You don't mind doing the washing up, do you?'

They left, laughing all the way to the courts, for he didn't do the washing up, didn't touch a thing until the police had been and gathered enough evidence to try them twice.

'When you've had your tea, Cooper, I've a little job for you.'

'I don't want it.'

'What's wrong with it, not good enough for you?'

'Cheese makes me sick.'

It wasn't the only thing but no sooner had I said it than Willie, a young Irish kid sitting next to me, had it off my plate and onto his and ate it quicker than he had salvaged it. Unlike today there were no special dispensations regarding diet, if you didn't eat it, you didn't eat.

Afterwards, I was made to polish the corridor floors but at least I had an electric polisher to do the job. Sadly, no one told me you had to put a pad under the brushes so when I switched it on it started bouncing around so violently I thought I was going to take off. Eventually, terrified I was going to be seriously injured, I let go and it went crashing into the wall, bringing the staff out of the office.

'If that's broken there'll be no pocket money until it's paid for!'

Nothing broken, just a small dent in the wall. I had arrived with a bang, which I hoped would grow louder and not by way of machines.

The evening's finale was a carol service involving captors, captives and invited voyeurs, seeking to wind down the year with a conscience feeding exercise that helps to unwrap the gifts. In truth it was nothing more than a showcase for Roberts, the deputy head, and his obese wife as they sought to fulfil the stereotype, both born and raised in the Welsh valleys. They could indeed sing but I could masturbate, I just didn't do it in public for gratification. As we headed off to bed, I was once again stopped by McKenna as he came out of the office.

'Cooper, your things are here. They've been checked so you can take them up to your room.'

He handed me a small bag of personal belongings that had instantly been liberated from me on arrival. There were fewer items than I had years on the clock but that's not how I counted.

'My radio's not here.'

'That's right.'

'What's happened to it?'

'Radios are a privilege, not a right. You've probably had the worst first day of any boy I've ever known at this school.'

Unsurprisingly, I found his comments more complimentary than inflammatory. I always felt I must be doing something right if my perceived faults troubled them into holding my things to ransom. After all, I'd already lost one radio in similar fashion.

'It's in the safe. You'll get it back once you've started to modify your behaviour in a way that shows a willingness to listen and learn.'

To get to the bedrooms you had to go through a locked gate and up the stairs where you were met by another gate. Once safely through, you were faced with a long corridor with single rooms on either side.

'Cooper, you're down here.'

A member of staff would sleep over every night should there be a problem, and a night watchman would patrol every half hour. As I was the new boy my room was directly opposite the night watchman's office. It was bleak in the extreme, uncarpeted, a bed nailed to the floor and a wardrobe befitting one who had nothing to put in it and in the corner, a plastic pot that even had a lid. Whoever said I didn't have a pot to piss in? The windows were a series of narrow slats that only opened a couple of inches, enough for temptation but nothing else, not even ventilation.

My room looked out onto the walled garden, a wall designed to keep everything in. To the left was a building housing the workshops, its roof covered in rolls of barbed wire that glistened in the light. The lights to the room could only be operated from outside in the corridor and would be switched off thirty minutes after lock down. The perimeter lights remained on until dusk and whilst not providing enough light to write or read, they were certainly an irritant.

I paced back and forth wondering if Franc knew where I was, I even held a conversation with him as if he was right there in the room. That was the funny thing, really, during such distractions I wasn't in a place, I was in a moment that didn't recognise its surroundings. I didn't know how far I was from anything I wanted to be near or how to get there so the change in circumstances held a far tighter grip than a roll of barbed wire that mocked at night. I spent the following days and weeks saying very little, doing just enough and even throwing in the occasional compromise, without being made to feel that I'd crossed over. I simply fed their need and allowed them to feed mine behind their egos. I had previously examined every lock, every crack in the wall, every corner of the building that might reveal a weakness but it was hopeless, there were none I could identify. I was so disappointed not to be able to execute what would have been my most spectacular and, without question, my most rewarding escape, but I could wait, so I would wear whatever mask was necessary.

* * * *

The unit operated a points system, whereby every Friday a meeting would be convened and each boy would be awarded a maximum of five points, although the average was between two and three. To get a five you'd have to sleep with the principal then show him the photographs. Mostly the meetings were an opportunity for the staff to publicly humiliate each boy in front of their peers but they were a necessary evil, for once you had reached a target of forty points you could leave the unit under escort. Once you had reached sixty, you could leave unescorted. That was my target and it kept the days short and the nights shorter; by ostensibly playing their game, I didn't need to pick the locks or wear several items of clothing to safely plot a route through rolls of barbed wire. Much better to have them throw open the gates with a shit-eating grin, than let them sit back and congratulate themselves for having picked your pocket, then giving back what they stole, disguised as a gift.

I accepted my worthlessness with humility, grateful that the staff were helping me to acquire the tools that would enable me to grow. The hours spent standing on the square weren't a punishment, they were a meditation and I learnt that the truth has no friends, that's why it's rarely heard, but I was never seeking to be popular, not on those terms. I was at war with an adult fraternity that never allowed the margins to expand beyond their own limitations. They hid behind walls and locked doors and preached a gospel that never stepped outside.

The gymnasium provided the greatest challenge, testing to the limit my ability to withstand the bullying mentalities that were falling over themselves to run each session. Each evening there would be a number of activities on offer, such as a reading group, drama and of course, sport. Before I had an opportunity to make a choice, a voice would ring out whilst staring into the clipboard.

'Cooper, you're in the gym, you need building up.'

Or stripping down, nevertheless I didn't utter a single word of complaint, despite my absolute loathing of these sessions. The first game I learned to fear involved a member of staff standing in the middle holding a football, which he would throw at the rest of us; if you were hit, you joined his team. I was hit several times in the face quite deliberately and never understood the purpose of the game, other than it satisfying a need that under different circumstances would be a crime. I once tried to sabotage the game by climbing to the top of the wall bars and was immediately ordered back down. Resourcefulness was clearly redundant in this game, for no one would see the blood.

Another, far more brutal game, was 'murder ball' and although no one actually died, it was very aptly named. It was a version of rugby without the discipline, a form of gang warfare that allowed personal grievances to be settled in the name of sport. There were only two basic rules, no punching in the face and no kicking at the valuables. Other than that, you had carte blanche to inflict as much physical damage as their cruelty would encourage. There was once a huge pile-up with several bodies laid on top of one another. the poor bastard at the bottom was desperately trying to release the ball so he could be free of the devouring pack.

I wanted none of it. Whenever someone threw me the ball, I would instantly throw it to somebody else, and with it my contempt for this barbarism. I stood watching the melee wishing I were anywhere but there. Suddenly, a member of staff grabbed hold of me and threw me sadistically on top of the pile, then stood back and roared with laughter.

'Now, we'll see what you're really made of!'

I lay there, defenceless, as they took full advantage of his extreme generosity. I didn't have much of a relationship with my peers, we only really shared space, now they were sharing something far more vicious, something that came from a place that would always keep us apart. When it was over I lay on the floor, bleeding from my mouth and with a couple of sore ribs, but the smug satisfaction that surrounded me couldn't easily be wiped off with a damp rag.

'Go and get yourself cleaned up, Cooper, that was pathetic, really.'

'He's like a girl, sir.'

At that moment I would have gladly fucking swapped! I jumped into the showers, wanting to hear nothing but the sound of the water cascading down on me. There was another boy stood with his back to me, eventually he turned around and was wearing nothing but a hard on. I didn't want that thing anywhere near me, yet he started walking towards me, smiling like it was a fucking done deal!

'Do you want to play?'

'No, I fucking don't, so get back in your own shower!'

He had continued walking towards me unperturbed, when salvation came in the sound of the rest of the boys leaving the gym. His smile vanished and he returned to his own shower without a word. Several weeks later whilst on home leave, he absconded and was subsequently convicted of sexual attacks against young boys.

Most nights, alone in my room, I would growl into my pillow without which I would have suffocated, trapped inside a medieval dungeon with only food for comfort, and sleep when it came. My resolve was weakening. I had compromised my entire existence in allowing them to believe that they owned me. Now I wondered if they did, if those points were scoring me, but when I finally hit the magical mark of forty points, all such feelings were vanquished, knowing what I'd had to endure just to make my own mark. It would still have to wait but it was the wait that allowed me to reaffirm my identity.

Nevertheless, I was impatient.

CHAPTER SEVENTEEN

'Come on, let's be having you.'

At weekends we would all be locked in our rooms for an hour or so whilst the staff went off and had their lunch. Most boys would talk to each other through a small gap in the door, I just lay on my bed listening to the radio, increasing the volume every time they increased theirs, not wishing the staff to return anytime soon.

'Where am I going?'

'Don't talk, just walk.'

Cowans was a diminutive Scotsman who bore a striking resemblance to Doug Henning, the American illusionist whose television shows were popular around that time. I followed him, my mind racing when it could be bothered to catch up. Once downstairs we were marched towards the air lock where another member of staff was stood waiting, key in hand. Cowans handed over his, which was a standard security procedure for any member of staff leaving the unit.

When we stepped out into the air I was momentarily disorientated and I turned to look through a window, just to see what it looked like from the other side; it was no different unless you'd never been there. It was over four months since I had been outside the unit for any purpose and that's where the difference lay. I couldn't see the signs of my arrival, the trees had colour as did the sky, even the birds sang. The grey was kept inside.

'You can stand there staring into space if you like or you can come with us. I know what I'd rather do.'

He was standing by the unit car with the driver's door open. The other boy had claimed the front passenger seat, so I climbed into the back. I stared at everything along the way, even a dog taking a crap on the pavement, it almost amused me. I watched the way people walked because they all walk differently when they're not being watched or herded.

Soon we were on the motorway, travelling at speed, my mind trying to keep up but it was hopeless, something was going on and it wasn't about to be revealed. I didn't know where the fuck we were, I just knew wherever I was heading, it was without any apparent reason.

We arrived at what appeared to be a hugely busy town or city, large numbers of people barging each other out of the way, streets full of shops inviting you in with promises of various discounts and credit opportunities. We parked and walked and I just followed, afraid of being swallowed up by a huge throng of people who swung their bags like weapons, but it became a kind of game trying to avoid being hit. By the time we had broken free of these mercenaries who, with store cards, help determine third world economics, I hadn't even noticed that the shops had begun to disappear. But when I saw it, I thought I must be dreaming, was sure I must be fucking dreaming for it couldn't possibly be real!

'So what do you think, is it better than you imagined?'

My imagination must have been hibernating for it never pictured this, a huge, breathtaking stadium with the words 'Manchester United Football Club' emblazoned on the façade like a voice that never goes away.

And who would want it to, who could deny the history that is taught through understanding? Who could deny the men, women and children, a place of worship with no promise of an afterlife or eternal well being? Yet still they flock to the altar because it makes this life a meaningful place, even on the bad days.

'Oh my god! Oh my god, I can't believe it!'

'Well, you can just stand and admire it if you like or we can go inside and sample the atmosphere.'

I was breathless and confused, it was all happening without explanation and therefore difficult to gauge. My usual reservations and suspicions had been replaced with an excitement that was being monitored but for once, I didn't care. What I wanted couldn't be taken once it had happened, not even with regret. What I wanted couldn't matter to anyone else, it was mine to own and treasure, like having sex for the first time. Even if it wasn't great, you imagined it to be, because you wanted something that was bigger than the occasion. We walked through the turnstiles and up the steps when suddenly it all came into view, the pitch so smooth it looked like a billiard table and the stands crammed full of people singing and rejoicing, and the game hadn't even started.

We were in the cantilever stand behind the goal, opposite the Stretford End and the visitors were Queens Park Rangers. We won, one-nil, but I missed the goal! Not being a regular to Old Trafford, I didn't really understand the protocol. We were seated and as our striker bore down on goal, the people in front of us stood up but we didn't. I only knew we'd scored because of the almighty roar that rang out, a noise I never wanted silencing, and it never was.

I slept badly that night, my senses had been saturated and over-fed. Mostly there's nothing, then occasionally everything, and in between there's wondering which comes next. It just depended on whose mood was the more playful.

Cowans clearly felt he had made some kind of connection because over the days and weeks that followed, he no longer stood off me, no longer spoke from a distance that barely resonated his intent, yet expecting me to read it. He began playfully punching me on the arms, at least on the face of it. He even invited me to do the same in full view of the entire unit. It became a contest to see if he could knock me off my feet. I, of course, couldn't trouble him. I didn't object because I was determined to hit him harder than he was hitting me and I had an endorsement, but also a disability. Even though he was hurting me, by withstanding the pain and coming back for more I was showing I could take it. Each punch that didn't put me down was everything I was.

One day whilst stripping off for football, the bruises on my arms were spotted. I was alarmed at the reaction, given that our sparring sessions were mostly held in the spotlight.

'Bloody hell, Cooper, how did you get them?'

How the fuck do you think? I beat myself up in the middle of the night because I'm bored! What the fuck did you see when you were laughing? It's not the bruises you're afraid of, it's who's pointing the finger and at who.

I was dragged into the office still bare-chested, and given a thorough interrogation. I objected to it because they'd all been a party to what they now pretended had never happened, yet they still expected an explanation other than the one they already knew. They would have taken anything other than that.

'Where did all these bruises come from?'

'Dunno'

'What do you mean, you don't know? They must have come from somewhere, they certainly didn't get there on their own.'

'I must have fallen out of bed or walked into a door, or something.'

I wasn't intent on protecting him, I just couldn't stomach the pretence and I wasn't going to tell them what they weren't willing to reveal. I was kept in the office for a good half hour as we covered everything from bullying to self-harm. Marry the two together and we'd have had something resembling the truth. In the end it would have been interesting to see what was placed on file, because the matter was never resolved, not in my presence at least.

* * * *

My attitude changed after that. Having now exceeded forty points, I was close to the target that would carry me north. It was all I could think of but it couldn't keep me quiet, in the end it was just a matter of time, theirs and mine.

One Sunday morning, the cook rang in sick, so the traditional lunch had to be collected by trolley from another part of the campus. Myself and another boy were dispatched, along with a member of staff, to fetch it. On entering the kitchen I was shocked to see that their cook looked like he'd been sleeping rough. His hair was greasy and unkempt, he needed a shave and a bath definitely had his name on it. He was carving the meat with hands that looked like they'd been digging coal. It was an outrage that went unmentioned, even when he cut his finger and started bleeding onto the meat.

'We can't eat that!'

'There's nowt up with it.'

'You've got blood on it.'

'Where?'

I pointed to a piece of meat as he sucked on the offending finger. He picked it up and tossed it into the sink.

'There, satisfied? Now, help me load this onto the trolley.'

'Well, I'm not eating any of it, I don't know what I'll catch.'

'That's enough, Cooper, you've had your say but you're going too far now. Any more and you'll be on the square.'

I'd have rather been hung from my ankles than be forced to eat a workhouse meal.

'Listen, Cooper, once we get this lot back to the unit, I want no more of your nonsense, okay?'

'I don't want any of it, it's rubbish and full of germs and you can't make me eat it if I don't want to!'

'Okay, Cooper, that's enough! Just remember who you are and it's this kind of attitude that brought you here.'

'I wouldn't eat any of that, it's got blood all over it.'

'Okay, Cooper, don't say you weren't given fair warning. On the square, lad, your dinner can go to someone who'll appreciate it.'

Someone who under the right circumstances would probably eat their own vomit. That's what they were relying on, and that's what they got. A bunch of kids who just wanted feeding, because between the food there was only the rules, their needs were more immediate and were catered for because it was simple mathematics.

I stood on the square, once again disconnected, there was only me now. I trusted what I saw and my reasons for speaking out but I didn't always trust my feelings for mostly they were trapped in a shapeless void. I had nothing to share because I no longer knew anyone who knew me.

CHAPTER EIGHTEEN

'My name is Stephenson. You can call me mister or sir and I'm your new Headmaster. I believe in discipline but also in fairness.'

A contradiction in terms, surely anyone who puts discipline before fairness has their priorities all wrong.

'With immediate effect, there are to be two new rule changes. Any boy who finds himself in seclusion will have whatever is on that day's menu in the form of a sandwich.'

His speech, delivered to assembled housemates and staff, left me in no doubt that the game was about to change. Afterwards, he asked for a word outside. My entire Saturday afternoon would be ruined without access to my radio and most importantly, the football, this being the second of the rule changes; radios only to be played in bedrooms. I followed him out of the common room and onto the square, already disliking him more with every step.

'Okay, Cooper, let me make myself perfectly clear. I know all about you and your nasty little habits. As far as I'm concerned, you need to prove yourself to me, lad. Today is day one, so whatever my predecessor may have promised you, it's cancelled.'

'What about my home leave?'

'You obviously weren't listening to me.'

'But I'm entitled.'

'I decide who's entitled to what. When you've earned it you can have it, until then, as a gesture of goodwill, you can have a week's leave in the unit.'

'That's not the same.'

'That's my offer.'

With that he was gone.

The unit offered a bizarre scheme whereby a person could be on leave whilst still remaining locked inside the unit. It was set up to cater for the section fifty-three people who would often be refused home leave by the Home Office for fear they might re-offend and cause a public outcry.

It was the summer of '78 and the 'Mario Kempes' World Cup was being staged in Argentina. He danced his way through endless defences looking more like a male model than a footballer. By being on 'leave' I was offered exclusive use of an upstairs lounge complete with a television set, perfect! I didn't have to rise with the rest of the unit, instead I would simply ring for room service to come and liberate me. Nor did I have to attend educational classes, such as they were, and I had first choice of the available leisure activities. As it was summer, most evenings there would be an escorted walk around the local countryside. A place on these walks was like a winning lottery ticket and they were always over-subscribed, but it wasn't the country air that was the allurement, it was the cigarettes that were regularly handed out. My name was first on that list every night of that week, the rest having to draw lots for the few remaining places. That was my week watching football, smoking cigarettes, missing breakfast and never allowing myself to enjoy it more than I should.

Shortly after returning to the ranks, a boy was caught trying to escape. He had been gardening and noticed that someone had rather foolishly built a compost heap right next to the wall. He positioned a wheelbarrow on top of the compost, hooked a rake over the wall and began climbing up the pole. The head of the rake snapped off, sending him crashing into the wheelbarrow and alerting the staff. We were all ushered into the gymnasium and made to sit in a line on the wooden benches, witnesses to a very public humiliation. The boy in question was stood over the vaulting horse, his trousers and pants down by his ankles and his hands held in place by a member of staff, stood either side of him.

Stephenson was standing at the far end of the gym, making whooshing noises with a wooden cane that sent everyone's nerves jangling. He then let out a demonic roar before running the full length of the gym and unleashing his own particular beast across the bare buttocks of a fourteen-year-old boy. After the first stroke, myself and most of the other boys looked down at the floor, unable to stomach it, but this simply enraged him further.

'Do not look at the floor, look at him! Any boy found looking at the floor can swap places with him. If we have to stay here all night then we will. Any boy who tries to escape from me better hope he's never returned!'

Not one member of his sullied brigade had the fucking balls to challenge him! They shared in the blood-letting and witnessed the screams that could have come from their child.

Several years later, the boy in question was one of the remaining five to finally come down off the roof of Strangeways prison, during the infamous riot of 1990. The pain he suffered in that gymnasium, he never inflicted on anyone else, he even baked me a cake once.

I lay awake all that night, afraid of what I needed to do, afraid of suffering the same fate, not sure that I could physically withstand it and wondering if anything was worth that amount of pain. But a far greater pain is to be an acolyte, to wander without honour or regret behind a cruel and vicious thug who wore a disguise provided by his employers. I could not live without reward.

During the week of my birthday, a case conference was convened to decide, amongst other things, if I could spend a week with my family at a Northern seaside resort. The request was flatly refused and sadly my family all went down with food poisoning, spending the rest of their holiday shopping for disinfectant. How Stephenson must have wished he could have changed his mind.

I just went back to waiting, I was getting used to it and was comfortable with the time it gave me to reinforce my belief that being scared was the motivator, not the detractor. Without the fear, there would be no reason for it that could make the waiting a meditation.

By the autumn I had been granted a weekend at home. I had been at the unit approximately ten months.

I was driven by the resident social worker to the service station near Brighouse and handed over to Grantham, my own social worker, who was accompanied by yet another fucking student! Without being offered any refreshments, I climbed into the back of his car and continued with the journey. They spent the best part of the journey discussing their various plans for the weekend, then moved on to holidays before finally being reduced to talking about me, though not to me. It was like twenty fucking questions!

I found my own entertainment in the form of the student's handbag, which was conveniently sitting next to me. I'd already shot it the odd furtive glance, now it was lovingly nestling against my thigh. I even put my arm around it. All the time I was glancing up at the rear view mirror but I needn't have worried, he used the wing mirror to monitor the traffic, everything else was monitoring her. It was nauseating, yet hugely rewarding. I liberated the purse, then part of the contents (no need for greed, it's so ugly!), finally sitting everything back neatly in place, including myself.

'You okay in the back?'

It was too late to ask, I wasn't going to put it back, it would have been a bigger crime than taking it and a bigger loss with the tick going into their box instead of mine. Too many of those and I'd be an example, and a liar.

'Yeah, I'm okay.'

There were no more questions, no more enquiries and no more reasons to think or feel any differently because there was no one to hang it on.

On arrival the social workers declined a cup of tea and after a brief introduction, departed for the eagerly awaited pub crawl. I figured the loss of the money would at some point be discovered and the usual interrogations would ensue. In the event it was never mentioned, no one ever knew because they dared not imagine how invisible they had been to mine. I wasted no time in heading to my room, eager to deposit the money in my safety deposit box, the spine of a Manchester United Annual. I carefully folded the money and was about to slot it in, when my brother entered the room.

'What yer deein'?'

'Nowt.'

'What yer hiding in that book?'

'Just some paper.'

'Let me see.'

'No, it's none of your business.'

'It's money and I bet you've nicked it. Give me half or I'll tell Dad and he'll take it off yer.'

The difficulty in trying to bluff someone who is willing to risk losing his share just to prevent you from having yours, is that there is no rationale with which to bargain. Nevertheless, I tried.

'There's fifteen quid here. I'm not giving you half, I took all the risks. I'll give you a fiver and you should be grateful, you've done nothing for it.'

'I want half or I'm telling Dad.'

'Tell him then, and when he gets here there won't be any money so you'll get nowt.'

'Aye, and neither will thee.'

I peeled off a fiver and held my hand out towards him, praying he wouldn't force my hand in a moment of pure greed and spite. I needed that fucking money more than he needed a distraction, mine wouldn't be spent on chocolate.

'It's up to you.'

He wasted no time in grabbing the money out of my hand and in taking it. At sixteen, he was two years older than me and whilst I had never felt physically intimidated by him, his capacity for betrayal was a constant concern, so I was seriously relieved when he took the money.

The following afternoon, my mother went shopping with my sisters and both my brother and myself went with my father to watch him play football. His team weren't a particularly impressive outfit and I never understood his willingness to play for them, given his outstanding ability as a goalkeeper. He believed in the game and its importance to the local community, he believed that men who worked hard trying to feed families most of them couldn't afford, should be allowed to be heroes for a while, if only in the eyes of their wives and girlfriends and fellow players.

No mention of children.

On that particular afternoon they were short of a linesman. The way it usually worked was that a member of the opposition's entourage would run one line, whilst the home side would provide someone to run the other, except the home side had no one available until my Dad approached the referee.

'My eldest lad can run the line, he plays for the school and he nahs all the rules, especially off side.'

'How old is he, like?'

'Almost sixteen.'

'Well, there's no one else, give him the flag and let's get kicked off, it's bliddy cold.'

The game kicked off with the usual frenetic start, every player on the park wanting the ball and everyone else full of advice. Halfway through the first half, I noticed my dad hopping from foot to foot before racing behind his goal to take a piss. My brother spotted him immediately and wasted no time in hoisting his flag high above his head and keeping it there until the referee approached him.

'What's up son?'

'My Dad went behind his goal for a wee, it's against the rules.'

The referee turned and marched towards my father who was instantly dismissed from the pitch, sent off for what I believe was un-gentlemanly conduct. It was an ignominious exit, as he walked the gauntlet past players and spectators alike, all jeering at a man sent off at his son's instigation. It was a short walk home, approximately a mile, every few seconds my brother would squirm and plead forgiveness as he received yet another crack around the side of his head

'I can't believe it, me own son got me sent off! Wait 'til the lads doon the pit hear aboot this, I'll be crucified!'

This would inevitably be followed by another, even louder crack. Sadly I had become accustomed to all of this, it neither shocked nor frightened, it was neither of anything, just the fucking norm.

During the weekend, my father had not bothered locking us in our room, but I figured as it was fast approaching bedtime on the penultimate evening, all that would change, so on the way up the stairs I grabbed one of my Mum's knitting needles and hid it under my mattress. It was the right call, I lay in bed that night wishing my mind could belong to someone else, wishing things could just be straightforward and not tangled up and wishing I knew what to do. Instead of what I was going to do, but doing nothing would just allow things to become even more tangled, and I couldn't just sit there picking at the knots whilst those who made them turned their backs. I rose early before the larks, it was barely light and I sat on the edge of my bed watching my brother sleeping, I wanted to stay a while but I couldn't risk the time so I quickly and quietly got dressed. I retrieved the needle from under my mattress and wasted no time in freeing myself.

The bucket was full of piss so I couldn't overturn it. Instead, I grabbed a pile of books and football magazines and stood on them. I wasn't quite five feet tall but thankfully the needle provided an extra few inches, so I slid it up the tiny crack in the door and flicked the sneck free. I stood on the landing, waiting for a response but there was none. I made my way down the stairs, trying not to breathe, believing if I did so my every step would be heard.

Once downstairs, I immediately undid the locks on the back door and returned to the lounge. My father had left his cigarettes on the table so I lit one and smoked it. The house was eerily silent and I was the only one awake, it was mine, but only by my thinking. I had no relationship with anything I touched, there was no smell that knew me, it was all borrowed, including the cigarette that now lay dead in the ashtray. I wanted to stay because that's what I was supposed to want, but I just didn't know anymore, I didn't know what it was like to do ordinary things without them seeming unusual, or painted on to another agenda with the response duly noted. I once again entered my own playground where the rules weren't a game.

I locked the door and posted the keys through the letterbox. I glanced up at the bedroom windows to see if any of my siblings were watching me depart but they weren't, they were enjoying the comfort of their dreams before heading off to school, and warm milk. The village was deserted and I made my way unchallenged towards my favourite café for a bacon roll and a cup of hot steaming coffee, my two favourite combined smells. After demolishing the bacon, I sat nursing my coffee when a great wave of sadness came over me and I almost started to cry. I had waited months for this moment, had walked through it a hundred times, each time the same, but Stephenson didn't seem so important anymore.

'So, young 'un, how come your mama don't make you your breakfast?'

'She's not very well.'

'She must be ill a lot, I see you in here plenty of times on your own. How come you don't walk to school with your friends?'

'I like walking on my own.'

'Well, it's no good for you. You should be talking with your friends, plenty of time for thinking when you get to school.'

Tony, the proprietor, was a sweet little Italian guy who always needed a shave. Sometimes he would let me play the pinball machine, even though I wasn't old enough. Occasionally, if I was a few pence short on the price of a meal, he would waive the difference. He was also intrusive, partly because he just liked to talk and because very often we were the only ones there. I never had anything to tell that could give him a link into another conversation but he never lost patience, he just lost me.

The street was starting to get busier and I stood there without a plan or protection and I needed both fast. I left before I'd wanted to but I needed to get away, it was the curse of my existence, responding to the need and not the wish. I headed for the underpass and a housing estate on the other side of town. I would be conspicuous for a while but only until I'd reached the disused railway line that stretched for miles, without a cop in sight. Having money increased my options and slightly reduced the risks. If I needed food I could buy rather than steal and reduce the chances of being captured. I also didn't need to travel on foot unless I wanted to, and mostly I did because paradoxically it was safer; no questions, no answers, no lies and no panic.

By lunchtime, I found myself stood outside the gates of St. Mary's school. It was a hugely dangerous venture but I was drawn to it and couldn't seem to move myself in any other direction. The kids were in the yard competing for decibels, my sister was playing a skipping game with some of her friends and a couple were leaning against the wall, watching but not seeing, how quickly one is replaced. I wanted to play my sister's game, wanted her to know I was her brother and not just an intruder who changes everything on appearance, but I could only view from a distance. I walked away from the school, walked the streets I'd walked so many times, yet still I didn't know their names and didn't bother to find out, I just knew the way without having to ask or be told.

As darkness fell and the temperature dropped, I began to question my reasons for doing this. A combination of the cold and extreme boredom had left me feeling miserable. Now I had to find somewhere to sleep and my resolve was under threat, but then it would have been had I gone back on schedule. I had no sense of time, only that it was dark. For some bizarre reason, I went to the back door of my house and tried the handle. It was open and in an instant my spirits rose. I walked into the kitchen and heard the sound of the television coming from the lounge and also my parents talking.

I froze. This was unexpected and I hadn't planned for it. I was trying hard to think, knowing that at any moment either of my parents could walk through that door and I'd be back where I started, just killing time to stay alive. In a moment of panic, I searched all around me, almost unable to breathe. Walking through to the lounge wasn't an option so I had to find an alternative and there it was, almost beckoning me conspiratorially: a plastic laundry basket, full of dirty laundry. I quickly removed the lid, climbed in, replaced it, then grabbed handfuls of clothing and covered myself with them. The smell was overpowering but at least it was warm. I just waited, waited for my parents to go to bed so I could climb out and light a cigarette, just to get rid of the smell and the nerves, which increased dramatically when the door opened and in stepped my father to make a cup of tea.

I tried not to breathe or at least slow it down to the bare minimum, afraid of being heard. Whilst the kettle was boiling he locked the back door. There were holes in the basket and I was able to watch him moving about the kitchen with a smile stretching all the way to Aldershot.

'I'll tell yer something else for nowt, I bet he's somewhere in this village and if he is, I'll find him and when I do, he'll get the hiding of his life.'

He often did that, left a conversation behind then started it up again as if he'd suddenly remembered what it was he really wanted to say. No one got off the hook, not even my mother. The threatened beating was reason enough to enjoy being right under his nose as he issued it. What had originally been necessary had now become profoundly satisfying and helped ease the stiffness I was feeling in my joints, quelling any uncertainty I may have been feeling.

'You know, when they catch him they'll stop him coming home for a while. Well he's brought it on himself, that's all I can say. And if they ask him why he did it, he'll just say I don't know, so how can they help him?'

By not asking!

As soon as my parents had gone to bed, I climbed out of the basket and sat in the lounge, absorbing the silence and grateful for the warmth and shelter my parents had unwittingly provided, having effectively trespassed in my own home. I slept in the tiny alcove under the stairs, beneath a pile of coats.

The following morning, I left through the back door, once again locking it and posting the keys through the letterbox. Now he'd know I'd been, but not how. I had no plans as I walked down the street, lost in a system of thought that at times was wayward and occasionally mournful.

I didn't see the cop drive past in his patrol car, but sadly he saw me. He quickly reversed until he was alongside of me.

'Get in, Michael, don't make me run after you and get this uniform dirty.'

I climbed into the back of his car and sat in silence as we drove the couple of miles to the police station. I was angry at the complacency that had allowed me to be so easily captured. So utterly immersed had I been in my own fractured existence, I had completely ignored the rules that were there to keep everything alive by keeping me on the move, and out of reach. Instead, I walked down a main road like a fucking plum!

CHAPTER NINETEEN

'Take your shoes off and if you have a belt, take that off as well, then empty your pockets into that bag. Everything, pens, tissues, we don't want you harming yourself and attracting undeserved sympathy.'

I doubted if I removed my genitals it would have been met with anything other than habitual disdain and punishment. However, I was not about to willingly spill my blood, not in that way.

'Right, in you go. How long you're in there depends on you.'

The door slammed shut and the room shuddered, as did I, but only because it was cold. It was also dark, so I just stood there until my eyes adjusted and the rest of me caught up. There was a thin mattress on the floor and an equally thin blanket, but no pillow. High up on the wall there was a window but it was too high to look out of, in the corner the obligatory piss pot.

It was the first time I had been in the seclusion room but I'd been well prepared for it, even down to sleeping in my clothes, but sleep was a rare commodity with the night watchman switching on the lights every half an hour. I didn't regret what I'd done, I would have regretted it far more if I had surrendered meekly on the designated day and offered myself up as the new sacrifice. Ultimately though, it was probably a pyrrhic victory. I got to say, "stuff you and your den of iniquity, stuff your violent masturbations and your inhumane degradations," but I only really said it to myself. They, on the other hand, carried on playing, but with renewed vigour and cynicism. I guess they figured they had me where they wanted me and weren't in a hurry to let go.

The following lunchtime the door swung open and Stephenson walked in carrying two plastic plates with a sandwich on each. All I could think of was how wonderful they would look crawling down the front of his suit. I was uneasy in his presence, my situation made me vulnerable, and he was an extremely unpredictable man who constantly needed second-guessing. It was tiresome and tedious.

'Here you are, liver and onions in that one, jelly and ice cream in the other.'

The smile never left his face, he was gloating and I was powerless to stop it. I was an audience of one, his favourite kind after his psychotic episode in the gymnasium that should have cost him his career and his liberty.

'I need to empty that pot.'

'You can empty it later. I'm sure by now you're accustomed to eating in a sewer, it should be home from home.'

'It's nearly full.'

He pulled the door to, careful not to slam it shut as it couldn't be opened from the inside, and the buzzer seemed to make people deaf.

'Then you'd better make sure you hold on to it because if any of that ends up on the floor, I will personally use you as a mop.'

He walked back towards the door and just before leaving, he turned to me once more. The smile had gone, replaced with a more menacing look.

'Don't even think about Christmas leave, it's cancelled, and as for your points situation, you're back to zero. You've nowhere left to go, Cooper, and I'm here to make sure you get there. Enjoy your food.'

He slammed the door shut and as soon as he had he gone, I picked up the plates and slammed them against the wall, then picking up a slice of bread I made a huge swirling motion with my hand, blending gravy and ice cream together. It looked like baby shit but I still stood and admired it, or perhaps I was just admiring myself. I had nothing but the tools I was born with to alleviate the boredom, and paint the walls the colour of my day.

I spent three days in that box, having been told I would remain there until I had cleaned the walls. Rather than play directly into their hands, the rest of the meals were left untouched on the floor and removed in the same condition. In the end, some poor fucker who was probably only guilty of a minor indiscretion was sent in to clean the walls whilst I sat watching in the corner. He asked me why I'd done it and I asked him why he was cleaning it.

By the evening of the third day, I was so hungry I was almost hallucinating. A hot meal arrived, it even came with a knife and fork. Cottage pie, jellied mince under a blanket of synthetic potato, it was sent to tempt me but it remained stuck to the plate. An act of kindness governed by abject fear, terrified of what would happen to them if the worst was to happen to me, even the promised cigarette never left the packet for if it had, that was my price. I was starving and cold but unmoved. What they couldn't resolve with a hot meal, a cigarette, or a multitude of threats, left them grasping for the manual, without which they were just you and me, with nothing more than the fear that brought them here and allowed them to hide.

'Right, Cooper, out you come. You've had plenty of time to think about your actions, now it's time to get to work again and I'll be watching you like a hawk, as will every other member of staff.'

Day four and an unexpected reprieve, but it wasn't a gift, just an ordinary way of getting back to basics.

'Well, come on, we haven't got all day! That pot needs emptying and you need a flaming wash.'

Having completed my ablutions I made my way down the stairs, along with the other boys. As I made my way along the corridor towards the dining room, I could smell toast; it had never smelt so fucking good in all my life!

'Cooper, don't just stand there like a moron, it won't walk down the corridor to you! Now, move or you'll be on the square.'

'He's like a statue, sir.'

'I'm well aware of what he looks like. On your way, lad, or you'll be joining him.'

I couldn't have stood on the square, I would have passed out, partly from malnutrition and partly from delirium, so I walked into the dining room and sat down. It was warm, almost too warm, but when the food arrived I forgot all about it. I had earned this moment but only I recognised it. I ate like there was nothing else to do because for three days there had been nothing else to do except masturbate. I kept hold of one whilst discarding the other, treating with contempt not the food itself but the manner of its delivery. Besides, I hate fucking liver!

'Cooper, for God's sake, it's not a flaming race, you know! You're not trying to qualify for the Olympics.'

'I know, sir, he's eating like a pig and it's putting me off.'

Willie, the young Irish kid, was sat next to me. He had been targeting me for several weeks, a punch here, a kick there, sometimes he would steal stuff my parents had sent in to me and as they didn't have a lot of money, this seriously pissed me off.

'Sit somewhere else, then, I'm not forcing you to sit there.'

'Don't get funny with me or you'll know what you'll get. If I want that toast, I'll just take it and what are you going to do about it?'

He was confident because he had every reason to be. He had so far acted with impunity, often pulling me around like a rag doll, but something had changed that no longer allowed my rational voice to speak, for there was no longer any protection in that.

'Try it and you'll see.'

And just like the fool he was, he did, but he never got to put it to his mouth. As soon as his grubby fingers tried rewarding themselves, I too became equally malicious, with an intent to match it. I'd had enough of words that only I knew, and had enough of laughter that was never a part of me, just aimed like a rifle. I stuck my knife into the back of his hand with all the strength and determination that I could muster and drew blood. He squealed like a pig, the expression of extreme shock on his face, matched those who sat nearby.

I was no longer the professor as I held his gaze whilst trying to push that fucking knife further and further into his flesh. Eventually several members of staff came to his rescue as they always do. They dragged me down the corridor and onto the square, not missing the opportunity for a little rough treatment. They barked out insults like they were instructions, it was always difficult to tell.

'Right, on your feet, Cooper, and stand there until I tell you to move, do you understand?'

He wanted an answer but he wasn't going to get one, not because I was unable to provide it, but because it was the acknowledgment of an authority that I no longer recognised.

* * * *

It took several months before I once again reached forty points but at least I was on my way. During that time there had been several attempts at petty-minded intimidation and cheap threats, but I drew comfort from these and the last thing I did each day was smile myself to sleep. I was becoming impatient as my excitement levels rose, when an unexpected surprise came my way.

'Cooper, you're in the printing shop today.'

'I thought I was banned.'

Several months earlier I had engaged in a boyish prank that had brought much laughter but was interpreted in more sinister fashion by those who never laugh. Out of boredom and mischief I had slapped some thick grease on the door handle, making it impossible to open the door without first having removed the grease. After being made to clean the printing shop for a day and a half, I was then banned from using it.

'The ban's been lifted but any more shenanigans and it will be permanent, understood?'

'Yeah.'

The printing shop was used to subsidise some of the other activities by charging various groups and organisations a nominal fee for printing tickets, invitations etc., but today it was hopefully going to subsidise me. At the helm was a bespectacled young man called Clegg. He had a serious disposition and believed young boys should share an adult's work ethic and he ran the shop on those principles. I generally found this experience profoundly dull and inhibiting but I hoped to change all that, whatever mask I was forced to wear.

'Mr. Clegg, I was wondering...'

'What?'

'My aunty wanted to know if we could print some tickets for her? She said she'll pay.'

'What kind of tickets?'

'Tickets for people to make donations. She helps at the church, cooking food and that, and they need some money.'

'Okay, but it will have to be next week, we've got as much as we can deal with at the moment.'

He was a solid, church-going Christian type who would have found it difficult to refuse, as difficult as I would have in passing it up. A week later, five hundred donation cards were safely in my possession, all I needed was a presentation to match the professional standard of the work. I lay awake all night, counting the minutes that counted the hours, having been told earlier that day I was going home tomorrow. Everything was packed, everything taken down off the walls, for the sooner they forget, the faster I could grow into someone they would never recognise.

CHAPTER TWENTY

'Oh, stop blubbering, I've hardly touched yer.'

I guess by his standards he hadn't, although the blow sent me somersaulting off the sofa and onto the floor, a tiny trickle of blood making its way down the side of my mouth to be met by my tongue.

'You's lot get to yer rooms, now!'

My siblings had been sat staring at the floor, fidgeting and shifting uncomfortably in their seats. They didn't need asking twice, they scuttled off, almost falling over each other in the process. Mum was in the kitchen, it was just me and him, like it always was. I climbed back onto the sofa and wiped the blood from my mouth and stared defiantly back at him, but he was in no mood to register such contempt.

'Right, I'll ask you again and this time I want the truth. Where did you get these?'

He was, of course, holding up the tickets I had printed. I had been at home little more than a day when, through a combination of extreme arrogance and stupidity, I tried my luck in the village for a little holiday money. But I was marked, and no sooner had I put on my best pious charm, there was a knock at my father's door. Having sent me on a fool's errand, he set about hunting for the offending items and having found them, his weekend was complete.

'I've told you, the school gave them to me so I could collect money for them.'

'So how come they didn't tell us, like? How come they didn't give you a letter to bring home?'

'They did but I forgot it.'

'Well, we'll see what the school says about it.'

'Do what you like, I'm not bothered! It's a waste of time talking to you, anyway.'

Not one of my smartest statements. His injured pride spat more venom than a cobra and attacked with more speed, and I rolled off the sofa in a pitiful attempt at self-preservation, but it just made him taller and me slower. I was approaching my fifteenth birthday and still wasn't yet five feet tall, I also weighed in at a pitiful seven stones. The only thing that hadn't shrunk was my tongue, or my willingness to use it.

'Don't ever try and make a monkey out of me.'

I couldn't even hear him anymore as I crawled around the floor, dishevelled and disorientated, not so much from the beating, which was pretty standard, nor the fact that he followed me with a well-aimed kick, it was having nowhere to go that made the pain my own. Everything began to shrink faster than I could comfortably squeeze into it, the house, the village, the school and every thought I ever had, lying side by side with my dreams that had already fallen into sleep.

Tea came and went but I no longer had any appetite for food, but thankfully this was simply put down to a childish sulk and ignored. Everything else would have to be, but I still refused to accept I had no name other than the one stuck to a locked door.

By early evening my father had softened somewhat, which was rather worrying; he was much easier to predict when ranting and threatening to bounce you off the walls. As soon as he appeared reasonable and tolerant, it was like talking to someone you've only just met.

'Fancy a walk?'

'Not bothered.'

'Haway, man, let's get some air, it'll do us good.'

I grabbed my coat, taking as much time as possible. I was never comfortable being alone with my old man, I always felt nervy and edgy. I was diminutive whilst he was a huge physical presence, towering over me. We walked to the edge of the woods, where he gave me a history lesson on the fate of the local colliery which had long since been flattened and covered with dog shit and broken bicycle parts. He then became nostalgic about his own childhood, how he and his brothers would roam the very woods we were stood by, building dens and taking birds' eggs from the nest, quite a collection they had too.

'You know those tickets you had? Whoever printed them, did a very professional job.'

The ego, with all its associations and vanities, can be as vulnerable as it can enlarge the truth beyond its own reckoning. My weakness wasn't that I wanted him to believe I was a master craftsman, it was wanting them to know my name was on the deed. It was all I was going to get now.

'Yeah, they did.'

'Five hundred tickets, and if everyone gave fifty pence, that's two hundred and fifty pounds for the school.'

The words almost fucking choked me, that and my own unbelievable stupidity. I couldn't bear to listen, stood on the edge of those woods, staring into wishes that ignored me.

'But the money wasn't for the school, was it? You were going to use it to run off. Tell me I'm wrong?'

'No, you're not wrong.'

Having gotten the confession he so dearly wanted, whereby his own ego would have placed him amongst the most skilful interrogators in living history, I was bounced all the way up the street and into the house, one whack per step.

'I told yer he was lying! What did I tell yer? Go on, tell yer mother what yer just told me.'

'Tell her yourself, you're the one who likes talking all the time.'

'Aye, that's it, try and be clever! Well, yer won't be so clever when yer in borstal!'

'Borstal?'

It was a threat we'd all grown up with; borstal wasn't a remand home like Redbank or Aycliffe, it was prison for the young.

'Aye, when they get to know down there, they'll probably send you to borstal and you've only got yerself to blame. You'll get five years for this.'

'Then, don't tell them.'

'I have to tell them.'

'No, you don't, nobody knows anything about it, they only know what you tell them.'

'I have to tell them so they can help you. If I say nothing and you do something else wrong, then I'm at fault.'

'No, you're not, you just want to look good in front of the social workers and you don't give a fuck what happens to me, so don't fucking pretend!'

I didn't see the first blow, as it swung its way to the side of my head, nor did I feel it, so full of adrenaline was my tiny frame. Within seconds it was business as usual, with fewer spectators, even my mother had left to attend to something else.

BORSTAL! BORSTAL! BORSTAL!

The words kept marching relentlessly until they had filled my room and had nowhere to go, except around and around, spinning my head and defying natural movement. They smothered and spat and stretched the night. I lay there before looking out of the window for relief but it kept coming back. Everyone was sleeping except me, everyone had a place that kept them. I contemplated suicide, albeit briefly, but as they slept in the next room comfortable in their dispatch, I wanted them to see me unafraid and alive, eyes blazing like a stranger who was once a guest.

I was to be returned in the morning and as well as being locked in my room, my father had removed everything before taking my shoes and clothes. I had only my pyjamas and my intent, but they were more alive than the simplistic intentions of waving goodbye.

I ignored the chaos of the breakfast table as each new item was delivered then attacked; cereals, milk, toast and a fry-up for my brother, who had started work as an apprentice plasterer. It was crowded and I needed room to breathe, and I became increasingly irritated by the routine chatter that would return the following morning and wouldn't notice the empty chair, or the toast that was missing. Eventually everyone departed, and I sat alone at the table amongst the remnants of family life but pushed my bowl into the middle. The chance had passed and the milk had run dry. My mother emerged from the kitchen with a mug of steaming hot coffee and sat down in her favourite armchair, but she wasn't comfortable. She leaned forward, nursing that mug like a wounded animal and refusing to offer any eye contact, as if afraid it might permanently blind her.

'Where's Dad?'

'He's in bed, he's been on nights, trying to provide for this family.'

She was ice cold both in speech and manner, and her voice came from a place only she knew. Or perhaps she was just angry because that's what the old man required and expected. Or maybe he was the one on the receiving end and she couldn't look at me for fear of exposure. It was confusing, not knowing who to avoid or detect.

'Where's my clothes?'

She placed her mug on the mantelpiece and disappeared off to some secret location that I was excluded from. Within minutes, she had returned carrying a small bundle, which she dumped on the sofa. I picked them up and waited for instructions but the coffee held her attention more than I could. So I made my way to my bedroom, not before spotting my shoes in the alcove; a surge of excitement ran through me and the countdown began.

'Michael, come in here please.'

'What now?'

'You can get changed in the bathroom and you can have your shoes when the social worker gets here.'

Which evidently couldn't come soon enough.

I dressed then went outside for a cigarette. I was outside of family, owned by the state who occasionally loaned me out to reluctant recipients, who dressed me and fed me, then handed me back.

I put out my cigarette, stamping on it until my foot hurt, then returned to the house and stood by the kitchen drawer. I was shaking, trying desperately to change my mind, but there was nothing except the betrayal. I opened the drawer and pulled out the biggest knife on show, and gripping the handle tighter than an olive branch, I marched into the lounge and confronted my mother, initially too shocked to speak.

'Just stay in that chair, Mum, I just want my shoes, that's all, then I'm off. I'm not going to borstal for five years for nothing.'

I was so nervous, the words almost choked me and my breathing was so laboured I felt like I had to breathe twice for every breath I felt.

'Michael, don't be stupid, you're just going to make things worse!'

'You and Dad have made it worse, just over a bunch of fucking tickets that I never even sold!'

'We didn't print those tickets, you did, so don't try and blame us.'

'No, but you could have thrown them in the bin instead of trying to get me locked up! It's not like anyone got hurt.'

I was terrified my old man was going to hear us and come down the stairs, so I ran to the alcove, found my shoes and returned to the lounge. My mother was sipping her coffee and looked almost regal. How I wished it could have been different, but I had to go.

'I love you, Mum, but I can't stay.'

Before she had time to answer, I disappeared out of the back door. I quickly tied my shoelaces and before making my way up the street, took one last look through the lounge window. My mother was making her way towards the stairs to alert my father, so I had no time to waste. I ran to the top of the street and cut across a field that led to the next village. My parents didn't have a telephone and it would take a while for my old man to get dressed and make his way to the kiosk.

Once I had reached the edge of the field, I took the knife, which I had hidden down the front of my trousers, and buried it in the hedgerow. I took a minute to catch my breath, trying to regain some sense of rationale and composure. I had crossed the line, massively and irrevocably, had torn down the boundaries of the family dynamic and now it lay scattered like ashes across a landscape that I was now using for refuge. I couldn't afford to remain stationary for too long. Now that the police were searching for a knife-wielding maniac, I was no longer simply a runaway, I was a disturbed individual who needed apprehending at all costs. I took one last look at the knife but I didn't want any further connection to it, it would forever have my mother's name on it.

My senses were now acutely tuned to danger and I made my way to Durham in a constantly high state of anxiety and nervousness, without a plan or the state of mind to execute one. I was lost, both in mind and in body, left with just the crudest elements of survival and a rationale that didn't question or accuse. I had to take the longest route to Durham, across fields and through woodland, because I knew the cops would be out in force. I also knew they would expect me to remain hidden, so I still felt exposed.

Strangely, the events of the morning had actually left me feeling ravenous when normally it would have had the opposite effect. I had just enough money for a bacon roll and a cup of coffee, but was immediately left contemplating my continued survival, and survive I must. I stole a book of raffle tickets from a newsagent's in the city and trawled the outskirts, determined to stay away from the city centre and its patrolling police cars, not to mention the odd foot patrol. By mid-afternoon I had made two or three quid from my bogus raffle.

I decided to head back to Craghead where it would be safer. As I walked through the city towards the bus station, I instinctively felt danger, knew something was wrong, and when I turned around there it was: a patrol car travelling slower than I was. In a moment of extreme panic and abject fear, I ran up an alleyway into a dead end. Road signs were scattered everywhere, and no way out, it was clearly some kind of council depot with only one building, but the door was open. I entered and quickly made my way down the steps. Halfway down and to my left was a door, which was slightly ajar. Inside, several workmen could be heard enjoying a break. I tiptoed past them, down the stairs into another room. In the far corner and again to my left, was another set of steps and to my right, a metal cupboard, next to which was a wooden box. It was my only hope and as time was running out, I climbed in and crouched down as far as I could; no sooner had I gotten into position, than I heard footsteps, heavy footsteps.

'Have any of you blokes seen a young lad come past here?'

'No, we've been here aboot twenty minutes, but we've not seen anyone.'

'Where do these steps lead to?'

'I'll show yer.'

They came down the steps and into the room where I was holed up. I tried slowing my breathing almost to a halt. I wanted to freeze time, movement, the fucking lot! I was convinced they would walk right over to the box, fetch me out and have me cuffed up faster than I could say pig.

'See, there's nowt in here.'

'What about those steps over there?'

'They just lead to the storeroom, there's noot doon there.'

'Any windows?'

'Just a skylight. It's possible to get up to it but I doubt a young lad could do it. He'd have more chance in the yard, the walls are easy to climb up and he could be away across the rooftops.'

'He couldn't have gotten away, he couldn't have!'

How I wanted to laugh for the rest of my life at the young constable who, having readied himself for the big arrest, ran into the invisible man who was only a few feet from where he stood.

'Well listen, if you see him hanging about the place, don't approach him, ring us.'

'What's he done, like?'

'He only pulled a fucking knife on his own mother!'

It all seemed so real when he said it, because it was fucking real! When the room eventually fell silent I was initially too afraid to re-emerge, convinced they were laying some kind of trap. When I did finally emerge, I could hardly move through a combination of stiffness and cramp.

Suddenly, I heard whistling and a soft swishing sound, eyes and ears went on full combat alert and then I saw the head of the brush. There was no time to get back into the box, nor could I have done it without being heard. The problem was the box was behind the cupboard and I was behind the box, not exactly the perfect fucking cover! When the head of the brush once again appeared around the side of the cupboard and stopped, I knew I'd been seen and was absolutely livid. The brush suddenly retreated and the whistling became faster and faster, as did my thinking. He quickly disappeared up the stairs and shut the door behind him. I stood for a moment, feeling a mixture of anger and desperation. There was only one thing for it, I would have to make a run for it and if the workmen tried to grab me, I would have to try and wriggle free. In any event, the police were on their way, and I was like a wounded animal wanting to strike first.

There could be no surrender.

I ran to the top of the stairs, taking them two at a time, then after taking a sharp intake of breath, I grabbed hold of the latch. It was the kind that pressed down and was commonly found on large wooden gates, but it wouldn't budge.

'Stay in there, kidda.'

The old bastard was holding on to the latch and I was trapped. I ran to the foot of the steps and frantically looked around for any avenue of escape, no matter how risky and all the time, the seconds were ticking away. At the foot of the steps was a box containing some rusty old tools. I picked up a monkey-wrench that was so heavy I could hardly lift it, let alone swing it. Nevertheless, a decision was made, the first cop to come through that door gets it, and if the second one follows him, then he can have it too.

I hopped from foot to foot as fear and indecision engulfed me, gnarling at my mind and showing me something I no longer recognised, something I didn't want to belong to. I dropped the weapon back into the box and had almost given up hope when I suddenly remembered their tea break. I entered the room and my prayers had been fucking answered: an open window.

I peered out to the left but the guy on sentry duty was out of sight. There was no one else around, so I jumped out of the window and tried breaking the speed barrier as I made my way up the street and through the back of the bus station. Suddenly, I was overcome with a fit of the giggles and it bent me double, the thought of the old guy saying 'in you go, lads, he's all yours!' Only to once again emerge empty-handed. That, coupled with the sheer relief, almost made me manic with excitement.

By early evening I was back in the village, largely because I had nowhere else to go and no one else to go to. The earlier excitement had worn off and been replaced with the hum-drum reality of a chilly autumn evening and the even chillier feeling that my presence there increased my chances of being caught. I was trying to avoid being captured by trawling the back streets in the dark, it wasn't a long-term solution to an immediate problem, but I was living minute to minute now, it's all I had, all that was safe.

My sister and her friends had befriended this guy who lived alone and was considered a little odd. Despite repeated warnings, they continued to visit him and would occasionally run errands, in return for which he would provide lemonade and chocolate cake. Having started to freeze my nuts off for longer than was reasonably tolerant, I felt a cup of coffee and a little warmth and conversation would be hugely welcome, and a piece of cake would be the final brick in the palace. I smoked my way across the village towards his house, which backed on to the spiritualist church and, unlike most of the houses, was privately owned. I knocked on the door and held my breath, hoping desperately for a reply. Eventually one came, and he stood there, looking perfectly normal to me.

I introduced myself and explained who I was and how I came to know of him, and he quickly invited me in. As soon as I entered his lounge the warmth hit me like a lover's breath and I resolved to stay as long as possible. He offered fruit juice and I think I surprised him by requesting coffee, black, strong and no sugar. Nevertheless, he made it and we sat chatting awhile, until we were interrupted by his phone ringing. He disappeared into the hallway to answer it, and sat invitingly on the top of his television set was his wallet. I took no time in procrastinating, afforded myself no opportunity to even consider the wickedness of my intent, I struck like a predator, swift, efficient and unseen, removing a five and three one's and stuffing them in my pockets before heading out the back, without morality or justice.

I had no defence. I couldn't persuade myself that it was a necessary evil, even though I was hungry and marked. I had behaved like a desperado, spitting back his kindness with poison. I had betrayed everything that I was and damaged myself beyond recognition by blurring the vision and confusing the argument. It was me I was fighting now.

I returned to South Moor and stood awhile in Aunt Jenny's yard, but it made no significant difference, except a feeling that stealing her money some years earlier had made her eat shit, although I doubt she had tasted it the way I had, so I left. I bought fish and chips, a penknife and yet more cigarettes before taking a bus back to the village.

Once there, I again tried my luck by trying the door to the house. This time, rather bizarrely, the door was secure but only on the chain. My parents had forgotten to lock and bolt it, or had they? I stood there, afraid they were laying an ambush for me. I opened the door the inch or two the chain allowed, and listened intently, but all I could hear was Kim's tail, banging excitedly against the door.

'Kim, it's me, don't get so excited, man.'

It was no use, he was bound to give me away, the amount of noise he was making. Captured by the love of a dog, it wouldn't have been the first time the family pet had gotten in on the act and betrayed me, the difference being it was done out of pure, unconditional love. I took out the penknife and quickly dislodged the chain and stepped inside.

I fussed Kim in order to calm him down a bit, then headed straight for the alcove, where I buried myself under a pile of coats. Having effectively broken into my own house, at the time it just felt like shelter. Within seconds, Kim had joined me and we lay there, comrades-in-arms, wanting only what we had. The peace was broken by a creaking sound that I recognised, my old man was making his way down the stairs. I lay motionless, one arm around the dog as I listened to my father make his way past our crypt and into the lounge, where he sat on the sofa and lit a cigarette.

I listened for any sign of footsteps drawing nearer but there were none, only the exhalation of cigarette smoke.

'Kim, come here, son.'

The dog wasn't remotely interested and that spelled danger for me. I lifted up one of his ears and whispered imploringly into it.

'Go on, Kim, go and see your dad.'

His response was to lick the side of my face, which on this occasion was neither welcome nor helpful.

'Come on, boy.'

My heart sank as I became convinced that an ambush had indeed been laid with the dog helping to confirm his suspicions. In a last-ditch attempt to throw him off the scent, I grabbed hold of Kim's arse and gave him a shove.

'Please, Kim, go to your dad!'

He wouldn't fucking budge and I was almost in tears as I lay there, my father's prey! I closed my eyes and waited to be seized. Miraculously, it never came and the surprise left me pondering my father's rationale. Having finished his cigarette, he simply rose from the sofa and disappeared up the stairs and back to bed. Having earlier commanded the dog to appear by his side, he now didn't even bother to investigate his whereabouts, and why wasn't he on nights?

I wriggled free of the coats, then I too sat on the sofa and lit a cigarette. It felt strange, sitting there with the mindset of an intruder and the fear to match. Eventually, I went back to the alcove and slept with the dog.

I woke early, a combination of anxiety and a basic survival instinct, but I still wasn't finished. I crept upstairs to take one last look around, already feeling I may never see this house again. I gently and quietly opened the door to my parents' room a few inches and peered through the gap. Although the light wasn't good, I was still able to see that the bed hadn't been slept in, nor had the single that was used as a spare. I entered the room and opened the curtains to provide more light, then I sat down on the single bed, confused and highly suspicious. My heart was racing as I once again began to feel I had become the victim of an elaborate trap, their room being the allurement as they slept or waited elsewhere. I felt nauseous and shaky and unusually, I began to feel defeat was only a moment away, but only if I hung around waiting for the inevitable, only if I gave up in abject dejection. I rose to my feet, preparing for a quick exit when I heard something and froze, unable to move, my mind remaining static with me. Footsteps coming closer, and still my mind had withdrawn and abandoned me.

I sat back down and in a moment of panic I took out the tiny penknife, unfolded the blade and placed it next to me on the bed. The door opened and I instinctively made a grab for the knife; it was my eldest sister, and I put my finger to my lip but still expected her to raise the alarm. I don't know if she saw the knife, I hope she didn't, but she simply whispered that she needed a book for school. After she left, I paced around the room, expecting my father to burst in and exact his own brand of retribution. I decided to go down fighting, having quickly regained my sense of purpose and will to be free. I just wished it didn't have to be so tough, I was battle weary and couldn't see an end to it anytime soon. I left the room without a backwards glance and quickly made my way down the stairs and through the house unchallenged.

I headed straight for the woods, the security providing time to regain my composure and try to work out my next move. The stakes had been raised beyond anything I had previously experienced, every cop in the district must be looking for me, it was essential that I lose myself and for that I would need money. I sat for a moment, in a state of utter confusion. Whilst not exactly enemies, my sister and I weren't particularly close, either, at that time in our lives. It was astonishing, an unexpected act of loyalty I've never forgotten, nor the countless other times she's been supportive.

On the move again, I made my way to St Mary's School and entered, intent on stealing some money. The office was busy, so I crept up to the staff room. I was busy looking around, when I heard someone coming up the stairs, so just like in the movies, I hid behind the door. The deputy headmistress came straight up to me and grabbed me forcefully by the arm and then began marching me down the stairs. Apparently, I had been spotted as I entered the building.

'You wicked, wicked boy! This evil has to stop!'

'I haven't done anything.'

'You were going to steal if I hadn't caught you! Well, I hope the police lock you away for a very long time.'

The word police was like a toothache that wouldn't go away and as she marched me into the office, I felt like I was sinking under a huge pile of shit as I saw my life drifting away.

'I caught him in the staff room trying to steal. Call the police.'

The headmistress sat behind her desk like a camp commandant. As she picked up the phone and prepared to dial, I once again pulled out the knife. It had now become a standard response to any perceived threat, betraying truth and arming my enemies, whilst disarming me.

'Get back! I'm warning you, I'll use it, just get back so I can get out of here and put that phone down!'

Pandemonium, as they both panicked and started screaming. I too panicked, not knowing what the fuck to do but still determined to flee! In the end, I pushed past the deputy headmistress and took off through a local housing estate, pursued by the caretaker. My legs suddenly felt leaden, a combination of the enormity of what I had done and the fear of being locked away for more years than I dared to imagine, so I turned on him.

'Get back!'

'Michael, don't do anything stupid!'

It was too late for that, I had passed the point of knowing what was real and what was imagined, what I wanted or what I needed.

'I'm telling you, get back now or you'll get it!'

He hesitated and so did I. I wasn't used to being in control but I didn't want to use the knife, it was a threat, not an end. I picked up a brick, believing it to be the lesser of the alternatives. Nevertheless, I hurled it in his direction. Escape was the only thing on my mind and he backed off.

'Now, fuck off, and leave me alone or you'll get more!'

He backed off completely and I went on my way unchallenged, still panting heavily, but I was alone, so I headed for the woods. When I reached them, I headed up the hill towards the allotments, believing myself to be safe, but already there was a policeman, talking to an allotment holder. I was shocked at the speed with which they had arrived and wondered where the rest of them were, but I wasn't willing to stand around and find out. I crept back down and hid behind a bush. Pretty soon, I heard voices and my position already began to feel exposed. I hoped beyond hope that I could become invisible, but they were all over the place and I knew I would be spotted, so I broke cover and fled.

'Stop, or we'll let the dog loose!'

Oh, fuck off! How many times have I heard that redundant threat, and there's never been a dog! Except this time, there was. I ran towards the allotments, but the dog grabbed my arm and dragged me to the ground, gnawing away.

'Fuck off! Get off him! Why didn't you fucking stop when I asked you to?'

I couldn't speak, I was traumatised as the policeman kicked the dog in an attempt to separate its teeth from my arm. I was arrested and immediately taken to hospital, where I was given a tetanus injection and the wound was treated. My mother complained to the police regarding their use of a dog, and the irony was not lost on me, given the criminal assaults she had previously ignored. I was charged with aggravated burglary and awaited my return to the Red Bank Special Unit, having made a full confession. What else could I do?

When I arrived back at the unit, they were awaiting me.

'Take that sling off.'

'The nurse said I have to keep it on for three days.'

'You're going into seclusion, now take it off because if I have to, I guarantee I'll be a lot rougher than you.'

No doubt he would have been, the man so corrupt that several years later he found himself in Strangeways prison, having been convicted of insurance fraud.

Over the course of the following few days, I would often be removed from class by a member of staff who would then re-enact a scene involving a knife attack. I wasn't sure what their purpose was, only that it wasn't good.

Then came the doctor.

CHAPTER TWENTY-ONE

'I've been asked to come and see you, Michael. I thought we could have a little chat about things, are you happy to talk to me?'

'Not bothered.'

He was Scottish and he blinked a lot and I really wasn't bothered. I had spent the best part of my life in similar situations; whatever I said, I would still be screwed.

'I see you've absconded on quite a number of occasions. What do you think about when you abscond?'

'Not getting caught, mostly.'

He scribbled furiously on his notepad as his eyelids went into overdrive and I was already bored. That was the pattern for the following three months, we covered everything from birth through to the Catholic church, the fires, and of course, my brief stint in front of the television cameras. It was the only time he smiled.

One evening, I was making my way to bed when another smiling assassin pulled me to one side. He was fairly new to the unit and I'd had very little engagement with him.

'Sort your things out, you're being transferred in the morning.'

'Where to?'

'You'll find out, but one thing's for sure, you won't be coming back here. We're through with you, someone else can have you.'

'Suits me.'

'Yes, and I should think it probably suits a lot of other people too, me for one.'

By lunchtime the following day my escort had arrived and the staff were so relieved to be rid of me, their kindness betrayed them. Once in the car, sat behind two social workers from the North East who saw me as nothing more than an inconvenience. I asked the question that nobody had yet answered.

'Where am I going?'

'Well, Michael, you know you've been charged with burglary? Well, your case has been listed at Newcastle Crown Court, so we're taking you back to the North East.'

'Am I going to a borstal?'

'No, you're going back to Aycliffe until the court has decided what to do with you and then you'll probably go somewhere else.'

I relaxed into the journey as my worst fears had been laid to rest. Not coming back was the one thing I needed to know, that and the fear of borstal. When we arrived, a new set of challenges presented themselves as the entire structure had changed and I didn't like it.

'I thought I'd seen the last of you!'

Roger Gibson was the new head of Royston House, and fresh from his wife's demise, had a new girlfriend, a glamorous woman who seemed to think it was her role to hang around the house being what she wanted, and not what she was.

'I've come back.'

'I can see that, but we don't want you anymore than anyone else does. Nobody wants you.'

'I'm not a little kid anymore, so don't think I am.'

'Would you mind explaining that statement?'

'You know what I mean.'

'Well, let me tell you something. Don't for a minute expect your new status to win any favours from me because it won't. Now get out of my office, I can't even bear to look at you.'

He wasn't around much and when he was, we hardly spoke. More significantly, there were no more beatings, he just didn't seem bothered.

Because I was due in Newcastle Crown Court in a couple of weeks, I was not allowed to leave the house under any circumstances, which meant having my meals brought from the dining hall and eating them under the glare of the entire house. Obviously, my parents were allowed to visit and they duly did, but the way they spoke suggested to me that what was going to happen had already been prescribed, it seemed everybody knew except me.

When I arrived at the Courtroom I was met in the foyer by my parents, who immediately began coaching me in the art of kissing the Crown's arse. Within minutes my barrister arrived.

'Right, Michael, this should be pretty straightforward. When you go in there, just plead guilty and we'll see if we can get you into hospital.'

'I don't need to be in a hospital, there's nothing wrong with me, I'm not ill.'

'Listen to him, Michael, he knows what he's talking about.'

He was asking me to take seriously a man in a robe and a funny wig.

'If thee doesn't do what he tells yer, yer'll be gannin ter borstal, now thee doesn't want that, does thee?'

My dad's feet pointed whichever way the fucking wind was blowing! Nevertheless, I followed the advice.

When I entered the courtroom I immediately noticed that there was no jury, further evidence that my fate was already decided. I entered my plea and sat down. I stared out of the window at the Tyne Bridge as the prosecutor briefly outlined the case, then it was my barrister's turn and he immediately summoned the doctor, who blinked faster than ever.

'Doctor, am I to understand that you've examined my client?'

'Yes, I met with him once a week for approximately twelve weeks, the sessions ranging between an hour and an hour and a half in length.'

'And were you able to reach a diagnosis?'

'Yes, I believe Michael Cooper is suffering from a psychopathic disorder.'

I wanted to laugh but if I had, it would only have helped them to confirm the diagnosis. I did, however, trawl the internet recently and discovered that the current research shows that a reliable diagnosis for this disorder cannot be achieved before the subject is eighteen, and preferably, twenty-one. I was fifteen years and four months old, and was sectioned under section 60/65 of the Mental Health Act 1959, without limit of time.

I was allowed a few minutes with my parents and my father asserted that just because I was going to the 'funny farm', it didn't mean I was nuts, in which case I wanted to know, what it did mean? But no one was willing to say. All I was told was that I would remain incarcerated until the doctors or a Mental Health Review Tribunal considered it safe to release me. I also learnt that the latter part of the section was a restriction order allowing the Home Office to exert almost total control.

I was immediately taken to Stanley Police station and fed cold fish and chips whilst awaiting my transfer to Moss Side hospital on Merseyside. I was about to be housed alongside some of the country's most dangerous killers and paedophiles, whose predatory instincts could only be satisfied through grooming and then assaulting young boys. I was four feet eleven and a half inches, blued-eyed and blond-haired, and I probably looked about twelve, but I was nobody's fucking picnic! Two plain-clothed cops were to be my escort and they were carrying handcuffs. I'd never been cuffed before but now I'd been condemned and they clearly weren't willing to take any risks with a psycho.

It was once again December, with Christmas only twenty days away and the weather was grim. Travelling over the Pennines we ran into thick fog and I desperately hoped we'd get lost, but you can't be lost forever, at least not this way.

Through a combination of the heat in the car and nerves, my left wrist began to itch and I used the teeth on the handcuffs to scratch it. Without any intent on my part the cuff slipped over my left wrist and I was free of it. I hesitated for a while, not quite knowing what to do. Eventually I thought it better to replace it for there was nothing in it that could better my position, except on arrival holding up my hand and saying, 'this is what I can do,' then quickly learning what they could.

We arrived by early evening and it didn't seem that secure to me, apart from a security barrier. There was nothing to fear and my hopes instantly rose, believing I would be out of here a lot faster than they had invited me in. We were escorted to an old building where I sat with the two cops standing over me like they were guarding a death that might suddenly wake up. Then came the doctor, a middle-aged woman, who smiled her way through the initial, if thoughtless, interrogation.

'You're very small, aren't you?'

I couldn't change my size, nor would I want to, it gave me everything I had without any form of impediment.

'Is it true you like being called Mini?'

I was disorientated by her lack of probing, her questions being those that a stranger might ask.

'Yes.'

I didn't understand why this caused so much amusement, but even the cops were animated and smiling, and I just sat there with nowhere to go and listening to questions that had no real answers. They just ticked the boxes that had already been ticked. We were eventually directed to where we needed to go and it was a huge shock, beyond anything that I had previously known: a wall circled the perimeter with a moat in between that and a wire fence. It was impossible to scale the fence and leap onto the wall, the distance being too great, and should you successfully climb the fence, you would stare up at a wall that had suddenly doubled in size due to that fucking moat. To gain entrance to the block, you had to negotiate a huge set of gates that seemed to resent my arrival, if they could have growled they probably would have done.

Once inside, the gates were locked, the cuffs were removed and I found myself standing outside a one-storey building. This was Firs ward, my new home, perhaps until I was old. The guy who had opened the gates now opened the door to the ward, using a key that was attached to a long chain. He wore a white coat over what looked like a prison officer's uniform, indeed I was soon to learn that most of the 'nurses' were members of that particular union and the few that weren't, were witch-hunted.

'Stand there and don't move.'

It wasn't a request but I was in no mood to mark my arrival with a grand gesture of defiance. This was fucking real and would require patience. The cops handed over the documents and wasted no time in getting out of there, they seemed more nervous than I was.

'Follow me.'

Perhaps he was beginning to melt a little for he almost looked at me as he spoke then marched off down a long corridor with me trying to keep up. Eventually we arrived at the washroom. He threw down a plastic mat right in front of my feet.

'Right, stand on that and don't fucking move until I tell you to!'

He was beginning to seriously piss me off with his barked instructions and obsession with movement. He disappeared then returned several minutes later, carrying a large paper sack.

'Right, get your clothes off and put them in there, and I want the lot, pants, socks, everything.'

I was accustomed to being robbed of my clothes but they were only garments, mere pawns in a game that attempts to strip away a layer at a time. Whilst I was once again following his instructions he ran a bath and I stood on the mat, naked and cold and obviously mute.

'Right, in you get and don't take all fucking day about it.'

There was about six inches of water and I didn't know whether to bathe in it or drink it. It was also tepid.

'Can I have some more hot water?'

'No, you fucking well can't! Now, get washed then get out.'

As I quickly set about myself with the soap he once again disappeared for good, I hoped, but his footsteps betrayed those hopes.

'Right, dry yourself off then put those on.'

He threw me a towel that almost landed in the bathwater, and dropped a pair of pyjamas into a crumpled heap on the wooden bench. As I was drying myself I took a gamble.

'Why do I have to wear pyjamas?'

'Why do you think? You're going to bed?'

'But it's early.'

'I couldn't give a fuck if it was first thing in the morning, if I say bed then bed it is. I don't like little fuckers who go around pulling knives on people, understand?'

It was rumoured that he had once been a member of the SAS but such stories always abound when minds lie predominantly idle. My exchange had exposed his intent, but reversing it was the problem.

'I said, understand?'

'Yeah.'

'Make sure you do, now follow me.'

We left the washroom and again set off down the corridor until we came to a door, which he unlocked.

'In you go. A few days in there will give you plenty of time to reflect on your crimes.'

A few fucking days! In a room with a toilet, a sink, a bed and nothing else, perhaps they had to drive you insane in order to have something to work with. Then came the screams, followed by a torrent of verbal abuse of a nature I had never heard before. This was insanity as a living experience and I buried my head underneath the covers, but I already wore the stain. They didn't scare me in the usual way, my concern was deeper, how to communicate with those whose minds were out of sync and were at the mercy of their psychopathic guardians.

I barely heard the door open and a plate of food arrived, at least that's what they said it was, but it defied rational description so I placed it on the floor and left it. An hour or so later a member of staff came to collect what he obviously hoped was an empty plate.

'What's this, then, a fucking hunger strike?'

He held up the plate and examined it minutely for any evidence that I might have been at least tempted.

'I don't know what it is.'

'It's not the fucking Ritz, you know, you can't afford to be too fussy!Oh, well, you'll eat when you're hungry, no matter what's put in front of you.'

'I wouldn't eat shit.'

'Oh, I don't know, there's a lad here who likes nothing more than a mouthful or two of his own shit, he'll eat yours too, if you let him.'

I spent three days in that room and I never ate any of mine, nor too much of theirs in whatever form it came. There was plenty of time for that, for now I paced nervously as my entrance into the bear pit drew ever closer. On the evening of the fourth day, I was thrown a dressing gown that could have fitted me and another, and invited as a 'favour' to spend a couple of hours with the rest of the ward. I was by far the smallest and also the youngest and all eyes were on me, but I wondered what it was they saw and what the voices were telling them? The ward comprised two large rooms, one of which was a lounge area with a snooker table and television. The toilets were at the far end of this room and would be opened every morning for washing and shaving, after which they were opened on the hour, every hour, with no exceptions. The other room was the dining area, and outside of mealtimes would form part of the lounge where people would go to listen to music or just get away from the television and snooker.

I found a table in the far corner that had been vacated and stood invitingly for me. However, no sooner had I sat down to try and clear my head and stop myself from sounding like a panting dog, I immediately had company.

'Do you like chocolate? You can have this Mars bar if you like.'

He was four, maybe five years older than me, but more childlike than adult, more childlike than me.

'No, you're okay.'

'I don't mind, I've got loads in my locker, I always give them to my friends.'

'Get away from him, Barker, give him a chance, for fuck's sake! He's only just arrived.'

'I only asked him if he wanted some chocolate.'

'Yeah, but it's not the only thing you want, now, is it, you queer cunt? Now, fuck off or you'll be going on the deck.'

The 'deck' was an identical set-up to the seclusion room at the Red Bank Unit. So far it was the only thing that was familiar, except that in more serious cases a large dose of legalised 'stun' juice would be injected into the backside, often using a glass syringe because the medication melted the plastic. It once burnt a hole in some poor fucker's buttock.

'Listen, lad, watch out for people offering you chocolate or cigarettes, it means they want to shag your arse. You look like a boy so you're going to attract a lot of attention, you'll need to be on your guard.'

'Thanks.'

Now I was truly frightened. I'd spent most of my life in environments where people wanted what I often wasn't willing to give but this was different, this was my fucking soul and it couldn't be bought, swapped, or taken. I returned to my room, grateful for the respite and an opportunity to galvanise myself, but I had little to feed off to relieve my anxieties. I was concerned at having to compromise my own ideals just to survive, concerned at becoming someone else. Earlier that evening, the member of staff who gave me the pep talk told me that the hospital had once been used to house victims of 'shell shock' during the war. I guess not a lot ever really changes.

CHAPTER TWENTY-TWO

During week-days most of the patients would be kept busy in a variety of ways, from work in the various workshops to a number of different educational classes that offered academic, arts and crafts, as well as sporting opportunities. New arrivals weren't allowed to access any of these facilities for the first three months and would remain stuck under house arrest, along with the small handful of patients who were simply too ill, or too dangerous, to be allowed any level of unsupervised activity. This is where my education started, where I began to realise how invisible I had ultimately become.

'Cooper, come with me, lad, I've got a job for you, you seem to have plenty of energy.'

The energy he spoke of was a non-stop stream of questions from morning until bedtime. I was thirsting and driven by uncertainty, wanting to know everything from the practical requirements of each day, to the hidden rules that re-invented themselves whenever the staff were bored. It also taught me the value of discernment, for the replies were a mixture of weapon and weakness, it helped sort the bullies from those in waiting.

'Right, put this on, you're going to need it.'

He handed me an all-in-one paper suit, identical to those given to murder suspects whilst their own clothes come under forensic examination. I put it on over the top of what I was wearing, still unsure of why I needed it but in no rush to find out. Then came the rubber gloves and a huge plastic bag. It was all a bit much for a simple cleaning operation.

'Now then, the bedding goes in that bag, the rest needs scrubbing.'

He pushed me into a room where the stench of shit immediately overcame me, threatening to have me spinning and vomiting. I ran into the corridor gasping for breath.

'I can't go in there, it's horrible! It'll make me sick.'

'Well, make sure you do it in the bucket or you'll have to clean that up as well. I'll be back in half an hour. If you're still alive, I might let you watch the telly.'

The door slammed shut and I heard him laugh his way up the corridor until all I could hear were my fears screaming at me, but no one else heard, there was no witness.

The shit was everywhere, in the blankets, on the mattress, on the floor and up the walls. It was in the sink and on the toilet, but not in the fucking toilet. I cleaned the lot because it was the only way out of there but all the while I fought back tears of utter hopelessness, knowing they were using my position to vindicate theirs. The room belonged to a guy who couldn't speak, had no social skills, only understood basic commands and was highly aggressive. Once, the hospital authorities sanctioned him being given a huge dose of medication in order to knock him out so that the dentist could remove all his teeth, the rationale being that his favourite mode of attack was to sink his teeth into people's necks and they were worried it might be theirs. Another time, he chased me around and around the snooker table and despite my terrified cries for help, none was forthcoming, the staff having locked themselves in the office in hysterics. Eventually one popped his head through a gap in the door.

'Get on the carpet, he'll not touch you on there.'

Around the television area there was a large square of carpet, housing several rows of chairs. This guy had an abject fear of carpet and as he was constantly barefooted, wouldn't go near it. He returned to the rocking chair he rode for hours at a time. It wasn't uncommon for the entire ward to be crammed together on that invisible barrier, however he developed a cunning method whereby he would place chairs together to form a makeshift bridge. Once or twice I, along with several others, would dash from the carpet, grab a vacant chair then dash back and pile the chairs in the middle. It certainly got the adrenalin rushing and the fitness levels rising, there are just better ways.

* * * *

Christmas came and went, hardly noticeable really, even the decorations hung there, already in a hurry to go back in their box until the following year. What must they have born silent witness to?

As the New Year slipped by without fanfare or applause, another shocking event was about to unfold. It was time to wake up to the reality of my daily existence and it struck at the core. I had always understood the predictability of institutional life and had always managed to manoeuvre myself into a position where I could count out the moves, by identifying the main source of danger.

During meal times I sat next to a young lad from Cardiff, a quiet lad with a heavy accent, so when he did occasionally speak, I could barely understand him. Completing a meal had already had its challenging moments: the guy who couldn't speak had to be fed in his room due to his penchant for running around the dining room, grabbing handfuls of food from every plate he could. Surprisingly, a number of people would continue to finish their meals seemingly oblivious or, quite frankly, not bothered that a shitty hand had just scraped across their plate. Another guy would sit alone because whenever he'd been placed on another table, he would attack the nearest person to him. These were threats I had quickly and obviously identified.

On this particular day I was hungry and wanted to eat. I collected my meal and returned to my table. Within minutes, I felt cold air on the side of my face. I turned to face the young man from Cardiff.

'Stop blowing on my face, I'm trying to eat.'

I returned to my meal, not particularly perturbed, but within seconds the blowing had been replaced with the kind of sound I'd never heard coming from a human being, high pitched and almost demonic, like he was possessed. I turned around in complete shock, it was like being a character in someone else's nightmare, or perhaps it was my own. He had gotten to his feet and had grabbed hold of the table housing our only sustenance.

'No, no, no, not the fucking table!'

It was in vain, for his instructions were coming from a source I couldn't bargain with, and sadly neither could he. The table went over, along with the food. The two other guys had remained seated and ended up covered. Their saving grace was that the food was never hot, often barely even warm. Several members of staff dived over the serving area and grabbed him before he could damage anyone, including himself, as during a previous episode he tore off one of his eyelids.

Remarkably, the staff showed a great deal of compassion towards him, although he was taken to seclusion and given the inevitable cocktail of drugs. They didn't man-handle him, instead they walked him, using just enough restraint for the purpose; not everyone was as fortunate. It seemed pretty clear to me that there was some kind of two-tier system unofficially operating on the ward. Those considered severely mentally ill, or 'low grades' as they were rather distastefully known, were given a level of care and shown the kind of humanity that everyone was entitled to receive, but didn't.

To resist was futile and often painful, defiance kept them smiling and that's what I intended to do, keep them fucking smiling, by disarming them through a combination of boyish charm, and affected eccentricity. All I needed was for them to start to like me, then it would be my turn to smile as, one by one, they took the nuts. It was highly manipulative, nevertheless, should I pull it off in such a cynical and massively suspicious environment, it may turn out to be the most important thing I ever did and without doubt, the most enjoyable.

CHAPTER TWENTY-THREE

'Min, the charge nurse wants you in his office, mate.'

I had been reading, something I had begun to do much of, as it would often keep the noises of the ward away from me. Things appeared to have taken an upturn insofar as I was still being given mundane tasks, but I now performed them with a little humour and clownish clumsiness, which resulted in my spending less time on the task than previously, with the staff laughing and shaking their heads. So when the call came to report to the charge nurse's office, it was a little worrying. Normally such an invitation would mean bad news from home, or a serious dressing down. I knocked on the door and stood nervously waiting to be invited in to discover my fate.

'Sit down, Michael. Is it right you like being called Mini?'

'Yeah, it is.'

'Well, that's going to take a bit of getting used to. Anyway, you won't know me because I've been off sick for a few weeks. I'm Frank Sugden, one of the charge nurses for this ward.'

He was disarming in that he was immediately pleasant and kind, albeit a heavy smoker in a small office.

'I noticed you got some magic tricks for Christmas, do you have an interest in magic?'

'Yeah, I suppose. I learnt a couple of card tricks, just simple stuff, when I was younger. My mum sent that lot in because she didn't know what to get me. She did ask but I wasn't really bothered about Christmas.'

'Let me show you my favourite card trick, I think you might like it.'

He held a deck of cards between his hands and turned over one red one and one black.

'It's easy, all you have to do is guess the colour of each card. If you say red, it goes in the red pile and if you say black, then it goes next to the black one. Now, there are fifty cards left in the deck, let's see how many you can guess right.'

I took it very seriously, almost convincing myself that I knew the identity of each card without actually being able to see it. About halfway through and with two lines of cards, he suddenly changed things around.

'Okay, let's move the red down to this pile and the black one up to this pile, then we carry on, same as before. Confident?'

'Yeah, suppose.'

Without any rationale to support it, he was making me feel as though the entire success of this trick rested on my shoulders and I was determined to rise to the challenge. By the time we had exhausted the entire deck we had two rows of cards, the top being separated by a red card in the middle, the second one being separated by a black card. The rest was anyone's guess.

'Okay, how do you think you've done?'

'Dunno.'

'Well, let's have a look.'

He gathered together the top row of cards, squaring them into a neat pile. Then turning them face up, he spread them across his desk.

'Well, this is where we started off, black, and as you can see there are only black cards, and when we changed over to red, there are only red cards. How did you do that?'

I was speechless, not to mention wholly impressed. When he spread out the second row it was the same, reds next to the red card and blacks next to the black card. In that moment I could have been in Vegas, I certainly wasn't in hospital.

'That's unbelievable! The most amazing thing I've ever seen with my own eyes! The tricks I knew were rubbish compared to that.'

'Well, you could do tricks like that, even better ones if you're willing to practice and work hard at the craft.'

'I am, yeah.'

'Then I'll make you a deal. Figure out how I did that trick then come back and show me and I'll get you some professional tuition.'

'What?'

'There's a guy works at the nursing school, in fact he's taught most of the staff on this ward. He's also a member of the magic circle and has performed magic all over the world. Conquer that trick and you may end up learning more than you can remember.'

He boxed up the cards and slid them across the desk towards me then with a smile and a wink he nodded towards the door. I stood up and prepared to leave.

'Be grateful, they are one of the few things you are allowed to keep and they're inexpensive. Always keep them in your pocket then you'll never be stuck for something to say.'

I already was, having swapped a mop for a deck of cards that no one seemed to want to take away, or hold to ransom. They had my name on them now and I would love them, for soon they would love me. I wasted no time in trying to bond with my army of Kings, Queens and Knaves, ably supported by a platoon of foot soldiers, with a couple of jokers thrown in to mask against complacency. I felt extremely self-conscious, sitting alone at a dining room table with the entire deck spread out in front of me. Hours turned into days, which frustratingly turned into weeks, and I began to wonder if I'd been set up. I wondered if the secret was so unbelievably complicated it had to be revealed.

One evening, I was sat alone despondently turning over card after card, I was getting so close I wanted to scream. Something was missing, some tiny detail that I kept overlooking.

'Min, there's a magic show on the telly.'

A member of staff casually popped his head around the door, oblivious to the rescue mission he had just performed. I managed to secure a seat fairly close to the television set which was situated high up on a wooden shelf. Some of the guys were playing snooker, others were at night classes. With great concentration, I prepared for my own.

It was a fantastic display of technique and showmanship that transported me to a place I could only dream of inhabiting, but it was worth the dream just to own the idea of its existence. It transfixed me and I wanted it to remain that way but if I had, I would have missed my deliverance, for there, right before me, was a deck of cards sat in the middle of a traditional card table. The magician, all smiles and with wonderfully manicured hands, sat behind them and to his right a member of his studio audience. As he began to perform the very trick that had kept me awake and unable to think, I kept my eyes firmly fixed on his hands. I didn't listen to him or laugh at his jokes, I just wanted to know how it was done. When it came, I couldn't believe that I'd missed it all this time, but it made the knowing all the more important to know because it came at a time when everything else I knew was a burden.

I went to my room that evening and practised and practised, and all I could hear was the urging of my heart. Every time I held those cards they felt like a perfect fit and it was hard to let go of them. It became mechanical, as I performed time and time again the very move that allowed the trick to dazzle, but it was the trick itself that would be talked about, not the method that nobody saw. I was ready to step up to the plate and have it shine and reflect my image. Not the one who stood on a plastic mat afraid to move, the one who now had the moves.

'Mr Sugden, I've cracked it, I know how to do it now! I want to show you, I've really worked it out, I can do it!'

I was so excited, tinged with a little nervousness, I'm surprised I didn't drop the cards all over the floor. He, on the other hand, was surprisingly calm and I felt he doubted me but rather than despair, it increased both my certainty and the thrill that would come from a perfect execution.

'Are you sure that this time you know the secret?'

He was referring to the two previous attempts when I had come marching into his office, only to have the trick fail and my confidence fail with it; but confidence can be restored.

'Yeah, I know how it works and I've been practising like mad, even in the dark.'

'Well, if you're suddenly that good, maybe you need an audience.'

Or maybe I didn't, I just wanted to show him the trick, to show him the work I'd put into it and the skill that came to me with it. I wanted him to know it was more than just cards,

'I just want to show it you, just want to show you I've been practising and working really hard.'

'Wait here a minute.'

I remained in the office as he disappeared. I took the deck out of my pocket and placed them on the table. It felt comforting, knowing that the outcome was guaranteed, it was almost impossible to fail. Unless I failed myself through fear, but the arena was marked and the cards weren't so nobody could hurt them and the trick was entirely down to them, of course, I simply dealt the cards.

Frank Sugden returned with a couple of nurses, one of whom had placed me on that mat, weeks earlier. It was an easy decision, he would perform the trick that would allow me to trick him. He would smile behind his hate and I would pretend he was amazing and thank him for it.

'Mini here has got a trick to show us. He's been working on it for a couple of weeks now and he thinks he's perfected it.'

I wasn't sure if he was setting me up to fail or giving me an opportunity to flourish in a hostile environment. Unquestionably, I was nervous yet in that moment I was more than I'd ever been; I was in charge and nothing happened unless it was directed by me.

'Is it okay if I sit here at your desk?'

'Sure, I'll stand here by the door.'

I removed the cards from the box and I was so nervous I had difficulty in swallowing and my hands were sweaty and shaking a little, but I kept my mind on the task and I knew the cards wouldn't let me down.

'This isn't a trick I can perform alone, it requires the help of another person, someone who can do the trick for me.'

I ushered him into the seat and he gladly took up the invitation. He sat comfortably and confidently and so did I. I removed a red card and a black card from the deck and looked over at Frank, who simply nodded.

'This is very simple, here we have a red card and here we have a black. Without turning over the cards, you simply have to guess which is red and which is black, do you think you can do that?'

'Yeah, I think I can do that.'

'Well, the trick depends on you, I don't do anything except what you tell me to do.'

He was smug, like he was suddenly in the know, and I tried hard not to laugh or to loathe him, but it was difficult. Halfway through the trick, I quite spontaneously introduced an element of my own. Having decided that a particular card should go on the red pile, I duly obliged.

'Are you sure this is red?'

'Yeah, I said it was, didn't I?'

'I would have put it on black, myself.'

'So, what makes you so sure?'

'Because it's black.'

I turned over the card to show it was indeed black as I knew it would be and his face crumpled although he tried not to show it. By the end of the trick he was indeed convinced he was the architect and that was enough of a recipe for me. I sat back and milked the plaudits. It was the first time I'd been applauded rather than bullied and I wasn't entirely sure how to respond, but I didn't want it to go away either, I was already addicted. It was the perfect illusion, for there was very little of myself in it, yet what they saw is what they thought they'd helped to create.

CHAPTER TWENTY-FOUR

The Industrial Therapy Unit was a huge, factory-style workshop with row upon row of long wooden tables where people would sit, descending further and further into madness, trying to confuse the boredom. This is where the chronically ill spent their days along with a small handful of disaffected or simply disinterested renegades. I was by quite a margin the youngest, and it was frightening to be surrounded by people who would constantly babble incoherently and then laugh at themselves. The work was uncomplicated, un-stimulating and lacked any real rehabilitative purpose, it was in any language cheap labour and hugely exploitative, more so because the workforce had no alternative. We would all sit at one of the tables, performing mind-numbing tasks in support of private industry. These could include receiving a large box of black metal trays with a bolt protruding from the bottom, requiring some poor fucker to sit all day, attaching a nut to each bolt.

My job was to sit with a pot of glue and a brush and wait for bundles of washing lines to arrive when I would stick a label on each one. Having been instructed to ensure that none of the glue stuck on the line itself, some invariably did. When I was found out, I simply played dumb, not difficult in that environment. It wasn't uncommon for someone to be sitting there with his hand under the table masturbating, nor was it that uncommon for someone to be masturbating the guy sat next to him whilst nonchalantly continuing with his work. Homosexuality was almost a second industry, absolutely rampant and as such the toilets were only opened periodically and heavily policed. Nevertheless, I never stepped inside and would often sit there in desperate need of a piss but determined to hold on until I got back to the ward.

The attention I had earlier been advised to guard against was now increasingly directed my way. Some of the guys had been there so long and had only known sex with a man, others were convicted paedophiles, chomping at the bit to sample my wares. Once or twice whilst queuing to leave, I felt someone stroke my arse but when I spun around angrily I was unable to detect who it was. Another was even bolder and certainly braver; having sat next to me, he placed his hand on my leg and made his way towards his idea of heaven. Needless to say, he never even reached the clouds.

'Alan Parker wants to know if you'll be his boy.'

I looked up and there, stood next to me, was a guy with a serious personal hygiene problem and wearing glasses stuck together with sticking plaster.

'No, tell him to fuck off!'

He took out an unopened packet of tobacco and slid it across the table, his smile sadly exposing what was left of his teeth.

'Do you want to be mine, then?'

Being someone's 'boy' simply meant you agreed to provide them with exclusive sexual favours in return for cigarettes and chocolate, any promiscuity and the deal was off. Some were just prostitutes and sold themselves again and again to whoever had the means to pay. For a while it was almost a weekly battle, fending of these predators, much to the amusement of the staff who assured me I would give in eventually.

Over the weeks I became more and more despondent, as the meaningful threads of my existence became increasingly frayed. Days were long and nights were longer, with nothing in between. It was once written that if you stare into the abyss long enough, it will stare back into you. Just as it was fixing its gaze on me, along came Gerry.

'I hear you like magic.'

He was a small man but with a captivating presence and he spoke with a soft Lancashire accent. We were situated in a small interview room with just a desk between us.

'So, what kind of magic do you prefer? The big illusions or the more intimate type of magic using things you can carry in your pockets or find lying around?'

'I don't know, really, I only know a few tricks and most of them are not that good. Besides, I'm locked up in here so there's lot's of things I can't have. I don't think they're going to let me saw anyone in half.'

He smiled and then removed something from his pocket, placing it on the desk directly in front of him.

'Do you know what that is?'

'Yeah, it's a thimble.'

Then began the most dazzling display of dexterity I had ever witnessed in person. It was breathtaking, and all for my private viewing. I did indeed feel privileged and already wanted what he had, just to share it with him. That thimble danced from finger to finger and hand to hand, disappearing then reappearing and as hard as I tried, I had no idea how he was making it happen. There followed a series of tricks involving cards and coins, all requiring a level of ability that seemed completely out of my reach. Thankfully he didn't seem to share my lack of confidence.

'Everything I've shown you doesn't involve any complicated equipment that can break down or be lost or even stolen. The best advice I can give you is to develop sleight of hand because once mastered, it's yours to keep.'

Gerry had quite a pronounced stammer but he didn't allow it to inhibit speech, nor did I allow it to distract from what he was trying to pass on.

'By learning just a few techniques, you'll start to develop a repertoire because most techniques can be used to master several different tricks, you don't have to learn a new one each time. It's down to you, if you're willing to practise every day then there's no reason why you can't master it. It's in your hands, and hands are the finest tools a magician has.'

I had never known myself to exhibit so much enthusiasm for something that required so much discipline, commitment and sheer graft, but somehow it didn't really seem like it was any of that, it just seemed like a better place to be. Gerry gave me some literature detailing some of the techniques he had spoken of as well as some magic magazines he said I could keep. In one half hour and in the absence of Franc Roddam, he had become the closest thing I had to someone wanting me to succeed rather than fail.

'Right, go away and practise some of these and I'll come back in a few weeks and see how you're getting along.'

I shook his hand, a good firm handshake, a contract we both understood and agreed.

'I'll practise until I get blisters on my fingers, I won't let you down.'

'Be sure not to let yourself down, Michael. I'll see you in a few weeks.'

He called me that all the time I knew him, the only thing he ever did that pissed me off. I practised daily, in between moving around the hospital, whilst waiting for my supply of washing lines and at all other times. Occasionally, my fingers would cramp but never my will. Days grew shorter and the nights just drifted by, and in between I was what the cards allowed me to be and that, it seems, was all anybody wanted, and it's all they got, in abundance.

Because of the high regard in which Gerry was held, word very quickly spread throughout the entire hospital and I was constantly being asked to perform tricks, which resulted in my having to learn new ones quicker than I could sometimes cope with. I learned from books, magazines and even bought a few from specialist mail order companies, all of which cost a great deal of money. I worked every job on the ward I could to make extra money and eventually was awarded the most sought after one, the kitchen.

This job was extremely demanding, in terms of the time commitment and was often extremely exhausting, therefore come bedtime, I often struggled for motivation, but I knew if I didn't practise, I would struggle in other ways that had long fallen off the radar. The job afforded me the maximum amount of money I was allowed to earn combined with my other work. Apart from basic provisions such as coffee and tobacco, all my money was spent on magical apparatus. I had quite a repertoire of close-up table magic but was also in the process of putting together a stage act. I had already begun to lead a more solitary life, refusing to become embroiled in the dynamics and petty mindedness of the ward and certainly avoiding the sexual politics that once threatened to derail me. Accusations were made against me that I had offered payments to a number of people in return for sex, the gay mafia had systematically set about undermining my position because I wouldn't fuck them, but it all fell flat when one of the fuckers broke down under interrogation. It changed the way I felt and in some ways, who I was. I became insular and although already driven, becoming more and more ambitious and even daring to believe that one day my audience would only want the magic. I began turning a blind eye to the iniquities of my job without a threat ever being issued.

So when staff began plating up food for themselves and secreting it in the hot plate, I never saw it. Even more disturbing was when the weekly stores arrived with items such as coffee, butter and breakfast cereals, I never saw those that were put in bags and taken home, I even lied about the shortfall. I was simply past caring what everyone else was up to, what they did or didn't do, they were all full of shit and I refused to subscribe to their idea of life, because it would never change. I had become flexible in a way that was in danger of making me pliable, not a comfortable position to be in, but necessary if my dreams were ever to be allowed out of their cage and sing.

There were other, more immediate, benefits to my myopia. Shortly after taking up my post in the kitchen, I was transferred out of the industrial therapy unit and moved to a much better workshop where I was taught to bind old and damaged books. I enjoyed this work, felt it had some meaning and clearly it had a genuine purpose other than to fill time or someone else's pockets. It was satisfying, putting back the words that had been treated so recklessly. Within a few weeks, more good news arrived when I was told I was moving to a better ward.

The Hawthorns ward was adjacent to the Firs but in many ways they were distances apart. At Hawthorns there were none of the petty mind games that came via a series of ridiculous tasks, neither was there a constant air of intimidation. The clientele also had more going for them, most were reasonably intelligent and one or two were even funny. In short, it was like being in an entirely different hospital, but of course the main similarity was the locks. I was shown to a room which was comfortable, and then introduced to the charge nurse, who I was led to believe was fair but firm, to both clients and staff.

'You've made progress, young Cooper, and now it's hoped you'll make some more. I know you like the magic and we want you to continue, but it's not life so you need to concentrate on other things as well.'

It was good advice had it been a college or some kind of halfway house, but here, making it work might mean changing all that you ever knew. Well, it wasn't impossible. I felt a little safer, which in itself bred confidence, and within a few days I had begun to come out of my shell and mix more than previously. I even learned to play snooker for the very first time.

Within twelve months my stage act was complete. The very first time I faced an audience, I was so petrified my voice was quivering and both my hands and legs were shaking, it's a small miracle that I was able to complete the trick but my presentation needed some serious work. It wasn't long before my confidence grew and grew, each time I performed I would pull a member of staff out of the audience and for three minutes they only did what I allowed them to, in between the audience's laughter. They weren't confident, sometimes even a little scared or unsure, and all the time I walked that stage like I'd spent my life on it, it was my arena and it's where I made things happen.

A couple of weeks after my last performance, in which a chosen card mysteriously disappeared from the deck and reappeared inside an Easter egg I had earlier placed in the care of a nurse sitting at the back of the hall, I was summoned to the charge nurse's office. The trick had caused quite a stir and some even suggested I was learning skills that would ultimately set me apart and set me free. They were right but not in the primitive way they were thinking. Their need to know and my already knowing was somewhere they couldn't reach. Somewhere they'd never been because their motives were never hidden, whereas mine were never revealed, because they couldn't see what was more than what they wanted, or could calculate.

'That was some trick the other night. Did you set me up by getting me to hold that egg for you?'

'No, really, everyone trusts you and I just wanted a real dramatic impact. I knew if you held it no one would think you were in on it. We pulled it off and you didn't know how I did it, so I knew you couldn't give the secret away.'

'Like secrets, do you?'

'Magic secrets, yeah, keeping them is the most important thing, otherwise you might as well not be a magician, or anything else, for that matter.'

'So, is it only magic you keep the secrets for?'

'I'll keep any secret if it's worth keeping.'

'Well, I've got one for you. You've got a case conference this afternoon and word has it, it could be the big one, you could be leaving us. Of course, you might want to keep that to yourself, but you might also want to keep your cool and not lose your temper.'

He was referring, of course, to a previous case conference some six months earlier, when I completely lost it under interrogation and went on the offensive, attacking all those present and their reasons for being there.

'Are they going to let me go?'

'I can't guarantee it but everyone seems to think you've earned it.'

I didn't know what I had done to earn my passage but I felt tearful all the same. Maybe it was just coming to an end and the knowing was more than the event itself because it asked more questions.

'I'll definitely keep my cool, I can't stand another minute in here.'

The case conference began with me pacing back and forth across the kitchen floor. My mind was racing, with me struggling to keep up, and all thoughts were beyond the walls, but were dreams, unless someone's signature could make it real by tearing them down. Eventually, I was invited in and I was almost distant, both in thought and presence. I didn't want to be there because I couldn't always explain myself to those who only convened on such occasions. My psychiatrist, who had rarely met with me, and whose most notable comment to date was that I should have taken up ventriloquism and not magic due to my hardly moving my lips when I spoke, chaired the meeting. There were others who I had never met and whom I didn't even know, yet they stared at me, just to see if I stared back and when I did, they turned away.

'So, Michael, we've had quite a discussion about you and the progress you've made whilst you've been with us.'

'I've done okay.'

'Obviously, we've talked in depth about the things that brought you here. What are your thoughts on that now?'

'I wish it hadn't happened. In fact, I wish a lot of things hadn't happened but they did and they won't just go away because I want them to. I was very young and in some ways very stupid.'

'And what ways were those?'

'I didn't always think, sometimes I just reacted.'

'How would you have reacted had one of those teachers stepped forward to try and thwart you?'

I was expecting the stinger, had been waiting for it, so I took my time and answered calmly.

'One of them did and I pushed her to one side, using the hand that wasn't holding the knife, then I ran out of the school. Escape was what I wanted, not a stabbing or a killing.'

'That's fine. Does anyone else have any questions?'

The clinical psychologist, who had never interviewed me yet presumed to know me, stepped up to the plate with a stern look and an equally stern gaze.

'Do you have a particular fascination with knives?'

'No.'

'But you agree that you have been involved in more than one incident involving a knife?'

'I've set more than one fire but that hasn't even been discussed, at least not while I've been in the room.'

'Okay, I've no more questions.'

Nor had anyone else and I was sent from the room in order that they could deliberate. I returned to the kitchen, and continued to pace back and forth. It seemed strange that my actions had come under such intense scrutiny when they were, predominantly, a reflex, but that couldn't be gone into or else there'd be no room for any of this. I was once again summoned, to be told that I had learnt so much from my stay that an application was being submitted to the Home Office, requesting a transfer to the Eastdale unit.

I had learnt to deceive, largely for the purposes of entertainment, but also to get out of there on whatever terms were available, so I learnt to say what they wanted to hear. Otherwise, I would have been talking to myself, for longer than I had the will to speak. Now I couldn't, because I could hardly breathe. I paced around with a funny humming sound floating through my mind. For years, I had never even considered or anticipated this, now I could almost touch it but I no longer knew what it was, only what the television and newspapers had shown me.

Within months of my application being submitted and accepted, I had a date for leaving. It was the beginning of the week and I was to be going at the end of the following one. A couple of days later I was summoned once again to the charge nurse's office; whatever he wanted, it no longer mattered.

'Listen, you know you were supposed to be leaving next week?'

'Yeah.'

The words barely left my mouth such was my nervousness, I hadn't often seen him this serious and it was disconcerting.

'Well, I'm afraid you're not, you're going tomorrow.'

I'm not much of a dancer but I gave it my best shot as I danced around that office, pure excitement racing through my veins! I even gave him a huge hug, which I had never done before, and I thought the smile would never leave my face. I never slept that night, afraid of losing that feeling, afraid of wasting a moment that may never be retrieved. I spoke to freedom through the bars as I had done every night for the past four and a half years, but this time it didn't speak back, it didn't need to anymore, for soon my replacement would arrive. I pulled back the curtains and the spotlights illuminated my room, as well as the compound. I wouldn't miss the view, I wouldn't miss anything about this place except maybe Gerry, who no longer stammered. I guess, ultimately, the excitement came from leaving when so many didn't, and from knowing that I didn't bend, I just altered my speech pattern and learnt to smile when I wanted to scream. They took the credit for the change that had occurred in me and I took the credit for them being able to. I glanced over at the Firs ward and remembered the night I stood naked on a plastic mat. I imagined I would suffer that indignity every day, that it would still be going on now but they soon get bored, it's the newness that turns them on.

I wondered, as I gazed out towards that room, as I travel down the motorway, whose turn will it be next?

CHAPTER TWENTY-FIVE

'Mini, isn't it?'

'Yeah.'

'I'm Pete. There's another two in the car, I think they were scared of coming in, in case they kept them.'

I was itching to get away, my stuff was neatly stacked on a dining room table and I'd stood guard over it most of the day whilst pacing around chain-smoking. I therefore wasn't really listening, wasn't even interested, but he was friendly and he didn't wear a uniform and for now that was enough. But I was still here, and that wasn't.

'Is this all your stuff?'

'Yeah.'

'Right, let's get it to the car. I shouldn't think you want to hang around.'

'Too right.'

I'd seen enough of these walls, had shared a secret or two with them but I said my goodbyes last night, they'll never be lonely. I made a grab for the box containing most of my magical apparatus, when several people descended on me all wanting to shake my hand and wish me luck. Even the available nurses put in an appearance but my hands were full.

'Look, I've got to carry this stuff out of here, I've got to go.'

I've never been in such a hurry to leave a place in all of my life and thankfully I did so without having to stain my hand. They'd had four and a half years to shake it and show some human decency, it seemed they were only capable when you no longer had to wait in line. We were escorted down the corridor by a nurse who let us out of the building and followed us to the gates, the final obstacle. I took one final look around, before staring up at the gates.

'Fucking hell, they don't look like they could manage a whimper, let alone a growl!'

'What's that?'

'Oh, nothing just something I once thought a long time ago.'

I had arrived on a cold December evening, handcuffed and frightened; I was leaving on a sunny July afternoon, frightened, having not yet decided if I was still in handcuffs or if they just got a little tighter. Once through the gate, Pete immediately headed towards the car, whereas I turned to face the nurse. There was an awkward silence for a second or two as history caught up with us.

'So, what are your plans?'

'I'm going to try and make it as a professional magician.'

'It won't be easy.'

'Nothing I've done was ever easy.'

'Well, take care of yourself, Min.'

He held out his hand for me to shake but I would have to put the box down on the floor.

'Hands are full, sorry.'

I am many things but not a fraud. He tapped me on the shoulder, which I could live with, and I turned around without looking back. I was halfway between gate and car when I stopped, suddenly realizing I'd been walking on my own. At least I'd gotten that far before it dawned on me, not in an air gulping moment, just relief that the gate was behind me and no longer me behind it, and I stood a moment just to be sure it was true.

'If you've changed your mind we can always see if they'll take you back.'

'Not fucking likely!'

He smiled, almost chuckled as he opened the boot of his car and allowed me to deposit my cargo. I'd never travelled with it before and was afraid it would get damaged.

'Honestly, you've just been released from a top security hospital not ten minutes since and you're worried about a few magic tricks! Most people worry about what they're going to do when there's no one there to tell them.'

They weren't just magic tricks, they were a disguise that had kept me hidden from such concerns, by absorbing all my energies. I hadn't even stopped to think about the journey ahead in terms of a plan, I didn't even know how I would map out a day, I just wanted it to be mine and not prescribed, it's all I knew and I'd already given everything in its pursuit.

Just to be here.

Shortly after pulling out of the car park and onto the main road that signalled we were finally off campus and on our way, the car pulled into a layby and I'm sure my heart stopped beating for a second or two.

'What's up?'

The words barely came out and must have surely betrayed my anxieties. The driver turned and faced me with a smile on his face.

'I thought you might like a minute's silence.'

'No, no, just drive, in case the fuckers change their minds!'

Everyone smiled and there was much chatter but it sounded like everyone was talking at the same time. I wasn't really interested in the conversation, feeling like I was missing out on the moment. It was a feeling that could never be imagined, if never experienced, so before it could pass me by I drenched myself in it, every second counted and I wanted to bank them all because it was all so new. I stared out of the window, remembering all the times I'd done that, wishing that the car would break down or we'd get lost. It was strange not to feel that way, stranger still not to have to. I saw fields that didn't have fences or walls around them and the grass really did seem greener and the sky bluer, and there was traffic and people. I wondered where the vehicles were taking them and if they wanted to go there.

'How come I'm leaving today?'

'We had to return someone to the hospital today, so his misfortune turned into your good fortune.'

It was a vicious cycle and the first words uttered by Jeff, the guy sitting next to me, words that immediately brought home the reality and shunted the initial thrill to the back of my mind. Suddenly I was unable to think beyond the dangers of a situation that watches with cynical eyes. I knew, of course, that the major condition of my release, and of those who had gone before me, was that the Home Office could recall you back to the hospital whenever it saw fit. The criteria was wide in scope and often changed, in accordance with the policy of the day, or the whim of those picking up the phone.

'So I'm taking the place of someone who's been sent back, someone who sat in this car?'

'If it wasn't you, it would be someone else. He knew the rules when he got there, no one forced him to break them.'

I didn't know what he had done, whether it was a minor indiscretion or a serious infraction, either way I was having his bed tonight.

An hour or so into the journey, we pulled off the motorway into a service station. As we got out of the car, Pete took a brown envelope from his jacket pocket and handed it to me.

'This is yours, I meant to give it to you earlier.'

It was the money I had been saving. A requirement of being accepted into the unit was that you had managed to save fifty pounds and I had a little more than that. Despite not having seen or held any money for several years, it neither excited nor scared me, it was just money, it never changes.

'Tea will have been served by the time we get there so you need to get something to eat now.'

Whilst having the money didn't throw me, having the choice did. Twenty-four hours earlier, the only decision I had to make was to hold out my plate and receive whatever was given, but now I got to choose what went on the plate and I couldn't decide, and all the time I was being observed. I eventually chose and was shocked at how expensive it was. Afterwards, I took a piss without worry and then went to the shop and bought a pack of Marlboro. I went outside and waited for the others, staring lovingly at the packet, the first I'd ever bought legally outside of the hospital. I looked out across the car park, looking through adult eyes but with a child's learning. When you leave an institution, you're effectively the same age as when you entered it, because everything you learn is only applicable to that and anything else doesn't belong. When we returned to the car I consoled myself with a cigarette.

'Can I have a light, please?'

'How come you haven't got one?'

'I haven't had one for four and a half years.'

'You're not in Moss Side now, you should have gotten a lighter or matches from the shop.'

'I didn't know I was allowed.'

'Okay, I'll give you a light, but in future you'll need to provide your own.'

Nobody tells you anything, you're just expected to know, yet had I bought matches and it wasn't allowed I would have been going back to Merseyside, as no one forced me to break the rules.

* * * *

The Eastdale unit was near the town of Newark in north Nottinghamshire, housed within the grounds of a local psychiatric hospital that catered predominantly for people with acute mental and physical disabilities, some being so poorly they couldn't tolerate solid food. The unit itself was largely experimental and only received clients from Broadmoor, Rampton, Moss Side and Park Lane Hospitals. These were euphemistically referred to as the 'special hospitals'.

On arrival, I was shown to a dormitory and that was basically that, no tour, no breakdown of the do's and don'ts, except a reminder that for the first couple of weeks I wasn't allowed to leave the building unless supervised by a member of staff. There wasn't a locked door or barred window in sight, the only security was a seclusion room at the back of the building to house those being returned. The first thing I did was to open a window all the way out. It was torture, being within touching distance of something so ordinary that most people took it for granted. I was bound by the rules and that was the test, to see if you accepted the boundaries or yield so easily to temptation just because it was right there, in front of you, but it wasn't so attractive knowing it could bite and knowing you would damage yourself for something that would eventually be yours anyway.

Towards the end of my stay at Moss Side I had been allowed to purchase magic tricks that used materials such as rope, which ordinarily wouldn't be allowed. These were locked away in the office and I was allowed access to them for practice and performance, but I wasn't allowed to take them to my room. Having unpacked everything and being ultra cautious so as not to infringe any rule, real or imagined, I marched down to the office carrying everything I thought I needed to hand over.

'I've got these. Back at the hospital they were locked in the office.'

'Not here, mate. I'll put them in the safe if you want me to, but I'm not going to demand it.'

'I can keep them, then?'

'What are they?'

I showed him what I had and he took a cursory look before handing them back as if they were worthless.

'I don't have a problem with it. This isn't a special hospital, in time you'll come to realise that.'

'What time's bedtime?'

'There's no set time. Obviously we don't want people staying awake all night then sleeping through the day, it's about being responsible.'

I stayed up until one a.m., just because I could, watching videos with some of the other guys, a couple of whom I knew from Moss Side. The videos were pretty grim but I stayed anyway, I'd been let out of my cage.

Over a period of several weeks I was shown around the grounds, where all the places that were out of bounds were pointed out to me, including the housing estate where some of the staff lived. This was followed by trips around the local village and then Newark itself, all the time being closely monitored as to general conduct, social skills and whether or not I displayed any anxieties that could lead to the type of behaviour that led to my being admitted to hospital. It was a lot of pressure, and any anxieties I did display were as a direct result of that. It's difficult, buying a cup of coffee when every aspect of the transaction is being noted on your file, even down to the way you handle your money. But it wasn't just trips to buy coffee and cigarettes, I had also been allocated work in a metal workshop which was absolutely unbearable, stretching the days, until sometimes I thought they would never end.

The week was split between the workshop and the education department. I had arrived without a qualification to my name and it was felt that I was capable of obtaining some. A tutor was brought in to teach me bookkeeping and accountancy, but I absolutely detest numbers, they just jumble my mind. I did enjoy the English classes, if not the teacher.

Eventually I was allowed out unsupervised, though rather oddly they didn't call it leave, they called it parole. Every time you left the building, you were issued with a card to prove you were legally entitled to be away from the unit, in case you got stopped by the police. I never quite got my head around that, why would the police randomly stop us? They didn't know who we were or where we lived, nobody did, we weren't fucking tattooed!

PART THREE
(20-33)

CHAPTER TWENTY-SIX

'Min, you're wanted in the charge nurse's office.'

I sat down in front of his desk but wasn't yet relaxed. I had earlier been advised that the magic needed to be kept in its proper place, purely as a hobby, and that I needed to focus more serious consideration on my future. I had been practising constantly, to help alleviate boredom and also to channel some of the anger and frustration I inevitably felt. Perhaps only I noticed the difference and that's why I ignored their advice.

'We've been searching for a new hostel for you down south. Unfortunately the only appropriate ones are all run by the Richmond Fellowship, a Christian Organisation, and you're adamant you don't want them, so we've found one that's run by the local authority, but it's in Mansfield.'

Mansfield, a small mining town in Nottinghamshire, the type of place I was hoping to escape from, but my options were becoming increasingly limited and I was desperate to move on. I therefore had no choice but to at least consider it.

'It will allow you to be closer to your family, but the news I'm sure you want to hear is that, as you know you recently resumed contact with your friend Franc, and he's invited you down to London for your birthday. Well, today we received permission from the Home Office, so you can go.'

With all the distractions, I had completely forgotten that some weeks earlier Franc had very generously invited me to spend my birthday as his guest. He offered to book me into a hotel to cover the day before, the day itself and the day after. The night before I was due to leave, I hardly slept, a mixture of excitement and uncertainty. It had been a long time since I'd last seen Franc and I'd learned to live without his inspirational guidance, even though I didn't want to.

The following day, the social worker drove me to the coach station.

'Listen, when you get to the coach station in London, ring us if you get into any difficulties. It's a big place and it can be quite overwhelming.'

He handed me a card with a phone number on it, and I casually tucked it in my pocket with a smile.

'What's funny?'

'I've been doing this since I was ten years old, I shouldn't think it's gotten any bigger since then.'

I climbed aboard the coach, uncertain and not even sure where to sit, because I had a ticket and it confused me, because without one there was danger and without that there was just boredom; I was an adult now.

The journey was long and convoluted, with many stops, and I rehearsed many conversations. I wondered if Franc had done the same, wondered if this was just goodbye in his style, gracious yet final. When the coach finally docked in London, I disembarked and stood looking around. I wasn't as confident as I'd been as a kid because I wasn't acting alone, I had instructions that I'd never known before, which changed everything by squeezing the lines closer together. Someone was supposed to be meeting me and I should have been grateful but in reality I could have done without it, I always knew my way.

I hung around the station, not knowing that across the road was the main concourse. When I eventually found it, a bearded man bearing the card, 'Mini Cooper' was stood waiting for me. I have to admit it felt pretty good, seeing my name displayed from a hundred yards away and watching the confused looks of travellers walking past and glancing up at the card.

'I'm Mini Cooper.'

The car was parked only a short distance away, a Mercedes, quite impressive, leather upholstery and various gadgets that would have taken me a week to figure out. It was a wonderful, sunny day, adding to my increasingly buoyant mood. The doubts had evaporated and I allowed myself the freedom to experience, unequivocally, joy without fear, the biggest step I had yet taken.

On the way to the hotel the car was a little hot, and I began to feel docile, so I decided to open the window. As I was fumbling around in search of the handle, the window suddenly opened and I stared in disbelief.

'How did that happen?'

'I pressed that little button just there.'

'Blimey, you can open the window just by pressing a button!'

'Yeah.'

He said it so blasé, like it was the norm, but even I knew that wasn't the case, and the knowing made the difference. We arrived at the hotel, which was probably the biggest building I'd ever seen, apart from those on American television shows, several stories high and quite frankly, it was fucking scary.

'Listen, do you want me to take care of formalities and get you booked in?'

'Yeah, do you mind? I've never been in a place like this before.'

'No problem.'

There was a doorman, replete with traditional uniform and cap, who would help people into any one of a fleet of taxis that were constantly in attendance. The carpet was thick and plush, and it already felt like I had walked onto the set of Franc's movie. This couldn't be for real, nothing had prepared me for it and I felt incredibly self-conscious, standing there in my cheap, outdated clothes, the only time such a thing had ever mattered and I was angry with myself for allowing it to.

We approached the reception desk and had to wait whilst a middle aged American couple were being rude to the staff. I watched them as they made their way to the elevator and I felt nothing but utter contempt. If that's what money buys, I'd rather be broke. I wasn't paying too much attention to the process, I never was that much connected to formality, I was always afraid that by recognising it, something far more valuable would be lost. Eventually, we found the room and entered. He put my bag on the bed and handed me the key, which was actually a card that slotted into the door and opened it electronically.

'Franc says anything you need within reason, just charge it to the room.'

He didn't need to say that, I wouldn't have exploited Franc's kindness. Still, I guess when someone has spent a great deal of time staring through bars, grateful for a glass of water that hasn't been spat in, there may have been a temptation to go a little crazy, just to join in.

'Do you want to freshen up before we head off to the studios?'

'Yeah.'

I went into the bathroom and had a quick wash. I had brought with me a towel and some toiletries but I needed neither, as everything was provided. I took great delight in using the products, feeling like they'd been put there just for me.

'Now, listen, this hotel is just around the corner from where Franc lives and I'm his personal driver for the duration of this movie. At the end of each day's shoot I'll drive you both home, which means you'll be hanging around for a while, is that okay?'

I figured it wouldn't really feel like hanging around. I'd done plenty of that already and understood its nature and how claustrophobic it could sometimes feel but this wouldn't choke me, it would allow me to pretend for a while. Who wouldn't want that when the alternative was crushing and largely irrelevant?

'It'll be fine, it's been a while since I last saw Franc, so just being here is great. How long will it take to get to the studios?'

'Forty five minutes, an hour, it depends on the traffic, really.'

Traffic dictated so much, I guess that's why I've always been fascinated by it. I'd spent many a dark, miserable evening watching a constant flow of bright headlights, brighter than the burning cigarette that was never far from my lips, afraid that if the traffic stopped, so too would everything else. I was eager to get there so didn't take long in getting myself ready. When we arrived I was shown into a private screening room. I felt incredibly privileged, as only those who needed to be there generally were, whereas I was a guest, but made to feel so much more. Franc was sitting amongst a small group of people, looking up at the screen where some footage was being shown.

'Hey, Mini, good to see you again, buddy! We're just watching some rushes, why don't you help yourself to some refreshments from the trolley over there and we'll speak later, yeah?'

'Sure.'

For those who don't know, which at the time included me, rushes are the previous day's footage and viewing them, I soon discovered, was an integral part of the film-making process, as questions surrounding the colour, the lighting, the sound etc., could be raised and then resolved. I walked over to the trolley and was staggered by the assortment of refreshments on offer. Such was the level of choice, it made the act of choosing impossible. In the end I settled for a bottle of mineral water, believing it to be a choice that wouldn't separate me from the others.

I then sat back and absorbed the detail, listening to all the ideas and noticing how they evolved and grew and deciding whether I agreed or disagreed, but obviously saying nothing, just grateful for the opportunity to think the same way. A day's filming doesn't take up an awful lot of screen time, and then it was back to the main studio to finish off that day's work.

As everyone filtered out of the screening room I sat there, not quite knowing what to do. Franc came over, clutching his copy of the script, and I stood and faced him.

'So, Min, I'm sorry I couldn't deal with you straight away, but we were in the middle of the rushes. But, hey, you made it!'

'I always make it to London, Franc.'

We hugged and in an instant I was given back the time that had been stolen. I just had to remember things differently, remember that I was no longer a child, yet not knowing how to have an adult relationship with him without having to plug all the gaps.

'So, you're twenty-one tomorrow.'

'Yeah.'

I almost didn't want it to be true, was afraid that he might think I didn't need him anymore, afraid that he might decide to step back. There was a hugely conflicting, complex group of emotions battling it out on the walk to the studio. I wanted it to be simpler, I wanted it to be as it always was but I wasn't Peter Pan.

'So, Min, I'm going to be pretty busy for a while. Are you going to be okay, just hanging out on the set?'

'It's okay, I'll enjoy watching.'

'Perfect.'

I walked onto the set with him and strangely, I didn't feel out of place or in any way overawed at the sight of actors and technicians who did this every day of their working lives and knew nothing of mine. I was shown to the director's chair, emblazoned with his name, and sat there like I belonged. The more curious the looks that came my way, the more comfortable I felt, because in essence, I was sat on the throne. Just by being there I, too, had entered a world of make believe. After a while, I fancied a cup of coffee and noticed the runner standing nearby, looking fairly redundant. I wasn't accustomed to having someone serve me because that was their role, and I wanted to know how it felt. I was hesitant at first because I guess I probably felt I had no right to ask just because I was in the director's chair, but it was a temptation that was difficult to resist, purely in its novelty.

'Excuse me?'

He turned and looked towards me, and with a wave of the hand I beckoned him over, but actually felt like a bit of a prick.

'What's up?'

'Could you get me a coffee, please?'

'Sure, how do you like it?'

'Black, strong and no sugar, please.'

He went off to fetch the coffee and I stared after him in disbelief. I couldn't imagine doing what he did, perhaps that's why I made him do it. It would have been no hardship for me to get off my arse and walk the few yards to the coffee machine and pour myself a cup, but I never did because I never had to, that's the fucking trap.

At the end of the day, I walked with Franc back to his office where he had a few things to attend to. Both myself and his driver sat in an ante-room, waiting for him to finish. His driver knew a little about me and we chatted; his questions weren't intrusive, he was simply interested. On the drive back to the hotel, Franc had his head buried in his script, yet was still able to hold down a conversation.

'So, Mini, I'm going to go home and get a shower and I thought maybe we could go for dinner with a couple of friends of mine, how does that sound?'

'Okay.'

He went back to reading his script and I kind of felt like I could just drop off and I struggled to stay awake for the rest of the journey. So much emotional energy had already been spent, and now I had to find more.

* * * *

'Mr Cooper, this is reception. There's a Mr Roddam waiting down here for you.'

'Okay, tell him I'll be down in five minutes.'

I hung up the phone and then panicked. I had returned to the hotel and gone straight up to my room where I lay on the bed enjoying all the sounds I couldn't hear, confident there wouldn't be someone banging on the door asking to borrow a cigarette paper or just wanting an excuse to come in. Then I nodded off.

I raced around the room like a lunatic and the five minutes already seemed like ten. I splashed a little water on my face, brushed my hair then checked where everything was in the room, an old habit from the days when my personal belongings would often be stolen. I then flew down the stairs, believing it to be quicker than the lift. Franc was stood by the reception desk and smiled when he saw me approaching.

'Listen, Franc, I'm really sorry, one minute I was admiring the room, the next, I'd nodded off.'

'Hey, Mini, it's been quite a day! I'm glad the bed's comfy.'

'It's the best birthday present I've ever had, it's a pity I can't take it with me.'

'I guess you must be hungry by now. The car's waiting outside and the table's booked. My friends will be waiting for us, you'll like them and they'll like you. It should be interesting, don't you think?'

It was the first time I had been formally introduced to any of Franc's friends as an adult, and my initial reaction was to wonder if they were merely curious to see how I had turned out, or were wanting something from the past that wore blonde hair and a cheeky grin. I had no real reason to think or feel this way but all the same I did, because the natural child had become a cautious adult. We arrived at a restaurant in Notting Hill, Franc, his wife and me, and I was immediately introduced to his friends who were already sitting at the table.

'Hi, guys, this is Mini. Min, this is Alan and Philippa, dear friends of mine.'

It was a full and proper introduction and I felt that the eyes of the restaurant were on me, wondering who the awkward looking young man was.

'Hi, good to see you.'

Although Franc had already kissed Philippa on the cheek, I wasn't ready for that so I stood there, stiffly shaking their hands, but at least I hadn't bolted for the door. Once we were all seated and the preliminaries were out of the way, wine was ordered and delivered. My glass became a prop as I played with the stem and rolled my finger around the rim. When the conversation came around to the film Franc and I had done, I began to relax a little, became more animated and even laughed at some of the answers I'd given to extremely loaded questions. Then came the waiter, hovering like a hungry bird of prey.

'Min, the steaks here are fabulous, do you fancy trying one?'

'Yeah, okay, I've never had it before but I'll give it a go.'

'How would you like it, sir?'

On a fucking plate would be just fine and how I wished I could have said that!

'I'm having mine medium rare.'

'Okay, I'll have the same please.'

Some garlic rolls were delivered to the table and the smell alone was unbelievable. I had no idea such food existed, it was almost too good to eat. When my steak arrived, I couldn't wait to try it. I cut off a piece but was horrified to see blood seeping out of it.

'Franc, this meat is bleeding!'

'That's how it is, medium rare.'

'I can't eat it if it's bleeding.'

I swear to God, if I had to hunt my own food then skin it and gut it, I would definitely be vegetarian, however on this occasion I simply swapped medium rare for well done.

Philippa had been listening without saying very much, but listening intently nevertheless. I don't know whether she was merely thinking out loud, or wanting a part of what was developing.

'Would you consider doing another documentary?'

I only had one mouthful of steak left but it certainly went down quicker than I had intended. It hadn't even occurred to me until now so I looked to Franc for guidance and support.

'Philippa's looking for a new project and she wondered how you felt about doing a follow-up to the last film.'

'I don't know.'

'Mini, I obviously don't know you as well as Franc and certainly haven't enjoyed the amazing relationship that you two have for the last ten years, but I think it would be interesting for you to look back on that time with an adult mind.'

I was immediately caught in a conflict. I desperately wanted to promote my magic act but at the same time I was being asked to hand everything else over to someone I had just met.

'I need to think about it.'

'Absolutely. Well, let me give you my number and if you decide it's something you might like to do then give me a call.'

She gave me the number and I spent the remainder of the evening feeling pretty subdued and a little confused. When we arrived back at the hotel, Franc came in with me and we had a beer together before both going on our way.

'So, what do you think?'

'I don't know, Franc, it's like we made a film together all those years ago that people are still talking about, you know? They're still interested in it but it's ours and if we were to do this it should be us doing it.'

'Hey, Mini, it would be great if we could do this together but I have different commitments now, it would be impossible.'

'Yeah, I appreciate that.'

'You know Mini you've had people make decisions about you for most of your life, the great thing here is that this one is yours, no one can make it for you.'

'Yeah'

'Don't forget, tomorrow you're on set, so don't stay up too late.'

We hugged, then he left and I stayed a while in the bar, drinking German lager from a bottle. I would be twenty-one after midnight but it didn't feel like it.

The following morning after showering, I went down to breakfast and found that the dining room was huge with an enormous array of food. I couldn't decide what to have so I settled for a slice of ham, unaware that the price was set, consequently that slice of ham cost five pounds and fifty pence! It was hardly a hearty breakfast and as I was due to be an extra that day I wasn't sure I'd eaten enough. I hadn't yet acquired the discipline for a full day's work or learned the requirements, nor it would seem, did I know how to look after myself in order to get the best out of me.

I was picked up around nine, still feeling a little sleepy, having lain awake most of the night, so when birthday greetings were offered I tried not to yawn back my thanks. Once at the studio I was introduced to someone who would be organising the extras for the day. First port of call was the costume department, that was run by a couple of gay guys, extremely camp but also very funny. Then came make-up. I sat in the chair, already feeling uncomfortable in my thick jacket and a pair of trousers that had more eyelets than a pair of Doctor Martins, not to mention some kind of scarf that had been wrapped around my neck half a dozen times.

'I'm not used to wearing make-up.'

'I should hope you're not!'

She was attractive and witty, and had an earthiness about her that added to the overall appeal. I was just another extra, moving along the conveyor belt, she didn't know my name or anything else, I was just another face to paint. When I walked onto the set, I felt there was no reason why I shouldn't be there, and I quickly blended in. In fact, as my confidence grew, the more ridiculous some of the others became.

The scene for the day was a glitzy ball so we were all paired off, one man to one woman, and it quickly became obvious which ones harboured acting ambitions. One guy in particular followed the camera wherever it went and I don't think his partner was overly impressed with being dragged around like a rag doll, but it was fucking funny to watch and made our job a whole lot easier! It was a ball, it was meant to be joyful and it was, but none of it was faked.

Not everything went according to plan. Franc had very sweetly positioned my partner and I at the top of the stairs, a crucial part of the storyline and therefore couldn't be edited out. The deal was that the star of the movie came up the stairs and we turned and bowed, and would be seen on film. It all seemed simple enough. Except I had my back to the stairs and relied entirely on my partner to give me the signal that he was coming, and I completely fucked it! It had to be instant and I was trying to be more considered, because I knew the camera had found me. Another problem was that the guy didn't have a lot of room to get by so it was essential I stood the other side of the tape. In order to do this, however, we would almost have to be cheek to cheek. This caused a lot of anxiety for me and as a result I kept stepping back onto the tape and blocking the path of the actor, which resulted in more rehearsals than anyone probably wanted, and on one occasion the actor lost patience and pushed me into the set. When the scene was finally bagged and in the can, I must have been close to turning blue and it had nothing to do with the weather. They had given me a long brass pipe to smoke and after every failed take, a technician refilled and relit it for me.

That was some karmic kick up the arse.

By the end of the day I was hot, sticky and exhausted. I walked with Franc back to his office and collapsed onto the sofa before realizing I was still in costume, so I trudged begrudgingly down to the costume department and exchanged it for my own. Once the make up was removed and my face was my own again, I remembered it was my birthday and this had been my party. I was close to tears as I returned to Franc's office because I could never hold on to the things that made me real, they came and went, leaving too many gaps that ate up the time. I was starting to drop off when I was woken by a chorus of:

'Happy birthday to you, happy birthday to you!'

Although a little dreary, I couldn't help but smile as first a young lady came marching through with a chocolate cake that was just begging to be devoured, followed by Franc carrying a bottle of Champagne. I had never even seen Champagne before, let alone tasted it, but I wasn't shy in holding out my glass. Chocolate cake and Champers, I needed two mouths!

'So, Mini, I guess this is where you make a speech, buddy.'

I looked at every face as they in turn looked at me, expecting. It was enough for me just to be there amongst them all, when a little over twelve months earlier I had slept behind a locked door.

'It's been an amazing day, it'll take some beating.'

I had taught myself to cover my feelings so well I no longer recognised when I didn't have to. The excitement was bubbling under the surface but I'd learned not to share what I didn't yet have, although it didn't stop me wanting more, to know the difference, and be allowed to, otherwise nothing had changed, except the time. I collapsed back onto the sofa and closed my eyes.

'So, Min, have you been paid yet?'

I opened my eyes but didn't immediately gather my thoughts. I had completely forgotten about the money, had forgotten about the work, because I was leaving tomorrow.

'No, I didn't know what I was supposed to do.'

'It's just down the corridor there, last door on the right.'

I entered the office and it was like walking into a miniature bank with a teller sat behind a glass panel counting money. I announced myself and a chitty was pushed through a gap for me to sign. It was unbelievable, one fucking signature in exchange for money! She counted it out, a little short of sixty-nine pounds. Back at the unit I worked five days a week for seven pounds, plus an additional six pounds from social security. That represented almost six weeks of bullshit labour to arrive at the figure I was holding, money for getting in the way and feeling the warm breath of a beautiful young woman caressing my face. When I was dropped off at the hotel, the money was already burning a hole in my pocket. Along the route I even took it out a couple of times and counted it, it was the most money I'd ever held. I hadn't got a clue how to look after it, how liberating!

I walked into the hotel shop, announcing who I was and what room I was staying in. I confidently strode up to the counter and ordered a couple of packs of Pall Mall cigarettes, I'd seen them on American television shows and in the movies.

'Could I trouble you for a light?'

The shop assistant pulled a book of matches from the pocket of her waistcoat, struck one and lit my cigarette.

'Thank you.'

'You're welcome, sir.'

'Mini's fine.'

I sat in the foyer and picked up a French newspaper. I couldn't even speak fucking French, but no one noticed or cared, because they didn't have to and I didn't know what to do next, because I had no one to ask. In the end I did what I always do in these situations, I went in search of a solitary space that didn't speak.

Having returned to my room and laid on the bed, I suddenly and inexplicably felt restless. I returned to the bar because I knew what to expect, it was the only decision I didn't have to analyse. I sat having a beer and began lamenting that in a few hours' time the bar would be a television room and I would go back to sleeping on a fucking mattress covered in plastic! I got to nibble on something I'd first tasted several years earlier and just like then, the plate was taken away before I'd finished. After a couple of beers, the events of the day and the machinations of my mind caught up with me and I retired to my room for a lie down. I woke around six the following morning, still lying on top of the bed and still fully clothed. I showered and dressed and then packed my bag but not before gathering a few souvenirs. I went down to the restaurant, had a full English then sat drinking coffee for a couple of hours. Franc and his driver arrived at the usual time and Franc paid the bill. I took a last look around the place before leaving with them.

'So, Mini, what time do you have to leave for your coach?'

'About lunchtime.'

'Well, don't forget to say goodbye before you go.'

'No, no, of course I won't.'

We drove on pretty much in silence, Franc pouring over his script and I was pouring over mine as I wrote it silently in my mind. I spent the morning hanging around the set and talking to the technicians. As lunchtime approached I waited for a break in filming then strode over to him with slightly drooping shoulders.

'Franc, I have to go.'

'Listen, you've got Philippa's number?'

'Yeah, I have.'

'Well, think about it and give her a call. You can trust her, she won't hurt you.'

We hugged and I just felt like a kid again, not wanting to go, but this was the set of a movie, a world of make-believe. Real endings meant real goodbyes.

'Take care, Franc, and thanks for everything, it's been a brilliant birthday.'

'Hey, Mini, you deserve it. Safe trip, buddy.'

At Victoria station I boarded the coach, took my seat at the back and lit a cigarette, a luxury still not denied me. It felt strange, returning without a gun being held to my head, even more bizarre was the fact that it never even crossed my mind not to. I must be getting old. A member of the unit staff met me at Newark station and drove me the short distance back to my very own world of make-believe.

On the way it was like twenty questions but I was in no mood to play. Walking back into the unit was a first-time experience for me, as it was something I previously would never have contemplated. I was handed some birthday cards from my family and took them down to my room for a private viewing. I immediately opened the one from my parents and a five-pound note fell out. My family had been on strike for the previous five months during the miners' dispute of the 1980's, and were entirely dependant on food donations and whatever financial help was available, which was very little. I picked up the money and felt like a complete shit. I had spent two days being indulged and had given little thought to my family and their struggle. This was a huge amount of money to them and held far more value than Hollywood's, and the human cost greater than the price of my labour.

CHAPTER TWENTY-SEVEN

By now the initial thrill and excitement of having been released from hospital had worn off and the stark reality began to bite. Within a few weeks I was spending weekends in Mansfield. I had already visited sometime earlier with my social worker and decided, come what may, to accept the offer of a place at the hostel. I was afforded a single room and coupled with the need to move on, both were huge selling points. Also, my family now lived only nine miles away so I could take a bus to visit them.

Bancroft House was a hostel run by the local authority, and part of the burgeoning 'Care in the Community' programme, whereby large institutions were being replaced with smaller units. Most of the residents were elderly and some had spent their entire lives in psychiatric care. On one of my visits, whilst browsing through the local rag, I spotted a talent competition being held at the Civic Theatre. I entered and the following week turned up for my heat. Usually my act was quite sophisticated and polished and I generally performed in a tailor-made suit, bought several years earlier as a Christmas gift from my parents. I had already performed a number of shows in the hospital but felt I needed to look more professional and so that's why I requested the suit. However for this occasion, I changed all that. On the eve of the contest, I created a new outfit, zany and colourful with a personality all of its own.

Johnny Oddball was born.

Thankfully, I won my heat and had to return the following week for the final, but as it wasn't really the judges who were judging me, it was more of a relief than a delight to have won through. In the end I was beaten by a ten-year-old girl, singing songs from some musical I hadn't even seen. She was good, I just doubt she needed it more than I did, but at least I made the final.

It wasn't a pipe dream.

A couple of weeks before I was due to move permanently to Mansfield, I received a phone call.

'Hello?'

'Mr Cooper?'

'Yes.'

'You don't know me but I'm producing Aladdin at the civic theatre in Mansfield this Christmas. We're looking for someone who can do magic to play the Genie, and your name was given to me by the theatre manager, would you be interested?'

I had lost the power of rational thought and was panting so heavily down the phone; I almost had a new career.

'Erm, well, er… yeah, of course I would.'

'I don't know if you're aware of this, but Mansfield hasn't had a professional pantomime for twenty five years so it promises to be quite an occasion. Anyway, it's a three-week contract worth two hundred and fifty pounds.

'Okay.'

I agreed to meet the producer several weeks later in Mansfield to sign the contract. All that remained was the broadcast and it was fucking loud, as I angrily showed off my contract to all those who thought I was a fantasist.

At the end of November 1984, I left the unit for Mansfield, carrying more props than clothes and not much else. It was a new beginning but no one had told me what to expect, and I didn't know what to ask. I wasn't even sure if I knew what to think.

I was simply on the move again.

* * * *

'I am the Genie of the magic lamp, your wish is my command, oh master!'

My opening line of the pantomime and I was so nervous I almost cocked it up. It was the Press Night, so the local media were in attendance and everyone was feeling the pressure to make the run a huge success. Everything was going smoothly until it became patently obvious that the villain of the piece was drunk. I shared a dressing room with him and often during rehearsals he would arrive carrying a plastic bag that only stopped clinking after he set it down on the floor.

Everyone was frantic, as he not only fluffed his lines, he wandered into scenes he shouldn't have been in. The producer finally managed to cut short his role without anyone really noticing. Sadly though, the press couldn't fail to notice that he was pissed and the reviews butchered him and were less than flattering regarding the production as a whole.

After the performance we all went across the road for a drink. Our colleague, far from being repentant, continued to drink himself into a stupor. In the end myself and another guy had to take him back to his hotel. I was roped in because I was the only one who knew the town and the location of his lodging. It was icy and we were slipping and sliding all over the place, but we got him there and dumped him on his bed. Something needed to be done, his role was pivotal so he couldn't just be axed and it was too late to replace him, but he obviously had a problem that wasn't just going to go away. There were three of us sharing the dressing room so in the end the producer collared me and the third guy and asked if we had seen alcohol being brought into the theatre. We both said no and were then asked to report any sightings directly to him. We spoke about it and both felt uncomfortable at having to inform on a colleague. In the end we decided to speak to the actor concerned and put him on notice, and if we saw any booze we'd hide it, with the help of certain other members of the cast. Several dressing rooms became makeshift off-licences for the duration of the run.

One weekend, I went home to my family. They were still on strike and times were hard, so the money I'd saved by staying away from the hostel I used to treat my parents to a night at the miners' welfare. There, after much discussion and my father telling anyone who was willing to listen that I was a great magician, I agreed to perform for free at the children's Christmas party. I owed them that and it was a way of handing back a five-pound note that was always more theirs than mine. After the performance, as a token of their gratitude, I was presented with a boxed set of miniature miners' lamps, which I gave to my father.

By the final week the work schedule and the stress of doing two shows a day began to take its toll and my health began to suffer. I had gone from having very little to do and virtually no responsibilities, to having to very quickly develop a conscientious work routine. Adrenaline alone had kept me going initially, but now I was getting pains in my chest that affected my appetite both for food and the work itself. During that week I also learned a sharp and brutal lesson about how ruthlessly competitive and resentful fellow artistes can sometimes be. During one performance, I was involved in a scene with two other characters. Instead of delivering my line, I threw in an ad lib which I thought was funnier. So did the audience, they fucking roared and I felt a sense of professional pride. Otherwise I thought nothing of it, until during another scene my colleagues set me up and I was made to look like an arse in front of a packed house.

Despite my health problems and the odd run-in with colleagues, the experience had been largely enjoyable and educational. I learned how to take direction, which I had previously been entirely resistant to, and I learned how to work alongside people I didn't like, but more importantly I learned I was good enough, if I was strong enough. By the time it all ended, however, I was no longer sure that I wanted to be part of something that I couldn't always control, or even like. That's what I took with me when the curtain fell on the last night, and I wasn't expecting or prepared for what happened next.

The following day, I woke early but didn't want to get out of bed. I lay there, unable to move, or think, feeling empty, emotionally fragile, but I felt if I started to cry, I might never stop. I had always been prone to bouts of melancholy, but this was the fucking black dog at its most fierce and I was afraid it might never go away! It lasted several days, during which time I contemplated suicide because I had become diminished; I would sit in the bath for hours until eventually I would notice it was cold. On one occasion, I went walking for miles, must have been gone for hours, yet I couldn't remember where I'd been or how I got back.

Yet no one noticed.

Eventually, the gloom lifted and clarity returned as the prospect of more work beckoned and I was desperate to keep the momentum going as well as having the added incentive of leaving 'home.' I had applied for holiday camp work, despite my earlier misgivings. Having written to all three major organisations, my first audition had arrived, at a venue in the Digbeth area of Birmingham. I took a coach and enough material for a ten-minute audition, my first ever, and an opportunity to spend the summer away from the hostel.

The audition went well as I once again found my confidence, but I then had to sit around waiting to be interviewed. I was far more nervous about that than I had been about the performance.

'Hi, I'm Ray, I'm entertainments manager at Sinah Warren holiday village. Have you worked in a holiday village before?'

'No, this would be my first time if I got the job.'

'So, what have you been up to recently?'

I was so relieved that he had said 'recently' as it didn't mean I had to go too far back. My greatest fear was losing my talent to ignorance.

'The most recent thing I've done was a pantomime in Mansfield.'

'Well, you understand you won't just be performing, there'll be other tasks such as organising social events and games. The hours are long and it's a six-day week. Now, what kind of fee were you thinking of?'

I went completely blank, I was totally unprepared for the question, believing that he would tell me what the job paid.

'Bearing in mind, of course, that your food and accommodation are provided free by the company.'

'Eighty pounds.'

It was a completely random figure and as soon as I'd said it I wished I'd said fifty. I just never know what to ask.

'I think we could do that. Okay, Johnny, you'll hear from us in due course. In the meantime, have a safe journey.'

I shook his hand then headed home, pretty confident but with the added security of another two auditions to come. Next was Manchester in a couple of weeks, but in the meantime, I was off to London again.

CHAPTER TWENTY-EIGHT

'Hi, Philippa, it's Mini. I've decided to do it.'

That was the beginning of a process that went on for several weeks, with endless discussions and the occasional meeting. My ultimate aim was to showcase my act and hopefully get some valuable exposure. Quite naturally, this was less of a priority for her but we eventually reached agreement regarding all aspects of the filming.

I caught a train to London, paid for by the British Broadcasting Corporation, whose budget didn't run to a driver so once there, I would have to make my own way across the city. I took a tube, it was a Sunday and I always remember how difficult it was to hide on a Sunday in the North East; trains would be empty and shops would be closed, but London always has to be fucking different! The tube was full, the shops were busy and there was a constant flow of traffic, both human and motorised. It was a drag, the earlier excitement and fascination had now been replaced with a more pragmatic and business-like approach, I just wanted to get to the hotel with something of myself still intact. Once there I checked in, having specifically requested the same hotel as before and even the same room. Surprisingly, I got both, but it wasn't the same, nor was I as excited about being there, I wasn't even sure why I had agreed to it. I certainly wasn't cute anymore and I couldn't have back what I never had to think about. I had very little money so was effectively under house arrest. A simple burger at some local take-away outlet took care of most of what I did have, what a miserable trip! Phillipa called at the hotel in the early evening just to run through the following day's schedule. She wanted to ensure there would be no fucking around as time was money and both were limited.

'So, as you know, we're going to film you watching the original film that you and Franc did ten years ago, then you'll be asked some questions afterwards. Have you had any thoughts about seeing the original film for the first time?'

I didn't know whether she was asking out of genuine interest or whether she was already hoping to frame her first question.

'I haven't really thought about it. I'd rather go in fresh and my response be more spontaneous, really.'

'I still think it might be a good idea to develop some kind of opinion as you're watching. You need to remember that you're going to be watching yourself on television, ten years after the actual event.'

I was beginning to feel slightly resistant to the whole project as it already felt like it was getting away from me. I didn't want to replicate the original film but I didn't want to have changed in a way that made the child pity the adult.

'I'll be okay once we get started.'

After she left, I ordered a couple of beers and charged them to the room. I didn't get the sleep she had hoped for and in the morning I felt so nervous, I couldn't eat breakfast. I checked out of the hotel but was completely unaware that the corporation had only paid for the room itself, so the beers came down to me. I was so accustomed to Franc taking care of everything that it simply didn't cross my mind that I would have to and I had no money. I therefore found myself in the embarrassing position of having to ask them to bail me out in front of the reception staff and other guests.

The BBC sent a car which drove me the short distance to Broadcasting House where I was ushered into a private viewing room, which was small and incredibly claustrophobic. Whilst the crew set up I sat there, chain-smoking. Then the moment arrived and I continued to chain-smoke my way through forty minutes of film.

I found it disturbing that I was somehow unable to articulate fully in the immediate aftermath of the screening. It was unnerving, watching my younger self and the fearless ripostes that followed each examination. There was an innocence about it that was natural and just, but still dangerously naïve. Intelligence that refused to hide and take the safest route, preferring a display that matched the questioners, but they were in a position to retaliate and they did, not only because they could, but because they didn't know how not to.

Between the actual screening and the questions that followed for the new documentary, there was only the time it took for the crew to set up, and these guys were pro's and were quick, which wasn't really helpful to me. I figured a day or two to reflect on something that ultimately had quite a cataclysmic effect on my life, would have been far more productive. Instead, I was left on camera questioning my own sanity.

'What's crazy about this whole thing is that I showed a great deal of insight into what I was doing but made no attempt to stop it, so I wonder, was I insane? Perhaps not as strong as that, but was I wired up wrong?'

These were the first words I delivered for Philippa's documentary on the BBC Two series, 'Forty Minutes', but whilst spoken by me, they did not belong to me and that was more frightening than the place they came from. The interview was edited in such a way that my adult responses were interspersed with those of the child in Franc's film. On one occasion, when I was being interviewed by a child psychologist and giving a detailed account of the science of fire lighting, the adult Mini appeared astonished.

'I never realised I gave it so much thought, I didn't know I went into that much detail, knowing the different methods of achieving the exact effect I was looking for. As I remember it now, I thought I just took a box of matches and lit something.'

It had only been ten years, could I really have so easily forgotten, or so readily?

'Although what I was doing was serious, I always seemed to know how far I could go. I mean, the fire in the house, I didn't know my father was there, I don't imagine for a minute that I would have lit it had I known. The nastier side to that, though, is maybe I would.'

Still a fucking drama queen! Always aware of the camera, the audience and the impact of such a well timed statement. Various shrinks and pretenders around the country would have been gleefully nodding their heads, saying, 'I told you he was a psychopath.' Worse still, was that I actually found myself agreeing with the decision makers, on the basis of my admission into a state mental hospital. At that point the interview should have stopped and I should have been readmitted.

I was driven back to Mansfield and then it was on to the Ritz ballroom in Manchester for round two of auditions for holiday camp work, which was far plusher and roomier than the dingy, cramped conditions of my first audition in Birmingham, and I was a little overwhelmed. In fact, I became so wracked with nerves, I felt cold and began to shake, not perfect for a sleight of hand magician. It was a growing concern and panic began to set in. Philippa, who was wearing a padded coat, wrapped it around me and as my body warmed so did my mind for the challenge. I had learned from my time in Birmingham and was far better prepared for the kind of response I was expecting. I used the audience without them really being involved, I spoke to them as if they had to me. It seemed to work, as there was fluency and professionalism about the act with none of the initial hesitancy from first time around. It was a proud moment as I had earlier wanted to leave, but had stayed.

Next came the obligatory interview and because I had enjoyed my performance, I was reasonably relaxed. I'd also learned on my arrival that the representative of the holiday company, the guy who would be conducting the interview, was the cameraman's brother, and as the interview was being filmed it left me feeling that sometimes the pieces really do fit.

The interview was warm and relaxed, even friendly. I was asked my age and the only time I almost stumbled was when I was asked how long it was since I'd left school. My reply was almost a whisper.

'Five years.'

'And what sort of work have you been doing in that time?'

'The only jobs I've had are entertaining.'

Not exactly a lie but not exactly a full diary either. There hadn't been that many jobs but I was still cutting my teeth. On his form he'd written, 'charming boy, good awareness of the job.'

A week later, I received a couple of letters through the post: I'd been offered both jobs. I took the first because the money was better and it was a much smaller camp, which was also in the county of my birth, the first time I'd been back. There were still a few weeks before the season started but there was plenty to do and much resting on decisions I had absolutely no control over. As the season ran for several months, it would require Home Office permission for me to take up the post. In the meantime, I was filmed in session with my regular shrink back at the Eastdale unit.

'We can talk about the future and putting things in place to deal with that, but what are your future plans?'

'Well, my immediate future involves a job offer, a definite offer, but the stepping stone between me and the job isn't whether or not I'm good enough, but whether the Home Office will approve me doing it.'

'I don't think it's a question of them approving you, I think as humans they'll be behind you and will want you to make a success of it.'

'Well, that's perfect, if it happens.'

'But, of course, they have to work within the framework of the law, so we'll have to find another social worker to supervise you and another psychiatrist.'

It was non-negotiable and therefore pointless trying to press more buttons. I'd already been a little naughty in agitating the way I had, and forcing him to confront the issue on camera, but I was trying to emphasise my position, that my future wasn't entirely in my own hands.

Permission was, however, granted and if and when my new chaperones were found, I'd be heading south. All I could do was wait.

* * * *

Filming was all but complete. We shot some more footage in and around the Mansfield area, most of which ended up on the cutting room floor. We also filmed an interview with a theatrical agent who confidently declared that he probably had more skeletons than me. Not wanting to miss an opportunity to raise his own profile, he arranged a booking for me at a local workingmen's club, which also went on film.

It was my first full performance where I was out there on my own, the show had been advertised and the audience were expecting. The spotlight I had craved in the dungeons of the North West was drawing ever closer, magnified by the presence of the crew, my parents and potentially my ghosts. It was time to deliver. Time to take it out of the bedroom, out of my parent's living room, out of my imagination and make it real.

The show began well with a good entrance, a warm reception and a few laughs. I was growing into it, the stage was mine, I was in no doubt about that and I walked it, inviting the audience to walk with me, which they mostly did. I was a fucking kid again, directing a show full of energy and vibrancy, innocence and play, without it being hijacked!

Except by me.

Halfway through the performance, without reason, understanding or even preparation, I completely changed my style. If the audience were taken by surprise they weren't as shocked as me as I suddenly began making it up as I went along. A new stage persona had emerged, an effeminate prancing figure who, hands on hips, did everything except blow kisses to the audience.

It seemed the pilot had ejected.

By the end, whilst not entirely disintegrating, the act lacked cohesion and simply petered out. The audience, who had earlier been enthusiastic, offered polite but somewhat muted applause. I was becoming a series of contradictions, each one pushing and pulling me and making it harder to decide who or what I was.

The crew returned to London with only one piece of filming left, an interview between myself and Franc. He was currently out of the country but it was hoped that he would return in time for the interview to be filmed at the camp. Everything was now fully in place, including my rail ticket which the holiday company had provided.

I arrived at the camp early in the evening and reported to reception, from where I was directed to the bar, which was seriously overcrowded. Many of these guys had worked the camps for several years and knew each other, whereas it was my first day and I hardly knew myself. I found a quieter space away from the bar and with drink in hand, just sat and observed the various dynamics. We were here for a three-day seminar in which the whole ethos of the company would be spelt out. As well as our duties, we would be offered additional advice on how to conduct ourselves and also to remind us that the good name of the company was in our hands and to treat it responsibly. As the drinks began to flow and people began to relax, so the competition began, everyone chasing the same dream but not everyone could have it. People became more and more animated as they talked themselves up, television work, cruise ships, deals with management companies that were only a signature away.

Yet they were all here with me, pissing in the same bowl.

The seminar was like any other, we were basically reminded of the fact that we were the face of a large corporate organisation and whilst I was willing to promote that in terms of them being my employers, I was only willing to do so within the terms of the agreement. I fully accepted that as well as doing cabaret in the evenings, I would also be required to organise games and sports throughout the day, and of course, keep smiling, even if you had a raging toothache. I didn't expect, nor did I sign up to a programme of sales, so when it was announced that we would be expected to wave booking forms under the noses of those about to depart, in the hope of securing their stay for the following year, I was extremely resistant. More so to a programme of guiding holidaymakers to the various bars and cafes around the camp so that they could avail themselves of the many offers.

It was one thing to deceive for the purposes of entertainment, quite another to take money because it was trapped.

I shared a chalet with a guy from the North East but that was the only similarity. He was the deputy entertainments manager so there was an immediate power imbalance. He also shaved his legs and I'd never known a guy to do this. The chalet was a basic bedroom with a door separating mine from his, and a shower we both shared. It was comfortable enough, given that we would only really be sleeping here.

Or so I thought.

Once the season was under way, I was in for a few surprises. The work was harder than I had envisaged but not beyond me should I get sufficient sleep, but this was proving impossible. I would lie awake at night, listening to the sounds of sex, and at first I was confused as to where they were coming from. One of the girls, an attractive young woman with an abundance of energy, was in an adjoining chalet and I wrongly assumed she was getting it on. It turned out to be much closer to home. This went on for a couple of days and whilst I didn't resent it for its own sake, I needed some fucking sleep!

'Listen, Shaun, I haven't got a problem with you going out on the pull and bringing someone back but, come on, I need some fucking sleep!'

'What's up, you jealous?'

'Actually, no, I didn't come down here to shag or shave me fucking legs, I came here to work, so show some fucking consideration!'

'You won't last five minutes here, I guarantee it.'

A few days later I was called into the entertainment manager's office where I had my first taste of how resentment can bind.

'Johnny, you look like shit! Sort yourself out.'

He began fiddling with my tie.

'Johnny, you can't turn up for breakfast looking like you've been clubbing all night, go back to your room and sort yourself out. And try running a comb through your hair, for God's sake.'

'I might as well have been clubbing, for all the sleep I got.'

'This isn't a country hotel, it's a holiday village. Get used to it, everyone else has to.'

'You don't, you're tucked away in a nice quiet spot.'

'A word, please.'

He took me into his office and closed the door. I thought he was going to hit me but I guess it wasn't in the manual.

'May I remind you who you're talking to?'

'You don't need to.'

'Don't try and undermine me in front of the staff, do you hear?'

He jabbed his finger forcefully into my chest and I brushed it aside with the back of my hand.

'Don't ever do that again.'

It felt good being unafraid, it allowed me to be angry.

'I don't see you lasting very long here, Johnny, so I wouldn't make any long-term plans. Now, go and sort yourself out, you're an embarrassment.'

I went back to my room, growling. My appearance had never been questioned in such a publicly foul way before and it really left its mark.

I had begun burning the candle at both ends, after work I would often go to the nightclub myself, figuring it was probably best just to get back to the digs when everyone else did. Since my run-in with the manager and his deputy I was now sharing accommodation with the bar staff and waiters and they kept irregular hours. Another problem was the lack of a shower, and because there was no hot water, I was reluctant to take a bath at the digs. I arranged with the manager of the leisure centre to use their facilities. The problem was that it didn't open until ten a.m., and whenever I had a break during the day it was often busy and paying customers, quite rightly, were given priority. Consequently, I didn't always manage to take a shower.

At lunch one day he once again pounced in brutal fashion, telling me to take a bath as I stank. My colleagues stared into their food in embarrassment, they knew he'd gone too far, yet weren't willing to challenge him. It cut to the core because I was the only one facing these difficulties yet still trying to do the same job as everyone else.

'What am I supposed to do? There's no shower and no hot water to take a bath. No one else has this problem and no one else seems bothered that I do.'

'There's plenty of showers on this campus, I'm sure you can find one. I don't want you coming in here smelling like that again, it puts people off their food.'

It was a difficult period, made even more so by the arrival of a couple of appointments, one to see the shrink and one to see the social worker. I rang and explained that obviously we would have to work around my schedule. It would have been impossible for me to sneak away for a couple of hours without my absence being noticed, yet they were completely inflexible, reminding me of my legal obligations and the repercussions of non attendance. I wondered why I had fucking bothered! Life was simpler when there was nothing to think about except the next meal. Now I had to lie again because if I didn't I would be considered unstable and unfit to perform my tasks, despite my popularity amongst the paying guests, many of whom would buy me drinks. I invented doctors' appointments, dentists' and even fucking opticians' and it almost backfired on me, anyway.

'Look, Johnny, it's been noticed that you're taking time off for medical appointments. If you're ill, we need to know about it.'

'I'm not ill, but we work long hours and so I just went for a check up, wanted to make sure everything is in good working order.'

'And is it?'

'Yeah.'

I just about got away with it, although I'm not entirely sure he believed me; perhaps he just didn't want to.

Then, I was walking through reception once when I saw the social worker standing there. I thought I would instantly stop breathing and was forced to think on my feet, when I shouldn't have had to.

'Hello, what are you doing here?'

'I just thought I'd pop by and see how you're getting on.'

I ushered her outside and was in danger of erupting. I was struggling to deal with something that was outside of its normal context.

'Have you any idea how vulnerable this makes me?'

'I told them I was a friend.'

'This is my workplace, for God's sake! I can't just have friends drop by whenever they feel like it.'

'Well, as you know, part of my role is to visit your workplace.'

'So is there any wonder why people fail?'

* * * *

'The company has received a letter asking permission for a television crew to come here and film you. So what is that all about? I mean, why would they want to film you?'

I had all but forgotten about Philippa's film, lost in a different set of challenges that weren't recorded but perhaps should have been. A more honest representation than a story wrapped in dreams, I wanted to tell him because I wanted him to know that he had gotten me all wrong, but I doubted it would have made any real difference.

'They're just doing a piece on Northern Working Men's Clubs and those who have worked in them, and basically just following their progress to see how far they can go.'

I was beginning to think I would never know the truth again.

'Well, they're coming here tomorrow to film you, that's how far you've gone and probably how far you'll ever go.'

'Yeah, but it's still me they're coming to see.'

As much as he knew it, he couldn't comprehend it, because for him it was all wrapped in stardom and for him I just didn't have it, I just had myself.

'They'll soon forget, they always do.'

'Yeah, just like they forgot you, eh?'

Probably not the wisest thing I ever said but he could only sack me for it, I guess that was the mark of how far I'd come.

The following day the crew arrived. Franc had just returned from the States and was driven asleep in the back of a car. The problem was the black dog had once again left its calling card and I no longer knew how to talk, in fact, I just didn't want to. We sat at a table in the sunshine and even before the cameras had started to roll I didn't want to be there. Franc was his usual, ebullient self but I just couldn't find it, not even around him. Then the camera started rolling and I couldn't stop it without getting up and walking away. There's no doubt now that's what I should have done.

The programme's narrator announced that having come down to the camp to see me, Franc found me depressed.

'You know, Mini, in all the time I've known you since you were ten years old, you've always said you wanted to be your own man. Now you have the chance to be your own man and you're still not happy.'

'I'm happy to be out of that place because I haven't got them breathing down me neck, I can't argue about that. I don't know, I just get frustrated.'

'Why?'

'Well at the end of the day, I'm a magician, not a kids' games organiser or whatever.'

'Yeah, but you can't always have what you want straight away.'

'Yeah I know, I mean, I'll cope with it, it might get better.'

I smiled but I guess I wasn't really convincing anyone, least of all myself.

'I'm just not very confident with the children and it's frustrating.'

'All the time I've known you you've always been disappointed with your circumstances. Do you think that's maybe because you're asking too much?'

'Maybe, I don't know. I don't know what I want, I don't know what I don't want, I think I'm just mixed up, that's all.'

Except I wasn't, I wanted things to be markedly different but they weren't; little pockets of institutions under different guises scattered across the country, different levels of authority and different ways to abuse it. Sometimes it just didn't feel worth it anymore, but that's not something you can articulate in a way that excites people or interests them. That's where it was the day Franc arrived and I killed the interview.

The final scene of the film showed me standing on the beach, looking mournfully out towards the sea with my own voice-over overlaid.

'I can't explain to myself how I feel, can't put it into a neat little package. Thirteen years is a long time, I've done longer than some people do for taking a life.'

When the film was broadcast, some footage was shown with me and the children. I appeared to ooze confidence and competence and the children responded to it, they even laughed at my jokes, but it felt illusionary as my insides would often be doing somersaults. Perhaps having spent so little time engaging with children whilst still a child myself, had left me without a template leaving me to rely purely on instinct, without the means of measuring success against failure. Shortly after the footage was shot, I developed stomach ulcers through self-inflicted stress, but it was more than that. Years of institutionalised life with poor diet and inadequate healthcare had also left me with bad teeth and periods of anorexia because deciding whether or not to eat was the only control I had. It was also another way of punishing adults, they could lock you up and throw away the matches but they couldn't force-feed you, and when their threats failed they would be forced to grovel. Now what fucking meal could ever taste better than that?

A little while later, both the general manager and the entertainments manager were given the push and were almost immediately replaced with much younger models, both of whom wanted to make their mark. After a couple of weeks of having my schedule constantly changed, I decided to go and see the entertainments manager.

'Can I have a word? There's some things I'm not happy about.'

'Listen, Johnny, I get paid a lot of money to make this place rock, if I get it wrong then I'm unemployed. But these suggest I won't be.'

He held up a large stack of questionnaires and waved them at me. Departing guests were invited to fill in their comments regarding the quality of their holiday.

'Not one of these is critical.'

I would like to have seen the ones that were.

'That's not why I'm here. I'm fed up being given all the duties that no one else seems to want to do. For instance, I deal with the kids every week when we were supposed to be taking it in turns.'

'Are you unhappy with your position here? Because you know magicians are two a penny.'

'Oh, is that right? Well, why don't you pick up that phone and spend a fucking penny?'

CHAPTER TWENTY-NINE

'Don't you think it would have been better if you'd just bitten the bullet?'

'You know that's a magic trick too, it's killed one or two, though.'

I was talking to my key worker, a member of staff assigned to you and meant to be your first port of call should you encounter any difficulties or problems. They also represent you in case conferences and basically fought your corner whenever necessary, at least that's what we were told.

'I mean, where would you rather be, back here or working at the holiday camp?'

'Is there a third option?'

There's no denying it was a shock to be back at the hostel just as I was beginning to forget the smell of piss and disinfectant. Having nothing to do and no one to do it with made the days extremely long and empty. I would wander for miles without any real purpose, sometimes wandering through the woods at night. I was once again ordered to sort myself out and to work within the established parameters and not seek to ignore or change them. I was prescribed anti-depressant medication and assured that it would help clear my mind.

But it didn't, it just made me sleep.

I spent weeks lurching between wandering, sleeping and only occasionally eating, believing rather bizarrely that it was a sign of weakness and that ultimately it was once again, the only part of my life I had total control over. One day, I went to cash my benefit cheque and nothing had really changed. I had been thinking for several days that I couldn't continue like this, couldn't go on feeling like nothing, it needed to mean something for this to be worth it. I was drowning in anonymity, because all I had were old stories to tell. I collected my money and headed for the bus station where I spent several minutes dithering before finally making a decision and got on the fucking bus! I was nervous and excited, so far I had done nothing wrong, but the rehearsal alone had left me feeling aroused. I reached Nottingham and headed across the city to the train station, heart pumping, mind still racing and senses alert and heightened.

Outside the station, I paced back and forth, breathing erratically. The next decision could mean I cross the line. I had no assistance or guidance, only what my soul was screaming at me. I could get on that train, feeling all the things I did back then but with the bonus of memory, the only time I had a true identity, the only time I felt alive instead of having it all eroded and ignored on the streets of Mansfield. I boarded that train and didn't give a flying fuck about the consequences, because sadly they were no longer a deterrent, more a rest home for disillusioned former wannabe's!

After changing at Derby, I settled into my seat for the ultimate leg of the journey, Durham. This time I was delighted at having a valid ticket, as I didn't want the journey to be interrupted. When we reached Durham, I disembarked, wanting it to feel like I had come home but it didn't and I didn't know why. That is, until I began to walk through the city. Everywhere I looked, there were streets where I had been apprehended, alleyways where I had hidden from danger. Even the riverside, tranquil and serene, beautiful and seductive, had only been enjoyed because I shouldn't have been there.

I boarded a bus because in that moment I needed to remember. So much had happened that I couldn't change yet it had changed me, and I needed to feel the importance of that. But it was another disappointment because everything was the same, except this time I was an adult, staring back at a child who didn't recognise me, because only the child truly remembered the place.

I was now an outsider, not allowed in without trespassing.

It saddened me deeply, as I stood outside the entrance to Aycliffe School, with no fear of being apprehended. It was like I was never there, not on the list, just forgotten, for there are always more. I wanted to step inside the place that I had always tried to escape, just to know how it felt to want to be there. To stare up at the windows of Royston House, knowing full well what was going on behind them and sometimes missing that, but I turned and walked away because what I wanted was pitiful and it embarrassed me. I was better off not knowing where I was going, than clinging to where I could always remain.

I headed into town in search of food. It was now a question of priority and primary focus. I bought a Chinese, then headed for the pub. It felt a little unreal, drinking in a place that had once seemed out of bounds. Bored and disillusioned, I once again boarded the bus for Durham, once again heading for the pub where I sat enjoying a pint or two, knowing I would never return to this region to live, because nobody does.

Unless sentenced to it.

By the time I boarded the train at Durham just after midnight, I was seriously drunk; not for the first time. I must have fallen asleep for the next thing I knew, the guard was shaking me violently by the shoulder.

'We're here, pal, you need to get off the train.'

I opened my eyes to bright sunlight, which did nothing to ease my hangover. I was confused and disorientated, but I grabbed my bag, weaved my way down the carriage, out of the door and onto the platform.

Fucking King's Cross!

I just stood there awhile, staring at a ticket that clearly said Nottingham. All the previous allurements were now obstacles, because I shouldn't have been there, the first time I'd recognised that fact with a measure of concern.

I walked down the platform, through the concourse and out onto the street. I didn't have enough money for a return fare and I didn't want to ask Franc, didn't want to explain as an adult that I was less equipped than the child so I spent the day wandering the streets of London and getting nothing from it. Everything looked the same, the buildings, the people and the traffic, congested but unable to change its course. Nothing was different anymore, nothing had the warmth of meaning or the excitement of its character resisting prescription.

As darkness fell, I returned to Kings Cross, no closer to sorting out the mess and too weary to be concerned. I went across the road to a burger bar and ordered a burger and a coffee and sat at the back, in search of a little privacy. I stared at the burger then pushed it away from me. I was becoming smaller and I didn't know how to grow back, I was just too tired. I took the pills from my bag and stared at them, transfixed, unable to divert my gaze or my intent away from the label. I began breathing a little heavier, but I also felt a huge sense of victory, as I could smell freedom and this time it was unconditional. I emptied out a handful of pills and swallowed the lot, washed down with lukewarm coffee. I then did the same with the remainder. It was the first time I had felt excited about life just as it was about to slip away, the first time I felt sure and certain.

I just wanted to lie down.

When I opened my eyes, I could hear train departures being announced. Although I was lying on a solid wooden bench, it felt as comfortable as a crib and I was in no hurry to move. I was doped on all the medication I had taken and was suffering a little cognitive dysfunction, but one thing didn't take a great deal of figuring out.

I had failed.

My bag, my money, everything had been stolen or lost, I had only what I was wearing, along with a thoroughly fucking miserable disposition. I looked up at the clock and it read ten past six. I figured it must be morning so I went outside to check. Euston Road was busy and I soon realised it was early evening and I hung my head in despair. I was defeated and would have to face the music, there was no point in putting it off. I handed myself over to the British Transport Police, not so much willingly as necessarily.

'So, what's supposed to be wrong with you?'

'Nothing.'

'There must be something wrong with you otherwise they wouldn't have sent you there.'

'They didn't know what else to do, I suppose.'

He took down the details, address, phone numbers, and then disappeared. When he returned, he was carrying a clipboard and a torch.

'Right then, young man, follow me.'

I followed him into an open cell where I was instructed to remove all my clothes, which he searched, right down to the last thread. I was then instructed to bend over whilst he shone his torch up my arse, grossly humiliating.

I imagined phone calls to the Home Office and a long trip back up the motorway. I don't know how long I sat there, drifting in and out of consciousness but when he returned he was accompanied by two other officers, and I feared the worst.

'Come on, there's no time for sleeping, you can do that on the train.'

'The train?'

'We've spoken to your social worker and he's going to meet you off the train at Alfreton and Mansfield Parkway. These two officers are going to see you get on the right train.'

I followed my escort and boarded the train, for once glad to see the back of this God-forsaken place. It had become a trap.

I spent the entire journey staring out of the window at things I couldn't see, then stepped off the train looking and feeling extremely sheepish, as well as deeply embarrassed. I had handed myself to them on a plate, meekly and without any resistance or argument and now they got to dissect me all over again, as a favour.

'Come on, let's get you back, the car's just around the corner.'

His manner was warm and gentle, given the lateness of the hour, and I didn't quite know how to deal with it, without totalling collapsing.

'We think you're probably suffering from clinical depression so we'd like you to come back to the Eastdale Unit for a while, just so we can keep an eye on you. It would be better for you if you came voluntarily.'

'Yeah, okay.'

I was barely audible as I stood staring at my shoes, unable to make eye contact. Eventually he took me by the arm and guided me towards the car. As we drove, I continued to shrink, as thought after thought came and went, none of them wishing to stay and be betrayed once more.

'You know, Michael, no one said it was going to be easy but we're here to help. If things get tough you need to talk to us, instead of bottling everything up and running away to London. Even for a young man, it can be a very dangerous place.'

Trying to speak made it harder to breathe and crying was easier than an intellectual debate on the legitimacy of this inquest, or of those charged with assessing the risk above the reason. So cry I did, in a way I had never done as an adult. It scared the hell out of me for I had never known such ferocity of emotion and was afraid it wouldn't stop until there was nothing left.

'I just wanted to die and I couldn't even get that right, without ending up in a fucking police station!'

He swallowed hard and temporarily lost the composure that was normally swathed in condescending pompousness.

'Are you saying you tried to harm yourself? You really need to be honest about this, Michael.'

'I took my tablets.'

'How many?'

'All of them.'

'When did you take them?'

'Last night.'

'Well, if they were going to kill you, they'd have done it by now, but you might have caused some other damage. You'll need to see the doctor.'

And that was that. I did indeed see the doctor the following day, who asked a couple of perfunctory questions, prescribed medication for my ulcers, my broken mind and ordered me to take complete rest.

I liked the sound of that.

For the next couple of days I was on holiday, long lie-ins, familiarity, sympathetic voices and hedgehogs. They came by the back door each evening to be fed and they gave far more than they took, along with the squirrels and the ducks whose mother had abandoned them. They took away the complications, made everything smaller.

Within days of my being there I suddenly went from one extreme to the other, nearly falling off the scale. From having the abyss wrap its insidious intent around my psyche, I entered a state of euphoria where the rules invented themselves faster than I could recognise their meaning, or place of origin, but I was grateful to be fearless again, to have back that uncompromising belief that was always stronger than the methods used to undermine it. Mischief became my closest ally and my funniest friend, and all that creativity that had been wasted and largely unappreciated, was about to reinvent itself outside of the boundaries and restrictive resentments of a simple stage act.

One day as lunch was being served, I was returning to the unit when I spotted a condom hanging from someone's exhaust pipe; it was an invitation I couldn't refuse, as each possibility fought with the other. I'd never held one in my hand before but I didn't intend hanging on to it. When I entered the dining room, some of the guys were already eating. I was so fucking giddy I could hardly contain myself. I sauntered into the kitchen and found the heated trolley used to transport the food from the main kitchens in the hospital and quickly dropped the condom into the container that held the custard. Everyone wondered why I was laughing so loudly at apparently nothing, until someone went to take a mouthful of dessert and found the offending item hanging from their spoon. I must have been going completely mad because I laughed so much I fell against a wooden partition that housed several ornaments. The whole lot went crashing to the ground, including me. As I was helped to my feet, it became fairly obvious who the culprit was and a few words were exchanged, but none from me as I continued to laugh and cry at the same time. I was on a roll, uncontrollable and with no concern for my future well-being, just maximising the moment to compensate for all those that had drifted by, observed but not interactive.

It felt good being a child, even though I was now too old to be allowed that freedom, and those mistakes.

Nevertheless, over the following few days I began a campaign of placing fresh eggs in various neatly made beds, hiding the kettle in the fridge and staying up all night writing a darkly comic novel entitled, 'Living Proof There is Life After Death.' The story centred around a child born wearing a full set of dentures, who travelled the country encountering, amongst other things, a violin-playing cow.

There was a number of discussions amongst the various 'professionals' in which schizophrenia was favoured by some, whilst others felt I might be suffering from manic depression. The eventual outcome was that no specific diagnosis was declared or recorded, nevertheless my medication was increased and I never wrote for the duration of my stay.

Somewhere in amongst the drug fuelled haze came news of the second film's broadcast date, and a spot on breakfast television's famous sofa, due to be broadcast live on the day the film went out. Despite it being Phillipa's film, they wanted to speak to me and Franc. I guess that film was never quite forgotten.

I was off to London again.

CHAPTER THIRTY

'Mr Cooper?'

'Yes.'

'This is your five o'clock wake up call, sir, the car will be with you in around half an hour.'

I had travelled down to London by coach and stayed the night at Phillipa's house. I was driven to the studios but did not feel particularly special or privileged, it was still dark and I was still a few hours away from feeling human. Franc and I were eventually ushered into the studio, where the presenter Frank Bough did a u-turn on what we had agreed to discuss and asked a whole series of questions I wasn't expecting. I did not present myself well as I stared at him with utter contempt, wondering how I could separate his head from his body without regret. It was left to Franc to rescue the situation, which he did confidently and eloquently but sadly I was left knowing I could no longer do it myself, I was no longer cute and I was no longer brave.

Just scared of all the normal things that seemed unusual.

Back at the unit a couple of weeks after the broadcast, I was awoken by a member of staff who stood over my bed and emptied the contents of a large, brown envelope over my bedclothes. Dozens of letters and enough postage stamps to reply to the nation, but the press had gotten there first and it wasn't pretty. They described me variously as morose and beaten up, and it was hard to stomach that in a few years I had gone from being a celebrated warrior of justice to an inarticulate messenger of blame. It was perhaps more an indictment of spirit than the system that had tried to destroy it.

I initially pledged to reply to all those who had written to me, believing that as they had taken the trouble I should at least do the same, it wasn't as if there were any real constraints on my time. However, a third of the letters came from religious nuts inviting me to subscribe to the kind of irrationality that would have sent me back from where I came, only to have to start again. There was one from a university graduate whose hypothesis was that I had basically been spoilt, another from a retired former army major who wanted to set me up in a flat, 'no strings', and a couple from teenage girls who appeared to have developed some kind of a crush.

All went in the bin.

Of the remainder, most received a few lines thanking them for taking the time to write but I did not include an address or any detailed information. There was one letter, though, that did catch my eye and I put it to one side whilst I pondered how to respond. It came from a thirty-three-year-old single mother of two young boys, the youngest still a baby. It was the only letter that came with a photograph and I guess I was curious, so I decided to reply less formally. Her letter had been sensitive and had stirred something inside me that I wasn't really familiar with but felt like sharing, if only to understand its nature, or mine in relation to it. I posted the letter, complete with my address and waited. I didn't know any women on a personal, intimate level and I guess I was a little seduced by her warm gentleness and her intelligence, not forgetting need.

It wasn't long before she had replied.

Over the following weeks, writing letters became a full-time pursuit, and an expensive one. Then one afternoon, lost in my own thoughts, I was summoned.

'Min, there's a phone call for you.'

'Who is it?'

'Marilyn.'

I was a little spooked by this latest development as I had not given her the number and units like Eastdale are notoriously difficult to locate through the usual enquiries. Nevertheless, I took the call, wanting to put a voice to the words.

'Hello?'

'Hi, it's me.'

'I know.'

Despite being raised in London and living in Essex she didn't have an instantly recognisable accent, it was more refined and easy to listen to.

'You know that place you're in, are you allowed out?'

'Yeah, of course, but I still need permission.'

'Do you think they'll allow you to come down here for a week-end?'

It was hugely seductive. I was a virgin and whilst I wanted to undo that, I didn't know how, I just knew that I'd learned to read and write without instruction, so I was hoping it would be the same.

'Yeah, okay.'

'There's just one thing, I only have one bed, it means we'll have to share.'

I was twenty-two years old and had never slept with a woman in any of the senses. My desire had already increased with every stroke of her pen and now it was her voice that almost had me gibbering.

'And I don't have any pyjamas.'

This may have been alien territory with rules and conditions I had yet to discover, but even I could grasp that a naked woman inviting you into her bed was offering more than just a resting place.

'Neither have I.'

I was already imagining what it would be like lying next to her, then it all changed and my mind went quiet.

'I've got a confession to make, I've cut your picture out of the newspaper and stuck it to my headboard.'

I laughed but not because I thought it was funny, I thought it was seriously scary and I was instantly thrown into confusion. On the one hand I wanted to satisfy a primeval urge, as well as enjoying what had so far eluded me. A normal healthy sexual relationship, that combined friendship, shared ideas and the merging of minds. But mostly I needed common sense to support a protective rationale that wouldn't capitulate just to satisfy convention, or nature's heritage.

'I talk to you every night before I go to sleep.'

It was time to go. I took her number and said I'd be in touch once the arrangements were made but panic had already set in. I spent the next few days ruminating, wondering how to avoid what I couldn't just run away from, but there were no strategies in place that I could rely on, I was a virgin in more than one sense.

The social worker agreed to drive me down to Essex and leave me alone with Marilyn, but only for a couple of hours. I still had reservations but didn't want to lose something before I knew what it was, just because it was outside of my experience. We found her house with a minimum of fuss. I knew what she looked like and how she sounded, I just didn't know how I would respond on my own level. She came to the door holding her baby who was quite poorly, but I was immediately taken with her love for the child. We were invited into the lounge and the social worker wasted no time.

'Listen, you two obviously have a lot to talk about and you don't want me getting in the way, so I'm going to pop into town for a while and I'll come back in a couple of hours.'

Marilyn showed him out and when she returned, the room seemed strangely quiet. She was keen to put the little chap to bed so I just sat there, studying the room. She wasn't well off as she survived on benefits but the house was comfortable and tasteful. Marilyn entered the lounge smiling. She had smiled when she had opened the door to us, in fact during the few minutes I had been there, a smile was never very far from her lips and it was a confident smile.

'How was your journey?'

'Long. You know, when I was a kid I used to travel from Durham which is in the far north of the country, all the way down to London, about four and a half hours but it used to fly because of the adrenalin. Now, I don't travel so well, because it's almost guaranteed.'

I was sat on her sofa, rambling because I was nervous, fiddling with my hands because I didn't know what else to do with them. She had taken a seat near the fireplace. I noticed she was casually but smartly dressed, she wore her clothes well.

'Are you hungry yet?'

'To be honest, I'm starving.'

She disappeared into the kitchen and I walked over to her dining table and sat down. She had already asked me if I liked Sheperd's Pie and I had told her that I did. What I didn't expect, however, was that she came through with only one plate of food.

'Aren't you having any?'

'I ate earlier.'

After lunch we had a brandy, and talked some more. We weren't exactly walking around each other and there was definitely something in that room that neither of us attempted to deny. Then came the knock at the door. We both smiled, not knowing whether we'd been saved or interrupted. Once in the car, he wasted no time in launching into his interrogation which felt intrusive, like a father questioning his teenage son. This should have been a private moment, but once again it was denied.

'So, how did it go?'

'Yeah, it was fine.'

'So, what did you talk about?'

'This and that.'

I was quickly learning the value of brevity. I was under no obligation to satisfy his voyeuristic manipulations, besides I deeply resented him thinking he had an absolute right to the information. I guess it's just a habit to them.

'Will you be seeing her again?'

'I don't know, there's a lot to think about.'

There certainly was! I was afraid that maybe all I felt when she knelt at my feet was lust and there was a strong possibility that had he not turned up when he did, we would have found out. It was all a little too surreal and my own reality was in conflict with that, offering more questions than answers, but it was something

I needed to work through on my own otherwise nothing that happened would be mine to enjoy, or regret. I needed to think and feel outside of the institution otherwise I would only ever be equipped to be there.

'Maybe you just need some time to think.'

'I've had plenty of time to do that and it hasn't produced much so far.'

* * * *

Shortly afterwards I was retruned to Mansfield, where I was informed that the only benefit I was entitled to claim was unemployment benefit. Despite apparently suffering from depression and having attempted suicide, the doctor considered me fit for work. I duly signed on and several weeks later the job centre sent me on a course intended to help improve my chances of securing employment. On the final day we were invited to fill out an application, which would be used to assess each person's suitability for training and employment.

When I was interviewed, they basically told me there was very little they could offer except a place on some government scheme. Should I refuse, my benefit would be withdrawn. I was required to work three days a week: Monday, Tuesday, Wednesday one week and Wednesday, Thursday, Friday, the following week, for six months for a weekly 'wage' of fifty-five pounds. After deductions it was approximately forty-eight pounds.

I started work on a Monday morning, having hardly slept the night before and my fears were quickly confirmed as I entered the depot, to be issued with a pair of protective boots and a donkey jacket. Most of the guys were around my age and had grown up together on the same estates and had attended the same schools. I didn't even talk like them and they initially didn't talk to me other than to ask my name. Perhaps that's what did it, that and them thinking I was posh, a bigger fucking joke than being there, only no one was laughing.

We were driven in the back of a truck to Hardwick Hall, a former stately home several miles from town, which was now owned by the National Trust. I enjoyed the wind in my face it was only thing I would enjoy. When we arrived, we learned that a lake was being developed and our job was to build a wall. This required us, firstly, to dig a fairly deep trench, whilst the instructors did the skilled work, such as cutting up the rocks that would form the wall. It was hard labour, straight out of a chain gang, which I wasn't built for and therefore struggled right from the off. Then just before lunchtime, they got something to cheer about. A truck turned up carrying bags of cement, which we were ordered to remove and deposit in the shed several yards away. I had never carried a bag of cement before and had no idea what it weighed but I took my place along with everyone else, and turned my back for the guy to load me up.

'You sure you can manage this, mate?'

'Yeah, I'll be fine.'

He placed the cement on my back and I grabbed it with both hands. I hadn't taken more than a couple of steps when I completely buckled under the weight and ended up face down in the dirt. The whole place erupted, with everyone falling about laughing. I tried to pick it up but it wouldn't budge, providing even more laughter.

'Cooper, leave it there! One of the other lads can carry it, go back to digging.'

When lunch was called, all the guys headed for the shed while I simply retrieved my lunch from the truck, found a huge rock to sit on and ate alone. I realize that in doing this I was further alienating myself, but I didn't know how to be any different, without being different. I opened the lunch the hostel had provided, a couple of corned beef sandwiches, a piece of fruit and a soft drink. That would have to change if I was ever going to manage one of those bags. When the shift ended I had to be helped into the back of the truck, then back in town I had to walk up a steep hill back to the hostel, it almost brought me to my knees. Despite my obvious exhaustion, I slept very badly. My body ached and so did my mind, the anger refusing to dissipate and the dread of the following day's work seemed to quicken the hours, rather than slow them down.

After a couple of months on the job and having now reached the stage where it was becoming more and more difficult to motivate myself, we were told to stop digging whilst the engineer inspected the work. He walked up and down the trench and examined part of the wall for a few minutes, then declared the work satisfactory.

'Okay lads, fill her in.'

'You can fuck right off!'

One of the instructors came bounding towards me, having to negotiate a path over a mountain of rocks.

'What did you say?'

'You heard. I've spent two months digging this trench out only for you to tell me to fill it in, so what was the point other than to waste my time?'

'If you don't pick up that spade right now I'll finish you and you know what that means.'

He might as well have held my balls in his hand and I felt like a child again, powerless and taking shit from people not fit to dispense their authority, and too stupid to argue with because it all came down to the same thing. Not what they knew, but what they could do unquestioningly.

If I'd gotten the sack, my money would have been withdrawn and there would have been yet another inquest so I picked up the spade. I began shovelling in the most desultory fashion I could hope to get away with, then in the best American drawl I could muster, began yelling:

'I'm shovelling the shit, boss, I'm shovelling the shit!'

And then:

'What we have here is a failure to communicate.'

It was my favourite line from the movie, 'Cool Hand Luke', and he was one of my favourite characters of all time. I began giggling like a lunatic, attracting some curious stares and the odd shake of the head, but they stayed away from my tiny, pocket-handkerchief area of land

As I walked down the hill the following morning, my boots heavy on the concrete and my jacket feeling heavier than me, I knew I couldn't do it anymore, because there was no more purpose than what had gone before, and I needed more. I turned and headed for the park where I sat on the swings, I was back to killing time and that's what I did in the absence of thought. I walked through the day and then returned to the hostel, changed and walked some more. Then I went to the cinema and when I returned close to midnight, having once more stopped off at the park, I was locked out.

'Where have you been?'

'What does it matter, I'm here now! I'm sick of people telling me I can't do what everyone else does. Am I an adult or still a fucking kid?'

'Don't you talk to me like that!'

'Yeah, well, don't you talk to me like you own me because you don't.'

I stepped inside and she ushered me into the office. I didn't enter willingly but she said she wanted a word with me.

'Right, I'd better ring the police and let them know you're no longer missing.'

'I was never missing.'

'You know the rules, the doors get locked at eleven and as you did not inform us that you were going to be late, you were officially missing.'

I noticed my address book sitting on the desk and wondered how it had gotten there when it had been in the drawer of my bedside cabinet.

'What's my book doing there?'

'I didn't know whether you'd gone to stay with friends or family so I rang them to check.'

I got up to go and she put her hand out to stop me. Ignoring it, I picked up my book and waved it at her.

'I won't forget or forgive this!'

The following morning I walked into the depot and handed in my notice. Another conference was convened only this time I was signed on the sick but not before I had to justify a decision taken by millions of other dissatisfied employees. I felt like my identity was being sculptured and moulded to fit their model and I began to question what I was thinking, afraid that it wasn't me.

I went to see a lawyer and changed my name by deed poll to Johnny Oddball. Although the act was well and truly defunct, I figured it was a powerful statement of intent. I began to reprise the role, dressing as zanily as I had done on stage with a few additions, a toothbrush sticking out of my top pocket and a baby's dummy hung around my neck. I was talked out of dying my hair half blue and half pink with a moustache to match, with the colours on opposite sides. I didn't really have the confidence to carry any of this off and it made me vulnerable, especially when I walked into a pub.

They thought I'd been let out of the local asylum.

I also grew increasingly disillusioned, believing that the earth didn't just turn on its axis but that we were turning with it, only faster and for no other purpose than to gather up all the things we didn't need, ignoring the things we do. One day I gathered up all my material possessions and decided to give them away, believing that all those who took them would help maintain the status quo whilst separating me from it. It was far harder than I had imagined. I owned a small portable television set and decided that was the first thing to go, I walked around town trying to give it away but most people recoiled in fear, a couple even ran away. I was sweating profusely, as it was a hot sunny day and the television set became just too heavy to carry, so on my way back up the hill towards the hostel, I dumped it in a bush, hoping that a passing thief would help himself to it. I took a break for a coffee and a fag then stuffed all my clothes into a black bin liner and set of again, but with similar results. Eventually, I dumped them in the bus depot adjacent to the hostel.

'Oi! You can't leave that there.'

'Oh, yes, I can! I've abandoned social norms, mate.'

I ran out of the depot, laughing like a lunatic, across the road and back inside the hostel. I gathered together the last of my possessions and stuffed them in the suitcase containing my magical apparatus and walked through town looking for a suitable drop-off point but in the end settled for where I stood when I was tired of walking.

The roadside.

When I returned to the hostel, I was handed the bag with my clothes in it; the depot manager had brought them back. I was asked what I'd done with the rest of my stuff and proudly told them. They rang the police and some of it had been handed in, but not the television. The next day I was at it again, re-distributing what had been returned to me, but I kept a couple of items of clothing. By the end of the day, I planned on leaving and taking to the hills but I never made it, I was returned to the Eastdale Unit, where I spent a further couple of months. Once again, the issue of my mental health became open to debate, once again manic depression was offered as a possible diagnosis.

Then came the news.

I'd been offered a two-bedroom apartment.

CHAPTER THIRTY-ONE

'As you can see, it's in need of some decoration but the association will be willing to offer you a grant to help with that.'

I had met a representative of North British Housing Association, my prospective landlords, to show me around the apartment. Also in tow was my key worker from the hostel, to ask relevant questions, because I was more used to being told.

The place was on the Bellamy Road estate, a large, sprawling wilderness approximately three miles from the town centre, which had been built to imprison the large influx of mineworkers moving down from Scotland, the North East of England and Wales during the sixties and seventies. Subsequently, only around a third of the population were indigenous. It was both a housing and an industrial estate, and not always easy to tell which was which.

My key worker had explained my circumstances, in particular that I would need to apply for a community care grant before I was able to move in. As this often took several weeks, she was keen to ascertain when the rent became liable, once I'd signed the tenancy agreement.

'Normally the rent is due in the first week but obviously under exceptional circumstances, such as his, then we can be more flexible.'

She never looked at me as she said this but it didn't really matter, I was already planning ahead.

'So what do you think, Min?'

'I don't know what to say.'

'Well, do you intend to sign?'

'Of course, do you have a pen?'

I signed the agreement and was handed the keys before she beat a hasty retreat. It was the first time my signature had recognised me.

'So, how does it feel?'

'A little overwhelming, to be honest.'

'Right then, lock up and we'll go, you've got the keys.'

'Actually, do you mind if I make my own way back? I'd just like a few minutes on my own, to take it all in, really.'

'Yeah, I understand.'

I showed her to the door, and she even stood back to allow me to open it.

'Listen, I really appreciate you coming here today. You asked a lot of stuff I would never have thought of and managed to buy me some time. I've a lot to be grateful for and I don't always show it, so thanks.'

'Bugger off, or you'll have me crying! I'll see you later.'

When she left I locked the door then opened it and locked it again. I could lock myself in or let myself out, awesome!!!

There was a pile of mail on the floor, all addressed to various people who had once lived here. One was from social security and without hesitation I opened it. Inside was a giro cheque for over one hundred pounds. I stared at the cheque containing this small fortune and was instantly seduced by its allurement, even though it belonged to somebody else. There was no battling of conscience, no conflict of morals, nothing at all going on that was going to encourage me to return it to sender, nothing going on that would allow me to, because I couldn't find a reason that was right for its own sake.

I've never been a particularly sophisticated thief, never gave it much thought really, and had certainly never been very skilled at it. I knew that for such an amount, I would be asked to provide some form of identification. I didn't have any in the recipient's name and even if I had, I would then have to forge his signature on the cheque. It was looking pretty impossible, a hundred pounds of government money beginning to slip through my fingers. I searched through the mail and found another couple of letters addressed to the same person. One was some kind of form involving a car insurance policy and it needed signing; I hoped it would be enough. At the back of my apartment was a small cluster of shops, one of which was the post office. I strode confidently up to the counter where a middle-aged woman was waiting to serve me.

'Hi, I've come to cash this, please.'

I slid the cheque under the counter with its bullet-proof glass, and stood waiting for her to disappear into the back and call the cops.

'Do you have any identification?'

It was standard practice and I didn't detect any heightened suspicion in her manner or her voice, nevertheless I was shaking a little and silently berated myself.

'I have this about my car insurance. I've just moved in and have sent my licence away for the address to be altered.'

She quickly glanced at it and then slid it back, before counting out the money. I couldn't get out of there fast enough and once outside, gulped the air like it was in seriously short supply. I needed a drink so I found the nearest pub and had several before calmly making my way back to the hostel.

* * * *

'I need a couple of signatures from you, this one here for your housing benefit and this one for the community care grant.'

Housing benefit allowed the rent to be paid by the local authority until I found employment, while the community care grant was monies awarded to people who had spent many years in institutional care and were now re-emerging back into the community and needed help with furnishings. I had no hesitation in signing both forms as I was in need of the help they provided. I didn't feel like a scrounger, I felt like a dependant, the state continuing to provide guardianship.

'I've also rung the electricity board and they're coming out tomorrow to switch your electric on. Because you've never paid for electricity before, you don't have a credit rating with them, so they are going to install a card meter and all you have to do is purchase the cards and slot them in the machine.'

It all seemed so very simple, so very straightforward and no longer someone else's responsibility. But everything was dependant on those fucking forms.

'Is there any point in organising anything until we know the result of those applications? I just don't want to get excited about something if it isn't going to happen.'

'You have a genuine offer of a tenancy and you're unemployed, therefore you fulfil the criteria for receiving housing benefit.'

I wandered from room to room, opening the windows just because I could and showing signs of excitement because no one could see or comment. It was all mine, and those who entered would have to knock first.

As soon as the meter had been installed and the guy had left, I returned to the hostel. It had been agreed that I would spend a couple of nights merely sleeping at the apartment in order to make the transition a little easier. The idea of sleeping in what effectively was a shack was, on the one hand, quite exciting, but also equally reassuring. It was like the old days, desperate for a roof and now I had one, but hadn't forgotten what it was like to search. The hostel gave me the loan of a single mattress and also boxed together some basic provisions. A couple of staff members then drove me to the apartment and helped carry the mattress up two flights of stairs and into my lounge. After they'd gone I'd been in the flat for several minutes before I realised that I hadn't locked the door. I guess doing it voluntarily was something I was going to have to get used to, but not right now. It was early evening so I still had a few hours to kill before considering settling down for the night, but I had come ill prepared, with nothing to read, nothing to write on and nothing to look at except the aging woodchip adorning the walls. The Social Club, which was directly opposite my apartment and could be viewed from the lounge window, was the central focal point of the estate and now seemed the perfect opportunity to introduce myself.

I stayed until closing time, observing and listening more than engaging vocally. I was asked the occasional question but nothing I was unable to answer or didn't want to. They were curious because they hadn't seen me before, and there's a certain amount of suspicion and paranoia attached to that, but on this occasion at least, they took it easy on me. When I returned home, I did indeed lock up and instantly recognised the different mindset when it comes to protecting your person and your property. It was the lateness of the hour that had provided the insight.

Just, as it always had.

I didn't immediately go to bed, preferring instead to sit on the floor of the hallway with my back against the wall, to enjoy what I seldom got the chance to, silence that could only be interrupted by my own thoughts taking me away, but there wasn't any. It was something I had never experienced throughout many years of institutional life, external sounds. I was totally unprepared for it because I wasn't expecting anything different, but there it was, loud music with no one to order them to turn it down with a threat of confiscation. A couple of drunken arguments could also be heard and a catfight that actually involved cats; welcome to the real world! The flat currently had no curtains and there was a streetlight outside shining its mockery into my lounge, so I checked out the bedrooms, but it was no different and there was nothing I could do.

Except remember.

That's what I did for most of the night, remembered the loneliness and the desolation and wondered if things really had changed that much, and if they had, were they any better?

In the end they were just different.

I returned to the hostel the following day but was no longer really there, now that I had my own set of keys and a mindset that wanted recognition of that. By evening I was back in the pub. I sat alone, lost in thought, trying to decide how I was going to fit in when I hadn't served the same apprenticeship. I began thinking about Marilyn. The last couple of days had helped soften my attitude towards her, and as much as I tried to fight it, I was in need of a little warmth, the kind only a woman can provide. I was just too afraid to ask outright.

I dropped a coin and dialled the number.

'Hello?'

'Hi, Marilyn, it's me.'

'Hello, I was just thinking about you.'

'Yeah, I was thinking about you. Guess what? I've got a flat.'

There was a pause and all I could hear was her breathing down the phone. It was so hypnotic I'm not sure I wanted to hear her speak.

'Would you like me to come up and spend a weekend with you?'

It was a gentle enquiry, a far cry from the intimidating demands that had sent me running for the hills only eighteen months earlier.

'There's nothing in it yet.'

'You're not getting out of it this time, Min! Every time I try and arrange for us to spend some time together you lose your nerve, I don't know what you think I'm going to do to you.'

'Yeah, alright, come up if you like.'

* * * *

That Friday as I waited at the bus station for Marilyn, there was a certain inevitability about the evening that was so far removed from both my experience and my emotional vocabulary that I didn't know how to feel about it, except abject fear. I was shaking even before she had arrived, as I stood observing the various couples gathered at the station and wondered what it took to arrive at that point of sharing and not understanding why it was so important.

She had travelled by train from Essex to Nottingham via London then taken a bus to Mansfield. I imagined she would be pretty exhausted when she arrived, but as she emerged from that bus she looked good, there was no denying it. I didn't know whether to shake her hand or hug her so in the end I took the easy route.

'Would you like me to carry some of that stuff for you?'

She had brought sleeping bags and a kettle, which I took and she held on to her own personal bag and also a plastic bag containing tea and coffee. She was clearly well prepared.

'So, are you pleased to see me, given how hard you've tried to avoid me, you bastard?'

The truth was, I didn't know because I didn't really understand what I was being asked to give away, just that you couldn't reclaim it once you had.

'Yeah, of course, I wouldn't have let you come otherwise.'

There still hadn't been any physical introduction but nothing about this meeting or its purpose came straight out of the manual. We took the bus back to my apartment and it still felt good, putting the key in the lock and showing her inside. She was the first person to step over the threshold purely at my behest.

'It's not like your place, I'm afraid. It's on a large estate and of course, it's not a house.'

'It's fine, stop apologising.'

She wandered from room to room and finally settled on the spare bedroom to lay down the sleeping bags, zipping them together to make one double bag. She then took the kettle into the kitchen.

'Listen, are you hungry after that journey?'

'Starving.'

'There's a fish and chip shop just at the back of the apartment.'

'Let me give you some money.'

'No, no my treat. Fish and chips?'

I would have felt like a complete shit taking her money. It's one thing to steal from the government but she was a single mother and she needed her money far more than I did, at least for today.

'Yeah, and if there's a shop open, can you see if you can get some milk?'

'No problem.'

When I returned she took the milk into the kitchen and filled the sink with cold water in the absence of a fridge. We then sat on the floor and ate our supper and she was indeed hungry.

'Well, we've still got the rest of the evening to kill.'

I gulped so audibly she couldn't have failed to hear me, nor could she have ignored the colour draining rapidly from my face, or the twitch that had resurfaced for the first time in several years.

'Well, I er… thought we could erm… go for a drink and I could er… show you a bit of the area so you can erm… see where I live, if you like.'

I was making an idiot of myself, talking loud enough for the whole estate to hear, and faster than I could keep up with.

'It's okay, I'm not going to pounce on you.'

'No, no, no I didn't mean it like that, I just meant…'

'Shut up, Min.'

'Yeah, I'll shut up, I talk too much.'

'I like hearing you talk, you just need to relax a bit more and just let things happen the way they're meant to.

I guess that was my problem, I wanted to know how things were meant to happen before they'd even occurred. We went to the club and then onto a couple of local pubs as I was in no hurry to return. She didn't seem entirely comfortable and whilst I didn't want to add to her discomfort, I didn't want to increase mine either.

'Can we go back soon? We can't stay here all night and we'll still have to go back at some point.'

I'd been rumbled but then my efforts hadn't been particularly sophisticated, I was very much a novice and it had clearly shown. Back at the apartment we had a hot drink and then it was time for bed. There was no escape now. She disappeared into the bathroom and I wandered into the bedroom, and stood staring out of the window, wondering how many similar scenarios were being played out across the estate. When she emerged from the bathroom, she was wearing a nightdress and carrying her clothes, which she put on the floor, before climbing inside the bags. She once told me she didn't own any nightclothes, but the fact that she did made it more interesting, as I was left to wonder what was underneath, without having it immediately exposed. I took my turn in the bathroom and stared into the mirror, a gift from my predecessor. As a kid, I used to love watching the television show, 'Some Mothers do 'Ave 'Em', featuring the hapless Frank Spencer. Towards the end of the series he and his wife, Betty, had a child. I was hoping this would reassure me.

'Come on, Min, if Frank Spencer can do it, so can you.'

I stripped down to my underwear, took my place in the bags and just lay there, rigid with fear. I didn't understand why I was so terrified of something as old as time, or why it was more intense than that which normally preceded a beating. Ultimately, my skills lay in the opposite direction and would be difficult to unravel. I had become expert in the art of keeping people at a safe distance, not inviting them in. Mostly I hadn't even shared a thought.

We lay there in silence for several minutes, the anticipation almost crippling me and then she made a move. I responded, uncertainly at first, but then instinct took over and several minutes later I was no longer a cardboard cut out. Unsurprisingly, it wasn't perfect but nor was it the absolute disaster I had anticipated. It wasn't passionate either, there was no kissing and no real intimacy besides the obvious, it was just animal instinct, just sex. I played my own part in it, I still wasn't able to just let go because I was unsure how much I was willing to give or how much I wanted in return, but sex for its own sake didn't really turn me on.

The following morning, we went for a meal, then I suggested we went to the cinema. As we stood outside and checked out the listings, I couldn't help but smile as I pointed up at the board, 'The Morning After The Night Before', starring Jane

Fonda and Jeff Bridges.

'It's got to be that one.'

The following day Marilyn had to return home. We stood in the kitchen, having a coffee when there was a loud knocking at the door. We both froze and looked at each other.

'Don't answer it.'

The knocking continued but we ignored it. I had no idea who it could be and it scared me. The flap of the letterbox opened and someone called out.

'Michael, open the door!'

'Fucking hell, it's me Dad! Just ignore him, he doesn't know I'm here.'

I was speaking in whispers, hiding behind my own door, trapped in my own apartment without privacy or the right to refuse.

'Michael! Come on, son, I know you're in there! Open up.'

'He's not going to go away until I answer. Stay in here a minute.'

I walked towards the door, safe in the knowledge he was about to enter my castle, and he could be asked to leave at any time.

'So, how did you find this place?'

'The people at the hostel told me. I popped in to see if yer wanted to come over for Sunday's dinner.'

'You'd better come in, there's someone I think you should meet.'

I walked him towards the kitchen where Marilyn was waiting. I would have liked her to have met him under different circumstances, would have liked her to have been better prepared.

'Dad this is Marilyn. Marilyn, my old man.'

'Pleased to meet you, pet.'

He held out his hand for her to shake. It wasn't often I had the chance to ambush him and rarely had I seen him looking so ill at ease. She, on the other hand, appeared surprisingly relaxed and calmly shook his hand.

'Pleased to meet you, Mr Cooper.'

'Are you the lass he's been writing to, like?'

'Yes, I am.'

'Aye, well, that's nice, it's probably what he needs.'

'Don't worry, Mr Cooper, I'll take care of him.'

'Right then, son, you ought to come over and tell yer mam.'

'I'm going to the train station with Marilyn, I'll catch the bus and come over later.'

I walked him to the door and saw him out, the invasion over, but not the inquisition or the lust for details.

'If yer like, I'll tell yer mam, then you can fill her in later.'

'Yeah, alright.'

After he left I explained to Marilyn that it was a northern working class thing, you weren't allowed a life separate from the family, except I'd already been living such a life and now resented having to share it out of duty rather than choice.

The scene at the station was reminiscent of the movies, with Marilyn hanging out of the window and me jogging down the platform. Eventually the train had more speed than I did, and I stopped and watched it as it disappeared down the tracks. I stared after it awhile, not really knowing how I felt or even how I wanted to feel. All that had happened over the last couple of days now seemed like it hadn't happened to me, like I wasn't really there. She knew everything about my past deeds, and not having to explain any of that was a huge comfort. There were no other circumstances where I could meet someone and still be free of that.

That was the draw.

That's what was on my mind as I took the bus to my parents' house, I knew I'd see her again because if I didn't, it might be a while before I lay next to a woman again, and then I would have probably lied. Because of the manner of our coming together and the strangeness of it all, the unquestioned acceptance that we would sleep together, that it was a given, regardless of any consideration that might have prevented it, I didn't even know if I fancied her or if it mattered. I had lost my virginity but still hadn't experienced the thrill of the chase. I had taken what was on offer, because I was grateful.

I entered my parents' house, feeling a little defensive. I was facing another example of my choices being questioned because they'd never gotten used to the idea that for the most part, I'd never had to ask.

'I take it Dad's told you, then?'

'Yes, he has but I don't understand why you had to lie.'

'This isn't the Victorian age, I don't need your permission.'

The lie she spoke of was me telling them I was staying at the hostel that week end rather than spend it with them. The conversation followed a similar vein, with question after question until my father asked if I would walk to the shop with him. Once outside the house, he slapped me so hard on the back I almost fell over. For years he had suspected I was gay and now he was beside himself with relief: I had finally made it to manhood with the help of a woman.

I hopped on yet another bus and made my way back to Mansfield and the hostel. Walking through those doors helped to put everything back into perspective; whatever happens still brings you back, contaminating everything that didn't belong there.

The following week I received my community care grant, a paltry fifty-nine pounds. I was staggered, but my key worker remained resolute.

'We'll appeal it, there's absolutely no way this is all you're entitled to.'

A couple of weeks later I won my appeal and received a cheque for a little over three hundred and fifty pounds. This bought carpet for the lounge and small bedroom, a second-hand cooker and the usual bits and pieces. My mother donated a single bed, my sister a fridge while my key worker kindly bought me a pair of curtains for my lounge as a house-warming present, and also managed to acquire, free of charge, a sofa, a wardrobe and a small coffee table from a charity organisation. But that wasn't all; her partner renovated old houses then rented them out. He had recently had to evict someone and so various cabinets also found their way to my place. Whilst at the hostel, I had purchased a small electronic typewriter and had begun writing again, encouraged by the feedback from my earlier efforts. The hostel had a quiet room with a desk, which I regularly used and she managed to persuade the hostel management to allow me to have the desk.

Firstly, the carpet needed fitting and my budget didn't stretch to that so my key worker and a student worker came and fitted it for me. All I could do was watch and make tea. Whilst there, the cooker arrived and was fitted then shortly afterwards everything else.

I now had a home, a place to make my own decisions in my own time, a place where everything was mine and not just borrowed.

'Good luck, Min, I know you can make it.'

In many ways I already had, by standing the right side of the door as they were leaving.

CHAPTER THIRTY-TWO

I had spent most of my life sleeping in beds that belonged to someone else and when I finally got the chance to sleep in my own it felt no different; I wanted it to mean more but it didn't. I never considered that reality could be so average. It had never been my experience, either side of the extremes.

There was, however, one notable difference in my living arrangements. When I rose in the morning and walked through to the lounge, there was only me, and not the noise and chaos that had been my regular introduction to the day. It was unbelievably uplifting just to have time and I made the most of it as I sat on my sofa, nursing a cup of coffee in one hand and a cigarette in the other. I was in no hurry to do anything else and that was the pattern of the first couple of weeks, regularly being offered reminders and sometimes being swamped by choice, particularly in the supermarket where I would take an age to do my shopping. I wasn't a particularly great cook but I could prepare a meal, though with such a vast array of goods and not always knowing what to do with them, it would sometimes confuse. Money was pretty tight but I managed. Franc had sent me a little to celebrate the move, which I used to pay for the telephone.

The social worker visited once a week and I offered him coffee and biscuits, keen to treat him as a guest in my home rather than an imposition on my time, or an obligation that was his entry. I spent my days mostly walking, writing and reading, in no particular order. I was resistant to formalised structure, didn't want to know what was coming next unless it was something I needed to hide from.

What came next was Marilyn. Her father had sadly died and left her some money, some of which she used to buy a car. She wanted to bring her children and spend the weekend at my apartment, thinking it would be a good idea for me to meet them on my own patch, that I would be more relaxed about it. I wasn't entirely sure this was a good idea, bringing children into an alien environment to meet someone who was a stranger to them. There was also the question of entertaining them and keeping them occupied. I lived on the second floor, so allowing them to play outside unsupervised was out of the question, which meant whatever they did, I would have to be with them and I wasn't sure that I was up for it, or even ready. But if I refused she would have viewed it as a personal attack on both her and her children so I agreed, lamely, for her and the children to spend the weekend at my place, and she drove the entire journey from Essex to Mansfield.

When they arrived, she wanted to go out for a meal, so I arranged for my sister to look after the children for a couple of hours. There was an Italian place that I had walked past many times but never stepped inside. We went for a drink then decided to give it a try, it was small and intimate and thankfully not too busy. Between mouthfuls of food, we talked, and I explained that there wasn't much for the children to do but there was a park nearby so we could take them there, weather permitting. I wanted to involve them as part of the conversation because I had so far only had a chance to say a quick hello, and they had looked terrified, which bothered me, but she was more intent on discussing what was on her mind.

'What do you want from this relationship, Mini? Because sometimes I think you're only willing to see me at your convenience.'

'I don't think that's fair! I mean, this weekend wasn't necessarily convenient but you're here.'

'Did you have other plans?'

'Not really, I just wasn't sure it was such a good idea to have the kids come up here for our first meeting. I mean, they've been stuck in a car for four hours, a quick hello, then packed off to my sister's for another couple of hours.'

'Don't presume to know what's best for my children! You don't even know them, yet you're acting like they're your responsibility.'

'If they're going to stay at my place from time to time, then obviously I do have a responsibility whilst they're there.'

'Oh, so you do acknowledge we have a future, then?'

I had been expecting some decent food, a glass or two and maybe a few laughs, not this level of intensity in what effectively was only our second outing. I felt like I was being bullied into making declarations at a time when I was still getting used to living with me.

'Listen, Marilyn, there's no point getting ahead of ourselves when really we've only just met, we're still finding our way.'

'Well, we'd have found it a lot quicker if you hadn't been so cowardly.'

I was bored and tired of a conversation that was completely at odds with my hopes for the evening. It was the first time I'd shared a restaurant table with someone I'd been intimate with, and I wanted the ambience to reflect that.

'Anyway, I want to go dancing.'

I was struggling to keep up with her and almost began to panic every time she went to say something. The first incarnation was difficult enough but the second was possibly limitless.

'Surely there's somewhere in this town where we can dance?'

'Well, yes, but I don't really dance. Anyway, I told my sister we would only be a couple of hours.'

'Oh, she won't mind, ring her.'

She seemed trapped between two worlds, hers and the one she was forced to inhabit, but what fucking world did I belong to, in agreeing to her demands and in the process betraying my own character?

'Hi, it's me again. Listen, Marilyn wants to go dancing, so do you mind if we pick the boys up in another hour or so? I really don't want to put on you, so if it's a problem, just say so and I'll come right over.'

I was urging her, silently imploring her to find a problem, real or imagined, hoping she would read between the lines, feed off my intonation and deliver the line I so desperately wanted to take back to the table, and go home.

'No, it's fine, the lads are asleep anyway, so just come by when you're ready.'

'Okay, well, we won't keep you up too late, we'll come by in about an hour... and thanks.'

The club was only a short walk from the restaurant. I was wearing a pair of white tennis shoes and a smart pair of white trousers. I thought I looked pretty cool, even a little groovy as I walked towards the entrance of the club with Marilyn alongside. I thought it would be as straightforward as walking into a pub, but clearly the doorman had different ideas as he put his hand across my chest and blocked my path.

'Sorry, mate, no trainers.'

I turned and walked away, silently and without argument, but at least I was still walking.

'Mini, what are you doing?'

'What do you mean, what am I doing? He says we can't go in.'

'Oh, and you're just going to stand there and let him talk to you like you're nothing, are you?'

'Marilyn are you fucking blind? He's about six foot four and somewhere in the region of eighteen stone of solid muscle, if he says we're not going in then that's good enough for me.'

'So that programme was all lies then?'

'I think we should get a cab and pick up your children, then tomorrow you should all go home.'

I walked with her to the taxi rank, she was still seriously pissed with me believing I had bottled it, but I wanted no part in any false reality. I walked away from her and yes, partly because I was afraid, I didn't want to suffer a beating to prove I was her man. I stared into shop windows trying to gather my thoughts and my composure, I was out of my depth in every imaginable way.

When I turned around she had gone.

This was seriously fucked up with all manner of responsibilities and repercussions raging through my mind, and my sister was still waiting.

I didn't know what had prompted her to disappear I just knew that if she didn't return I would have to take a decision that I never imagined I would have to, handing her children over to the police so that they could contact social services. I decided not to wait for a taxi and would walk the couple of miles or so to my sister's house, she had been absolutely brilliant in helping to facilitate this night out and I didn't want to burden her anymore.

I was almost there when a taxi suddenly came to a halt and a door flew open and there was Marilyn.

'Mini, what are you doing, why did you run off like that?'

I couldn't believe I was hearing this, nor was I sure I wanted to get into the taxi and travel with her.

'You have got to be fucking shitting me!'

I climbed in but was so consumed by anger that I could hardly speak and so I didn't, I just stared straight ahead.

'Why did you leave me on my own when you knew I had to pick up my children?'

'We'll talk about this when we get back. I'm not discussing it in the back of a cab.'

When we pulled up outside my sister's house I was relieved to be getting out, if only for a moment's respite. I raced down the garden path and into the house, breathing heavily.

'Are you alright, you look stressed?'

'I can't talk about it now, there's a cab waiting outside.'

We gathered up the boys who were sleeping, and headed for the cab, my sister carried the youngest, then handed him over to Marilyn, who thankfully had remained in her seat. I helped the oldest to make his own way and showed him the back seat whilst I climbed in the front.

'Listen, thanks for everything, I'll call you tomorrow.'

'Okay.'

She had concern written all over her face and I wished I could have told her but it just had to wait. When we arrived at my apartment, Marilyn got the boys bedded down whilst I made a coffee. When she came through her demeanour had changed once again, she seemed charged, like she was looking for a fight, but I was looking for some answers to this growing insanity, without wanting to feed it further.

'So, are you going to tell me what all that was about?'

'I was hoping you could tell me, Marilyn, because I've never experienced anything like that before. First, you try and get me beaten to a pulp by a bouncer, then you were rude to the people queuing for taxis, what was that about?'

'Oh, I don't need to listen to this, I'm going.'

'No, you do need to listen because tonight was totally fucked up and whatever the game was you were trying to play, I won't have it! I don't need all these complications.'

'Oh, I'm a complication now, am I?'

'You're not even listening!'

She turned and went into the bedroom where the boys were sleeping, gathered up her things and then woke the boys.

'Marilyn, you can't leave tonight, you've had too much to drink.'

'Don't tell me what I can or can't do!'

'It's too dangerous, especially with two kids in the back.'

'Oh, so now you're accusing me of being a bad mother?'

'Oh, what's the point?'

I returned to the kitchen and continued making coffee. I could hear the youngest boy crying and wondered what they both must be thinking and how confusing it must have been for them. There was no question of me wanting her to go, but not under those circumstances, not when the risks had shot through the scales.

'I'd like my kettle back, if you don't mind?'

I didn't hear her appear in the doorway of the kitchen and her voice made me jump. She had left the kettle on her previous visit and said I could keep it. Rather childishly, I refused to hand it over. I guess I must have been trying, in a rather primitive and unsophisticated manner, to wrestle back some semblance of control, having had a tornado sweep me off my feet and dump me flat on my arse. She made a grab for the kettle at the same time as I did, and so began a tug of war with boiling water slopping everywhere.

'Marilyn, let go of the fucking kettle, someone's going to get scalded!'

'You let go, then.'

Neither of us did and then I slapped her. She stepped back, looking thoroughly shocked, and so was I, as I stared at the offending limb.

'Why are you doing this, Mini?'

'I'm sorry, I panicked I just wanted you to let go!'

When it would have been just as easy for me to.

She carried on organising herself and the boys and I met them in the hallway.

'Marilyn, this is madness!'

'Well, you're the one who's been sectioned, not me.'

She pushed past me, opened the door and was gone, followed by her brood.

I returned to the kitchen. I stared at the kettle and in a complete turnaround to before, decided I didn't want the fucking thing! I ran out of the apartment, towards the car park and got there just as she was pulling out. I hurled the kettle as hard as I could and bits of plastic flew off in all directions as it bounced off the concrete.

'Have the fucking kettle!'

Something had to give, better that it be the kettle.

I returned to my apartment, locked and bolted the door, the first time I had done both, sat on the sofa and buried my head in my hands. I was breathless, not because I was out of shape, but because I was out of touch. I had been involved in a situation where I had no strategy for dealing with it, because I had been taken completely by surprise by its very existence, not being aware that such behaviour wasn't just confined to an institution. But I couldn't play by the institution's rules anymore and that's what concerned me, the fear that I might have been left bankrupt.

CHAPTER THIRTY-THREE

I spent the next couple of days walking around in a daze, unable to concentrate and unable to understand. My mind began to punish me for my complacency and lack of instinct, which had never before failed me. I had surrendered to the availability of sex without the usual consideration and caution; I had given myself away cheaply when everything I was should have prevented it.

But it only worked on a clear day.

I was lying on my bed one afternoon, listening to some music when the telephone rang.

'Hello?'

'It's me, Marilyn.'

'What do you want?'

'I just want to talk to you. I've missed you.'

'Yeah, and you were lucky you missed everything on the way home that night.'

'Why are you so angry with me when I've done nothing but care for you?'

'What fucking planet are you on?'

I slammed the phone down so hard I missed the cradle and grazed the back of my hand. I replaced the phone, ignoring the temptation to pull it from the socket and hurl it across the lounge. Just as I walked back into the bedroom it rang again. I could have easily ignored it, believing it to be her, but I didn't because she couldn't damage me over the phone and it was easier to be assertive.

'Okay, you've made your point.'

'There is no point, Marilyn, that is the fucking point!'

'You bastard, you just fucking used me!'

I hung up again because what I wanted hadn't yet wanted me, I was no longer grateful, except for the fact she was many miles away. What I wanted, was peace and someone who needed it more than chaos. When the phone rang yet again my patience was threadbare. I snatched it from its cradle and couldn't have cared less how I was perceived, but sadly I gave no consideration to her feelings, she was still entitled to that.

'Listen to me, you raving lunatic, if you don't stop calling me I will go to the police and report you for harassment, now fuck off!'

'I'm not going to call you again, Mini, I'm going to see my father.'

She spoke calmly, with a gentle inflection and then she put down the phone. I stared at my own receiver, thinking how strange the message had been, but otherwise was unconcerned. Until about thirty seconds had elapsed and it suddenly hit me that her father was dead and she could only meet him on the other side.

'Oh my God, oh my fucking God!'

I fled my apartment, went down to the hostel and spoke to the staff there. Unfortunately I had to explain the details of my relationship at a stage when I would rather have not. The member of staff concerned was someone I'd had a number of confrontations with and quite honestly I didn't particularly like. Her response, however, was quite astonishing, both in the way she swung into action yet still had time to offer me some emotional support, seeing how distressed I was and how impotent I felt. She firstly rang the Essex police who agreed to call back should they have any relevant information to report. Whilst we waited she praised the speed with which I had sought help and generally massaged my ego a little. Several minutes later the police did indeed ring back to report that there had been an incident at Marilyn's house involving both police and paramedics. She had attempted to cut her wrists and had been transferred to a hospital in Colchester, for treatment and assessment under the Mental Health Act.

'I've got the doctor on the line, he wants to talk to you.'

'I'm the doctor treating your girlfriend and we have managed to stabilise her.'

'Well, actually doctor, she's not really my girlfriend any more. I tried to explain that to her today and she's gone and done this.'

'I'm sorry, my information was that you're both really close and that it was the death of her father that resulted in these actions.'

'What's happened to her children?'

'They're fine, they're being looked after by a close friend.'

'Look, doctor, tell her I'll call her tomorrow but I'm not promising anything, that's the best I can do.'

The following afternoon, I rang the hospital and was put through to Marilyn's ward. I was nervous as I waited for her to come to the phone, I didn't want to add to her problems, but I didn't want them to be mine, either.

'Hello.'

'Marilyn, it's me.'

'Oh hi, Min, thanks for ringing.'

'It's okay.'

'They're letting me out today, so when are you coming down to see me?'

She was bright and breezy, leaving no clue to the events that had occurred only twenty-four hours earlier. It was astonishing and I was struggling to keep up, as I had my own position to defend.

'Well, I just rang to see how you were, really.'

'So, you're not coming down, you're just going to desert me?'

'Well, I wouldn't put it like that, exactly.'

She started crying, violent sobs that burned my ears and I had to move the receiver away from me but still she wailed so loudly I couldn't decipher what she was saying. She was fucking angry and it was aimed entirely at me. I hung up and pulled the phone from its socket.

A couple of days later, I returned the phone to its socket and it rang constantly but she had changed tack, warm and loving, and I just didn't know which way to turn, didn't know which was the real personality and which was the fake. Eventually, worn down by indecision and beaten into submission, I acquiesced and took the coach to see her. There was also another reason. I wanted to see those wounds. They were superficial, just as I had suspected, now it was my turn to be angry and less than twenty-four hours later I was back on the coach. It was exhausting and I couldn't understand why I just didn't cut my losses and consign her to history. Perhaps it was just too close to home and too difficult to reject her out of hand.

Making me no different to those who had found it so easy.

* * * *

So I continued to see her on and off. Her father had left her a house on the North Circular road in London, which she had difficulty selling, but when she eventually sold it at a knock down price, she used the money to by a place in Mansfield. She then offered to take me on holiday to Menorca with her boys. I sorted out a passport and she took care of the rest but a couple of days before we were due to fly I backed out. Unsurprisingly, she was pretty angry with me, accusing me of being a coward and a worthless piece of shit that should have stayed locked up. There had been times when I wished I had. I was beginning to feel increasingly small in a world that often felt too big for me.

I was terrified of travelling abroad to a country whose language I didn't speak or understand and whose customs I was ignorant of. If things kicked off, I would have been stranded without having the means to return home. I didn't expect, nor did I receive, a postcard from her but a couple of days after her return she invited me out for a drink. We met at a pub near her home which we had often frequented as it had a children's room full of toys and games. Her house was only a fifteen-minute walk from my place and although she encouraged me to spend time there, I often felt like a lodger because she had paid cash for it and every time we rowed she would order me to leave and as she owned the property outright, I had no rights. Just as well I didn't give up my flat.

'I don't know where this relationship is going any more, I mean, we don't even live together.'

'You keep asking me to leave, Marilyn, I don't know where I am with you half the time.'

'I don't think you're much of a man, I think you're cowardly.'

'Would you rather I be the kind of man your ex-husband was?'

'Don't bring him into it, he's twice the man you are!'

'So why aren't you with him?'

And that's how it went, until eventually she threatened to invite him over to sort me out. I just laughed. We had both had quite a bit to drink and I was feeling a lack of inhibition, so when she invited me to stay the night, I naturally agreed. As soon as we returned and the boys had gone to bed, she rang her sister-in-law and began mocking me, calling me pathetic and once again reiterating her threat to have her ex come over and rearrange my face. I had had enough, I marched towards her, intent on grabbing hold of the phone and putting an end to it.

'Give me that fucking phone!'

We both grappled with it, yet she was still intent on rubbing my nose in it whilst extracting as much drama as she could.

'Can you hear him, hear what he's doing, the big shot attacking a woman?'

During the struggle I stumbled and fell backwards onto one of the stereo speakers, damaging it. I got back on my feet, grabbed the phone and hurled it across the room, watching as it smashed against the wall.

'Don't take the fucking piss!'

She stood, staring at me for a few seconds, while I waited for her reply. Instead she ran out of the house, screaming like a lunatic. I sat down and lit a cigarette, staring at the broken phone. It was seriously fucked up, I had lost control and put myself at risk, and I was still angry when the police walked in.

'Michael, isn't it?'

'I guess it is now.'

He asked what happened and so I told him but I could see where his sympathies lay, which angered me even more.

'Your partner wants you to leave.'

'What about what I want, don't I get a say in any of this?'

'Not really, this is her house if she wants you to leave, then you have to.'

'Oh, right, so when people lock you up and treat you like shit, you have rights, but now I don't?'

'Look, I don't want to arrest you, I'll even give you a lift back to your flat. I can't be fairer than that.'

He spoke calmly with no hint of the threat normally associated with a police officer's questions but it was entirely lost on me. I had sunk so low I had lost the ability to reason.

'I'm not going anywhere. I'm fed up of being pushed around.'

'Michael, did you break that telephone?'

'Yes, I did.'

'Michael Cooper, I'm arresting you on suspicion of causing criminal damage.'

He then proceeded to read me my rights when up until then I'd had none. He took me to a waiting car then onto the police station where I was charged and thrown in a cell for the night. Okay, okay, so it was fucking stupid, but it was familiar and I needed that right then to give me something to cling to that couldn't be denied. When the door of the cell slammed shut, a level of calm returned to me, and the uncertainty had gone.

The following morning I was offered breakfast but declined. I was then called out of the cell to speak to my solicitor. I gave him the full details and he made a note of it.

'Will I go to jail?'

'I shouldn't think so, you'll probably get a fine and be ordered to pay for the damage. Just go in there, give your name but don't offer a plea, we'll sort that out later. I'm sure you'll be fine.'

I wasn't particularly keen on the idea of prison so I was comforted by his reassurance. I did what he instructed so the case was adjourned and I was released on conditional bail, the main condition being that I didn't contact Marilyn, either by telephone, by letter or in person. I asked the lawyer if that meant she couldn't contact me and he said it didn't, as she hadn't been arrested or charged. Even so, I figured the scales of justice were on tilt, yet again.

CHAPTER THIRTY-FOUR

On my return home I paced back and forth for hours on end, indulging my feelings of anger, watching it build until it couldn't be contained any longer. I felt like a child again, forced to take responsibility for someone else's shit because I refused to tolerate it. Whilst I fully accepted my culpability for the damage that was caused, I felt hers in the events leading up to it hadn't been recognised at all, and I rather stupidly, not to mention arrogantly, believed I was entitled to an explanation.

But I didn't get one.

She was out or refusing to answer; either way, I was left standing on the porch and eventually decided to go back home. I turned to go just as a police car pulled up and two cops climbed out and came walking towards me. One of them had once worked at the hostel and would often call in for a coffee and a chat.

'What are you doing, Mick? You know the terms of your bail.'

'I just wanted to talk.'

'Well, you can't and I don't know why you're even bothering. Go home and forget about her.'

I struggled with the notion that if she was considered such bad news, why was I the one being exiled?

I trudged home feeling lost. The last few days had taught me how little I could shape the things I didn't accept by ordinary means, and there seemed to be no justice, only law, which was entirely discriminatory. I felt like a burden on time because I had begun to walk through it with my eyes closed, trying to ignore it and trying to opt out.

A few weeks before my arrest, I had applied to the mental health review tribunal for an absolute discharge. Should I be successful, all the restrictions I was currently living under would be revoked. Due to changes in the Mental Health Act the Home Secretary could no longer veto the panel's decision, he simply had to accept it. We thought we had a strong case, particularly as I was now living independently within the community and there had been no issues surrounding risk. Nevertheless, my solicitor advised me to agree to voluntary supervision, as this would strengthen my case even more. Quite naturally I had agreed, but to my surprise, when the time came, the panel didn't seem at all interested in examining any possible risk indicators, they just wanted to discuss my relationship with Marilyn. Even when I explained that the relationship was over, they still wouldn't let go of it, wanting to know in detail what strategies I had put in place should she try to contact me.

'So, should she make a nuisance of herself, I would have no hesitation in contacting the police, and if she began to harass me then, with the help of my solicitor, I would launch the necessary legal action.'

After two hours I was granted an absolute discharge.

I walked out of there expecting a fanfare but there wasn't one, just an ordinary day that I now belonged to. My social worker dropped me off at the bus station and I caught a bus back to Mansfield. On the way back, the full reality suddenly hit me: I really was on my own now, something I had often dreamed of but never experienced. I would have to learn all over again and I wasn't sure I had the enthusiasm for it.

I began to notice things more acutely and their impact was more profound than it had been when I had an army behind me, because I had been stripped of the protective layer that sometimes offered a rescue plan. Conceit had made me hasty and in turn more vulnerable, and I began to retreat more and more into myself, because I knew how to live there, knew the landscape better than anywhere else.

A group of youths would often hang around the shops, yelling abuse at me as I went by. I didn't know them, nor did I understand why I had become a figure of fun, except perhaps for the way I dressed, which occasionally was quite flamboyant. Sometimes they would stand in front of me, pulling at my clothes and generally trying to intimidate. Whilst I was nervous, I would keep walking in the direction that I was going. I had never known how to deal with anyone physically. I had no weapons except silence and no feeling other than utter contempt, but over the course of several weeks all the old feelings of hopelessness I'd suffered through my incarcerations, resurfaced. I was dealing with threats, perceived or otherwise, that I couldn't always identify. I was living in fear without having a single strategy to change it, everything I knew had been left behind. I was socially illiterate.

One afternoon I went into town for a drink. On my return to the estate, I popped into the club for another one. The ringleader of that particular group was playing pool. He noticed me but said nothing. I went up to the bar, ordered a pint and then put my name on the board for a game. I was next up and if he won, I would be playing him. I sat there, drinking my beer and willing him to win. Adrenalin surged through my body as such a prospect was looking more and more likely. I didn't just want to beat him, I wanted to humiliate him and I was already beginning to set my focus. Several minutes later, I had completely destroyed him, without even breaking sweat. I just wished his friends could have witnessed it. Through a combination of sheer elation and the alcohol loosening my tongue, I became reckless.

'You might think you're a big man when you hang around shouting abuse at people in a gang, but on this table I'm the fucking man!'

'Do you think so?'

He grabbed hold of me and marched me out of the club as I struggled to hold onto my bladder. Once round the back, he threw me against a wall and head-butted me. I thought I had been launched into orbit as I slid down the wall and slumped to the ground. Blood was pouring profusely from my nose and formed a large red patch down the front of my white sweater. I didn't know if my nose had been broken, I just knew I wasn't in any hurry to get up.

I couldn't stay there forever, nor would I have wanted to, as it would only act as an encouragement to others, so feeling groggy and disorientated I got to my feet and went home. Once there I cleaned myself up, trashed the sweater then went to bed where I remained for several days, when I returned to court. The prospect of prison no longer troubled me.

I registered my arrival and sat in the waiting area to be called into the courtroom. I'd only been there a few minutes when my solicitor appeared.

'I've just been handed this list for damages. As well as the speaker and the phone, there's a broken kitchen window and smashed crockery.'

'Hang on, the argument happened in the lounge, we never went into the kitchen and I certainly didn't break any windows or smash any crockery. If I plead guilty then I'm admitting everything and I'm not willing to do it. I'll hold my hands up to the damage I caused, but nothing else.'

'I'll have another word with him and get back to you.'

Those were the good old days of being able to smoke in public buildings, so I promptly lit up and observed my fellow deviants as they tried to outdo one another with tales of exploits, with one significant omission: they got caught.

'Okay, I've had a quick word and told him you were willing to plead to the phone and the speaker and he's going to drop the claim for damages.'

I went into the courtroom and pleaded guilty. The prosecution were good to their word and withdrew the claim for damages, claiming it was disputed and impossible to prove. Once again it was adjourned, this time for a fucking social work report! After my beating, I rang both the social worker and the doctor for support and was told the health authority wouldn't afford them the time to see me, as I was no longer officially on the books. It also turned out that Marilyn had locked herself out of the house several days before my arrest and had gotten her neighbour to break in by smashing the kitchen window; as for the crockery, I can only speculate but it wasn't me.

* * * *

After the hearing I began to shun daylight hours. I was living in a world I didn't recognise, a world that continued to threaten. The beating had traumatised me and I felt more alone than I ever had previously. I would write through the night and sleep through the day; often I would wander across fields and through the streets without encountering a single soul. I was creating a world within a world and I felt out of place in both. I guess ultimately I was searching for a place I could safely inhabit rather than the one bereft of imagination. For whilst the blood might drip from my pores, the ink dried quicker on the page, it was comfort for a while a different expression, but in the end a child with a pen in his hand needed to be an adult with a sword.

One evening whilst working, I picked up my typewriter and hurled it to the floor, angry and frustrated that my words caused more pain than joy. They had become secrets, sharing my confinement and like me, only coming out in the dead of night. I stared at the bookcase, the television and the furniture and I no longer had a relationship with any of it. I tipped over the bookcase, violently ripping pages out of some of the books. I was on a roll and nothing could stop me in my quest to destroy the illusion of sanctuary and put an end to life in a bunker. The television went crashing to the floor and I was really getting into the swing of it, even allowing myself the odd shriek of laughter.

Then the phone rang.

'What?'

'Mini, it's me, Marilyn.'

'Well, what the fuck do you want?'

'I just want to talk to you.'

'Well, I don't want to talk to you, so fuck off!'

I slammed down the phone, pulled it out of the socket but rather than hurl it across the room, I merely dropped it on top of the debris that was piling up. I then went into the kitchen, took the chip pan and poured the contents over the lot. This was followed by a bottle of tomato ketchup then finally some cornflakes, placed around the edge to form a perimeter wall. Satisfied with my work, I took a knife from the kitchen and began to hack away at my clothes whilst still wearing them, and by the end I was well and truly shipwrecked. How fucking symbolic! I wrote my last will and testament, leaving my entire estate to Franc Roddam, although I doubt he would have liked that little lot delivered straight to his door. Finally, I went to bed to plan a spectacular exit.

I was woken around seven-thirty the following morning by a loud banging on my front door. I got out of bed and walked into the hallway to look through the peephole, two cops were stood outside.

'What do you want?'

'Just open the fucking door!'

'Michael Cooper?'

One of the first things I did after moving into my flat was to go and see a solicitor and change my name back.

'Yes.'

'You're under arrest, get your clothes on.'

'Under arrest for what?'

'Breaking your bail conditions.'

'She rang me.'

'You shouldn't have answered.'

'Well how the fuck do I know who it is unless I answer?'

'Just put your fucking clothes on, you're coming with us!'

I went into the bedroom followed by one of the cops. I put on a pair of shredded jeans with a sweater to match.

'You can't wear those, put something else on.'

'You're going to throw me in a cell yet are concerned as to how I dress! How strange you are.'

He pushed me hard against the wall whilst the other one walked off into the lounge. I could almost hear the clock.

'Steve, come and check this fucker out!'

'Don't fuck me about, put some different clothes on!'

As soon as his back was turned and he'd left the room, I grabbed the last will and testament and stuffed it under the mattress.

'What the fuck happened?'

'I was bored.'

'You were bored so you trashed your flat, are you some kind of nut job?'

'We're all nut jobs, we just don't all wear a uniform to confirm it.'

I was past the point of choosing what I said with consideration, preferring whatever came to mind with mischief. He took out his cuffs and walked towards me. I offered my wrists without being invited and he slapped them on, making sure that the teeth cut into my skin. Then he grabbed me forcibly by the arm and marched me towards the door.

'Where are the keys?'

'In the pocket of the jeans you were so offended by.'

The other cop disappeared and returned a few seconds later with the keys. Outside on the landing, he locked up and I was escorted to the car, which was parked on the grass, adjacent to the shops. I was on public display as people came and went, fetching their newspapers and their milk, whilst others passed by on their way to work. I was driven to the station, processed and thrown into a cell. Everything suddenly went quiet, thoughts came and went but nothing seemed to stick, I was watching myself pass by.

I was kept in the cell for the best part of the day, then just before the close of play I was escorted up to the court and stood in the dock with the bullet-proof glass, all for breaching bail. The prosecution stood up and outlined his case, pointing out the state that both my clothes and my apartment were in, and suggested I needed remanding in custody for my own protection.

When he had finished, my solicitor came over to the dock to speak to me and I leaned forward to hear him through the holes.

'Do you want to go to prison?'

It seemed a strange question, stranger still that it caused a moment's hesitation. I didn't know what I wanted because I didn't know what I could have. Eventually I just shook my head.

'This is a case in which the girlfriend of the accused rang him and as soon as he knew it was her he hung up. Now with regards to his flat, I have spoken to the original arresting officer who is willing to make a statement saying Mr Cooper needs help, not punishment.'

I had never known such a robust defence before and in light of recent events, I felt reassured by it.

'To that end I have contacted the Millbrook Clinic and they said he had to be referred by his GP who is currently on leave. I also contacted the police surgeon who refused to come and see him as he hadn't been charged with a serious offence, nevertheless a spell in custody would in my view be harmful in the extreme.'

My solicitor sat down and the magistrates huddled together but I had no idea what they were saying, then the chairman spoke.

'Stand up please, Mr Cooper.'

I stood up with sweaty palms and a heart beating faster by the second but noted he had been polite.

'We agree with your solicitor and will continue to bail you but you must adhere to the terms. You do understand the terms, I take it?'

'Yes, I do.'

'Good. Now may I suggest that if you get into emotional difficulties you might like to consider contacting the Samaritans?'

I didn't know whether to laugh or cry and a quick glance around the courtroom showed I wasn't the only one. In the end I simply muttered.

'Yes, I will.'

I even managed it without laughing.

CHAPTER THIRTY-FIVE

'Fuckin' hell, Michael, you never do anything by halves! What were you thinking of or shouldn't I ask?'

My eldest sister had come over after work to help me salvage the wreckage and hopefully tidy up the mess. I don't think she realised the size of the task until she saw what remained of all I had disowned. It was embarrassing, allowing her a sneak preview into my frailties, knowing it would be reported back to the rest of the family and my aura of strength and 'never say die' doggedness would be pricked. I'd never been allowed human weakness but it was seductive, letting go of all that control and trusting to luck.

'I don't know, really, it just sort of happened.'

'Well, the best thing you can do is get out of the way while I get on with it. Go to the shops and get some milk then you can make me a coffee.'

I was reluctant to go, but knew I would have to as I was wholly reliant on my sister carrying out the work, so I was in no position to barter. Before leaving I glanced through the kitchen window; I could see the shops and was able to check if any potential threats were lurking but there was none. Nevertheless my senses were still heightened as I took the short walk from my apartment. As I made my way towards the mini-mart, the guy who had head-butted me came out and I froze momentarily.

'I want you a minute.'

He came strolling towards me and I swallowed hard but was determined not to succumb to any more threats of violence.

'Listen, I'm sorry about the other day, I didn't know who you were but your sister told me. If I'd known, I wouldn't have done it.'

'My sister?'

It turned out he'd been seeing my youngest sister for a couple of weeks. I wasn't sure if his apology was out of respect for her or out of concern that I might tell my father, or perhaps it was fear of what he perceived I might like to do to his house. Either way, it meant nothing to me in the same way that he didn't. I went to go past him but he stopped me.

'I've told the others to lay off you so you shouldn't get any more trouble.'

Perhaps I should have dropped to my knees and meekly surrendered to his generosity and spirit, but I would rather have eaten my dinner off the pavement.

'Yeah, thanks.'

* * * *

A couple of weeks later, I was back in court.

A report had been submitted, asserting that the relationship had been difficult and that we were both equally to blame for that. The magistrates agreed and granted me a conditional discharge with twenty pounds costs payable at two pounds per week. I left the courthouse feeling angry and betrayed; three court appearances and two spells in the cells, not to mention being dragged in handcuffs from my home early in the morning, for something that was dismissed within seconds.

I had a few beers then returned home to write. Miraculously, my typewriter had survived its collision with the floor so I sat up all night putting the finishing touches to a play I had been working on for months. Over the years I had, off and on, written some poetry, but now wanted the added challenge of a much larger project, besides I quite fancied the title of playwright. I had been introduced to the new creative team at a theatre in Leicester, in the East Midlands. My introduction came via Phillipa when we were negotiating the making of the second film, and they were keen to work with new writers and directors. On the basis of a novel I'd written some time earlier, which one of the team had been shown, I was invited down to the theatre and offered the chance to write a play. A payment of two hundred and fifty pounds was mentioned, however when I rang several weeks later it was denied, but I still wrote the play based around magic, torture and deceit. Now I had but a few hours before I was due to deliver it and I worked all through the night without a break. By nine am it was done and I splashed some cold water on my face and set off.

I was greeted warmly and offered some lunch, which provided me with the perfect opportunity to sell my play and to demonstrate my understanding of the various genres. Most significantly, it helped to reinstate my true identity as a creative rather than destructive force. As I launched into my spiel about themes, the complex nature of certain types of behaviour and what might motivate it, the guy who was going to read it and ultimately pass judgment on it, began casually flicking through the pages. I didn't break stride and my arms were flapping about in truly animated style as I passionately tried to promote my ideas, it came naturally and without affectation and there wasn't a hint of uncertainty.

'So ultimately, I've developed a structure that mirrors the complex, sometimes fragmented nature of these types of fractured relationships, rather than merely experimenting with style.'

He looked up from the manuscript and studied me for a moment. It was the first time I had remained still, and quiet.

'It sounds like a very ambitious project for a new writer.'

'I guess it is ambitious but also hugely exciting, not to mention potentially ground-breaking.'

Okay, so I was talking it up but it was an opportunity to restore my belief and I wasn't going to have it shaken or diluted. As a kid I was often told I lived in dreamland; better to live them.

'There's no doubting how you feel about this work, but obviously it's only the first draft, so I anticipate a period of development then hopefully we'll have a script we can all work with.'

It was a meeting I didn't want to end because I was able to speak my own language and feel good about it, but it wasn't enough to be part of an experiment, I wanted the lifestyle. Without it they would just be words that pass away the day. I collected my expenses and left the theatre with a mixture of excitement and concern. I wasn't convinced he shared my enthusiasm, had hoped for a more complete sharing of ideas and energy, but it certainly wasn't unique, in fact it was all too familiar, allowing the doubts their feeding frenzy.

Nevertheless when I returned home and walked through the estate, I did so with a different mindset, confident and unswerving. It had been a long time since I had felt it and never in this new life that I thought would be so easy. All I could do was wait but I wasn't willing to do it to the exclusion of everything else so I continued to write. When the call finally came, it was brutal in its destruction of the work and mindless in its delivery. He basically attacked everything I had tried to do and made no excuses for his ignorance, and lack of bravery.

'I hope I haven't butchered it.'

'Well, you claim it is completely without merits and that it broke all the rules of structure and form. I'd say that was pretty much a hatchet job.'

'Well, I just want to guide you, I think your ideas are good but you need to learn the principles alongside of that.'

'Well, I think you're trying to make a big deal about the new writing thing because it's in vogue but you really want the same as it's always been and there's nothing new in that.'

'Well, you know, Mini, whilst your history is fascinating, it won't sustain you on its own.'

'I've never expected it to but I wasn't the one who suggested it as a basis for this play.'

I hung up, more stunned than angry. I didn't slam the phone down nor was I tempted to pull it from its socket. Once again, I found myself having to fight to legitimise what I was attempting to do, but at least on this occasion I got to decide when the conversation was over with none of the usual repercussions.

I didn't write for two or three days afterwards, I just pounded the streets trying to wear down the disappointment. One afternoon, I returned from my quest feeling somewhat deflated and picked up the letter lying on my carpet. It was from Franc and it contained a cheque for two hundred pounds and a note saying, 'spend it frivolously'. I could have cried but instead I picked up the phone to thank him. It was great hearing his voice again, and I never failed to draw inspiration from him, I told him what had happened with the theatre people and he gave me a much needed reality check. Of course things don't always work out first time and in this game rejection is part of the norm. I guess I just wanted things to be a little easier for once, perhaps my history made me feel that way.

A week or so after speaking to the theatre people, I received an unexpected phone call. The theatre were planning a number of workshops which initially involved working with a director to develop the script, then being part of a five day workshop involving actors and I had been invited to participate. It was an exciting prospect, which I never thought would happen in Leicester after criticising their treatment of new talent. I had a number of meetings with the director involved and I was impressed with his willingness to take risks. We agreed on a format and a timetable and I went home and got on with the work. Once the first draft was completed and had been read by the director, I returned to the theatre for yet another meeting. It was beginning to feel like work, which was excellent.

The meeting went well, with just a little tinkering required and I sat in the bar having a drink when another young director approached my table. I'd already spoken to him a couple of times in passing, but had never seen his work.

'Hi Mini, I hear you're doing one of the workshops.'

'Yeah, hopefully.'

'How's the script coming along?'

'It's good, I've just got to make a couple of small adjustments and it'll be ready.'

'Good, because I start rehearsals for a new play in a couple of weeks and I need an assistant director. There's no money involved but obviously we'll pay your travel expenses.'

'Yeah, I'm up for it.'

'Excellent, I'll be in touch nearer the time.'

It was difficult to comprehend the speed at which events can change but I was ready, I had been for most of my life.

The script was completed and accepted just before rehearsals were due to get under way and, as the workshop was still to be finalised, it allowed time for me to fully embrace my new role. The play had been performed in America but was having its European premiere in Leicester. The job title sounded creatively stimulating but was in fact a misnomer. I spent my first day on the job phoning Heathrow airport trying to track down a cashmere sweater belonging to the playwright. Midway through the afternoon I finally tracked it down, grateful that I wasn't paying the phone bill. The rest of rehearsals were similar in fashion; I made the tea, nipped out for lunch and various other errands, but it gave me an invaluable insight into the whole process, from script to performance, and it re-ignited my passion. The director was only a year or two older than me. Having gone to the theatre one evening and been totally captivated, he gave up his economics degree for a career as a theatre director and had been largely successful. He had a gentle, persuasive manner that coaxed rather than demanded, and when the theatre later set up a youth project he was given the job of running it. As opening night approached, I was given some money and dispatched into the city to buy cards for the cast. This was one errand I was anxious and nervous about, I really didn't want to do it.

'I don't know what to get, you'll be better off sending someone else who knows what they're doing. I've never bought cards for actors before.'

'Min, they're just people like you and me, just get something classy.'

That was the fucking problem, I'd never really done classy before and wouldn't recognise it if it were the only thing in the room. When I returned an hour or two later clutching a handful of cards, his disapproval was obvious, so much so he was unable to hide it.

'These are no good, I'll have to get some more.'

I stood there feeling like a complete pariah and a bit of a fraud. I was playing at it whereas they belonged to it. By the end of the first night my work was done. I was walking through the foyer when the director called out to me.

'Min, wait up. Listen, thanks for all your work on the play. You may be interested to know that Channel Four are producing a new show to replace *The Tube*.' This was a late-night culture show aimed at the youth audience. 'They want ten minute plays by writers new to television, using directors new to television. Each play has to be submitted through a production company and I've just set one up, so if you're interested send me your play and I'll forward it on.'

'What can you say in ten minutes?'

'Well if you talked constantly without interruption for the next ten minutes, you'll probably find you'd have quite a lot to say.'

'Yeah, I suppose you're right. I'll think about it and let you know.'

I'd never had so many offers in such a short period of time and I didn't have to go chasing them, they seemed to follow me, leaving no time to ponder. I even dared to think I was alive. I gave little thought to Channel Four, preferring to concentrate on ironing out the faults from an earlier project. During a coffee break I was waiting for the kettle to boil when I had a Eureka! moment. I raced to my desk and twenty minutes later I had a ten-minute play, based around magic, madness and a burnt-out house. As I sat back and enjoyed my coffee, I nearly jumped out of my skin when the phone rang. The voice on the other end made me jump even more.

It was Marilyn.

'How are you?'

'I'm fine, Marilyn. How come you've rung me after all this time?'

'I've missed you. I wondered if you fancied coming over for some dinner tonight?'

I shouldn't have had to even think about it, really. It had been several months since she'd been in touch so I should have told her to take a hike. My life was busy, largely satisfying and fairly uncomplicated, but I did lack a little female company.

'Okay.'

I wrote down her address and hung up. I stared at the piece of paper for a while, wondering if I was doing the right thing. Sadly where my life is concerned, that can often be the attraction.

So I had dinner with her and her boys but I didn't really know how to play out the rest of the evening, didn't fully understand what was expected of me, I just figured I'd hang around for a while then when it got to around nine or ten, I'd bid them all farewell. Eventually, the lateness of the hour meant it was time to do the polite thing and return home. I went into the hallway and collected my coat, thanked Marilyn for a wonderful meal and then opened the front door. I stood on the porch and noticed how well the light framed her features and the way she was dressed. And I wanted her.

'Listen, maybe sometime I can return the favour, you and the boys come over to my place and I'll cook for you all.'

'You don't have to go if you don't want to, you can stay the night if you like.'

I guess in some ways we were as bad as each other. Every strand of rationale was pointing me away from there, but everything else marched me through the door and up the stairs.

The following day she told me that she had enrolled for nurse training and had arranged childcare for the boys but it was expensive. I offered to do it without really considering what it required. She wasted no time in ringing the childminder to cancel, who apparently wasn't happy at losing the work and of course, the money. Once I'd had time to think about my decision and the manner by which it had come about, I wasn't particularly happy, either. Perhaps I was just being paranoid or cynical, or maybe I'm naturally suspicious, either way I couldn't help thinking I'd walked right into an ambush. I'd never had anyone depend on me before, never experienced that level of responsibility, or developed the discipline to maintain it.

I was fucking terrified.

The eldest lad walked himself to school but the youngest had just started nursery and naturally had to be walked there and back. He only attended in the mornings, which meant I had to be up early. I would make him some lunch then keep him entertained throughout the afternoon, with videos and games. He liked playing hide-and-seek around the house and he loved going to the park so when the weather was suitable that's where we would be. He was great to be around, chatty and questioning everything, often with more questions than I had answers to. When the eldest came home from school, I would prepare them an evening meal and occasionally have to sort out a squabble. This gave me the opportunity to do things my way rather than perpetuate the type of discipline I had been regularly subject to at their age.

It took some working out but I never once went for the easy option of giving them a clout to make me feel better, because I wouldn't have done. Sometimes I would speak to them and just calm the situation down, and occasionally some form of punishment would be necessary. This usually involved depriving them of something they were guaranteed to miss for a day or two. I would always discuss this with Marilyn, mindful that they were her children and her ultimate responsibility. Sometimes the eldest boy would invite his friends over after school. Whilst I was responsible for every person in the house, I often felt like a gatecrasher and often felt invisible, even when Marilyn was around, sometimes even more so, but I'd signed the contract, I was morally bound through naivety, stupidity and testosterone. It seemed easier to stay than start afresh with all that baggage to reveal then unload. I split my time between her place and mine

One afternoon, I was typing away when the phone rang.

'Hey, Mini, fantastic news! Your script has been accepted, you need to call Working Title straightaway.'

I was stunned into silence. I had completely forgotten about the script, having become so wrapped up in domestic manoeuvres and just trying to hold on to my sanity long enough to recognise it. Once I began smiling I wasn't sure I knew how to stop. I don't remember ever feeling that good before and as such I didn't quite know how to respond to it, or how to switch it off.

So let it run.

Working Title were the production company who had secured the contract to produce the plays for Channel Four. He gave me the number along with the name of the person I needed to speak to, a former employee of the theatre. I wasted no time in dialling the number and within seconds I was put through to the relevant department. I was determined to sound confident, believing I now had every right to be. I was about to be paid for something I'd written whilst waiting for a kettle to boil. That's my kind of work!

'Hi, it's Mini Cooper, I was told to call you.'

That was the name on the script the same name that was attached to all of my deeds, only the court papers claimed Michael but by then I was always somebody else, and that's what they wanted to see, it's all they understood.

'Hi, Mini, thanks for submitting the script, everyone who's read it has loved it.'

'Well, that's promising.'

'Okay, well the contract is worth twelve hundred and fifty pounds, five hundred to be paid on signing the contract and the remaining seven hundred and fifty pounds to be paid on the day of filming.'

I tried to sound like I had these conversations all the time but the fact was she had thrown me. I expected the issue of money to come at the end not the fucking beginning! It was a staggering amount insofar as I hadn't come remotely close to earning this kind of money before and I was in my twenty sixth year, but I didn't want her to know that so I kept it simple.

'Yeah, that's fine.'

I figured there would be some changes required as this was fairly standard, it could also be pretty contentious so I didn't want to delay the inevitable. I was hoping it could be dealt with quickly and smoothly.

'So, are there any areas of the script you want changing, any dialogue you're not happy with?'

'No, no, no the script is perfect as it is but you forgot to put your address on it, that's why I wanted you to get in touch, so we could mail you the contract.'

* * * *

'What the fuck is going on?'

'What?'

'Why is there a Christmas tree in this scene?'

'Well, you wrote it.'

'Yes, I fucking did write it, so show me where it says there's a Christmas tree before I go fucking mad!'

I shoved the script in his face, ignoring the usual standards of etiquette and forgetting I had a writer's palate.

I had wanted an active role and to be part of the entire process, and whilst I quite naturally respected the director's vision, I had my own as I wrote it and was willing to defend it vociferously if necessary. We had met a couple of times where we presented our individual ideas and were able to arrive at a point through mutual negotiation that satisfied us both. The principal agreement was that as magic was involved we should cast an actor who could perform to a high standard rather than use camera tricks, so after auditions in London, with lots of kids performing card tricks although not one of them could act, we finally found one who could, but he didn't know a single magic trick and there wasn't enough time to teach him.

Now I sat in an ante-room, watching the action unfold on a monitor.

'Look, I haven't got time for this right now, I need to get this filmed.'

I was manhandled off the set by a couple of burly technicians. This was my career in somebody else's hands, like so much of my life.

A member of the production team came over.

'Are you okay, Mini?'

'No, I'm not. Let me ask you something, if you were shooting a ninety minute movie, would you shoot it in nine days?'

'No, of course not.'

'So why are we shooting a ten minute play in a day?'

'We have a very tight schedule for this, everyone's under a lot of pressure.'

'That's why he's just fucked up the whole film!'

'I think you're being very unfair, I'm sure he knows what he's doing.'

I returned home, consumed with anger and frustration and was not easy to live with those first few days. I resented returning to the mundane and was eager to put right the mistakes that had occurred during filming. In the end there was little I could do except wait for it to be broadcast and hope the edit had removed the problem. Every Wednesday evening I would switch on Channel Four and hope to see it, but it was always someone else's.

I didn't get to experience the theatre workshop either, as I had lost all confidence in the director and didn't want to lose another piece of work to panic. I was losing trust in a process that became independent of the work itself. That day in the studio everyone was given a voice except me and I was still smarting from that, still seething with rage. I began to question my whole commitment to what I was doing and needed to step back for a while to protect an increasingly fragile mentality. I rang the people at the theatre and told them I couldn't attend the workshop and made some excuse about being mentally frail; they simply cancelled it.

On a personal level, life with Marilyn was also becoming increasingly difficult. Her money was tied up in the house and all she had to live on was the meagre amount she earned as a student nurse. She was putting increasing pressure on me to find a job as Christmas was fast approaching. I felt I had enough to deal with, taking care of the boys, how the fuck could I do a job of work, come back to them and try and fit in time to write? She clearly didn't share my ambitions and was quite mean in her dismissal of them, nor did she appear to understand that I was running my own home and therefore couldn't provide as much money as she wanted me to.

I split my time between my place and hers so I didn't feel as though I was a drain on her resources. Nevertheless I capitulated because I was becoming tired of coming into conflict when all I wanted was a little peace. But it wouldn't be my work, just something I did for money, and sleep. I subsequently signed on with an employment agency, who simply asked a few basic questions and said they would be in touch. A couple of days later I received a phone call and was offered four twelve-hour night shifts, Saturday through until Tuesday, at the Barr soft drinks factory, on the estate where I lived. Marilyn nodded her approval from the dinner table, so I was set to start. Eight pm until eight am, for two pounds fifty an hour, less if I'd worked days and roughly half of what the factory employees received for doing the same job. I reported to the security office and was handed a boiler suit, a cap and a clocking in card, along with a locker key.

I punched my ticket to register my arrival and start the clock ticking currency. I found my locker, stashed away my food, then turned to the guy standing next to me.

'Listen, this is my first time here, who do I need to see?'

'Are you with the agency?'

'Yeah.'

'You need to see the supervisor, his office is over there.'

He pointed it out to me and I climbed into my uniform and made my way there. The supervisor was a small guy in his forties from the North East of England with a huge chip on his shoulder.

'You don't look like you've ever done a day's work in your fucking life!'

'Why, have you been following me?'

I swept the factory floor all night, wondering if I would make it through to dawn without going completely insane, and struggling with the notion that out here was something worth having because it improved your chances and gave you quality of life. An additional problem was that once the weekend was over I was still expected to take the youngest boy to nursery and then fetch him around lunchtime, which meant I couldn't go to bed, having just finished work, and nor could I leave him alone on his return.

I was basically putting on videos to occupy him whilst I nodded off on the sofa for an hour or two. It was an unbelievable situation and whilst he was brilliantly behaved, it was completely unfair to make me his responsibility when it was meant to be the other way around.

I drew my first week's wages, having worked a forty-eight hour week on nights: a little over ninety one pounds. Even by the standards of the day, it was pretty abysmal and I wondered just what the fuck was happening. I was being controlled when I had a choice, but maybe it was more familiar than being in charge, maybe I hadn't yet figured out how to be or knew the territory and could claim it. Added to the mix was the fact that I had developed a special relationship with her youngest son and he had started calling me 'dad' without any prompting from me, which was hugely flattering and an enormous privilege, and difficult to just walk away from and disappear. I continued like this until Christmas, but not without the occasional row and its explosive aftermath, although there were no police or the obligatory demand to pack my things and leave. On New Year's Eve I threw a party at my apartment, mainly family, as I hadn't yet acquired any friends other than fellow detainees. After everyone had left, Marilyn started having a go at me over how much I'd had to drink.

I stared at her for a moment then I completely lost the plot, but not in a violent or threatening manner, I started laughing and my whole body laughed with me, jerking and trembling.

'Look at you, sat there laughing like a lunatic! You're just a piss-head, Min, I don't know what I ever saw in you.'

'Do you honestly think I could do this fucking sober? Under the circumstances I think I've shown remarkable restraint, but the night is still young.'

'Well, don't think I'm sleeping with you tonight, you can have the sofa.'

'Well, like you're always saying to me, this is my house so you can take the fucking sofa!'

'You bastard! You're going to force me to take the sofa?'

'Well, you're happy for me to.'

It was all pretty immature, really. I guess the sofa had become the only space I felt able to control, give that up and I'd just be her puppy, betraying everything I once was but had latterly sold to the lowest bidder. Now I wanted it back.

'You can fuck off! I'm going and you won't see me again.'

'Well, don't leave anything, I'd hate you to have to come back for it.'

She picked up a bowl of peanuts from the table and hurled them at me with real venom. I ducked and the bowl hit the wall behind me, putting a sizeable dent in it before breaking into several pieces. I walked over to the debris on the floor and started gathering up the pieces, ignoring the nuts for the time being.

'Oh, this is a surprise. Aren't you going to start smashing the phone or kick over a speaker?'

'I don't have any speakers, Marilyn, but I could always smash the kitchen window and claim it was you.'

I continued to gather up the pieces, leaving them in a pile on the floor and then scraped the nuts together to form another pile. When I picked up the ceramic fragments of the bowl I cut myself.

'Oh, dear, have you cut yourself?'

'Yes, I have.'

'Good.'

She turned and stormed out of the lounge and I could hear her rousing the boys and wanted no part of it, I didn't even want to see them leave. Instead, I went to the kitchen and ran my thumb under a cold tap before applying a plaster. When I came back through they had gone and maybe it was irresponsible of me not to have tried to stop her, given that she had drunk quite a bit herself, but experience is the great provider. A few minutes' later, I had a call from my mother who said Marilyn had just turned up in a hysterical state, apparently parking the car half on the pavement and half on the road. She was lucky that was her only mistake.

My mother put the boys to bed then it was left to my eldest sister's partner to deal with Marilyn, who was stomping around the lounge. He eventually, and rather firmly, insisted she sit down, and surprisingly she did. I never did understand why she drove nine miles in an intoxicated state when her own house was only five minutes away by car. Perhaps she needed an audience, irrespective of who they were.

A few days later I received a series of phone calls from Marilyn, accusing me of betraying her and her boys and of jeopardizing her career in nursing. I refused to accept this.

'But you agreed to do that work to help us out.'

'Who was helping me? I mean, it's pretty basic arithmetic, I work twelve hours and get two hours kip on the sofa, yet you're accusing me of letting you down. You're unbelievable!'

'Well, if that's what you think of me and my children, then we don't need you.'

'I doubt you ever did because all I'm hearing is what you and your children need and you don't seem that bothered about those who are providing it.'

'You're selfish.'

She hung up and I wasn't disappointed that she had, she didn't want a conversation, she wanted continuance; same terms, same conditions.

Same pain.

CHAPTER THIRTY-SIX

I was now in a strange place. I knew what I didn't want but what I did rested with others and I'd already felt the pain of that. I began thinking that my ideas, whether on paper, or locked in a room with a plastic piss pot, had the same journey to make with the same explanations to preserve them.

I just wanted them to dance on their own, unmarked.

I spent a couple of weeks grappling with my frustrations and fighting the black dog of depression but it was no good, it knew when to pounce: when the phone didn't ring and the typewriter no longer typed. I once again took to wandering the streets in the dead of night and sleeping through the day, living entirely outside of regular society, of this world but not really in it, yet having nowhere else to go. I was eventually referred to another psychiatrist and prescribed yet more medication. I went home and emptied the entire contents of the packet into a wine glass and had no reservations regarding what I was about to do, it was selfish, but nobody else could be me and I was tired of trying. Then the fucking phone rang and in that moment it was the one person I didn't want it to be, the one person I couldn't be angry enough with, to just say why don't you just fuck off and leave me alone! Anyone else and I would have done.

'Hi, Mini, it's Franc. How you doing, buddy?'

It had been a long time since I had cried like that. I felt part rescued, part prolonged and didn't know whether to hug him or hate him, but I never could hate him, I just didn't want to believe him anymore because it was easier to give myself up to failure and blame someone else. So there I was on the other end of the phone, pouring my heart out and feeling embarrassed yet safe. He urged me to pour the tablets down the toilet and flush them away and I did, with some regret. But I didn't regret his intervention because if there were no one worth listening to then it really didn't matter.

I went and stayed with him for a couple of days but it wasn't the same because I wasn't, and I didn't know how to change back. I felt awkward and constantly ill at ease, because I was diminished and further weakened by his knowing. He tried to communicate with me through music, he was very enthusiastic and chose well. First up was a track by a band called 'Was Not Was' with a powerful opening verse:

'On the day that I was born my daddy looked at me he said, you look like corn and your feet are made of clay and then he turned away.'

Followed by the chorus:

'Don't you know that I was knocked down made small, treated like a rubber ball, knocked down made small, treated like a rubber ball?'

Whilst I was there I got him to switch on Channel Four television. I thought it would be a great moment if we could watch my play together, a real arrival and a chance to discuss, one artist to another.

But it wasn't on.

'Listen, Franc, can you ring Channel Four and find out what's going on? Because I've not been notified of anything and I don't want to have to put this on every week, just to try and get a glimpse of my own fucking play!'

I was seriously agitated and hugely disappointed. I desperately wanted him to see it and to know it came from me.

'Sure, I know a couple of people I can speak to.'

He made a couple of calls and was eventually directed to the person with the answers so he called them. When he placed the receiver back in its cradle I knew it wasn't good news.

'The executives at Channel Four didn't like the production, they felt the character was all wrong and they've decided not to show it. But everyone else thinks it was probably the pick of the bunch.'

'I fucking specifically asked them if they wanted any rewrites and they said the script was perfect!'

'Hey, Mini, this happens all the time in the movies, you know? You develop a script, everybody's happy, then you shoot the movie and there's a problem.'

'Yes, but Franc, you make a couple of great movies that everybody loves, then you hit a situation like this and you still have your reputation to fall back on, but I don't have that. I'm still trying to get off the ground because some dumb fuck didn't know how to read a script!'

This was the one occasion he couldn't make me feel better, because I felt like an arsonist and not a playwright.

The following day I returned home. I descended rapidly into self-pitying mode, caring very little for my own well-being. I ate very little and wandered aimlessly when I could be bothered to climb out of bed and venture out.

I eventually returned to my previous routine of writing through the night and sleeping through the day but after a while, all I really wanted to do, was stay in bed and mark time. I began to imagine life on death row, counting out the days with no plan other than to want it over, in order to leave the state behind for good, that's where I was at. I could think of nothing else and quickly began sticking sheets of paper to my lounge wall, each one numbered from one to fifty-six. I don't know how I arrived at that figure but my death row diary had begun. I don't recall what I wrote, I just remember that far from it being a timetable of death, I was searching for a reason to live but I needed to believe that I could, I just couldn't find what seemed lost. I couldn't find what the child had possessed in abundance, I just kept finding moments of uncertainty, tinged with madness. So I returned to my bed and spent several days lying unwashed in my own private Bedlam.

Then one Friday afternoon there was a knock at the door. It had been several months since Marilyn had left but I still suspected it might be her so I didn't bother getting out of bed. When my father called through the letterbox I was even more reluctant, I hadn't seen a single soul for days and was in no mood for his inquisitorial approach.

'Bliddy hell, have you just got out of bed?'

'I've been up all night writing.'

I invited him in and he stood and stared at the pieces of paper stuck to the wall.

'What are yer writing about death row for?'

'Why not? People write about war.'

'We're driving over to Tesco's, we wondered if yer fancied coming with us? It'll get yer out the flat for a bit.'

'Yeah, alright, let me get washed and dressed.'

How ironic that I agreed because I felt safe having him walking by my side! I didn't feel entirely comfortable leaving him in the lounge, though, afraid of how much of my stuff he might be reading. Finally we left the apartment and it felt good to be out in the open air. My parents did their shopping then as we left the store my mother handed me a bag of groceries, there were even some beers.

'I'll give yer a lift back.'

'It's alright, I'm going to walk, I really need the air.'

My mother came over and slipped a ten-pound note into my hand then gave me a hug. It took all of my strength not to crumble.

'We're coming back tonight to go to the club, yer can join us if yer like?'

'Yeah, okay.'

I watched them drive off then made my way home. Back home I was feeling pretty pumped up and in a mood to party. I wasted no time in cracking open a beer, but it had been a while since I'd had any and it went straight to my head. Pretty soon I was feeling seriously charged and became more and more uninhibited. I found myself dancing maniacally around my lounge with rock music blaring out of a portable music system then I tore down every sheet of paper and threw them in the bin. When the beer ran dry I was determined that the feeling it had helped to manufacture was maintained, so I went to the pub and had a couple of pints.

Later that evening and already intoxicated, I went to the club and met my parents and had another pint. I was in a counterfeit place but it seemed more real than real, because real never smiled so much. My parents spent the best part of the evening playing bingo, and I spent my time flitting between them and the lounge. Whilst there I discovered that a guy I vaguely knew was holding an engagement party for his son after the club had closed, and I asked if I could come along.

'Sorry, it's just for close friends and family.'

It was fair to say I wasn't a close friend or even just a friend, I'd had a pint with him a couple of times at the club and met him once at another party. He smoked a bit of dope but I always felt he was more excited about being known to smoke it, than the benefits it provided.

'What if I bring a bottle, can I come then?'

'Yeah, if you bring a bottle you can come.'

I had exhausted my funds but I wanted the night to last forever, wanted to party the way my heroes did, in the delusional belief it would unlock my talent, believing their success came from an uncompromising lifestyle.

How truly fucked up and lost had I become?

'Mum, I've been invited to a party but I need to bring a bottle, can I borrow a couple of quid until Monday?'

I wasn't in the habit of tapping my mum for money, they didn't have an awful lot and I didn't want to be dependent on them, however the alcohol seemed to have no conscience or pride as I held out my hand and accepted the money. I hurried to the bar before last orders and bought a two-litre bottle of beer. I tried handing back the change to my mother but she told me to keep it.

I walked my parents to their car and thanked them for their efforts.

'So, have you enjoyed yourself, son?'

'Yeah, Dad, it's been the best day I've had in ages.'

Saying it brought it vividly to life and it nearly overwhelmed me. All those days trapped under the bedclothes, thinking I was dying and wishing I had, now the beer made me feel alive, and wanting to be.

A battery-operated toy.

'Well, enjoy your party but divin't get into any trouble.'

'I won't.'

As they climbed into the car I thanked my mum for the money and once again thanked them both for the evening. I felt like I wanted to keep on thanking them, afraid of losing the closeness I had briefly felt.

Then they were gone.

* * * *

I arrived at the party and there was a full house. I wasn't fazed by the fact that there were people there I didn't know, mostly they didn't know me and I was intent on keeping it that way.

So my companion for the time being became the kitchen, where copious amounts of alcohol were stacked up and waiting to be liberated in the true spirit of adventure, without bounds. As the night wore on I became increasingly drunk, as did most of the other guests. I found myself sat next to a young woman who had something of a reputation on the estate for being an easy pick-up. I was feeling invincible and sufficiently drunk not to care, so I began flirting with her and pretty soon I began to move through the gears until the flirting became more suggestive. She wasn't remotely interested, my ego had been mauled but mostly I suspect, it had been self-inflicted. There's nothing very classy or sophisticated about a drunk looking for a fuck.

I was sat licking my wounds and staring into the bottom of a glass that was eager to be refilled, when an unknown voice belonging to someone I hadn't even noticed changed the shape of everything.

'Have you got a brother who lives in Ollerton?'

'Yes, I have.'

'You were on the telly a couple of years ago. I watched it, you set fire to your mam and dad's house when you were little.'

All around me people were watching and listening and I felt extremely uncomfortable. I had spent the previous three years working hard to avoid such an encounter because it could never be explained here.

'What made yer do that, like?'

I stood up, on my way to the kitchen for yet another drink but he seemed reluctant to let me pass.

'You must have had a reason.'

'If you want to know ask my fucking brother, he always tells a good story!'

When I reached the kitchen, the beer had been drunk so I poured two generous helpings of wine. The first never even touched the sides and the second only just. I then poured another and returned to the lounge.

Through a combination of excessive amounts of booze and a little dope, I could have been walking naked down the street without a single reservation. I might even have posed for photographs. I hadn't entirely forgotten my earlier encounter and still felt a little exposed by it but no one else seemed to be paying me any undue attention. I was who I always was, the stranger who never came with anyone, perhaps that's why he made his move. I was sat staring into my glass, lost in thoughts I was trying to unscramble, when the guy sat directly opposite me started growling and hurling abuse. At first I wasn't aware that it was directed at me until I looked up. This seemed to enrage him even more and I began to feel threatened but also angry at this unwarranted attempt at bullying me, a reminder of the inexcusable, inarticulate acts of aggression that had once formed part of my daily life. His brother, whom I knew quite well, quickly spotted what was going on and intervened, standing in between us.

'Listen, you, we're all having a good laugh here, if you fuck it all up for me then you're on your own!'

His brother's words seemed to silence him but there was no telling what was going through his mind as he continued to glare at me. In one final act of conciliation, I walked over to him and held out my hand, but he didn't take it.

'Hey, you, he's offering you his fucking hand!'

'Listen, if I've offended you in some way, then I'm sorry.'

He reluctantly shook my hand but did so without any sincerity, just like I'd apologised. It ate me up, having had to in the first place and I couldn't shake free of loathing myself whilst resenting him. We spent the remainder of the evening casting furtive glances towards one another.

Then I became bored.

'Come on, for God's sake! This is supposed to be a party, not a funeral, let's dance.'

I leapt to my feet and started flailing my arms about like someone possessed. Within seconds I went crashing to the floor, taking the television with me. Thankfully the television survived the ordeal but my party was over. I was manhandled and then frog-marched to the door and thrown out into the garden where it was raining, yet miraculously I managed to stay on my feet.

'Go on, fuck off, you fucking idiot!'

'Yeah, fuck off, shit for brains, no one wanted you here anyway!'

'Don't worry, I'm going. I'd have had more fun in a fucking crypt!'

As I turned to make my way down the garden and out through the gate, my earlier abuser followed me. He pushed me and this time I wasn't so lucky, I fell backwards hitting my head against the gate, and muddied my clothes.

'You're nothing, you!'

His comment stung more than the indignity of having to pick myself up off the floor amidst laughter and stares.

'I might be nothing to you but you're nothing to anyone who ever knew you! I don't even know your fucking name!'

I turned and left, and despite the taunts and the baying, no one came after me apart from the rain. I returned to my apartment and paced relentlessly back and forth across my lounge, choking on anger and frustration and strangled by impotence. I was sick of being pushed around by people whose only vocabulary were their fists. I wanted them to start walking around me instead of through me, wanted them to be more afraid than I was, but for that to happen they had to hurt in the only way they could. I didn't know if I was capable, more importantly I didn't want to be because in that moment there would be nothing to separate us, but I was sick of playing hide and seek. I went into the kitchen and grabbed a long knife with a serrated edge and tucked it into my belt. I left the flat without giving myself the opportunity to change my mind, and headed back to the party, breathing heavily.

I stood under the porch of a bungalow directly opposite the house, chain-smoking my way through layers of uncertainty. I didn't want this, didn't want what it was about to make me in an attempt to feel safe. It was seriously fucked up but these were the streets I now walked, forever at their mercy. Visibility was poor, it was dark, raining quite heavily and the street was dimly lit. A young man emerged from the house and all I saw was him pushing me over for the very last time. I quickly pulled out the knife and in the process cut my belt in half and my trousers fell down. I reached down to pull them up and caught myself with the knife, cutting the thumb of my left hand.

The young man disappeared up the street, oblivious to the pantomime unfolding behind him. He wasn't even the intended target. I returned to my apartment and changed my trousers, but I couldn't change anything else and I would never be welcome here, I was a refugee. I picked up my benefit book and also my passport to present as identification at the post office and set off on the long walk to Liverpool and Moss Side hospital. If they took me back, I would promise to stay.

I walked by the soft drinks factory where I had once worked. Several months earlier a guy from the estate climbed the fence and made off with several crates of pop. He sold it in the club, one hundred per cent profit. Bizarrely, in view of my original intention and having no desire to hang around any longer, I decided to do the same.

The fence was made of chicken wire and once you reached the top you met with three rows of barbed wire. By pushing the top of the fence forward you could create a sufficient gap to crawl under and drop down on the other side. Unfortunately the fence sprung back and catapulted me through the air. I came crashing down on my back, severely winding myself but at least it was grass and not concrete.

I walked into the main warehouse and took a look around but all the branded stuff was stacked too high for me to reach. I felt despondent, everything I had attempted to do mirrored my failure to exist, and not just breathe. In the yard away from the main warehouse were some wooden palates, stacked several feet in the air, each wrapped in plastic. I stood amongst them, hidden from view and had a cigarette. It was still raining and I was still pissed off. I began messing around, holding a lit match to the plastic covering the crates. There was no real intent or the formulation of a particular plan, just boredom and uncertainty. Eventually my matches ran out and I sauntered over to the canteen, I was hungry and there was a vending machine there. However, when I got there the machine was empty and I sat at a table and smoked another cigarette.

It felt strange, sitting there without the sandwiches that had so often helped me through a shift just by giving me something else to think about, but now I was a trespasser like so many times before. As I got up to leave I spotted a handbag sitting on the windowsill. I took it just because I could, for no other reason.

I climbed out of a window, which was directly opposite the security barrier and the hut that housed the guards. I ducked underneath the barrier and ran as fast as I could all the way back to my apartment. Once there I examined the contents of the bag and found a pair of socks and a bottle of cheap perfume, terrific!

I decided on making a cup of coffee and having yet another cigarette before going to bed. The kettle was empty so I took it over to the sink.

'Oh, my fucking God!'

I stood, staring out of my kitchen window as flames lit up the entire sky, despite being several hundred yards away. I was dumbstruck, for when I walked away from the factory there was no fire. My mind was scrambled. As the panic set in there was only one thing for it: I would have to disappear for a while. I stood on the balcony of the flat, drinking coffee, when two police officers arrived. It couldn't have been more than twenty minutes after the event.

'Michael Cooper?'

'Yes.'

'Can we come in?'

'Do I have a choice?'

'Not really.'

I turned and went back into the apartment. I claimed the centre ground by sitting in the middle of the sofa. I didn't invite them to sit but they quickly found somewhere anyway.

'Are you aware there's been a fire on the estate tonight?'

'Yeah, I've just seen it through my kitchen window.'

'So, where were you an hour ago?'

'I was at a party.'

'And where did you go after you'd left the party?'

I was trying to second-guess them. I was convinced they knew enough to have arrived at my apartment so quickly and so confidently, I just didn't want to believe it or acknowledge my guilt.

'I came back here.'

'What would you say if we told you we have a witness who says a person matching your description was seen running from the premises at the same time that the fire was started?'

'It could be anyone.'

'Michael Cooper, I'm arresting you on suspicion of arson.'

He read me my rights but surprisingly didn't cuff me. I figured I wouldn't be offered the Samaritans this time around, just when I most needed them.

CHAPTER THIRTY-SEVEN

I felt like a murder suspect as I stood stripping off in front of the cops. Every single item of clothing was placed in a paper sack to be sent away for forensic examination. I was given a paper suit to wear but was nevertheless naked. When the door finally slammed shut I felt a huge sense of relief that the circus had taken a time out, the previous few hours had been completely manic and I was struggling to separate truth from reality.

But it could and would be denied.

After a couple of hours trying to analyse and then re-analyse everything whilst still battling with intoxication, the door opened and a cop came in, holding a piece of paper and a pen.

'I need you to sign this.'

'What am I signing for?'

'To give us the authority to remove your flat keys from your property and conduct a search. You can refuse but we can apply to the magistrate for a warrant, and as you are a suspect in a serious crime, it will be granted, so you'll save a lot of time by signing it right here.'

He seemed absolutely certain of his position and whilst it may have been helpful to gain some legal advice on the matter, I ultimately decided it was probably pointless to refuse so I signed. Of course, once he had left I knew everything was about to change; the stolen handbag was still in the apartment and would inevitably be found, thus placing me at the scene of the crime. My mind raced as I tried desperately to come up with something plausible. One thing wasn't in any doubt, I would have to admit that I was there but it still didn't prove that I started the fire.

The following day my father turned up to see me but was refused. Because I had spent part of the previous evening with my parents, they were viewed as potential witnesses. A member of the Bancroft House staff, however, was allowed to see me, despite my not having been a resident there for several years. How ironic I had to speak to her through a bullet-proof screen. I continued to deny any involvement in the crime but it didn't seem a very convincing display. Perhaps she had already decided that I was guilty by reputation, I guess everyone else had, too.

It had already made the local news.

After several hours spent stewing in my own repugnance and ultimate shame, I felt entirely empty for this one was just a crime. When my solicitor arrived we had a brief conference and I again denied involvement but admitted being on the premises for the purpose of stealing soft drinks. He then casually informed me that the police had a valuable piece of evidence but they hadn't told him what it was. This information and the manner with which it was delivered temporarily froze my mind and I was in danger of going into meltdown, but just as casually I told him they were probably bluffing. We went into interview with the detectives and it was classic 'good cop, bad cop', with my solicitor taking up a fairly anonymous position at the far end of the room where he proceeded to work on another case.

Sitting with his back to me.

'Michael, when you were arrested you claimed you hadn't been to the soft drinks factory where a fire occurred last night, do you still maintain that?'

He was bristling but so far all he had was words and he needed mine to condemn me.

'No, I was there, but I didn't start that fire.'

He hesitated slightly and the much younger officer took the opportunity to further his own career.

'So, what were you doing there?'

'I was going to steal some pop.'

'And did you?'

'No, all the good stuff was stacked too high and I couldn't reach it.'

'Tell me about the security guard who chased you down the street. I mean, surely you're not going to invent some wild story about that as well?'

'I didn't know I was being chased.'

'Well, you were, you were chased all the way to the corner and he stopped when he saw the flames and ran back to dial nine, nine, nine. Don't you think it's a coincidence that you were being chased minutes after the factory yard was engulfed in flames?'

'Yes, but they happen all the time.'

Bad cop sat back in his chair and sighed heavily. He was starting to become agitated and I was sure it wasn't part of the act. His case wasn't being made for him and it obviously caused frustration. Good cop leaned forward.

'Michael, you're making things very difficult for yourself. I think you probably need help and we'd like to get you that help so you can get better and get on with living your life. You're still young.'

It was almost fucking laughable, watching and listening as he struggled to sound sufficiently empathetic, whilst his colleague looked on intently, silently imploring him to gently dissect my heart so he could force-feed it to me!

'You see the thing is, Michael, if you didn't start that fire then why were you running away so fast?'

'Because I'd stolen a handbag from the canteen, then I climbed out of the window, ducked under the barrier and ran off in case the security guard had spotted me.'

I told the truth about all of my movements, simply omitting the crucial detail of putting a match to the plastic wrapping. It meant by keeping it simple I didn't have to rely on an already faltering memory, nor did it provide an opening for them to exploit, so they reverted to type by refusing me a light for my cigarette. The second interview continued in the same vein. They questioned and challenged my movements and introduced more witness testimony, but so far not one piece of forensic evidence had been put forward to show that I, and only I, could have been the cause of that fire.

'Do you remember seeing a red car?'

'I probably saw lots of cars.'

'No, this particular car stopped you and you spoke to a woman.'

'I've no recollection of that.'

'Are you telling me you can't remember talking to her when it happened only a few hours ago?'

'Yes.'

'So you're denying ever having had a conversation with this woman?'

If I said yes and they were then able to prove such a conversation had in fact taken place it would have been hugely damaging for me.

'I'm not confirming or denying it, I'm saying I don't remember.'

It was a cause of some anxiety that I had absolutely no recollection of this woman or the security guard chasing me, it gave them ammunition they weren't expecting through my inability to offer an explanation.

'Well, this woman stopped you and asked if you had called the fire brigade and you replied, and I quote, 'I hope the bastard burns'. Now, does that help to jog your memory?'

'No.'

At this point it would have been prudent to have asked for an identity parade to see if this woman picked me out. If she didn't, her evidence would have been worthless. Neither myself nor my solicitor, who was still busy with his other case, even considered it. In any event it was never tested and I still don't know to this day if it was me she spoke to, or whether I said what she claimed.

In between interviews I would be returned to the cell to stew for a few hours more, the whole process designed to wear you down slowly and torturously, exposing you like an open wound. Sensory deprivation leaves only your mind but with anxiety and paranoia doing battle with each other, it becomes your most feared enemy. By the third interview the police had upped the ante. They were still relying on witness testimony but it had become more cynical in an attempt to establish a pattern they would make the bedrock of their case.

'Tell me about the guy at the party, or have you forgotten that you were there, too?'

'Which one, there was a lot of people there?'

'The one who recognised you, said you'd been on the television. For the benefit of the tape, Michael, what was the programme about?'

This was a desperately cynical attempt to forge a link between the past and the present and merge them into one uncontrollable urge.

'Well, you've obviously spoken to him, so you know already.'

'I know the basics but I'm trying to give you the opportunity to explain your side of things.'

'If you want to know, ring the Beeb. They'll sell you a copy of the tape.'

'Do you know what I think? I think you're a pyromaniac, a fire bug who can't control himself.'

'You can't talk to me like that! You know nothing about me, you're just grabbing at tiny fragments and trying to stick them together!'

I turned to face my solicitor who was still sitting with his back to me. He hadn't been remotely disturbed or alarmed by my outburst, despite the fact that I had raised my voice.

'He can't talk to me like that!'

He finally turned to face me, a little surprised that he had been asked to offer some legal advice. As he turned back towards his work he meekly offered:

'You don't have to answer if you don't want to.'

Interviews four and five concentrated on trying to demonstrate that I had premeditation and had planned weeks in advance to start a fire. They had found some of my earlier writings in which there were references to deliberate fire lighting, no surprise given that it was part of the play I had written for the theatre. Next up was the fact that I had changed my trousers. People at the party had given a description of what I was wearing, which of course wasn't what I was wearing at the time of my arrest. I had to make a spontaneous decision within seconds so I decided to tell them what I had really intended and how I came to lose my trousers. They quite simply didn't believe me, thought it was laughable and sadly I probably wouldn't have believed me either, had I not been there. That's just it, no one was ever there, yet they acted like they were, spectators in the gallery who apparently knew more than I did, because they only had to speak to be believed.

By the end of the fifth interview I returned to my cell feeling pretty beat up. I had been there the best part of two and a half days and I just wanted out, just wanted to give it all up. I took a deep breath and was ready. I had no idea where it would take me but my mind was made up and there was no turning back. I rang the buzzer and a young constable came to the door.

'Now what do you want?'

'I want a light.'

'Give you a light? You must be joking, it's too dangerous giving you a light.'

'I want to confess but unless I get a light, I'm saying fuck all!'

'You want to confess to the fire?'

'Yes, now can I have a light, please?'

He passed me a light through the flap in the door then scurried off to find the detectives, but not before I threw one more spanner into the works.

'I want to quote the Fischer report.'

The Fischer report was commissioned in the mid-eighties after a mentally ill man spent years in an asylum for a crime he clearly didn't commit, but the police, recognising that he was vulnerable, persuaded him to confess. Fischer recommended that anyone who had been sectioned under the mental health act should have an appropriate adult present during interview. Well, that included me, it was my time to play.

'You don't look nuts to me.'

'Well, I spent four and a half years in a top security hospital. Look it up on your computer, because I want my old man to be present and if he's not, then anything I say may be deemed inadmissible.'

This time he did scurry off and I lit another cigarette off the butt end of the last one, but somehow I figured obtaining a light wasn't going to be so difficult during the next few hours. Sometime later I was ushered into an interview room where both my father and the two detectives were waiting for me. My father gave me forty Marlboro and a large bar of chocolate, courtesy of my mother. I was touched by the gesture, it was their way of showing support and it didn't go unnoticed. I was in need of every comfort I could find.

We went through the preliminaries, I was making my confession without undue influence and then I proceeded to explain how I got into the factory, stood by the pallets and intentionally struck a match.

'What made you do it, Michael?'

The question wasn't unexpected but my response to it was. I had rehearsed what I was going to say and how I was going to say it, calm, articulate and with a hint of underlying anger. I didn't expect to find myself overwhelmed and broken, unable to resist the tide or pretend it no longer existed.

'I was eight years old when they took me away, and I was twenty three when I moved into my flat, but they never told me what to do, they only ever told me what not to do. When there's no one to ask, what will I have for dinner?'

'Are you saying you found it hard to adapt to outside life?'

'It wasn't me they released, they took all that away. If they hadn't, I'd still be there.'

'I understand the problems you might have been having but that doesn't give you the right to jeopardise the lives of twenty-six night shift workers.'

Suddenly my mind relocated its concentration and focus and was once again on the offensive.

'Don't you pretend to understand, you understand instruction, that's all! As for the night shift, I've already told you, I checked the building first to make sure there was no one around, then I lit the pallets several feet away. But you can't resist, can you? Nothing changes.'

The machine was switched off and the tapes were sealed and packed away, my old man didn't seem himself but he held himself together.

'Listen, son, whatever happens, we'll be behind you.'

'Yeah, I know, Dad.'

I tapped his arm. I didn't want another mental collapse but it was hard to say goodbye at a time when I wanted him to rescue me. Then I was taken back to the cell with the chocolate and cigarettes. I lay on the bed, stuffing my face, having not eaten a single thing since I arrived. A couple of hours later I was escorted to the custody desk and surrounded by enough cops to quell a small riot.

'Michael Cooper, you are charged that on September twenty-second, nineteen-ninety, you committed an act of arson at the Barr soft drinks factory, Bellamy Road Estate, Mansfield, with intent to endanger life. Do you have anything to say in relation to this charge?'

'No.'

I was marched back to my cell where I smoked several cigarettes, paced awhile, then finally found sleep.

CHAPTER THIRTY EIGHT

'Michael, I'm Doctor Sharma from Arnold Lodge Regional Secure Unit in Leicester. Your solicitor has asked me to talk to you, are you happy to speak to me?'

It was Monday morning and I was due in court. I just wanted the talking to stop, wanted to go back to sleep, didn't want to have to explain anymore. I felt empty and unmotivated. Also present was my erstwhile social worker but I wasn't sure which of us he was trying to help.

'So, Michael, how are you feeling now?'

It was the first time I'd heard him speak in almost a couple of years; same bullshit spoken at you.

'Tired.'

The truest thing I'd said in a long time, I was tired of being me, dissatisfied with what was left but still trying to hang on to it.

'Michael, I see from your custody records that the doctor prescribed you some medication, do you know what it was?'

'Anti-depressants.'

'And do you know why you were taking them?'

'Well, they're anti-depressants, why do you think?'

Every answer I gave was hurriedly scribbled on his pad and I would simply sit there and wait for the next question. It wasn't like I had anything else to do, I didn't even know what the weather was like outside.

'Your social worker tells me that you've already had a lengthy spell in hospital and that you also tried to kill yourself. Tell me about that?'

'It didn't work.'

'Are you disappointed?'

'I am now.'

In that precise moment I really was because I knew I was about to be sub-let once again. All I would own was what I didn't tell them, but they'd already banked what they didn't tell me.

'Do you think you might have been depressed when you started the fire? Do you think you're depressed now?'

'I don't know.'

'Do you think you need to come into hospital?'

'I don't know.'

I was deliberately being non-committal because I didn't want to limit my options before I'd discovered what they might be, nor did I want to diagnose myself by walking there on my own.

'Well, I'd like to have the opportunity to assess you for a while. How do you feel about that? I think you should take this opportunity, Michael, you could receive treatment and it may help to keep you out of prison.'

He speaks again. Blame it on the mind and let's all go home, just another breakdown that couldn't have been predicted.

'Okay.'

I returned to my cell and a couple of hours later I was summoned to the courtroom, still wearing my paper suit. The hearing was all over in a couple of minutes, no application for bail was made and I was remanded to HMP Lincoln until a bed became available at Arnold Lodge. On returning to my cell my clothes were waiting for me. I dressed but didn't know how to think or feel, having my own clothes didn't have the usual attachments as they were an integral part of all this, having just returned from being under the microscope, handled with indifference. I guess I must have been really nervous. I generally am when I don't know what's coming next, especially when it applies to everything.

I was taken firmly by the arm and escorted out of the custody suite to a waiting mini bus and instructed to take a seat. I grabbed one by the window. I hadn't seen the sky or natural light in three days. A young guy sat himself next to me but was unable to remain still, constantly looking around to see who else was getting on the bus. It clearly wasn't his first time as he bantered with the officers who were escorting us. He was a petty criminal taking a short vacation and like all holidaymakers he just wanted to reach his destination. Before long he would be coming home again, without the friends he called brothers.

'You been to Lincoln before?'

'No.'

'You been in jail before?'

'No.'

'Got any burn?'

'Any what?'

'Burn, tobacco.'

'A bit.'

'Give it me and I'll give it to the reception orderly. He'll give you it back after you've been processed.'

'No, you're alright.'

'I know the lad on reception, he's safe, he'll take a cut, I'll take mine and you get the rest. Otherwise the screws will take it off you and you'll end up with fuck all!'

'I'll take my chances.'

Within an hour or so we pulled up outside the gates of Lincoln prison, an old Victorian jail on the edge of the city. I watched as the huge steel gates opened but it wasn't an invite, it was a command. We drove around the back towards reception and as we left the bus several prison officers were stood in a line with German shepherd dogs on leashes. As we walked past the dogs they began rearing up, snarling and snapping their teeth.

Once in reception, it was reality that began to bite as we were herded into a large holding cell, with each instruction being issued as if already obeyed. For every question there was a ready-made answer, the trick was matching them up, not making them up.

Within minutes of arriving, a young afro-Caribbean kid walked into the cell, which wasn't locked, asking if anyone had any 'burn' they wanted him to hold until they were processed. He was the orderly and pretty much had the run of the whole reception area, a trusted prisoner. I wasn't about to wait for the deluge so I got up off the bench and walked over to where he was stood, and looked him squarely in the eye, trying not to blink too much, or shake too much, either.

'Yeah, I've got some.'

'Fags or tobacco?'

'Fags.'

'How many?'

'Fifteen or sixteen.'

'I'll take five, the rest are yours.'

'Five?'

'Listen, guy, when you walk up to that desk the screw will take them off you and you'll have nothing and when you get on the wing you'll be banged up 'til the morning.'

'Okay.'

I had taken note of how the guys spoke to each other and it was always with an edge, no politeness, just decisiveness and anything wanted was never requested, you were just expected to deliver. I tried to emulate this but I suspected he knew this was a whole new seat of learning. I figured ten was better than none and I tried not to hesitate as I surreptitiously slipped the box into his hand and returned to my seat.

I was staggered by the amount of good-humoured banter that seemed to surround me. Many of the guys knew each other and appeared to be treating the whole experience like a school reunion, rejoining their fraternity. Even the screws joined in, seemingly oblivious to the merits of their employment or the worthiness or veracity of its aims, given how many kept coming back more dependent than ever. It quickly became apparent that the favourite topic of conversation was, not too surprisingly, crime. Guys were eager to discuss their various charges and the merits or otherwise of the case against them. Group discussions took place whereby the evidence would be dissected and suggestions offered as to how to combat it. There was also a considerable amount of gloating regarding evidence the police may have missed, or the skilled way someone dealt with them in interview. There was no show of remorse, no admission of guilt, that was for deadbeats, for as one guy proudly and loudly proclaimed, 'anyone who confesses deserves to be in prison.'

'Cooper, let's have you, lad.'

I strode up to the desk and just stood there, awaiting instructions.

'Empty your pockets onto the counter, there.'

All I had in my pockets was a used tissue, which I removed and threw onto the counter. I tried to make it drop off the end so he would have to pick it up but sadly it didn't quite make it.

'Is that it?'

'Yes.'

'No fags?'

'No.'

I kept my answers short, I really didn't want to talk to him because he wasn't talking to me.

'Well, you've not come with any sealed property so there's nothing to sign for. You've been remanded in custody until there's a bed available at Arnold Lodge, so how did you manage to swing that one?'

'I didn't, it swung me.'

'Right, pick up that box and go over to one of those cubicles, take your kit off and put on what's in the box, then put your stuff in and hand it over to the officer there.'

I picked up the box but left the tissue where it was, which he didn't notice as he was already preparing the next one. I walked over to a cubicle where a screw was standing directly in front of it. I pulled the curtain to, but just as quickly it was pulled open again and the screw walked right up to me.

'This isn't a fucking changing room! That curtain stays open so I can see you at all times.'

'So what's it there for?'

Apparently it was for those being released who, having suffered the indignity of this dehumanising process on several occasions throughout their stay, were then afforded a little privacy and the return of their dignity on the day they were unleashed back into society.

'Less of the attitude and start stripping.'

'Enjoy this, do you?'

I was nervous, he was a big powerful guy with plenty of backup and that thought made it hard to swallow, but I just couldn't help saying it.

'As a matter of fact I do, every fucking minute of it! Now, get your kit off.'

I stood and stripped, determined not to give any eye contact, I didn't want to see my humiliation in his eyes. Afterwards I bent down to pick up my clothes and put them in the box.

'Not so fast, turn around and lift up the sole of each foot.'

It became mechanical, I was no longer able to attach anything to it that would have made any difference so I didn't even try, I became silent again.

'Right, turn back around and open your mouth.'

He came towards me and started poking around inside my mouth with a gloved hand. I thought I was going to grog but I fought it off and gave little sign of my distress, or at least I hoped so. He then ruffled my hair to be sure there were no weapons or drugs concealed in my follicles.

'Right, put those on and you're done.'

The prison uniform consisted of denim trousers, a denim jacket, a tee shirt, a blue and white striped shirt, socks, underwear and shoes, all of which had been worn by many before me. The prison service clearly weren't expecting many pint-sized law-breakers because the clothes could have housed both myself and my brother.

'Fuck me, you look like you were born to wear those!'

This time I did offer eye contact and I hoped it was as penetrative as it felt.

'Ditto.'

'Okay, Cooper, back in the pen, I'll be watching you.'

On the way back to the pigpen I managed to retrieve my cigarettes and slipped them into my jacket pocket. I was instructed to pick up a bedroll and a pillowcase full of plastic utensils. Several minutes later my escort arrived.

'Cooper, come with me, lad.'

As we made the final leg of the journey past the kitchens and the area where the food was served, a couple of inmates were hanging around, interested in the fact

I was heading for the hospital wing. They were neither threatening nor intimidating and I stared straight ahead, trying not to betray any sign of myself.

The hospital was right at the far end of the prison and was located on two floors. I was marched up the stairs and shown to a single cell. I walked in and dropped my stuff on the bed.

'If there's anything you need, get it now so I can get you banged up.'

I noticed inside the pillowcase there was a plastic jug with a lid on it. I grabbed it and showed it to the screw.

'Some water.'

'There's a recess at the end of the corridor, straight there and straight back.'

As a new arrival I was entitled to emergency canteen and just before lunch I was escorted to the prison shop, which was housed in a disused cell. As I didn't work I received unemployment wages of approximately one pound and seventy pence, which afforded me half an ounce of the cheapest tobacco, a packet of papers and a box of matches. The tobacco was full of twigs and was like smoking wire wool, how ironic that it was called 'Hiltons'!

Later that afternoon I had just settled into another mind-numbing, bird-watching session when the door opened.

'Cooper, you've got a visit.'

'Who is it?'

'How the fuck do I know who it is! Do you want it or not?'

'Yeah, of course I want it, a bit of human contact would be welcome.'

I was escorted in silence and entered the visiting hall, where I was given a table number like I was expected to know its location. I looked around for a familiar face and at the far end of the hall I saw them, looking more uncomfortable than I did.

My parents.

I strode over to the table, wanting to hug them but also feeling shitty at having to put them through this all over again. They tried to look dignified but were probably feeling the same as I was.

Another fucking waste!

'Thanks for coming.'

My father did what he always did in these situations, what he did in any situation that was outside of his control: he cracked jokes, and having been both a soldier and a miner, gallows humour was his speciality.

'Well, at least the car should be safe here, unless someone manages to escape.'

'Better hope it's me, then.'

I said this because I'd never been behind the wheel of a car, never even considered it, never wanted it because I thought freedom came from not always knowing how to get there, not being trapped by certainty.

'So what's it like?'

'To be honest, it's not much different to Red Bank or Moss Side.'

'Are you eating properly?'

Jokes have been told about mothers wanting to feed their offspring by proxy but there's nothing funny about prison grub, not unless you entered it for the Turner prize, should it survive the journey. Surviving the journey could even be its title.

'Yeah, I'm alright.'

An obvious lie, given that I'd hardly eaten anything but there was no value in telling the truth. My mother then slid a raffle ticket across the table and I stared at it in disbelief.

'Mum, I'm not being funny but what good is a raffle ticket to me?'

'It's not for a raffle, pet, we've got you some cigarettes. When you go through you have to show the ticket and they'll give them to you.'

CHAPTER THIRTY-NINE

'Take them off, please.'

I had arrived at Arnold Lodge, the psychiatric unit, under a two-screw escort. I was handcuffed to one whilst the other sat in front of me. We had passed through the air lock and had been shown into a secure waiting area. A female nurse had been summoned to fetch me and admit me to the ward. She was referring, of course, to the cuffs. The screws at first appeared a little hesitant but this wasn't their domain and they couldn't call the shots.

'Some of our clients have issues with the police and if they see those, along with your uniforms, it could cause us a few problems.'

Once the cuffs were off, their job was done so they left, whereas I was escorted through a series of doors until eventually I reached the ward. The first thing I noticed was how claustrophobically small it was, with most of the clients gathered around a television set. Having spent the past week locked behind a door, to now be exposed in this way was already causing me concern. I was shown into a small interview room where I went through the usual formalities. I was asked if I understood why I'd been sent there, what I'd been charged with, etc. I was then given a plastic mug; a number of clients would self-harm, cut themselves, so porcelain was out. They also went through my property and removed the matches, so if I needed a light I would have to approach a member of staff, as did everyone else.

'For the first two or three nights you'll be sleeping in this room. It's just procedure, everyone who arrives is observed for the first couple of days.'

The room in question was adjacent to the television set so I wasn't expecting too much sleep. Insomnia had been a common feature during various phases of my life and it didn't take much to keep me awake.

Whilst I had been working at the theatre in Leicester I had come to the lodge to visit a guy I had known in Moss Side. Now I was sharing a building once again, I was deeply embarrassed and wanted to get it over with as soon as possible. Just off the ward and through a door that remained open from 8.30am-8.30pm, was a larger area that housed a table tennis-table, a pool table and a music system. It was a communal area shared by all four wards. I went and sat out there, dreading the moment when he would appear, yet strangely I felt less conspicuous away from the prying eyes of nurses and clients alike. Sadly, I didn't get to enjoy it for long.

'Mini, what are you doing here?'

He had emerged from his ward along with the same staff member who had supervised when I visited. They both looked visibly shocked, and I don't expect I looked that great myself as I stared down at my shoe-laces.

'You're not going to believe this, but I've been admitted.'

'Fuck off, you're having me on!'

'I wish I was.'

'Really, you're a patient?'

'Yep.'

The member of staff looked on but said nothing, but I felt sure he'd have plenty to say once he was safely back inside his fortress.

I was eventually rescued, in the loosest sense of course, by the doctor who had interviewed me in the police station. That's how I spent my first couple of days in camp la-la, being interviewed by doctors and various other therapists. The nights were spent locked in my dungeon being observed every thirty minutes. I largely passed the time pacing back and forth, listening to the television, but more often than not the conversations were more entertaining. My file at the time must have made pretty dull reading with a whole series of one-line entries.

'Constantly paced back and forth.'

During the day there would be various structured activities, full participation was rewarded with an additional nine pounds fifty a week on top of the money received from social security. I quickly fell in with the routine and spent my days watching videos, playing in pool and table tennis tournaments, alongside bingo and quizzes.

Killing time.

But one inalienable truth began to quickly emerge: whilst I had struggled to meet the challenges of the free world, I knew exactly how to live in an institution.

There was quite an eclectic mix of characters and personalities. One guy was convinced the security services were trying to kill him and that his doctor was part of the conspiracy, so he took him hostage in an attempt to make them back off. He was in a pretty poor state, often chain-smoking and staring into space for hours at a time, yet he played table tennis brilliantly. One day he was sent for electric shock treatment (ECT). He came back an incoherent, dribbling mess. Another young guy would sit in an armchair and just piss because he was too fucking lazy to go to the toilet. Once when he was instructed to take a bath and had been in there a while, a member of staff went to check on him only to find him lying in an empty vessel.

'What the fuck are you doing?'

'Drip drying.'

This kid had a very strong accent and I couldn't always understand him, but it didn't help that his brain had become addled through years of sniffing glue. Sadly, he died of renal failure before he reached thirty.

Whilst I was there, a number of family members came to visit me and I noticed during these visits that my mood was extremely elevated, at times even elated, the symptoms being overly talkative, switching constantly from one subject to another and showing an apparent disregard towards my situation. It was possible that this may have been due to the sheer relief at no longer being in the toxic wasteland that was prison; it certainly wasn't due to excitement. The problem of course, is that when you're so deeply, so absolutely immersed in the chaos, when you're unable to complete one task without starting another half dozen, it's difficult to take a step back and analyse what's going on. However it did occur to me that my symptoms were pretty much identical to the ones that had manifested themselves prior to my giving away all my possessions, therefore it seemed fairly clear to me that I was suffering from Bi-Polar Disorder (Formerly Manic Depression). I didn't know what to do with this information, didn't know how best to represent this moment of self-recognition, because no one else had seen it simply because they weren't looking. Having previously been diagnosed with a psychopathic disorder, their entire assessment focused on either confirming or rejecting that diagnosis.

* * * *

'Mini, there's a woman on the phone wanting to know if she can come and visit you, what do you want me to say?'

'Who is it?'

'She says her name's Marilyn.'

I was a little unhinged by the enquiry; it was like falling out of bed in the middle of a beautiful dream.

'Yeah, tell her it's okay.'

'Are you sure?'

'Yeah.'

It had been a while since I had last thought about her and I certainly didn't expect to see or hear from her again. Psychiatric wards are at best unpredictable with unprovoked violent attacks commonplace. At worst they can steal your identity by encouraging you to doubt yourself. Therefore any source of comfort, no matter how remote, adds something different, something that can help to preserve your humanity by allowing you access to that part of yourself that can't be denied by the stroke of an expensive pen.

'It's good to see you.'

'It's good to see you, too, but you know we can't delude ourselves. It seems increasingly likely that whatever happens I'm going to be locked up for quite a while, so obviously you need to think about that.'

'I don't care, I love you! I've never stopped loving you. Whatever happens, we'll deal with it together.'

'Well, you say that now but you know, it could get pretty tough.'

'Mini, I haven't come here just to walk away again, we'll find a way.'

I guess I was testing her a little, trying to establish the truth and sincerity of her conviction. There was also an element of doubt on my part, being cautious about wanting to reinvest emotionally whilst living in an environment where, by necessity, such feelings are hidden. I did, however, agree to see her again and in between visits we wrote and spoke on the phone.

I had been there almost a couple of months when I was summoned to the ward manager's office. Until that point I had been fairly complacent, not giving too much thought to the outside world other than what the media allowed me to see.

'There's a doctor from Rampton Hospital coming to assess you tomorrow, but you do know that whatever happens, you're probably going to be locked up for at least ten years?'

'Maybe.'

I turned towards the door. As far as I was concerned this conversation was over, I didn't fear his reprisals, I just loathed him and his hideaway allowance that kept him delivering his own brand of psychopathic safety management.

'Oh, Mini.'

I turned and stared back at him. He was wearing the same smile he probably wore after every highly enjoyable, and successful masturbation.

'Good luck.'

'Actually, I've never needed luck and I've never really had any, it's not something I've ever had to rely on to get by.'

He knew he was holding my balls in his hand and gently squeezing them, and I knew that too, so despite a primitive urge to punch his fucking lights, out I didn't.

After a disturbed night's sleep, I emerged the following morning having resolved to resist and even disrupt any continued attempts to detain me in hospital.

Throughout all of my detentions there was one common thread: they were all indeterminate, I never knew when I would be released, if at all. I was completely at their mercy, they chose the music for me to dance to, so I decided to take my chances on trying to secure a prison sentence, a fixed term, knowing that on the final day the gates would open and I would walk out, unfettered and hopefully regrouped.

And I wouldn't have to dance.

I had never crossed swords with this particular doctor before, had never even heard of him. He interviewed me for ninety minutes and it was like going right back to the beginning as we covered my family history and my formative years. I almost knew what the next question would be which gave me time to decide how I wasn't going to answer it. He was looking to interpret everything I said and I was trying to cut off his supply, without any real knowledge of where that might lead. Despite my best efforts to limit his options, he still managed to compose a damning eighteen-page report. It was difficult, reading a stranger's words, knowing he'd probably already forgotten you, but I wasn't afforded that. He kept the best until last.

The court must regard Mr Cooper as a dangerous individual, who presents a significant risk of offending, in a way that is detrimental to others if thwarted or if he feels that so doing, will result in him achieving his desired objectives.

He has been made the subject of a number of interventions over the years, none of which have been able to modify his behaviour.

I do not believe there is a method or approach available that will ever have this effect.

His actions on a number of occasions have taken the form of abnormally aggressive or seriously irresponsible conduct but I'm unable to say whether this arises as a persistent disorder or disability of mind.

I therefore have no medical recommendations to make.

I had played an outrageously bad hand, naïve in the fucking extreme! I tried to be smarter, more authentic, questioning his ability to compile such a life-determining report in such a short timescale, I even tried to be charming. In the final analysis, I could have been as charming as I once was, and as smart and as cute, but the words on the page wouldn't have changed.

I walked around in a daze for a couple of days, trying to work out all the permutations, particularly how many extra years that report could add to my eventual sentence, and could we obtain another one and try to refute it?

A week later I was returned to prison.

CHAPTER FORTY

'Cooper, you're at Nottingham Crown Court tomorrow. You'll need to take all your property with you.'

'Why? Aren't I coming back?'

'Yeah, you'll be back, but if you get sentenced you'll be moved across to the convicted side.'

When the door slammed shut the full reality began to sink in and I had a heavy feeling deep in the pit of my stomach. I'd been coasting along for the past couple of months, just finding my way through each day. I sat on the bed, staring at the floor. Tomorrow might bring riches or it might leave me bankrupt. Then there was the issue of being transferred to the convicted side; once a sentenced prisoner, visits were limited, as were privileges.

I wasn't alone, there was a whole coach-load of us being taken to Nottingham that day. We sat in pairs, handcuffed to one another, with a handful of screws strategically placed throughout the coach. I didn't know the guy I was chained to, nor did I want to, I just wanted to look out of the window and dream, because dreams don't talk. On arrival, we were split into two groups and housed in two large holding cells. Midway through the morning I was called out to see my barrister who greeted me with a yawn, looking like he'd been sleeping rough.

'Obviously, you've already admitted to the offence so you have little choice but to plead guilty. Besides, given the evidence against you, a jury would convict in any event.'

Actually, the only evidence against me was my confession, which sadly was irrefutable. When a person is being prepared for trial they are handed their depositions, effectively all the evidence the prosecution intend to present to the court. This includes forensic evidence such as fingerprints, fibres from your clothes and witness statements. My clothes had been sent to the laboratory and came back negative, my benefit book had been found outside of the canteen, having fallen from my pocket as I climbed out of the window. This, of course, supported my initial statement that I had entered the premises and then stolen a handbag from the canteen, but there were no witnesses to the crime itself, only the security guard who chased me down the street. The fact that I was carrying a stolen handbag, which was later recovered from my apartment, was in itself evidence of why I was fleeing, but it was all academic, I wasn't playing a game of 'catch me if you can'.

I wanted to enter the coliseum with my hands held high, I just didn't want to stand alone in the dock, but I was the only prisoner.

'So if I plead guilty, what sort of sentence can I expect?'

'Five to seven years but given how damaging the medical evidence is, probably seven.'

'I was thinking more like ten so I guess that's a result.'

Within minutes I was called to the courtroom. It was a long walk along several corridors, deep in the bowels of the building. I was shown into an anteroom and given the opportunity to splash some cold water on my face. I didn't really feel the need, yet at the same time felt I was being asked to fulfil the role of the condemned man, so I did.

The young man who had entered the courtroom before me emerged full of smiles and gave me a high five.

'You'll be alright, he's in a good mood. I was expecting two years and he only gave me nine months.'

Judge John Hopkins was known locally as 'the hanging judge' so for him to be in such a generous mood was indeed good news. I entered the courtroom quite relaxed, thinking I might get the five and not the seven. As I walked through the door and into the dock I spotted my mother, eldest sister and Marilyn sitting in the public gallery. I nodded and smiled at them and they smiled back, nervously. I stood before the Clerk of the Court and was asked to confirm my name and address, the charge was then read out and I was asked how did I plead? I replied, firmly and loudly.

'Guilty.'

I thought if I said it like I meant it rather than being afraid of it, I might not fear what was coming next and wouldn't have to pretend it was just. The prosecution rose and began to outline his case. Normally his role is to portray you as a complete bastard in the hope of seeking the maximum sentence permissible for such a crime, but he didn't.

Everyone was in a good mood; well, it was Friday.

As he was addressing the court, the solicitor's clerk came over to where I was sat and whispered.

'Your barrister has just read the medical report again and he said don't be surprised if you get off.'

At least that's what I thought she said, or perhaps it's just what I wanted to hear. Either way, the adrenalin was pumping faster than I could compute.

'Sorry, say that again.'

'He's just read the medical report again and he said don't be surprised if you get life.'

Time really does stop when it too struggles to breathe. Everything I'd ever known became irrelevant, including myself, as I was the only one there who knew me. When the prosecution had finished, my barrister went to rise but with a wave of the judge's hand he remained seated.

'I've consulted the authorities in this matter and I'm minded to impose a life sentence. Do you wish for a short adjournment so that you too can consult the authorities before preparing legal argument?'

'Yes, my Lord.'

'Very well, we will adjourn for lunch and resume this afternoon.'

The long walk back seemed even longer and no matter how many times the word life was mentioned, it didn't seem any more real.

But the betrayal did.

I wasn't feeling self-pity, I was feeling anger and resentment. All the old feelings resurfaced but I was an adult now, not a cute kid who the public had once adored.

There was nothing to applaud now.

The authorities in this case were the various law books and statutes, along with sentencing guidelines and the criteria that needed to be met in order to impose them. I hoped my barrister could stay awake long enough to study them, but it felt like the deck was stacked and I wasn't the dealer.

I was given sandwiches, which I gave away, preferring a nicotine lunch, it nourished anxiety if not hunger. I told the guys in the cell what the Judge was considering and they were virtually unanimous in their contempt, insisting it was just a ruse.

'Listen, star judges always pull that kind of shit just to scare you! They want you to think you came that close to a life sentence to put you off doing it again. You won't get no life sentence.'

'Yeah, man, you ain't killed nobody and you ain't hurt nobody, don't be letting that bullshit get inside your head.'

Their support was a little overwhelming. Some of those guys were on my landing and I knew them just to say hello to really, others were semi-literate and I would write letters and poems for their girlfriends or wives. Unlike some I never charged a fee for this service because I couldn't imagine not being able to do it and

I was unwilling to trade in misery, because then I would have been a prisoner who wore the colours.

Not just a man occupying a cell.

They were right too, of course, I couldn't afford to let them get inside my head but I wanted to scream and there was nowhere to do it where I couldn't be heard, so they didn't need to be in my head, when they were where I stood. I was eventually called out to see my barrister, with the clerk once again in attendance. Their body language showed all the hallmarks of defeat and I immediately felt despondent.

'I've studied the authorities and sadly you fulfil the criteria for the imposition of a life sentence.'

'So are you saying it's inevitable that I'm going to receive a life sentence?'

'Yes, probably.'

'And there's nothing you can do?'

'I'm afraid not.'

'Well, there must be something.'

I was so exasperated that my voice rose a couple of octaves; even before the proverbial had happened, my voice was never that high.

'I'm afraid there isn't anything that can be done.'

I sat there feeling utterly hopeless and the frustration was unbearable.

'Listen, do you remember when I came to visit you in prison, you told me that you fancied doing an Open University degree because you had no qualifications? Well, now you'll have the opportunity, then when you do get out, you'll have something to show for it.'

I had never seriously contemplated throttling anyone before but when I heard those words I could easily have made an exception!

We went back into the courtroom and the judge asked my barrister if he had consulted the relevant authorities to which he replied that he had. He was then asked if he needed a further adjournment and he replied no, yet in fact he could have asked for a further twenty-eight days.

'Michael Cooper, stand up, please.'

I was nudged in the back by the screw sitting behind me. The judge outlined the details of the case, that I had entered the premises of a soft drinks factory and started a fire that caused a considerable amount of damage.

'Now of course, it's not necessarily the amount which is important in any case of arson but it is perfectly clear that this was a determined attempt and a number of persons may well have been injured.'

I knew what he was building up to and at that point I just wanted him to do the deed and let me get out of there.

'I have before me a most helpful report and so far as the author is concerned you are a dangerous individual who is not amenable to any form of treatment, therefore it is not appropriate for you to be detained under the Mental Health Act. The court is therefore left in the position where you have committed a most grave offence and where, so far as the doctors are concerned, you are subject to a degree of mental instability and which is not treatable by them but which is likely, in the future, to result in further grave offences.'

I hardly recognised myself in his words because I might have been everything he said I was, but he made it sound like a career.

'I have already, during the course of discussion with counsel, applied my mind to the various authorities on this matter and I have no doubts on the facts before me, so far as you are concerned, that you fall well within the guidelines laid down for the imposition of a life sentence.'

I hadn't read them but I didn't need to because the words can't move, they just sound themselves out.

'Accordingly, in relation to the offence of arson, the sentence upon you is life. In relation to the burglary, nine months concurrent. Take him down, please.'

I glanced towards my family but it wasn't a pretty sight, they were as helpless as I was. Although I was desperate to get out of there, when the moment came my legs seemed to fail me and I needed to be helped but I didn't surrender. I was once again walked through a series of corridors and they were expecting trouble but they got none. I was allowed a brief visit with my family through a bullet-proof screen and there were some tears. It's pretty tough when you can't touch the hands of your family and try to reassure them. Even tougher, witnessing their pain whilst feeling sorry for yourself.

We once again boarded the coach and I had already started preparing myself for the long haul. It was dark and the streets were littered with people scurrying about but I only really noticed the shapes. They were nobody that I ever knew, likewise the buildings, the roads and the fields I could no longer see. I had rented them all for a while but now they were like images in a glossy magazine of places I couldn't afford. At least that's what I told myself because I couldn't see over the wall and didn't know if or when I ever would, or even if I would want to again.

On my arrival I was immediately allocated to the hospital wing, which I deeply resented; I was a life sentence prisoner now, no longer the product of one of their failed cleansing programmes. I was immediately shown into an office where the senior officer (S.O.) was sat with his feet on the desk.

'You've just been given life. Arson, wasn't it?'

'Yeah.'

'Anyone killed?'

'No.'

'Anyone hurt?'

'No.'

I was already bored and starting to lose patience because I wasn't interested in his questions or his motives for asking them, I just wanted to hide behind a locked door to collect my thoughts and assess my sanity.

'So how come they gave you life?'

'Because they couldn't first time around'

'So you've done it before?'

'Yes, when I was about eight.'

'Yeah, but presumably you were too young to be prosecuted back then?'

'They have very unforgiving natures.'

There was something about him that made me uneasy, his questions appeared supportive rather than a mere lecture, but there was no warmth in his tone and no real sign of empathy.

'If I was you, I'd appeal.'

It hadn't even crossed my mind as it wasn't something I'd ever had recourse to, nor had it been suggested by my legal team. I felt sceptical as to why it was now being recommended, and of course by whom. Prison officers are well known for their liking of mind games but they are generally not very sophisticated. If this was some kind of ambush I wasn't able to spot it, and in any event my options weren't exactly increasing as we spoke.

'Maybe I will.'

'Well, you're going to be here at least over the weekend, we can't place you on normal location until the doctor gives the nod.'

Normal location! Row upon row of cells like fucking market stalls, each housing a different product and every price negotiable! Heroin, dope, sex. It was state controlled hedonism, paid for by a restless society.

'I'd like to know why I'm here when the doctors made it perfectly clear in court today that I'm not amenable to any form of treatment.'

It was the first time he had smiled and I instantly got the joke.

'We're not here to treat you, we're here to keep an eye on you. Suicides create bad publicity.'

The truth is, I had considered it, torn between the conflict of saying, 'Up yours,

I'm out of here!' and their pleasure in seeing me remain. Ultimately, that would be my pleasure too, because every day I was alive, was a day with possibilities.

I was shown to a cell and was relieved to hear the door slam shut. Sometimes you just need to ask yourself the questions without having to record the answers. I wasn't planning on making this my home so apart from making the bed I did nothing to make it more comfortable, I didn't want it to be. Instead I wrote to my parents in an attempt to reassure them that everything was going to be okay. It's no easier lying on paper as opposed to in person but it wasn't for my benefit so it didn't really matter. The door opened and a screw walked in, carrying a form like it was about to bite him.

'The S.O. has told me to give you this, he says you need to get it to your solicitor within twenty-eight days.'

He didn't wait for my reply. Having complied fully with his instructions, I put the form to one side, it would give me something to do in the morning. I spent that entire weekend bemoaning the fact that I was being contained on the hospital wing, and I only ever came out of my cell to collect food. On the Monday morning I badgered the staff to have me put in front of the doctor and I think they were only too happy to oblige, as my whining had probably become unbearable.

'I want to go back on the wing, I'm a lifer, not a mental patient.'

'We need to be satisfied that you have no suicidal thoughts, no thoughts of harming yourself in other ways, or of harming others. Sometimes the impact of a life sentence isn't immediately felt.'

I stood up and reached into my pocket. I removed a disposable razor and threw it onto his desk.

'I was given that by an officer immediately on my return from court, despite having a beard. Now if I was paranoid, I'd think he wanted me dead but as I'm not, I just prefer to think he must be stupid. Either way I don't think I'm the one who needs monitoring.'

He picked up the razor and studied it for a second or two then dropped it into his waste paper basket.

'How do you feel about your sentence, do you think it was fair?'

How could I answer that without adding a few more years to an already long sentence, or a few more days to the one I couldn't serve?

'I just want to get on with it.'

Later that afternoon I was transferred to 'B' wing, a mixture of long and medium term prisoners. My landing held no-one serving less than five years, which was a comforting thought, for those with nothing to lose are often willing to risk it all. I was shown to a cell and I fully expected there to be another occupant, but when I saw only a single bed I knew it was mine and I could have cried. There's not much to explore in a prison cell but nevertheless I tried.

What else was there to do?

Within an hour the door opened and the landing cleaner walked in, carrying a huge pile of newspapers which he dumped on the unmade bed, along with some cleaning materials for the cell, and a wick lighter, an absolute fucking godsend! Disposable lighters weren't then allowed in prisons, so most inmates relied on matches which, with the help of a razor blade, would be cut into four, a tricky business at the best of times, without any guarantee that they would light. A number of prisoners would smuggle in the ignition wheels from those lighters known as clippers and sell them on. The more craftsman-type prisoners would then fashion a body with two holes, one for the wheel and one for the wick. This was simply a strand from a mop head, which would be lit from a naked flame then extinguished. Having now created a charcoal effect, the sparks from the flint would ignite it, providing a bright red glow. Strictly speaking, such lighters were contraband and their possession could result in disciplinary action, yet the flints were available from the prison shop.

Around teatime the door opened, just as I had finished cleaning. It was tradition when occupying a new cell, to wipe away all traces of its previous incumbent. Two screws were standing in the doorway and one was holding what I thought looked like a passport.

'Cooper, you've been put on the book. From now on, wherever you go, two officers will go with you. It can be as easy or as difficult as you want it.'

The book they referred to was the category 'A' book. A category 'A' prisoner is defined by the prison service and home office alike as someone whose escape would pose a serious threat of harm to the public and for that person to have the financial resources and the necessary contacts to orchestrate such an escape and possibly even flee the country. The book itself was, in effect, a passport containing my photograph and all relevant details. Whenever I moved around the prison, I would have a two-screw escort, which included trips to the toilet and shower room, though thankfully they didn't step into the cubicle with me. Whenever I was handed over to someone else for them to assume the responsibility, the book would have to be signed with both the date and the time entered in the relevant column.

For the first couple of days it was quite novel, being escorted around the prison, never having to queue for a meal and always given plenty, and never having to queue outside the prison shop, gagging for a cigarette. After that it became tedious.

Back then a category 'A' prisoner wasn't allowed to work or attend educational classes so I was once again surviving on unemployment wages, not to mention killing time without a repertoire. Unlike remand prisoners, monies sent in could not be used to purchase tobacco and food items so there was no way of making my confinement more tolerable and after a while I stopped counting time, because it wasn't even numbers anymore. I only emerged from my bunker for meals, ablutions and an hour's exercise each day, weather permitting. When this was first offered I jumped at it, despite it being bitterly cold and not having a coat. I was escorted to a metal cage and locked in to walk in circles until either dizzy, crazy, or until I remembered that I still had pride some fifteen minutes later. Needless to say, it didn't form part of my daily routine. Instead I paced up and down with the window open, still a cage but with limited exposure.

My friends from London and Leicester continued to write, as did Marilyn, and I was sent books and writing materials. These were essential in continuing to maintain some sense of self and helping to concentrate the mind, keeping it safe from the dogged framework that only supports those who deliver it. Within days I had received a visit from my family. Whilst on remand I was entitled to daily visits, now I was entitled to a statutory visit every twenty-eight days and a privileged visit also once every twenty-eight days. The trick, obviously, was to organise it so that you got a visit every fourteen days. As a convicted prisoner you had to apply for a visiting order, which would be dispatched to the address of the person intending to visit and because of my heightened status I had to submit the names, addresses and my relationship with each individual who may want to visit and security checks would then be completed to see if any had a criminal record. They weren't interested in anyone caught speeding or convicted of some petty theft, they were only concerned with those who might pose a threat to security by trying to spring me, but they were all clean. Nevertheless, when I entered the visiting room I was positioned adjacent to the platform where the screws sat and observed. It's not easy, trying to have a conversation when you're more concerned by them.

On this particular day the visiting room was half empty yet they still told us to wrap up after just half an hour, which was hugely disappointing and frustrating, given that there was much to talk about, and much to jettison. I had some weeks earlier formally written to the housing authority, serving notice to quit my apartment. It was fairly obvious that I wouldn't be out in time to resume my tenancy so there seemed little point in prolonging the inevitable. Now various relatives and friends of relatives were after the contents, which made perfect sense, of course, it just didn't give much time to talk about anything else, didn't allow me to show them that the uniform was borrowed. After they'd left I was shown to a cubicle where I was given a full strip search. The screws were bristling because they were expecting trouble purely because of the fucking book! In an attempt to soften me up they gave out the usual rhetoric of how they hated having to do it, then began making small talk, asking who had visited me when they knew full well. I remained silent throughout the inquisition and not even offering eye contact, that's why they prolonged it.

An hour or so after I had been returned to my cell the door opened and an elderly screw, who had clearly seen better days, stood there wheezing, with a book in one hand and a small transistor radio in the other. Before the visit had taken place I had written to my family asking if they could buy a small, inexpensive radio, because I was afraid of completely losing touch and emerging without even knowing who the government was.

'Your visitors brought this in for you, you need to sign here for it.'

I was aware that they had handed it in, I just didn't expect to receive it so soon, it wasn't the normal way of things. I signed, took the radio and turned my back on him. He needed a signature and I wanted the radio, it was the length of our relationship.

During this period my solicitor contacted me to say he wanted to commission a further report to present to the appeal court but Legal Aid wouldn't pay for it, so he wondered if Franc would be willing to foot the bill. Franc generously agreed but I had serious reservations about the tactics being employed. According to my lawyers, there had, for some time, been an ongoing debate amongst psychiatrists as to whether psychopathic disorder was in fact treatable. The doctors in Rampton were virtually unanimous in declaring that it wasn't, only to change their minds several years later, whilst some doctors in Ashworth believed it was, so it was to them he now turned. The burning question was why did he initially approach Rampton in search of such a diagnosis, when it was patently obvious it would fail?

And why was he still playing doctors and fucking nurses!

Nevertheless, I agreed to see the doctor in question but only because Franc had paid for his day out. I quickly became bored, however, and largely uncooperative because his questions were textbook and could just as easily have been posed to my guardians, who may have found them harder to answer. There was no real investigation into the events that had brought me to this place, or the motivations that might have kept me there, he simply wanted to know if I had intended to kill my father twenty-one years earlier. I completely lost interest and began playing games, but those fuckers were pretty sore losers.

I returned to my cell to find a letter from Marilyn waiting for me. It was two pages long, the first page was chatty, the second page had no real news, just a declaration in large letters:

WILL YOU MARRY ME!

It was a bold declaration, not to mention a serious proposal, and it was delivered within weeks of my being sentenced. I was still treading water as I struggled with the paralysing effects of life imprisonment, the words still echoing through what was left of my mind. I was in a state of some confusion, which brought with it a certain amount of conflict, and I cursed her timing. I had already begun the process of closing myself off from the rest of the world, not that I'd ever fully embraced it, and now here she was, asking to share my world at a time when I was at my most insular, hoping to remain impenetrable, keeping everything hidden except from myself.

That night I lay on my bed, staring up at the strip light hanging from the ceiling. If you stared at it long enough then looked away, you could no longer see what was in the room so you had to invent it. I got to thinking about some of the other guys. A number of them lived for a letter from their girlfriends or wives or a visit from their kids and whilst some weren't looking for anything other than that which could be rolled, smoked and create a state of amnesia, others chose to remember. Some chose to remember they were still men and that their conviction wasn't the sum of who they were, it didn't define them. Yet each were capable of grave acts of violence, sometimes on a whim, sometimes pre-emptive and always extreme. They were prisoners, husbands, boyfriends and fathers, men who had blood on their hands, who could hold a newborn child like it was the most precious cargo in the land. The contradiction wouldn't leave me alone. Nor would the notion that if you could find a way of expressing the unfettered, unconditional joy of love, in such a soulless, loveless place, then everything might just be transformed, leaving these walls a mere instrument of the courts, as cold as the statutes that had built them.

The following morning I wrote to Marilyn accepting her proposal, and several weeks later I was taken in handcuffs to Lincoln Registry Office. A small group of family and friends were gathered and the cuffs were removed for the duration of the service. I felt a little fazed throughout, such was the duality of it all. People I'd known for years now acting as unpaid extras in a surrealist film lacking any real direction. A number of photographs were taken, one of which found its way into a Sunday newspaper and friends commented on how happy I looked. I think delusional would have been a far more appropriate description. I had allowed myself to become seduced by an idea rather than being driven by an emotional need that wouldn't stop bleeding. I hadn't given a single thought as to how I expected to maintain a marriage from within a prison cell. More significantly, I doubt we'd ever really been in love, more in need, nevertheless three months after being sentenced I was now a married man.

It was insane!

CHAPTER FORTY-ONE

'Cooper, you're off the book, go down and get your tea.'

Just like that, after a month of being closeted without explanation, I joined the rest of the prison population and queued. Later that evening, when the flap on my cell door opened, I thought it was just a security check so I remained sitting with my back to the door.

'Cooper, you're in court tomorrow, you'll be given a knock at six-thirty.'

I spun around so quickly I almost fell off the bed, sure he must have got it wrong and therefore irritated by the interruption.

'I've already been to court, I got life, remember?'

'Well, you're on the list for Nottingham Crown.'

There was no reasoning with that, no possibility of error because the list never lies, nor is it ever questioned.

'It must be a mistake.'

'Tell that to the judge.'

He closed the flap and I went back to answering Marilyn's letter. I had spent most of the evening trying to find the words whilst battling my own rationale. We were separated by the judiciary, unable to enjoy anything more than letters and the occasional visit. Prison cuts you off from warmth and humanity. There were a number of pen pal schemes, which a lot of the guys signed up to because the list was almost exclusively made up of women. It allowed them to stay in touch with themselves, a reminder that no matter what they had done in a moment of madness, it didn't stop them from feeling.

I just felt ambiguous.

The following morning I boarded the coach and was once again bound for Nottingham. Once there I was ushered into an interview room where my solicitor and barrister were waiting. My original advocate had been replaced and the new one smiled rather than yawned.

'No one told me I was coming here today.'

'I'm afraid it was rather hastily arranged. I don't know if you are aware, but when a person is sentenced to life they can return to court within twenty-eight days and present new evidence to try and persuade the judge to change his mind.'

'So do we have any new evidence?'

'Well, we were hoping to present the latest medical report but because of the weather, he's unable to make it.'

It had been snowing for several days and the doctor was unwilling to make the trip so we had nothing at all to present to the court except folly. Court time is expensive and the Legal Aid board would have been billed both for his appearance and for the few minutes he spent with me.

I walked into court and awaited the arrival of the judge. He entered carrying a handful of files. When he saw me standing in the dock he clearly wasn't expecting it and in that moment I really didn't want to be there. As expected he erupted and slammed his files down so forcefully they were sent crashing to the floor and had to be retrieved by the usher. Lacking in instruction I didn't know whether to remain standing or to sit down.

Eventually, I sat; this wasn't my argument.

'What's this man doing in my court?'

My barrister, who himself was clearly intimidated, gingerly got to his feet, head slightly bowed in feigned reverence.

'My Lord, we were hoping under the twenty-eight day rule to present fresh medical evidence, however, due to the inclement weather conditions, the doctor concerned is unable to make it to court.'

This simply inflamed the situation even further and the judge's already flaky patience was being stretched.

'Haven't these people heard of fax machines? Get him out of my court, get him out now.'

A tap on the shoulder was my cue to leave, not that I needed any prompting. Curiously the judge seemed to hold me responsible for the whole debacle, he obviously thought I had nothing better to do with my time.

* * * *

Lincoln Prison is really just a holding pen and eventually everyone gets moved on. Initially, those sentenced to life are transferred to a lifer centre and there are only three in the country, Wakefield, Wormwood Scrubs in London and Gartree in Leicestershire. Wakefield was notorious for housing a large number of sex attackers and was euphemistically referred to as the monster mansion. Any inmate arriving at a jail having first been there was immediately viewed with suspicion and would have to provide documented proof that he wasn't a 'nonce.'

Thankfully, I was allocated Gartree.

Whilst waiting to be transferred my friends from London and Leicester tried to drum up support for my appeal. A young woman who had worked in the press office at the theatre was now working as a freelance journalist and she agreed to write an article which she sold to the Independent On Sunday. Back then, I had often received complimentary tickets and would need a bed for the night. On one occasion she let me have her spare room, so it came as a huge shock when she completely crucified me. She basically portrayed me as delusional regarding my writing ambitions and reported that the people at the theatre tolerated rather than actively encouraged me. The guy who directed my television play even colluded with her, saying I bounced around with a copy of Screen International under my arm.

Absolute bollocks!

She also courted Marilyn, taking her for dinner on several occasions and eliciting, amongst other things, details of my alcohol consumption. The most shocking revelation, however, didn't come from Marilyn or any of my former colleagues, it came from my lawyer, and I quote:

'I don't know what she sees in him, he's a homosexual.'

When challenged by the journalist he claimed another client of his had told him that we had been lovers whilst incarcerated in some Godforsaken institution. When I challenged him he steadfastly denied it. The newspaper provided me with a transcript of the interview and also informed me that it had been recorded, but he still fucking denied it! I sought independent advice and was told that it's almost impossible to get legal aid to sue for libel. There was nothing I could do.

Except fire him.

Having enjoyed a relatively cordial relationship with the media, this left a sour taste in the mouth. It was ugly and it made me feel ugly and betrayed. I still remember the final paragraph.

He spends his time alone in his cell writing long eloquent letters to his friends, and hope beyond hope, he's writing another play.

I felt isolated and strangely alone, almost invisible in my impotence. For a while, every time I wrote, I felt like I was pretending, like maybe the hope was indeed beyond me, until I remembered that I only wrote to believe and not, thankfully, to be believed. A number of prisoners on my landing had also managed to gain access to the article and I was concerned that the homosexual fraternity might consider me easy prey. In the end I had no cause for anxiety, I guess ultimately they recognise their own; in any event, they left me alone. As for the rest, their support was both welcome and comforting.

Being taken off the book allowed me the same freedom of movement as all the other guys on the landing, and of course allowed me to get to know them a little; in prison, that's as much as is safe. There was an interesting mix of characters, the cleaner was a Dublin man called Liffey. Apparently when he was a child he fell into the famous river and nearly drowned, hence the nickname. Then, of course, there were the Budgie Brothers, although how they came to be named that remains a mystery. They were both bald, except for long ponytails and they both sported goatee beards, and looked like twins, but weren't. They were both serving six-year sentences for armed robbery, the youngest had only been out three weeks from a previous sentence. They had attempted to rob the Post Office where they used to cash their giro cheques. The postmaster recognised them and told them to clear off or he would release his dog. They fled in their getaway car, a beaten up Skoda. Whilst sat in a field enjoying a spliff, they found themselves surrounded by armed police; Britain's most dangerous. Tyson was so named because of his tendency to use his fists instead of his tongue. This tough guy was so terrified of cockroaches he used to attach a mirror to the end of a broom handle and search his cell every night before bang up. I actually liked him a lot, his toughness masked his weakness, he was a convict but only whilst he was there. Finally there was the art thief serving a twelve-year sentence for walking into a trap a twelve year old would have foreseen. He'd stolen a painting that couldn't be sold on the open market, and when he tried, he was arrested. The young offenders, those aged between sixteen and twenty, eulogised this guy but he was nothing more than a clown wearing different coloured paint.

It was a depressing time, surrounded by human waste. Prison was their education, life was their battlefield and one fed the other. Alone in my cell, I was just alone, I couldn't even help myself. I was no longer sure if I even wanted to, I was beginning to enjoy being hidden.

'Cooper, you're off to Gartree in the morning.'

The voice seemed distant and when the flap opened and closed I thought for a moment I must have imagined it, almost believing that I would remain there forever, because time never seemed to move.

It just waited.

CHAPTER FORTY-TWO

The reception area at Gartree was much smaller than at Lincoln, which had large numbers of prisoners arriving and departing each day. Gartree was a dispersal prison, so named because years earlier some government minister decided that high-risk category 'A' prisoners should be dispersed amongst ordinary prisoners, some of whom were serving shorter sentences. Nevertheless, eighty per cent of the population were lifers and some of those had very high tariffs. The tariff was the minimum period you had to serve before being considered for parole, the period required to satisfy the public's need for retribution, at least, that's what it says in the brochure. However, only in extremely rare cases could a lifer hope to be released on tariff. If, for example, someone had a ten-year tariff, they could expect to serve closer to fourteen years. Those serving fixed term sentences of say, five to ten years, would only come to Gartree if they had caused problems elsewhere. It was easy for them because no matter how much shit they caused, when their sentence expired they had to be released by law.

Ours had no sell-by date.

When I eventually arrived on the wing it was a complete culture shock. Lincoln was an old Victorian prison whereas in contrast Gartree was more modern. Victorian prisons have large cells with high ceilings, in Gartree the cell was no bigger than a fucking rabbit hutch with a low ceiling. Despite it having a bed, a piss pot and a table and chair, I somehow tried to convince myself that it was just a holding cell and I would soon be moved but then the door closed on another day.

I spent the first couple of days walking around in a daze. In Lincoln I had spent the vast majority of my day locked in my cell and was comfortable with it, now I had the opportunity to spend most of the day out of it and didn't know what to do, and occasionally felt helpless. The landings consisted of what were called spurs, which basically comprised one long corridor with many cells and two shorter ones with only a handful. I was on one of the shorter ones and my fellow detainees were all part of the London gangster scene.

I almost felt like a fraud.

I would occasionally say hello in passing but would invariably get no response and I began to feel a little paranoid, believing I must have offended them in some way and worrying about any possible repercussions. They always ate out in the corridor, having placed several tables together, but I was never invited to join them so I ate alone in my cell.

The food was of a much higher quality than I had previously experienced and there was plenty of it. Gartree's security status ensured that it received a much higher budget than some prisons. Food has always been a contentious issue, there are more arguments and fights during mealtimes than at any other time. Clearly the authorities recognised this and didn't want to upset the troops, especially not those who would never see the light of day again. Perhaps that was why they also had cooking facilities, so that prisoners could prepare the food of their liking. Inmates were allowed to use their prison earnings to buy meat and vegetables through the prison shop. Most prisoners earned very little through the work that they did so they would often form consortiums with as many as half a dozen guys each contributing a couple of quid each week, thus providing enough funds for a couple of decent meals over the weekend.

Even in prison the working week comes to an end.

Another benefit was being allowed to wear your own clothes but rather strangely it created its own class system, because those who continued to wear the uniform did so through a lack of resources. I begged, borrowed and almost stole but I never wore that fucking uniform!

After a couple of days wandering around, looking and feeling pretty lost, a Bernard Hill look-alike wandered into my cell with a message.

'Liffey's upstairs, he wants to say hello.'

I'd completely forgotten that a few weeks earlier he had been the first to land there but wasted no time in following his messenger up the stairs. He had secured work in the officer's mess and his cell was awash with all manner of goodies that they hadn't managed to consume that day. He would return each day with bags of sausages, sometimes, fresh cream cakes, but rarely empty handed. I was a vegan at that time, though not for any moral reasons, it was the healthiest diet with lots of fresh fruit, pulses and grains. It also caused some inconvenience to the prison in providing it and they resented anything that was outside of their normal control, anything they couldn't refuse, but they would have done if they'd caught me eating meat. Consequently I spent many a torturous evening watching everyone else devour these treats; it was the best reminder of the need for a strategy that gave me something without taking anything away.

Pretty soon most evenings were spent in Liffey's cell. High security prisons are by definition dangerous places, so it was important to quickly become part of an existing group. One that was already accepted. It provided some much needed camaraderie, moments of shared experience to remind ourselves that we didn't always occupy such a small space. I guess I took a little more convincing. There's much paranoia and suspicion constantly sweeping those landings so the group also offers protection against threats and intimidation, but mostly just by being seen to be a part of it. Anyone keeping their own counsel immediately activated the whispering committee and without any evidence to support it they will automatically assume he has something to hide. The first port of call is sex offending but this would sometimes be dismissed if the person in question didn't look like one, for example, if he didn't wear glasses or look unusual in other ways. So that might make him a police informant or someone who thinks he's better than everybody else because his accent doesn't come from the ghetto and that's why he refuses to associate with those who do. Had I chosen to stand alone, slightly built and with an accent and intelligence that wasn't representative of my current peer group, I would have instantly been condemned as being at least one of those things. Prisoners constantly cry out against injustice but some are equally quick to perpetrate it.

And mostly they get it wrong.

Initially I did come under the radar of suspicion, as I spent most evenings smoking dope with everyone contributing to the re-defining of reality. A lot of the guys would do anything to escape their current reality, which for some, hung in the air like a toxic gas. But I wasn't one of them, preferring to abstain because my reality was my guide and my anger towards it kept me concentrated and honest, and it was the only thing that gave me any sense of hope.

Because it was still me and I still owned it.

I did, however, eventually capitulate some weeks later. There were enough hours in the day for both and ultimately whilst in prison you had to quickly develop a prison mentality, civilian values were worthless in this hate-filled wasteland of human dereliction.

I quickly secured employment as a cleaner on the landing below where I was living, back then some of the guys used to make hooch, illegal alcohol made primarily from yeast, sugar and usually fruit juice. The prisons baked their own bread so yeast was always available at the right price. During the festive period when demand was at its highest, you would go to fix a sandwich and the bread would just fall apart through a lack of yeast. They buy it in now.

I had been given strict instructions that when the gallon containers containing the cleaning detergent were emptied, I was to clean them and stash them. These were to be used for the brewing and if left empty the screws, on their daily security round, would find them and slash them with a penknife. One day I forgot and was met with a tirade of abuse with the odd blood-curdling threat thrown in, just to reinforce the issue and his position.

'You just remember whose fucking side you're on or I'll cut you up, you cunt!'

I was on the same side as I'd always been on, my own, there was no egalitarianism amongst the prison population, I adhered to my own standards and would never have swapped them, but I never made the same mistake again.

I continued with this routine for several weeks, being largely ignored by the wing oligarchs then one Saturday morning everything changed in the most bizarre circumstances imaginable. The prison operated an inter-wing football league that ran for the duration of the season. Liffey and I were waiting to be allowed off the wing, when an altercation occurred between our goalkeeper and a screw. Threats of violence were quickly made and he was just as quickly marched mob-handed down to the punishment block in the bowels of the jail. Only those in attendance truly knew the horrors of what took place in that hidden dungeon. It even housed a cell within a cell so the screams couldn't be heard. But for now, the only noises being made were the rest of the players in full-scale panic as kick-off drew ever closer and nobody wanted to go in goal.

'Well, some fucker has to do it or we'll get docked the points!'

So spoke the captain but he was fighting a losing battle, with ten glory hunters all wanting to bag a few goals. No one wanted the responsibility of protecting the goal at the other end.

'My mate can play in goal.'

At first I wasn't aware that Liffey was talking about me, or that he had suddenly assumed the role of agent.

'What, him?'

I stood there feeling like a bit of a prick with them all glaring at me with obvious contempt. That's when I decided I wanted to play.

'He's a fucking midget!'

'I can reach the bar.'

I got the gig and as I changed into my oversized kit I was already berating myself for no longer being able to enjoy the anonymity of the spectator, but since when had that ever been an option? Despite Liffey's assertions, I hadn't played in goal for a number of years and I soon wished he had kept his fucking mouth shut, as I stood there in total disbelief at was unfolding. Had there been weapons, it would have been total carnage, but as it was I cringed every time there was a tackle. This wasn't football, it was blood sport. On one occasion the ball was played towards my goal, the pass was over-hit and I had plenty of time to gather it. The forward had carried on running but I wasn't alarmed, at least not until he ran straight into me, knocking me clean off my feet. I was slightly winded, not to mention a little nonplussed as I gathered up the ball and prepared to take the free kick. He stood right over the ball and I asked him to stand back so I could take the kick.

'You got a fucking problem?'

'No, no problem, I just want to get on with the game.'

He smiled and began walking backwards. At the time, the smile bothered me but I was told later that he had simply tried to intimidate me and as it hadn't worked, he had given me his nod of approval.

Some time later I had come out to claim a cross and was elbowed in the side of my head. My team-mates retrieved me from the back of the goal and I was so dazed I could hardly stand, let alone walk. I quickly conceded a couple of goals to go with the two I'd already let in and was instantly abused. If I was expecting sympathy I guess it's true what they say, it's in the dictionary between shit and syphilis. I played a poor game, a combination of rustiness and not quite knowing what the fuck was going on! I limped off the pitch, bloodied and battered, but I wasn't being carried, and on that day it was far more memorable than keeping a clean sheet. I staggered onto the wing where one or two of the oligarchs were gathered, along with a handful of foot soldiers. Suddenly they formed a line and began applauding, and at first I was so astonished I thought they were taking the piss, the midget being made to feel even smaller.

'This boy has got the heart of a lion!'

I walked past them with a wry smile and received the odd pat on the back but their congratulations were unwarranted. By taking the blows without complaint and by getting up ready to receive the next one rather than staying down, I had passed their test and earned the right to be there.

But for me, it was just business as usual.

* * * *

Although I was no longer under the microscope and wasn't constantly looking over my shoulder, nothing else had really changed, the aches and pains were reminders of that. I carried on as normal, working through the day, smoking through the night and occasionally, even managing to sleep.

Except the night before a game.

Sport became an integral part of my daily routine. During exercise periods there would be five-a-side games on the plastic pitch, and there were also a couple of tennis courts, available during the summer months. Pretty soon tennis replaced football. As a child I had fallen in love with the game the very first time I had watched Wimbledon on the television. The grace and artistry of the most skilful exponents completely mesmerised me. There was no one to rely on, no one to let you down, except yourself; perhaps this is what appealed most. I needed a racquet but I didn't have any money, nor did my family, so I wrote to Franc and asked him if he could send an inexpensive one. I was always reluctant to do this, as I didn't want him thinking that I only contacted him when I wanted something, but within a week, a racket and a set of balls arrived. That evening, alone in my cell, I practised my very weak backhand and was reluctant to put down that racquet, even when I began to feel tired, because as long as I held on to it, I felt something other than despair, and the world was bigger than the space I stood in.

I had just started getting a handle on things, understanding the nature of my day, when it all changed. I'm pretty much a creature of habit; I like routine, it cuts out indecision, whereas change restructures everything and there's more to have to remember. The prison was downgrading to category 'B' status as of April 1st but this was no joke. The changes were swift, all the guys who were still on the book were transferred to maximum security prisons such as Whitemoor in Cambridgeshire, which hadn't long been open and had a number of vacancies. So too the dogs, which had only ever known the inside of a prison. I guess they were also serving a sentence, particularly as some of the handlers stayed behind and new ones would have to be found. Staffing levels were also reduced with a large number of screws being transferred to various parts of the country. A great many had come down from Liverpool newly qualified, and naturally had applied to go back.

One of the more significant changes was in the budget, which had now been slashed. Almost immediately the quality of the food deteriorated, along with the amount on offer. Other services were also affected, in particular within the education department. A number of courses that had been freely available, such as Open University degrees and 'A' levels, were now restricted. Many long-term prisoners chose to do an Open University degree as it provided intellectual stimulation in an environment that didn't ordinarily promote it; alone in their cells they were students. Due to the volume of work involved, these guys didn't work in the prison workshops, they attended classes all day, every day, Monday to Friday. Education was the poorest paid because the prison service needed to maintain their industries in order to support itself. Therefore the lack of a financial incentive discouraged some from even attending the most basic literacy class. Now, due to financial restrictions and a regime change, the prison service finally got its way, abolishing full-time education, so those wishing to attend classes could do so for half a day, the other half was spent working.

For a while the prison had the feel of a local jail such as Lincoln, for example, with a constant flow of traffic, people coming and going on a daily basis and there being no real sense of stability. It unnerved me slightly as I felt I was in a different jail and had to re-establish myself all over again, which probably meant more bruises, but then fate lent a helping hand when I least expected it to.

Liffey had secured the 'red band' post of barber, despite having no previous experience of cutting hair. This wasn't uncommon in prison, if you were a successful landscape gardener you may well end up working in the kitchens. A red band however was something many prisoners aspired to, as it was the most trusted position available, allowing the bearer to move around the prison unsupervised. He had given me advance notice of his intentions and had encouraged me to apply for his old job in the mess, which I did successfully. This was massively important for me as I was beginning to feel swamped by all the changes and was once again looking for an escape route, anything just to slow things down a little, anything that kept me from where I really was even if I couldn't shape my mind to it.

The job was seven days a week. I left the wing at eight thirty am and didn't return until around six and the only inmate I came into contact with was the guy I worked with, who was also part of our group. He had been promoted to the red band position whilst I took on his previous role as the cleaner. The job required me to wear whites, white cotton tee shirt, trousers and jacket to match. All that was missing was the fucking hat, but this wasn't a kitchen as such, it was where the screws fed themselves for a few bob, yet constantly complained about the price. At the far end of the mess was a little backroom where we took our meals and this is where I went to change. As I stood in my underwear, waiting to step into my trousers, my colleague entered the room.

'Very nice.'

He was obviously coming on to me and for a second I was tempted. It had been a while since I'd enjoyed any sexual gratification, further still since I'd felt any human warmth, but ultimately I needed to feel the soft, warm breath, of a woman, however long I had to wait.

'Behave yourself.'

It was never an issue again.

What quickly became an issue however, was my diet. The mess was staffed by auxiliaries who were basically support workers, one of them was actually married to a screw and was nicknamed the Soup Dragon. When my appointment was announced she was heard to say:

'Well, I'm not cooking for a vegan, I don't know what they eat.'

This was a problem as I would be taking all my meals there. Even those who were willing to provide a meal had no real idea about nutrition, and for a while I was essentially surviving on the supplements that were given to me each week. The Soup Dragon had clearly decided she didn't like me even before I had arrived and would make a point of complimenting my colleague's work whilst ignoring mine and I was the donkey. One day my colleague went to the hotplate to get his lunch. Having retrieved it, he began to look for mine.

'Where's yours?'

'What do you mean, where's mine? It should be in there with yours.'

'There's nothing in here apart from mine.'

Without saying a word, I simply grabbed a cup of coffee and my tobacco tin and retired to the backroom. That evening I made a formal complaint, along with an official request to be employed elsewhere, believing my position was unsafe.

I lasted a mere six weeks.

I was offered work in the slipper factory in the mornings and educational classes in the afternoons. Whilst the noise and tedium of the factory drove me crazy, the classes were an outlet I sorely needed. I became a full time factory worker, sitting at my machine, constantly wishing that it would break down, and those wanting slippers would have to walk barefoot through the corridors of blame. My mind was always in flight, rattling the bars of its own cage, seeking its own remedy to the slow strangulation of tedium.

We were becoming estranged, as were me and Marilyn.

Whilst we both continued to write, letters were becoming shorter and less frequent with the content being more documentary than feature film. Visits became a series of entirely separate conversations as we both clung to our respective worlds, unwilling or unable to split ourselves in two. There were long periods of silence punctuated only by the loud inhalation and exhalation of cigarette smoke, it was clear to me that we both knew we could no longer maintain this fiction. I eventually took to removing my wedding ring and only replacing it on the day of the visit, sadly I guess there's no bigger statement than that, nothing more certain or guaranteed.

Within a year or so we were divorced.

CHAPTER FORTY-THREE

Psychedelic cars abound like houses set on Mars
Today I dine with angels in a cavern filled with stars.

This wasn't the start of my meltdown. By the time I had written these lines, it already had me in its grip. It began in almost identical fashion to that period when I was living in Mansfield, giving away all my material possessions. I had once again tried to embrace the simple life and had become interested in Buddhism, but the rigidity of the routine and the strict adherence to the principles rendered me resistant and I quickly became disillusioned with the notion of absolute reverence to fallible concepts. One evening I went to collect my meal and promptly slapped the food down on top of my head. I wasn't expecting it to be so hot and it burnt my scalp but I tried not to show it. Meat and gravy cascaded down the side of my face and dripped onto my clothes as everyone looked on, dumfounded. The guy who served me the food stared at me then stuck his finger in the gravy before licking it off.

'You're off your fucking trolley, mate!'

The following day I once again began giving away all my possessions and there was no shortage of takers; cassette tapes, my stereo and even my typewriter were all handed over to whoever wanted them. Having rid myself of all the things that never brought comfort, I headed to the library. However, once there I couldn't find a single book that caught my attention but was fascinated by a potted plant that was sitting on one of the shelves. I picked it up and it was love at first sight, I marched over to the librarian and placed the plant on the counter.

'Are you having a laugh, Min?'

'No, I'd like to book this plant out, please.'

'This is a library not a fucking garden centre!'

'Yes, and the only thing of interest here is the plant, which has sat on that shelf for God knows how long, just being ignored. Even plants need a little tenderness from time to time.'

'So what are you, the plant man of Gartree?'

By now a sizeable queue had begun to form behind me, and the natives were restless and probably in need of nicotine.

'Boss, just let him have the fucking plant or we'll be here all day!'

'I don't want to keep it, I just want to book it out for three weeks then I will return it.'

He glued a piece of paper to the side of the pot and stamped it, everyone was happy but it didn't end there. I began to dress increasingly flamboyantly, and both my speech and general manner caught up. One evening, whilst wearing odd shoes and with back to front question marks on either side of my face, I stood at the head of the food queue, imploring everyone to hand it back. I was becoming increasingly vulnerable as I continued to put myself at risk, apparently oblivious. The question marks were written on whilst looking in the mirror and the shoes were just another way of trying to break out of the mould and redefine the rules. The screws were convinced that I had simply been using some dodgy drugs and as soon as the effects wore off everything else would calm down, but things were far from calm in that dinner queue.

'Listen mate, if you don't get out of my way I'll wrap this tray round your fucking head!'

It was unusual to be given advance warning of an impending attack but I brushed it to one side, seemingly unaware of his threat.

'I will not be intimidated by these primitive threats, they won't hide your greed.'

At that point Liffey stepped in and ushered me away, marched me up the stairs and threw me into my cell. He got one of the guys to stand guard over the door with the instructions:

'Whatever happens, don't let him out of here, otherwise he's going to get himself killed.'

Apparently, he went downstairs and told everyone I'd gone nuts then he persuaded the screws to contact the hospital wing. Whilst waiting for an escort one of the guys came over to me.

'Listen, Min, you need to sort yourself out, mate. I mean, how long is this going to go on for?'

'I don't know, I don't know how long I've got.'

I didn't breeze onto the hospital wing, I took it captive and held it in my grip. After fifteen minutes the psychiatrist was exhausted and by the end of that day, so was everyone else. Except me. I stayed up all night, working on a new paper, the content of which changed every few minutes. I was pumped full of some very heavy medication which had some seriously vicious side effects. I would lie in bed all night, crossing and uncrossing my legs before losing patience altogether and getting up to pace the cell. I was constantly restless and often wanted to scream in frustration, believing that the effects of these drugs were damaging me more than the condition they were being prescribed to control.

My family came to visit during this time. Visits lasted approximately two hours and you were expected to remain seated at your table for the duration, otherwise the visit would be terminated. It was pure hell, having to force myself to remain seated when every part of me was screaming to be on the move. It required such an intense level of concentration I could barely speak or even hear what was being said to me.

I had finally become the stranger I so often thought I was.

I also received a visit from Franc who had brought a couple of his children along, one of whom was little more than a toddler. The guy at the next table asked if he could give her a crisp. Franc's children had never eaten crisps before but Franc said he had no objection to the guy offering her one. It was an amazing moment and hugely moving; this guy had been convicted of what is disingenuously called an 'honour' killing. He had killed his daughter, yet wanted Franc to remember him for the kindness he had shown to his, wanted him to know he had still retained some humanity in spite of his crime, that he could still smile at a child. It was more than I could manage at the time and I envied him.

One day my cell door opened and a hospital screw walked in, carrying a large brown envelope.

'The lads on the wing sent this over for you.'

He handed me the envelope and I emptied the entire contents onto my bed. I was shocked at the sight of all the goodies that lay before me. Due to my now being a patient I wasn't able to work and therefore couldn't earn any money, relying largely on what was being sent in. The rules had changed, allowing prisoners to spend monies sent in on those things that previously could only be purchased using prison earnings, but I didn't have a bottomless pit and had to be frugal. Not this week at least, as I stared in disbelief at the pouches of tobacco, chocolate and even a handful of coffee sachets. It was staggering generosity from a collective group who ordinarily frowned upon any form of mental weakness, believing the recipient to be handing their mind over to the authorities without a struggle. Indeed, the hospital wing was even nicknamed, 'Fraggle Rock'.

Then Liffey arrived in his capacity as the library red band but before performing his duties he stopped by my cell and returned everything I had given away, and which he had set about retrieving. It almost reduced me to tears, it was like having a father without the scars.

One day I was listening to the radio and pacing my cell as an aid to concentration, when the presenter boldly proclaimed:

'One of Cooper's shoes is missing.'

I wasted no time in organising a search whilst at the same time being intrigued as to how she came by the information. I wandered into a corridor and immediately emptied the contents of a large dustbin onto the floor. Within minutes I had company.

'Min, what are you doing?'

'I'm looking for my shoe, one's gone missing.'

'But your shoes are on your feet.'

'Yeah, but one's missing.'

'No, Min, look you have two shoes on your feet, they're the ones you arrived in.'

'Yeah, but they're odd, if I find the one that's gone missing then I'll have a matching pair.'

'It's probably back on the wing somewhere.'

His rationale, whilst completely reasonable, didn't really provide any answers so I assumed he was just making it up for convenience.

'So how come the woman on the radio knew it was missing? You can't answer that, can you?'

'Min, you're not very well, what you heard on the radio was probably just some form of hallucination.'

'No, you're just trying to confuse me because you probably already know where it is and you don't want me to find it.'

I was convinced of that, convinced that the missing shoe would provide the balance and I was therefore desperate to find it, because if they got there first, I could never wear it again, because it only mattered when the thought was mine. On another occasion, I was watching football on the communal television set and was convinced that it was faulty. I asked the same nurse to fix the set but he was adamant that there was nothing wrong with it.

'So, why is the ball moving so fucking fast then? This is Italian football, they never play fast, you're just trying to wind me up and make out I'm fucking nuts or something!'

I asked a couple of the other guys who were watching if they had noticed how fast the ball was moving, but they said they hadn't. I truly believed that everyone was involved in a conspiracy and it made me feel important. I spent the vast majority of my time in the hospital working on a new thesis. I had already tried to persuade anyone who would listen that I was the new messiah, based in part on the way I looked, long hair and a beard. Most found it amusing, some even irritating, but none believed, especially not the visiting chaplains who amused me far more than I did them.

But their job was to listen.

Once I'd exhausted their well-trained patience and polite tolerance, they would move on to the next cell, where the incumbent would invariably ask if they had any cigarettes. Eventually, after several weeks of searching in every crevice I hadn't managed to fall into, I was sufficiently patched up to return to my wing and start a new life as the court jester, but it had its compensations, for there was no kudos in hurting someone who had apparently lost his mind. I had more protection than ever because those who frowned upon it were equally grateful it hadn't happened to them instead of me.

Then came the news I'd been waiting for: I was off to the Appeal Court where I felt sure that justice would finally be served, I just hoped it wasn't too late to know the difference.

CHAPTER FORTY-FOUR

As the Royal Courts of Justice are based in London, it was common practice for an appellant to be moved to Brixton prison the day before his appeal was due to be heard, so I was relieved to learn that I would be driven down on the day in question.

The early start was immaterial, as I'd hardly slept the night before. I was reasonably confident that we had a fairly strong case, certainly an arguable one. The prison psychiatrist had prepared a report stating that I was more likely to be suffering from a manic-depressive illness as he had tested me and felt I didn't meet the accepted criteria for personality disorder, and opined that a hospital transfer might be more appropriate. The psychologist also wrote a favourable report, although she didn't make any specific recommendation.

But I still played down my chances when asked, too afraid to believe.

It was a ninety-minute journey, which I spent handcuffed to a screw who rolled his own cigarettes. Every time he fancied a smoke my wrist got yanked in his direction; I should have rolled them for him and saved us both the hassle. Another screw sat staring out of the window, commenting on virtually every fucking vehicle that passed us as we sped down the motorway. At one point he showed particular interest in a car that was about to overtake us.

'I've not seen that one before.'

He pulled out a tiny pocket book and began hurriedly thumbing through the pages whilst glancing up at the car's registration plate.

'Blimey, its come all the way from Cardiff!'

We arrived in London around ten a.m. and once beneath the courts, I was thrown into a cell. It was a relief to be off that van and able to stretch my legs a little, along with my mind. Just before lunch, I was summoned. I climbed the stairs to the courtroom, flanked by the two screws who had travelled down with me and was shown through a door straight into the dock, which was in an elevated position. Three judges were sat at a podium to my right but they never looked at me or addressed me directly. The walls of the court were wood-panelled and the shelves were full of law books and I couldn't help noticing, with some degree of nausea, that there was a certain aesthetic quality to what over the years had often seen ugly proceedings, especially in the days of the hangman.

As the appeal was against the sentence but not the conviction itself, the crown did not provide an advocate to challenge any of the assertions that were about to be made. It was simply a case of my guy trying to persuade the panel that had the trial judge been in possession of all the facts, he would have imposed a different sentence.

Approximately three years after appearing at Nottingham, I finally had my day in court as I sat listening intently while my barrister argued eloquently and passionately on my behalf. Occasionally, a member of the panel would interrupt to challenge some point he was trying to make but he simply offered a second argument in support of the first. At no time did he appear flustered at having his momentum disturbed, and he certainly wasn't overawed. When he had finished, the panel were prompt in announcing their decision and I could hardly breathe. They held up the reports that had provided the reasons for being there and whilst accepting that there were a number of differences between the various documents, they felt the most recent weren't unequivocal.

So I had to endure yet another assessment.

Ordinarily I would have been anxious as I awaited the outcome of such an intense examination, but on this occasion I felt that everything I said was of more use to them than it was to me. Without redress there was no persuasion but I hadn't tried to anyway, that was my satisfaction, knowing it was futile but real, if only to me. The eventual report stated that I was grandiose, delusional with some paranoid thinking and should be assessed under the Mental Health Act to confirm or deny a diagnosis of manic depression. Three months later I was on my way to Yorkshire.

* * * *

Stockton Hall was a privately-run psychiatric hospital but it was certainly no health spa for the rich and spoilt. Just a few miles from the ancient city of York, it could have been anywhere in England because once inside there is no sense of geography. Just the same old space and the same old smell, even the fucking staff have the same look in their eyes.

Within three days of arriving I decided I didn't want to be there. The prison routine was predictable if tiresome and dull, whereas at Stockton Hall I was constantly on edge and couldn't settle. As it was an acute ward, which also doubled as admissions, most of the clients were obviously seriously ill with all manner of psychotic conditions, resulting in various types of bizarre and sometimes violent behaviour. One young guy who came from a very well-to-do family heard voices that kept imploring him to kill people. He was waiting to be transferred to Broadmoor, such was the nature of his illness and his perceived level of dangerousness. Wherever he went, a member of staff followed him; if he sat down, they would sit next to him and at night he slept with the bedroom door open with someone sat outside. The room was also virtually bare, as he was not allowed anything that could be fashioned into a weapon. One afternoon I was sat quietly reading a newspaper when all hell broke loose. He had somehow managed to get his hands on around a dozen pencils and without warning, flew across the room and began stabbing a young Indian chap. The guy sitting next to him had only been in the job a couple of days, having previously been a carpet-fitter, and he completely froze with fright, despite this poor fucker lying on the floor being repeatedly stabbed in the face. Reinforcements quickly arrived and dragged the attacker off to his room but he wasn't secluded in the real sense of the word, which was somewhat surprising.

Mental illness doesn't discriminate.

The ward was basically square shaped with a lounge and dining room combined. Either end were doors leading to the corridors that housed individual bedrooms. These doors were locked between nine am and four pm. Having been used to walking a much bigger space, it felt claustrophobic. I also resented being forced to live in conditions that provoked anxiety and fear with no opt-out facility. I quite literally felt trapped and it was hugely stressful as there was no escape and very little protection. I had been prescribed a drug called Carbamazepine, used primarily as a treatment for epilepsy but also as a mood stabiliser. I was given it in liquid rather than tablet form, and it seemed more experimental than definite. One evening, shortly after being given my dose, everything went crazy. I was sat watching television and I went to stand up.

'Oooh, I think I'm going to fall down.'

I almost did and probably would have done had a member of staff not caught me and sat me back in the chair.

'You okay, Min?'

'No, everything's moving like I've been drugged.'

With the help of another member of staff they escorted me to my room and laid me down on the bed. I felt like I'd been on a three day bender; the room was spinning, my head was pounding and I felt like I was going to throw up. I emerged several hours later, barely able to walk due to the pain in my head. I bounced off the walls and eventually made it to the medical trolley.

'Can I have a couple of paracetemol, please, my head's killing me?'

The nurse in charge of dispensing the medication picked up my drugs card, looked at it, then replaced it on the pile.

'You're not written up for it so I can't give it to you.'

'You've got to be kidding me! Since when do you need to be written up for a fucking headache tablet? I don't know when I'm going to get a headache, do I?'

'If you're not written up for it, I can't give it to you, that's the law.'

I stormed off and found a seat next to the television. I had been there only a matter of minutes when a young female client who never spoke ran into the middle of the room, pulled down her trousers and took a piss right there in front of me. No one was going to convince me that my mental well-being would be best served by remaining here, so I effectively withdrew into myself. I was acutely aware that my every word, every gesture was being recorded, so I attempted to starve them.

But they always find their way to the feast.

I even took to showering twice a day, the only way to prevent the contamination from permanently clinging to me, and the only opportunity to continue to maintain my own standards. But it also served as a constant reminder of how self-preservation had begun to outlaw me. The clients ignored me, as I did them, and the staff resented me for not adequately fulfilling the role, leaving them to decide on the merits of their invention.

The following morning I went to collect a dose of my liquid straightjacket to be told that the dose had been reduced as a consequence of what had happened the previous day.

'So are you saying the dose was too high?'

'Sometimes a dose that suits one person doesn't always suit another so it's altered accordingly.'

'So what is it, guess work? I could have been overdosed.'

I took the juice, showered and prepared for another day of bingo, daytime television and the usual histrionics. Finally, after three months, they lost patience with me and gave me the news I was desperately waiting for: I was being returned to Gartree.

CHAPTER FORTY-FIVE

When I arrived back at Gartree I was shown into the reception area. For the first time in three months, I knew what was coming next and it was strangely reassuring. I removed my clothes, endured the indignity of the search but it didn't last long and it was soon forgotten. I was quickly returned to the wing and it was like I'd never been away, all the usual faces were hanging around but I didn't want to. I was shown to a cell which, as it turned out, was right next to Liffey's. I performed the usual ritual of scrubbing out the cell but it would take longer to rid my mind of its debris. I spent those first few weeks coasting a little, I had no work and was in no hurry to re-enter the slave trade. It gave me more time to think but in prison that's not always healthy.

I had once again been informed that I was returning to the appeal court. It was difficult to get excited about it as I felt it should have already been disposed of, it was becoming ludicrous in its tightening of the boundaries, they were now so narrow it was impossible to walk through them without bouncing off the sides. The judges wanted a deterministic evaluation of risk that could no more be applied to them than it could to me, it was inherently corrupt, not to mention impossible to determine.

Within minutes of arriving at the Royal Courts of Justice and being thrown into a cell, the door opened and I was called out to see my barrister. He looked sterner than usual as he sat fidgeting with the latest medical report.

'This report isn't what we were hoping for, in fact in terms of the appeal, it's worthless, as he doesn't believe you are suffering from a treatable mental disorder. I'm sorry but I can no longer put forward an argument in this case.'

I was stunned and sat there battling with the natural disappointment of failure whilst trying to control my growing anger at having been dragged all the way to London to provide him with a payday and me with a sore arse.

'That's it, then, we just give up?'

'I'm really sorry, you shouldn't be in prison but we no longer have an arguable case.'

His words no longer had the same impact and I got to my feet, no longer wanting to hear him tell me I shouldn't be where he was helping to return me. It wasn't his fault but the waste of my time was.

'You could have sent me a letter.'

I headed towards the door but he wasn't done yet.

'Michael.'

'It's Mini.'

'I thought it important to discuss the report with you in person.'

'But we haven't, it was decided before I got here. All you've done is pass on information.'

Within minutes I was back in the dock where the barrister formally abandoned my appeal. In order to demonstrate that I had insight, he made a case for my having seen how futile it was to continue to pursue a lost cause, aided and abetted by the appeal court judges themselves.

He just didn't mention that.

As I climbed aboard the prison van to once again make my way back to Gartree, I realised I had been in the building approximately one hour, less time than it took to get there.

* * * *

'Aaah, yer back, yer little fucker! Come in, the lads are waiting for yer.'

I had only been back an hour or so and was lying on my bed, confusing what should have been simple, looking for reasons that didn't exist, trying to restructure the ones that did, but ultimately just feeling miserable and lost, when Liffey appeared, beaming his trademark smile.

'I just want to lie on my bed for a while.'

'There's plenty of time for that when we bang up, and you wouldn't want to be wasting the lads' hospitality now, would you?'

I followed him into his cell where all the usual suspects were present. Each had killed in various ways, each had their reasons and each was brutal as I suspect most murders are, and I sat amongst them, as men.

'So I take it the appeal went down the shitter, then?'

'You could say that.'

He handed me a spliff and was ready with a light before I'd even put it to my lips. I took a drag, aware that all eyes were on me. It almost blew me away and made my eyes water, it was seriously well loaded and reserved specifically for occasions such as these, or any other form of bereavement. The guys had all helped to contribute to the kitty but I wasn't expected to do anything other than to help smoke it, and contribute the odd bullshit story to compete with the rest. Never before or since have I been in the company of men I thought of as brothers.

Now that the appeal process had run its course everything else swung into action and I struggled to keep pace with it. I received my tariff, which was five years, which I'd almost reached. I was thirty-two but felt older.

* * * *

One area I flatly refused to cooperate with was my parole hearing. I refused to appoint a lawyer, refused to call any witnesses and refused to submit any written representations. This might look like petulance, but it wasn't, it was defiance. By removing myself I was refusing to acknowledge the method of their disposal. On the day before the hearing was due to be heard, I told the doctor I would not be attending.

The parole board had a legal obligation to inform you in writing of their decision within seven days of the hearing. On the seventh day I was in a meeting with the doctor and a visiting psychiatrist, who had been the clinical director of Arnold Lodge when I was there several years earlier, and had returned me to prison saying there was nothing wrong with me. He visited me once a month and was now working at a private hospital. He wrote a report where he now claimed:

There is clear and un-refuted evidence that Mr. Cooper is suffering from a manic depressive illness.

Followed by:

However, it is my contention that he developed this illness whilst in prison.

It was arrogance personified, because he obviously couldn't contradict his previous diagnosis. There was no surprise in the statement itself, or the feeling of vindication that came with it but he handed me a copy like I'd forgotten. He'd fucking bent the truth, like we'd never met. I read it then slid it back across the desk.

'I only use these to write my canteen lists on and I've got bundles in my cell.'

During the meeting between the two of them, the prison doctor left to go to the administration offices because I had told him it was the seventh day and I still hadn't received a reply. He returned sometime later, holding a sealed brown envelope, which apparently had just been faxed through. The board decided not to direct my release and concentrated on the mental instability that had occurred over the preceding months, but didn't offer any suggestions as to how best to manage or treat it. Instead they opined that it was necessary for me to meet the challenge of a new environment and recommended that I be transferred to another category 'B' prison, as I was considered too dangerous for a move to conditions of lower security.

Both the doctors read it then looked at each other.

'So what are we going to do?'

'I think the time has come to sign the Section 47/49 papers and submit them to the Home Office as soon as possible. We need to get the ball rolling and get him moved to Arnold Lodge.'

It was a statement rather than a discussion, but one I was no longer willing to interfere with. The papers were necessary to facilitate a move from prison to hospital, the only chance I now had. I remained on the hospital block, awaiting assessment by the medics from the Lodge.

If I had remained in prison I would have died, certainly spiritually and intellectually but also in the traditional sense because the temptation, each time it arose, was increasingly harder to negotiate with, I just wanted to die more than I wanted to live, if this was my living. Conversely it's not always easy living amongst broken souls trying not to get too close, afraid that who you are wouldn't fit, but would somehow be encouraged to, but at least it offered some hope where the former didn't.

* * * *

'Min, your Mum's just rung, she wants you to call her straight away.'

'Okay.'

I instinctively knew what she was going to tell me as she had never left such a message before. I grabbed my phone card and marched down to the telephone kiosk.

'Hi, Mum, it's me. When did it happen?'

'Yesterday. He had his operation and they said it was a success but when they were waiting for him to be taken down to intensive care he suffered a massive coronary. At least he was still under anaesthetic so he didn't suffer.'

Although she wasn't tearful, she was clearly upset and trying valiantly to hold it all together. I on the other hand, was a little confused. I felt I should have cared more than I did, wanted to feel more than I did but I wasn't comfortable with a lie that deceived me more than him.

'Well listen, as soon as you know the details regarding his funeral, let me know and I'll apply for permission to attend. I must warn you though, I'll be handcuffed and there'll be a couple of screws in attendance.'

'That's okay, it would just be nice if you could be there.'

My father had been ill for a while. Twelve months earlier he had suffered a heart attack and having ignored medical advice to quit smoking and change to a healthier diet, he suffered another, which was immediately followed by a stroke. He spent months in hospital receiving physiotherapy, speech therapy and even occupational therapy designed to help him adapt and cope with his disability. He had come to visit me whilst I was in hospital in York. My mother and eldest sister brought him, wheelchair-bound although able to walk short distances with the aid of a stick. He climbed out of his chair and with great determination walked around it, one hand on his stick, the other on the chair, before collapsing back into it, proud and extremely satisfied. Despite everything that had gone before, I took no pleasure at all from seeing such a strong, proud man, often stubborn, often pig-headed and more often than not brutal, reduced to the vulnerability of a child. Now he was dead, aged fifty-six, having not smoked for a year. Perhaps he should have, it seems to keep me alive.

When I came off the phone I turned around and was faced with a screw looking decidedly uncomfortable. Their training doesn't include bereavement counselling, only how to play down the situation in order to prevent a violent outburst.

'Everything okay, Min?'

'Everything's fine, thank you.'

I marched straight past him towards the office.

'My old man has died, I need a form to apply for permission to attend his funeral.'

'The Home Office will only allow you to attend the funeral if it's a member of your immediate family, so was he your real father or your step-father?'

'Don't take the fucking piss! Of course he was my real father.'

'Well, you need to put his details down on the form.'

I filled in the form within minutes and submitted it. A couple of days later, permission was granted for me to attend the funeral, with additional permission granted for me to have an appropriate set of clothing handed in on a visit. All that was left was for me to inform Franc.

'Hey, Mini, how are you?'

'I've been better, Franc. Listen, there's something I need to tell you and I just wanted you to hear it from me. My old man died a couple of days ago.'

'Oh, my God, Mini, I'm so sorry.'

'No, no, it's okay, I'm not about to join him, I just wanted you to know, I just needed someone to tell.'

Franc brought balance to a situation that went in search of every direction but still came back empty-handed. He made it real and not just some idea that could be erased if it didn't fit.

'You know, Mini, you shouldn't blame your old man for everything. I know that's tough but who knows what pressure was being put on him?'

Since I had received the news, I had thought of a great many things, some outlandish, others that had carried a grain of truth not easily thrown away. Franc had helped me to validate those because they weren't hidden, they'd been there all my life.

'I'm not blind, Franc, I know there were times when he was probably being manipulated, just as I was.'

'Well listen, stay in touch and if you need anything just write me and let me know.'

On the day of the funeral I was taken to reception so I could change into a set of smart clothes. My escort was waiting for me and I was fortunate to have a couple of screws with whom I'd enjoyed a pretty good relationship. Once dressed, I was handcuffed and then double cuffed to one of them. We then climbed into a waiting taxi and awaited our departure. Before we were given the green light to pass through the gates, a member of the security department came over and checked everything.

'Under no circumstances must these cuffs be removed, do you understand?'

'No problem, sir, they'll be staying on.'

The gates opened and we were on our way. The taxi driver never spoke and after an awkward silence it was left to the screws to try to lighten the atmosphere a little and make the trip at least bearable.

'So, Min, have you been to a funeral before?'

'No, can you believe it? My first ever funeral and it's my old man's.'

Various members of the family had passed away over the years, during my many incarcerations, but it was considered too risky to allow me to attend the funerals, and they were probably right. It had been six or seven years since I had visited my parents' village and I didn't even know where the Catholic church was. When we pulled up outside, I realised that I must have walked passed it many times without even noticing.

We stepped out of the cab and one or two people were passing by. I smiled at them but they scurried along. It was a beautiful autumnal morning and I doubt they had even noticed. Inside the church we were entirely alone, apart from the smell that never seems to change with time or absence.

'Where do you want to sit, Min?'

I chose a pew somewhere in the middle, the decision obviously governed by my circumstances. I didn't want to sit at the front under the voyeuristic glare of the entire congregation, nor did I want to sit at the back, so ashamed I needed to hide. But I didn't want to turn it into a circus, either.

My father's coffin sat on top of a trolley just a few feet away from me and I couldn't take my eyes off it.

'Can I go over to the coffin before everybody else gets here?'

We walked over to it but the situation was all wrong, with handcuffs and uniforms, and I felt unable to say what I wanted or even feel something outside of this contrivance.

'Listen, Min, you're not going to do anything stupid, are you?'

I shook my head slowly and deliberately.

'No, I'm only here to bury my Dad.'

He removed the handcuffs without another word, and he and his colleague then returned to their seat, allowing me a private moment. It was a gesture I've never forgotten, a moment of humanity I hadn't expected. I stood there alone, without fear or anxiety, the only time I'd ever felt that way around him. I expected to have more to say than time would permit, but I simply placed my hands on top of the coffin.

'You're not a monster, you're just a man in a box.'

I walked away and returned to my pew where I sat lost in it all, questions I couldn't ask and answers I'd never hear, not from him, at least. I wondered if he'd ever really known life and not just the breaths he never counted; would he miss it, or was it all just the same?

Pretty soon everyone started to file in. I saw people I hadn't seen for years, some I hadn't seen since I was a boy and it still felt distant. I recognised their faces, some ravaged by time, others waiting for it to catch up but that's all I saw, a crowd just like any other. The service seemed to last longer than my old man lived, at least that's how it felt with the young Irish priest, fond of hearing his words echo then settle above a nodding congregation. In the weeks leading up to his death, my father apparently attended the odd Mass, sitting at the back in his wheelchair. It seems he too wasn't immune to the odd pang of fear.

During the service the hymn 'Abide With Me' was sung; it had been specially requested and the tears began to flow. We often sang it together during the F.A. Cup Final, the only time we ever connected. Football, a universal language and the only one we actually shared, where our disagreements didn't descend into violent one-upmanship. There were plenty of them but he respected my opinion on football, believing he had sown the original seed. When the hymn finished it became instantly real and recognisable. He wasn't coming back and for a couple of hours on a Saturday afternoon, I would miss him but still enjoy the beer. After the service I was allowed to stand, unfettered, at the entrance to the church and greet people as they came out. Then it was off to the crematorium and when the curtains closed, it was like he'd never been here, a life still waiting to be lived. I waited as everyone else began to file out but I wasn't allowed to follow the others back to my mother's house for the traditional raising of the glass, instead we headed straight back to the prison, without them realising they had actually rescued me.

The following week during a cup-tie between Newcastle United and Oldham Athletic, several members of the family travelled to the North East, carrying my father's ashes. Minutes before kick-off they walked across the pitch and scattered them in the goal he used to stand behind as a boy. My youngest sister had initially tried to arrange this and had been refused, then my brother, who was estranged from my father, took up the challenge. He explained to club officials that the old man had been a lifelong supporter of the club and should they continue to refuse, he would go to the press; they relented. I'm sure he would have been smiling, for ultimately he had achieved his greatest wish. He hadn't been laid to rest in 'scab county', as he often referred to Nottinghamshire.

* * * *

Within a few weeks, a doctor from Arnold Lodge came to assess me. I was expecting a fairly robust examination but it lasted no more than twenty minutes. Finally, he looked me squarely in the eyes and said:

'I'm going to get you out of here and all being well, you won't be coming back.'

I was stunned to say the least, not to mention sceptical. I wanted to believe him and in many ways needed to believe him but it was safer not to. I had fought long and hard for this moment but I wasn't used to getting what I needed.

I was told I was top of the waiting list and as the weeks went by I began to lose all hope of ever moving. One Tuesday I went to the treatment hatch to collect my medication at the end of another prescribed day.

'Good news, Min, there's a bed for you at Arnold Lodge.'

'Blimey, I'd begun to forget all about it! When am I going?'

'Thursday morning.'

I had waited almost a year to shrink my world so that I could fit into it more comfortably, and I was about to find out if it would nourish and sustain, or leave me wishing there was more.

PART FOUR

(34-45)

CHAPTER FORTY-SIX

'So, Mini, how does it feel to be outside without a huge wall spoiling your view?'

'Bigger.'

It had taken approximately nine months between leaving prison and being granted that first supervised trip around the grounds. We passed through reception, first stopping so a description of what I was wearing could be recorded. My escort announced our destination and was then issued with a radio that could be used to contact the control room, should I do what had once been top of my list.

It seemed a long time ago.

Arnold Lodge was one of a series of buildings situated within the grounds of an old Victorian asylum that under different circumstances might have passed for a country retreat, but now much of it stood empty in various states of dereliction, just waitng for the property developers to move in and once again re-write history.

That first trip was like my first memory of being taken to the park by my parents when I was probably five or six years old. I was enthralled by everything that moved but equally excited by the things that didn't. I tried counting all of the leaves on all of the trees, just to see which one had the most, but in the end there were just too many of them and I kept losing count. On the occasion of that first outing I wanted it to feel fresh and clean, like I was once again viewing it through the innocence and imagination of a child's perspective. I wanted to count those leaves again, knowing I could count them all, but in the end I satisfied myself with simple comparisons and simple tastes, the difference in air quality and the constant smell of prison that hadn't followed me because it had to remain where it was, like a ghost, so I returned to the unit and walked back onto the ward, but everything was different. I had been outside and knew I could be again, I had reached the upper tier and it had changed the shape of my tenure.

When I first arrived from Gartree I spent those first few weeks largely observing and surprisingly finding little to criticise, although like most institutions, no one really informed you about the routine or anything else, for that matter, it was trial and error and getting things wrong was often the way to find out. The first time I attempted to post a letter I asked where to find the post box and was simply told to hand my letter in at the office.

'Min, you haven't sealed it.'

'I didn't know I was allowed to.'

He handed it back and I just stared at it, feeling a little embarrassed at having spent so long outside of normal experience; I no longer questioned it. I quickly sealed it then gave it back.

I also discovered quite by chance that clients were allowed television sets, which they kept in their bedrooms. I loved watching Wimbledon and the thought of two weeks of uninterrupted tennis almost had me feeling delirious. My birthday was only a few weeks away and as an early gift my family sent me sixty pounds so I could purchase a second-hand television. The staff rallied round on my behalf, their enthusiasm was so unexpected and so entirely against the grain, that I momentarily forgot I was still incarcerated and allowed myself the luxury of a little unguarded excitement. As soon as the television set arrived, having been collected by a member of staff, others joined in, helping to tune each channel. Once the set was safely housed in my room another staff member fiddled with the aerial until the picture was watchable. I thanked everyone individually and without regret, it was good knowing that I could. In a few weeks I had gone from a strictly punitive regime, where requests were often met with obstruction, delays, or even ignored. Now I had my very first colour television, made possible by those who wanted it to happen just because I did. They had changed everything through kindness, generosity and human decency. I hadn't forgotten they were still my custodians, but it was no longer the first thing I saw.

Another significant incident was a change to my medication. I was still suffering mood disturbances and the doctors were keen to put it right and within a couple of months and for the first time in many years, I began to experience some genuine stability of mood.

After having been there approximately six months, and having fully settled in and adapted to marked changes in both regime and daily life, I began working with a number of different therapists. They helped to break down the barriers that had consistently enabled me to defend my parents, often making excuses for them. The breakthrough came not from acknowledging that they were a pair of shits, but through understanding they were fallible human beings. In a sense I needed to apply the same principles to myself. The sessions became increasingly intense and frustrating with lots of anger and inevitably some tears. I was desperately clinging to a notion that they were equally determined I should let go, but it's all I had and I was afraid that if I gave it up, only the tears would remain and quite possibly I might drown in them.

I needed to believe, **had** to believe that it had all meant something, the incarcerations, the beatings and the cold hungry nights negotiating with death, I was still here for fuck's sake! I refused to reason with the idea that none of it was of any greater significance than my name being plucked arbitrarily from a hat, when it could just as easily have been yours. After several more sessions exploring this theme I was eventually persuaded that in all likelihood, what kept me from death whilst taking someone else was indeed a lottery. It was a shocking realization that left me broken for a while, I guess I'd been thinking I'd served a tough apprenticeship, successfully navigated my way through the most extreme tests of character and strength, to now reasonably expect my future to burst into life, but it's not ordained it's just fucking life.

Now was the time to apply for unsupervised trips, again within the grounds. The response was quicker than the first time and I was once again successful, this time being granted a dozen one-hour sessions. It was like hooking a duck and every time I did, it revealed a winning number but I still guarded against complacency, still believing a fall was just around the corner. That's what came with me as I walked alone across that same car park, and past the trees and open spaces that now seemed even bigger. It was easy, not to mention tempting, to just sit absorbed in the feeling that for sixty minutes I owned the time, but I didn't want to just sit around smoking cigarettes whilst staring out at the horizon.

I began jogging, initially as a means of working the time and making it something other than just another test. I was, of course, a complete novice with no real knowledge of the demands or indeed the requirements of such an exercise therefore it wasn't long before I got into serious difficulties. I enjoyed the challenge of running circular laps around the grounds and not succumbing to the tedious repetition of counting them out or the dizzying monotony of covering the same landscape, only to do it again and again. On each occasion I would set myself an additional challenge of increasing my distance by another couple of laps, which provided self discipline and motivation as I also began to introduce little mind games to help keep me concentrated. I would read out loud the registration number of a parked car and would try to identify the various species of trees and shrubs. I don't know how many I got right, but it didn't matter.

By now I had such a varied portfolio of leave that, apart from sleeping, I was off the ward more than I was on it. I had unlimited unsupervised leave to the local high street which allowed me to plan a more varied and interesting running programme. More crucially, I was allowed unsupervised leave into the city once a week for a maximum of eight hours and that's where I was headed next. I found the running store without too many problems. The store made use of a machine that measured your gait in order to help the staff advise on the best type of shoe to match each individual's needs; I didn't know such machines existed. It simply consisted of a mat placed on the floor which fed information onto a screen. I was instructed to walk over it several times in my stockinged feet, then run over it a couple of times. It turned out that I overpronated, which in layman's terms meant my feet turned too far inwardly as they pushed off from the ground. This required me to purchase shoes with added support to help prevent injuries to the knees and lower back. I had enough money for the shoes, the socks and a coffee and sandwich at my favourite café bar.

Sitting with my usual coffee order, I noticed, not for the first time, that the place was full of same sex couples so I figured it must be a gay bar. I'm certainly not homophobic but it was a concern as I always sat alone and it seemed only a matter of time before I began to attract unwanted attention. Sadly, I made the decision that it was the last cup of coffee I drank there, which was a loss because the place made me feel sophisticated.

Life was starting to feel good because slowly, over time, I had begun to put the various elements together and I could take them anywhere. I was acutely aware of the void I had experienced back in Mansfield all those years ago. Still conscious of wanting to fill each day with something of sustainable value that didn't rely on others to provide, only my body could now prevent me from running and only my mind could halt my growth. But I no longer needed to fill it with mindless examples of how the state needs to compensate me, nor did I need to crowd it with unhealthy preoccupations of failure when I'd already succeeded. I had defied death many years earlier and had battled mental illness and the cruel stupidity of circumstance.

But I was still here.

Having so much leave helped the normalising process. Whilst on the ward smokers were not allowed to carry a lighter, instead a member of staff would be called upon to provide the necessary, however once unsupervised leave was granted, a lighter could be purchased, carried, then handed over on your return. Just having it signalled progress, a convicted arsonist lighting nothing more than a cigarette.

CHAPTER FORTY-SEVEN

My trips into town had become such a part of my routine I no longer got excited by them, which was kind of exciting in itself. I guess when you start taking things for granted, they lose their grip on you. However, one day I received an unexpected surprise that did turn back the clock and excitement raged once again. Some weeks earlier I had spoken to Franc over the phone, outlining how much leave I'd been granted, and of course how it was shaping the future. Then a letter arrived that I was only too eager to sign for, having instantly recognised the handwriting. It was, of course, from Franc and he was coming to Leicester to spend the day with me. It had been many years since I had seen him walk alongside me on a busy city street, but never on streets where I would be the guide, and finding somewhere decent to eat might create a problem. I asked around and got a few ideas then on the day itself I set off briskly to meet him from the train. I paced impatiently back and forth along the platform for what seemed like the entire length of my sentence. Then the future became the present as the train slowly emerged from the tunnel. I was already smiling, already forgetting where I'd left to be there.

'Hey, Mini. How are you?'

We hugged, then made our way out of the station. As we busied ourselves with the standard introductory small talk, I suddenly realised we had emerged from the station and were heading towards the heart of the city and I wasn't entirely sure who was following who.

'So, Mini, I hope you're hungry, I've found a restaurant that looks quite exciting, it could be fun.'

I asked him the name of the place and it wasn't on my list. I felt an instant pang of disappointment as I wanted to recommend somewhere myself, to show him that I knew this city and the best places to eat. But unless he liked curry, I didn't. So in reality he had probably rescued me from further embarrassment. He had found the place in one of those good restaurant guides and when he gave me the name of the street, thankfully I knew how to find it. The restaurant was situated above a small row of shops and accessed via a side street. Interestingly, the restaurant was called, 'The Case.' My initial disappointment instantly evaporated. There was stuff on the menu I hadn't tried before so it was exciting and the ambience made me feel daring, that and wanting something other than fucking chips!

'So Mini, they've got you in the hospital again.'

'Yeah.'

'Ever since I've known you the authorities have been saying you were unstable but I've never believed that.'

'I don't know, Franc, I've done some pretty wild things.'

'Sam Peckinpah, you know the Hollywood director, wrote to me after the film was shown on television and he said you were a brilliant child and in the right circumstances you could grow into a brilliant adult. I still believe that.'

He had almost moved me to tears but I fought them off, as this wasn't a time for indulgence.

'I don't know, a lot's happened, Franc, and I'm thirty-something now, not a cute little kid.'

We continued to eat and to talk, we discussed what constitutes a good life, and I explained how my needs were much simpler now, and how I now measured success was very much at odds with how I had twenty years ago.

Fame and fortune replaced by warmth and courage.

Franc had brought along his mobile phone and placed it on the table. I had only ever seen one on the television, never actually held one in my hand. Some mutual friends of ours were holidaying abroad and knew of our meeting, so it came as no real surprise when the phone rang and it was them, wanting to speak to me. Franc handed me the phone but for some inexplicable reason I felt like I'd been handed some space-age gadget. Instead of holding it to my ear like a regular phone I held it out in front of me and spoke into it before then putting it to my ear so I could hear the reply. After performing this ritual a couple of times, Franc tapped me on the arm.

'Mini, you don't have to do that, just hold it like a house phone.'

After lunch I showed him around the city and we talked constantly. It was hugely stimulating and exciting as I relaxed my guard and exposed myself to ideas that seemed a galaxy away. When the day was over and his train disappeared back down the tunnel, I thought of the time when I would have been following behind on the next one and I couldn't help but chuckle and enjoy the feeling of not wanting to. There was no temptation to resist, I stood there almost waiting for it but it never arrived, a clear sign that I had.

When I returned to the Lodge I was excited about my day and desperate to share it. I spoke to several members of staff and a couple of clients then the next thing I knew the ward manager wanted to speak to me.

'I hear you spent the day with your film-maker friend.'

'Yeah, I did, it was a good day.'

'Well just so you know for the future, if you plan to meet family and friends in town, you really need to put it to the ward round first.'

I was staggered, it never even occurred to me that I would need the blessing of my custodians, nor should it have done.

'Mini, you know how the system works, we liaise with the Home Office all the time and they're sticklers for details.'

CHAPTER FORTY EIGHT

I was now thirty-five years old and had been at the Lodge for three years. Under Mental Health Law, I was advised that I would soon be going in front of the Mental Health Review Tribunal, which was compulsory. The problem was, due to my lifer status the tribunal did not have the power to release me, they could simply recommend that I continue to be detained in hospital, or be returned to prison. This in turn posed a dilemma for the doctors; if I were to remain where I was, the panel would need to be convinced that I was still in need of continued treatment, whilst all the time preparing me for eventual release. The alternative didn't bear thinking about, but think about it I did, day after day, wondering if my days of semi-freedom at the Lodge were coming to an end. In the weeks preceding my appearance in front of the tribunal, I continued to exercise all my leave options, and whilst the threat of prison was never very far from my mind, thoughts of absconding were, because then it would have been guaranteed, and an extreme failure on my part. I can't ever remember viewing it that way before.

I was so nervous on the day in question that I could hardly speak and I felt cold and shivery, despite it being the middle of summer. The chairman of the panel was a high court judge and also present were an independent psychiatrist and a layperson. I was legally represented and my own psychiatrist was also in attendance, to present medical evidence in support of my case. He and the judge engaged in some clever wordplay as the legal complexities were addressed and the inherent difficulties were ironed out. He continued by outlining his plan to eventually have me transferred to an open hospital, no bars, no locks, adding that a return to prison would undo all the valuable work that had so far been completed. My lawyer presented evidence of my progress during my time there, including a number of therapy sessions and of course the amount of leave I currently held without there being any problems that might cause concern. I spent most of the hearing listening, which suited me fine. I was asked the occasional question and tried to keep my answers short and to the point, as I'm very talkative when I'm nervous, and prone to waffling.

The entire hearing lasted no more than forty-five minutes and when it was over I felt pretty good. I had the distinct impression that the judge liked me and that he felt some genuine sympathy towards my situation. The protocol was that I would receive their decision in writing within seven days but I felt the pressure had been lifted so for me, it was business as usual, although I still counted the days. Finally, when it arrived and I read it, I couldn't have wished it any better; if I'd been allowed glass I would have fucking framed it!

It is the view of this panel that Mr Cooper should not be returned to prison, instead his progress towards eventual release should be directed via the psychiatric route.

It wasn't a view that was binding upon the Home Secretary but in the face of all the evidence, should he have rejected it, there would have been a case for a legal challenge: in the end it wasn't necessary. The decision took away any uncertainty I might have been feeling and allowed me to concentrate fully on moving through the system. If I expected it to be swift, however, I was sadly mistaken.

The following few months offered no indication of a move, nor was it even discussed. I continued with my well-rehearsed routine but became despondent, feeling my life had stalled just as it seemed to be gathering momentum. Then during ward round one day, I was unexpectedly asked to start thinking about where I wanted to live and it didn't take much thinking about.

'Leicester. I grew up in the sticks and as a city it's not too big. It's also got a lot going on in the arts which is of great interest to me.'

'The problem you've got with Leicester is that there are three prisons in the county and a lot of guys are settling here on release and the local authority are picking up the tab. We might have difficulty in persuading them in your case.'

Only a psychiatrist could chain you to an open door.

'You also have to consider the possibility that as a convicted arsonist, not everywhere will be willing to accept you.'

I didn't object to the reality check but I was seriously pissed off at being offered a choice that wasn't, made to believe I had a role in the decision-making process when clearly a decision had already been made.

A few weeks later I was informed that a referral had been made to Bassetlaw Hospital in Worksop. I had a vague idea where it was and was certain as to what it was, another former mining town, another fucking Mansfield! A road I had hoped would be full of adventure with new and exciting challenges, but instead I was being returned to the melting pot of a racist, bigoted community that respected only what you did with your hands and not with your mind. There was little to do in such places except visit the pub and once there you were expected to share their views or be considered a threat to them, and any kind of threat would invariably be met with aggression. It was guaranteed to make life difficult. For the first time during my stay at the Lodge I became uncooperative, feeling I owed it to myself to provide some kind of protection, because the body of work I had undergone needed to be put to work, was entitled to be given a chance.

'You've got no chance, there's no way I'm going to Worksop, it's just another fucking mining town and I've lived in them most of my life!'

On this occasion I was in conference with one of the junior doctors who had evidently been sent to persuade me to change my mind. I had already made it clear to anyone who would listen that I would rather piss my pants than piss in their pot. I guess what I resented the most was the bullying albeit without fists, but I wasn't being heard because expedience mattered most, more than me being allowed a plan of my own.

'Worksop was chosen because it's a fairly small town with a very good network of psychiatric services.'

I played their game through clenched teeth because I had long since learned that if they didn't get what they wanted, they made sure you didn't, but I wasn't willing to throw in the towel completely.

'Will I have my own room?'

'Well, we can't guarantee that, but you know this could be a very good move for you. We would anticipate you spending only a couple of weeks on the ward before being transferred to the Stepping Stones hostel and then eventually released into the community, so I don't think it would be the end of the world if you did have to share.'

'I'm not willing to share a room. If this is the progressive move everyone says it is, then I want what I've already got in terms of my private space. If I give that up it doesn't leave a lot.'

Perhaps part of me was hoping that my uncompromising stance would help to sabotage this move and bury it once and for all, or maybe I was just trying to get something for myself out of this deal. They left without saying much and they certainly didn't give anything away, but they must have spoken to someone because pressure was almost immediately applied to get me to change my position regarding a single room. I was accused of making unreasonable demands on a small, overstretched psychiatric ward and was reminded of how grateful I should be at being offered this opportunity. I managed to contain my anger and simply reiterated what I'd already said, adding how ironic it seemed that I was now being called a bully.

* * * *

Several weeks later I received the news that I had been accepted by Bassetlaw and shortly after that, a visit to the hospital was quickly arranged. Myself, along with a couple of nurses, were driven in the hospital minibus with its iron grill designed to protect the driver from a violent attack. As we passed through reception and the nurses gave our destination, the guy in the control room said, 'What kind of workshop is it?' I thought about that the whole journey.

It took around ninety minutes to reach our destination, Bassetlaw and District General Hospital, which was built on the top of a hill, approximately one and a half miles from Worksop town centre. The first thing that struck me was how small and chaotic the ward appeared to be and despite our visit having been prearranged they seemed genuinely taken aback by our arrival. We were eventually shown into a small interview room and were each offered a hot drink, which never arrived. I later discovered that the ward manager had intervened, declaring that the tea and coffee facilities were for patients' use only. After what seemed like an age the ward manager did finally appear. She preferred the term matron, but I could have thought of one or two more.

'I can show you around the ward if you like but there's not really that much to see. I can't show you the patient's bed space so really there's only the lounge and the smoke room.'

She begrudgingly marched us to the lounge which, apart from a television set and a few board games with half the pieces missing, had very little else to offer except space. The smoke room was tiny and littered with cigarette butts and chain-smoking psychotics.

'As you can see, we're basically a very small, very busy, sub-acute ward.'

She was addressing my guardians, not me, the pattern throughout the tour, such as it was.

'You can say that again about it being an acute ward! It's not often I get mistaken for a cop and one guy thought my name was Brian and I worked for MI5! Is there much call for an international man of mystery in these parts?'

She didn't even smile.

'I'd also like to raise the issue of my own room.'

'Bed space is allocated as it becomes available, you'll probably have to spend some time in a dormitory at first, then be put on the list for a single room.'

'Without a room to myself I won't be leaving Leicester to come here.'

'That's entirely up to you.'

As we left, one of the nurses turned to me.

'So what do you think, Min?'

I looked at them both and instantly got the feeling that they wanted me to articulate what they were thinking so they could record it as coming from me rather than them, even though we were clearly in agreement.

'I've seen worse.'

'What about Nurse Ratchet?'

'I'll just have to reserve judgment for now.'

Within a couple of weeks I was on my way to Worksop again, only this time on my own. It was deemed necessary for me to familiarise myself with the town, though why I couldn't have done that once I had arrived there was beyond me, surely there wasn't that much to see? I was to travel by train and for the purpose I was issued with a journey planner, detailing train departures and arrivals, and of course which particular trains I needed to catch. As much as I felt compelled to, I managed to resist the obvious reminders offered with a hint of sarcasm. My journey planner has always been my instincts and my eyes.

The town was much smaller than I had even imagined and much filthier, strewn with litter and dog shit and litter from the previous night's fish and chips lying on the floor, inches from a waste bin; inexcusable, but hey, they're fucking rebels! I quickly found the local library where all the usual suspects were haphazardly stuck to a notice board: flower arranging groups, poetry readings, brass bands and of course, a missing cat. Wandering around town, I began to think that every other shop was either run by a charity, or was a discount store selling everything for a quid. There was also a large number of cafés but these weren't the café bars I'd experienced in Leicester, they were euphemistically referred to as greasy spoon cafés.

I soon discovered why.

I also couldn't help but notice that there were far too many pubs for the size of the area. I counted fourteen without venturing towards the outskirts, along with two or three nightclubs. But no cinema, and no proper theatre or arts centre, just a run-down council offering they kept trying to offload. After a couple of hours I trudged my way up the hill towards the station, finding it increasing difficult to feel positive about this move, except the more I put behind me, the closer my reach for what was still in front. I just hoped such thoughts would be enough

* * * *

'Mini, the doctor wants to see you.'

I had only been at Bassetlaw a couple of hours and I'd already had one minor confrontation when, upon arrival they had locked away my television and portable stereo, insisting they needed to be checked by an electrician and passed fit for use. I explained that I had already gone through this process down at the Lodge and therefore it was ridiculous to have to do it again just to satisfy someone else's paranoia.

'It's all to do with health and safety. If we allow you to have that equipment and you get electrocuted then we're liable and the NHS can't afford a lawsuit.'

'Well, in the unlikely event that I do get electrocuted, I'm willing to take the risk.'

'Look, I don't make the rules I just have to follow them, the same as you do.'

The perfect cop out, suggesting we were both victims of the same capricious legislators and bound together by their authority. It was pointless trying to reason with someone who was afraid of saying anything he hadn't been told to, but the net result was that I was without my television for the first time in over four years, nor could I listen to the football, a Saturday afternoon ritual for more years than I could count. But I had been given my own room, except there was nothing in it except me, and my notebook, my constant companion. In terms of in house entertainment there was a stereo in the smoke room that constantly blared out music to cut your wrists to, and the only television was in the lounge, offering the soporific effect of daytime programming. Now the head honcho wanted to see me and I wasn't expecting an unconditional welcome.

'I know you've only just got here today so I won't keep you longer than necessary. How was your trip?'

'It was okay.'

'Well, I just thought I'd hook up with you to explain how things are going to work. As you already know, you'll be on the ward for a couple of weeks then you'll be transferred to the hostel.'

'What about leave, will I have the same amount that I had in Leicester?'

'Unfortunately all your leave will have to be re-applied for. Because you've left Arnold Lodge, the process has to be gone through again. It's a quirk of the system, I'm afraid.'

I hadn't expected that and I struggled to understand the rationale behind it, I figured progressive meant moving forward. Still, after the spat over the television I was in no mood for another round of jousting, instead I just smiled, which came perilously close to a mocking laugh.

To demonstrate her sensitivity to my situation and the toughness of it, she relented and granted me unsupervised access to the hospital grounds. Perhaps I should have been grateful and to some degree I was, as it allowed me to escape the ward whenever it became impossible. The problem, of course, was that it was predominantly a general hospital with only the one psychiatric ward, whose existence was both known and feared by the locals. Subsequently anyone entering or leaving stuck out like a bare breast. Added to which the grounds themselves were about as exciting or as interesting as watching a couple of tortoises mate, but it's all I had and I wasn't about to give it back. It gained me access to the hospital shop where I would buy a newspaper and saunter over to the coffee shop to read it.

One hour a day of normal living.

One afternoon I returned to the ward having been for a jog, when I was met by one of the mangers.

'Mr Cooper, I understand you were meant to be moving to Stepping Stones next week?'

'Yeah, that's right.'

'Well, unfortunately we need your bed and they have a room available for you now so you'll be leaving today.'

'Well, I've just been for a run, I need to take a shower.'

'That's fine but I need you gone by tea time.'

I had been on the ward no more than ten days and whilst I certainly wasn't unhappy to be leaving, I was offered no assistance in making the move except for a fucking wheelchair! I was expected to load my belongings onto it and wheel them down to the hostel; needless to say, I didn't hurry. I took a long, luxurious shower, changed, then headed into the smoke room for an equally luxurious fag.

The room was small and therefore difficult not to engage in some way with anyone else who might have been in there. Apart from myself there were two young women having a conversation. I was particularly struck by one of them. She was well spoken, smart and immensely attractive, the first time I could recall ever noticing such a thing, and it puzzled me that I had. It all suggested to me that she wasn't a client, rather a doctor or social worker and the woman she was talking to must have been her client, fucking typical! I extinguished my cigarette and left the room but I couldn't help taking a final look and wondering. Outside in the corridor a nurse was sat, observing the various goings on in the television room.

'Who's the really well spoken woman in the smoke room?'

'Oh, that's our resident solicitor.'

'Solicitor!'

I'd never met one yet who had made it onto my Christmas card list, and was almost ashamed at having met one that I fancied, but the law is the law and the divide was there to protect. I marched down to my room without another word, packed my stuff and loaded it onto the wheelchair, not sure whether I should be angry or grateful. Angry because when it had finally happened, the object of my lust was unattainable; grateful, that having experienced it, it now existed, making me more three-dimensional than two.

It took two or three trips to move everything from the ward to the hostel. The room they had allocated me was right at the top of the house with no wheelchair access, therefore each of the large items had to be carried individually up the stairs before making the next trip. Until then I had always considered myself as a light traveller, possessing so few things, but I guess the longer you walk amongst society, the more you gather along the way. The room itself was tiny but it came with its own toilet and sink, which for me was perfect. However, by the time I had finally transferred all my stuff I was drenched in sweat, a combination of stress and physical effort. During the transfer the hostel manager was quickly on the scene, sitting on my shoulder, clucking away.

'I understand you're fully conversant with the current leave arrangements?'

It wasn't easy, trying to organise your things whilst becoming increasingly agitated by such an invasive and unwanted presence.

'Was there anything else? Only as you can see, I'm trying to sort my room out.'

'Yes, the television set needs to be locked in the staff room until it's been tested by the electrician, no doubt the ward staff have already pointed that out to you.'

'It's over there.'

I had my back to him and pointed towards the balsa wood wardrobe. The television had almost toppled over.

'Well, perhaps you could bring it to the office when you're finished.'

'I can see this is going to be a real barrel of laughs.'

'What makes you say that?'

'Experience.'

An hour or so later and still waiting for the television, he sent a support worker to my room to collect it. I then went downstairs to the smoke room and had a well-deserved fag.

I was amongst the old who just kept getting older. Without knowing how to keep some kind of record, they seemed to have no idea of the length of a day, only what time their next cigarette was due. The hostel was little more than an annexe to the hospital, housing a number of clients who were in need of care but not sufficiently ill to warrant admission to the hospital. As most would never leave, the name 'Stepping Stones' was nothing more than a PR exercise.

CHAPTER FORTY-NINE

'This came this morning, it's from the parole board.'

I was attending the offices of the local probation service, just another part of my weekly routine. Refusal would put me in breach, as would refusing to attend any of my other appointments unless I could provide a good reason. Any breach could result in recall and it was far more likely to happen in the first few months than in the first few years. I had been at the hostel just under twelve months and hadn't missed one, it was a minor inconvenience in comparison.

My stay at Stepping Stones had been eventful for all the wrong reasons, it was beginning to feel like a pattern. The first few weeks were spent ordinarily enough, acquainting myself with all the various professionals I would be in regular contact with, familiarising myself with the hostel staff, and trying to avoid the clients. After a month or so of sitting around my room, feeling pretty sorry for myself and jogging so much I was in danger of losing a couple of inches off my legs, I was offered a place at a day centre for the mentally ill. Ordinarily, I would have asked for a bag to puke in once I'd stopped laughing but I still had no leave at the time and was going a little stir crazy. Several applications had been made to the Home Office but as the medical staff had no previous experience of how to approach them, they kept coming back. I lost count of how many times the very first application went back and forth until successful. Therefore the day centre suddenly seemed attractive, as I was willing to tolerate whatever nonsense came my way just to have the freedom to walk there and back three times a week. It was, however, a hugely undermining experience. The staff were generally patronising and occasionally condescending, making it difficult for people to succeed and move away from mental health services. Perhaps some of the clients would always be what they already were, which was pretty frightening, but others could potentially have had more if only they had been encouraged to believe, and not reminded of why they were there.

It was fucking depressing and the walk wasn't even that great.

Despite appearing to be taking my place within the community, it was pure illusion. I was still on a leash, still being held as a patient under the Mental Health Act and until I was released on life licence, everything would remain as it was, because those who governed my daily life didn't have the authority to change it.

The search was also on for a new lawyer as my previous lawyer was a specialist in mental health law and he felt the legal services commission wouldn't pay for him to represent me in a criminal justice matter. In the end, my social worker recommended a guy who worked for a firm in Nottingham so I went to see him and was immediately impressed by his thoroughness. He had vast experience of these panels and the way in which they worked, in particular the importance of presentation.

The general consensus amongst professionals was that it would be far easier to persuade the panel to release me should I be offered a place in a supported housing scheme rather than just being dumped in some tiny bed-sit alone, and quite possibly afraid. Therefore once all the reports were completed a referral was made to the Turning Point hostel right in the centre of town. Although still a hostel, it had an entirely different ethos to Stepping Stones. It was independently run, by a charitable trust rather than the local authority, there were no patients and no sections, clients prepared their own food, laundered their own clothes and generally learned to live outside of the rigid controls and institutionalised abuse that is prevalent in many psychiatric hospitals. The interview wasn't as tough as I expected and I was accepted with very little fuss, a fact that took a little while to sink in. It was beyond my normal experience for such a major decision to be passed so effortlessly. In the meantime a successful application was made to the Home Office for me to spend two days a week at Turning Point, the purpose being to gently ease me into a more liberal routine and allow me to acclimatise to a strange world of decision-making.

Some months earlier the young woman I had first encountered on the ward had also been moved to Turning Point. I had seen her a couple of times since, when I had returned to the ward to visit. Whenever she saw me she would smile and in that wonderfully cultured voice would say:

'Hello, Mini, how are you?'

'I'm fine, thank you.'

My replies were invariably curt and abrupt, but stopping just short of being rude. Her legal status still troubled me and so did the way I felt, which was often the reason for my being there, I just didn't know what to do once I'd passed through the gate.

On Boxing Day I had been invited to a buffet that was being held on the ward and was surprised to see her moping around, looking incredibly lost and pained. I understood my situation perfectly and had spent so many festive seasons away from my family it was no longer an issue or a thought, but this was different and it puzzled me as I rather naively expected the middle classes to take a different view of such things.

'Would you like a game of Scrabble, Mini?'

'Oh, no, I don't play word games.'

I felt like a bit of a shit, standing there in the face of her disappointment. Intellectual stimuli is difficult to come by in such places, so are the type of distractions that might help you forget, if only for a few minutes. The truth was, I was a little afraid of her. I'd once seen her engage in a heated exchange with a member of staff and she was fearsome. It was then to my astonishment that I discovered that she wasn't a solicitor, she was indeed a client, but she did have a law degree which she often used to render her victims impotent, hence the title. This was a feisty, passionate woman and whilst a little scary, I was already desperate to discover what would happen if her passion was ignited. I'd also heard she was a fabulous Scrabble player and I really didn't want to be on the receiving end of a publicly humiliating thrashing. But now it would be impossible to avoid her, as we would soon be sharing the same building for more than just a couple of weeks. The reality, of course, was that the more I tried to avoid her, the more intrigued I became. I wanted her, I just didn't know how to make it happen. I was experiencing thoughts and feelings that I'd previously been spared from and I couldn't decide whether to embrace them and indulge their wondrous liberating quality, or resist for fear of drowning in a flood of ignorance and inexperience.

Safe but not saved.

My room at Turning Point hostel was at the top of the building, small but adequate, with a bathroom I would be sharing with two others. On arriving, I took a look out of the window; having spent so many years behind a wall, I always hope for a better view but on this occasion I was disappointed. The window looked out onto the sidewall of a domestic residence next door. It was grey and dreary, just another fucking wall! I dumped my bag on the bed and headed downstairs towards the lounge on the pretext of familiarising myself with the general layout of the place but it also provided a harmless way of seeing her without making it blatantly obvious. I opened the lounge door and there she was, sat in the corner, dressed predominantly in black. She had gained a little weight because of all the junk they were pumping into her but it made absolutely no difference, I still thought she was incredibly attractive and her voice soon became my addiction.

'Hello, Mini, are you living here now?'

She smiled and I temporarily stumbled through my thought processes until I eventually managed:

'No, I'm just coming down a couple of days a week for now. I just thought I'd stick my head through the door to see where the lounge was. I'm going to go back upstairs.'

'Well, come down later if you like, if you're not busy.'

I did come down later, in fact I made my way down almost every time I knew she was there.

The name 'Turning Point', was a complete misnomer. Very few of the clients were given any real encouragement to turn their lives around, a great many of them had poor diets but little if anything was ever done to help to improve their culinary skills. The staff were lazy, preferring to hide away in the office, playing on the computer, rather than involving themselves with clients.

For me it was perfect, almost utopian, but others were simply left to fester in an ubiquitous cloud of cigarette smoke. The first time I walked into the kitchen to prepare a meal I almost threw up and stormed into the office, outraged that I could be expected to cook in a refuse site. The member of staff I spoke to was at best apathetic and due to the way he responded to my concerns, clearly hadn't seen the state of that kitchen, or the pans and utensils, which still had the previous week's food stuck to them. Realising that I was getting nowhere, I told him if it wasn't sorted I would contact the environmental health team. The following week the problem was resolved, at least by their definition it was. I don't know if the kitchen had been fumigated because I never saw it, instead I was met by the manager

'Follow me, I've got a surprise for you, I think you'll be pleased.'

He unlocked a door leading into a two bedroomed, self-contained apartment I didn't even know existed. This was to be my new home and I would be sharing it with a young woman, but not the one I had in mind. It seemed an odd arrangement and not one I was particularly comfortable with. The situation was further compounded by my flatmate's habit of walking into the lounge late at night scantily clad, in order to have a cigarette. Having been deprived of such images for such a long time, I might have been forgiven for wanting her to take her time but I didn't, I had no interest in her on any level nor did I enjoy such exposure in a way that offered no protection. Rather than fix the kitchen they tried to fix me and I resented it because they were playing with my future. Thankfully she moved out after a couple of weeks to take an apartment above a butcher's shop.

By the time I'd reached the stage where I was effectively spending half my week there I finally received the news I was waiting for, my date with destiny.

* * * *

Although the hearing was still a couple of months away, it was all I could think of.

Since the papers were prepared and passed onto the parole board I had been almost mechanical in my approach, jumping through hoops like a well trained circus animal in search of the next treat. Now it was suddenly real and I was frightened of wanting what might be denied and afraid to believe that this life could be mine when it still felt borrowed. Before the Parole Board was willing to hear my case, the psychiatrist had to first submit a report saying I no longer required hospital treatment. Once again I was in a position whereby if they refused to release me, the only remedy in law was a return to prison. I struggled to understand how I could have spent so long moving amongst society without a blemish, only to disappear as if I'd never been there. Five years after vacating my prison cell it was still awaiting my possible return.

Privately I tried to encourage myself to believe in my own worth and that it would be enough because it couldn't be denied, but even I struggled to believe me. Then my lawyer called. He had just been issued with the names of the panel members and wanted to inform me, should I be familiar with any of them. The judge was unknown to me, which I considered a blessing, and I'd never heard of the layperson, but the independent psychiatrist was someone I'd hoped I would never come across again. He was the author of the report which condemned me to a life sentence and was clearly **not** independent, particularly in view of his own words.

'I do not believe there is a method or approach available that will modify this man's behaviour in a way that will reduce his risk of re-offending.'

I pointed this out to my lawyer, fully expecting him to immediately canvass the parole board.

'I don't think he'll be a problem but if it turns out that he is, we can always appeal.'

'Yes, but to appeal you first have to lose and if that happens, I go back to prison.'

My earlier impressions had now been replaced with a familiar feeling; win or lose, it makes no difference to them, it's just a unit of work, and whilst they enjoy the winning, losing won't spoil their appetite.

On the day of the hearing I could barely speak. I had chain-smoked my way through the previous night, afraid to sleep, afraid that if I did I would lose the opportunity of locking away my final moments should I need them for future comfort. I was gripped by fear and concerned that it would restrict my ability to present myself as myself, which was all I had left and without it, if I lost, it wouldn't be me they were returning to prison and I'd have no one to tell. I entered the arena and was invited to sit directly opposite the judge, flanked by my team. Two representatives of the Home Office sat at the back, their role simply to observe the proceedings. The judge addressed me directly as he introduced himself and the remaining two members of the panel.

'Okay, Mr. Kelly, should we begin with your opening address? Though I should point out you might find you're pushing at an open door.'

It was a phrase I'd never heard before. That and the cerebral paralysis that was threatening to engulf me meant it took several seconds for me to work it out and in an instant my mind was reconnected, free from anxiety and doubt. My lawyer also took the hint, and knowing he didn't have a fight on his hands he kept his presentation short and to the point. He spoke of the length of time I'd already spent outside of prison and the way in which I'd utilised that, he quoted from the various reports and asked the various authors to confirm that their position hadn't changed since submitting them. It was unanimous.

The panel then turned towards the witnesses and put to them a number of not-so-challenging questions. Nevertheless it was an invaluable experience now that I'd woken up, to witness what indeed was a rare sight: both my psychiatrist and social worker were so overcome with nerves they were barely audible. Whenever I visited them in their closeted little cockpits that seemed shut off from everyday reality, they spoke with confidence and assuredness, but removed from their comfort zone and with the balance of power no longer theirs, they were left with nothing but themselves. Finally, I too, was examined by the panel. The judge asked a number of standard questions that didn't really trouble me but the lay person came after me like he was chasing down a fox.

'Mr Cooper, we've heard a lot about your progress but what I'm interested to know is what you would do if the same set of circumstances arose once again?'

'I would think that's hardly likely.'

'But what if they did?'

'There were a number of factors involved in the original offence, for them all to converge at the same time, at the same place would mean I've been sleeping for far too long.'

'Would you care to elaborate?'

'Well, for the scenario you're describing to actually happen, would mean I would have to ignore all the early warning signs.'

'So what strategies do you have in place to ensure that you don't?'

'Well, look around you, these people are not here out of curiosity, they're here to demonstrate the network of support that I currently have access to.'

'What I'm wanting to know is, what if you needed to contact someone and they weren't available, what would be your plan B?'

'All of them? That would be pretty unlucky, but it wouldn't be the end of the world, I have others who are willing to offer support. I also have a determination to ensure that any difficulty is dealt with in its infancy.'

'Indeed, well, I think Mr Cooper has answered the question adequately.'

The judge intervened just as I was becoming extremely irritated. I don't mind being genuinely cross-examined for the purpose of assessing my suitability for release, but not just to give someone the fucking floor before they returned to their life of anonymity!

My final moments were spent locking horns with Dr Woods and it came as no real shock. He talked exclusively about my past misuse of alcohol and suggested a clause might be inserted into my licence forbidding me from future use. I countered firstly that I hadn't had a drink in several years and that such a clause would be superfluous, given the probation services' authority to have me recalled at any time they feel my risk to the public is increased.

'I agree, I don't think there's any need to insert any additional clauses into the licence at this stage.'

Once again the judge intervened, before spelling out the usual formalities. The hearing lasted a little more than ninety minutes, an unusually short time.

'As you are no doubt aware, Mr Cooper, we will make a decision and you will be informed in writing within seven days. However, if you and Mr Kelly care to wait outside for a few minutes, we may decide to call you back in.'

We all filed out of the conference room where the hospital managers would meet to decide the fate of their 'customers.' The mood was celebratory, with everyone clearly feeling they had played their part. I had even broken with tradition and dressed formally, I just hoped it wouldn't become a habit. Both myself and my lawyer were called back within what seemed like seconds but was probably longer. I stood in front of the judge, trying not to sway too much, a side-effect of the medication.

'Mr Cooper, we've studied the reports and of course have listened to the evidence given by yourself and a number of witnesses. We also note that the Home Office itself supports your release on licence and we find no reason to reject this application. Accordingly we direct your release and whilst you will be formally notified of this decision we see no reason to keep you hanging on. Congratulations.'

'Thank you.'

I actually meant it and almost smiled at the thought. I wasn't sure if I was thanking him for giving me what I wanted, or for allowing me to be successful without having to battle to prove my worth, or have it questioned. When we re-emerged no one had left and we gave them the news. I received their congratulations nonchalantly but that's not how I was feeling, I just didn't want to appear too excitable, as if surprised and overwhelmed.

Or even lucky.

Despite receiving the news from both myself and having it confirmed by my solicitor, my psychiatrist was unwilling to formally discharge me until she had received notification in writing; what a difference an hour makes. I didn't resent having to wait another week, in fact I almost relished it, knowing that my position was secure. There was no immediate afterglow, just a feeling of continuance. By the time the paperwork was completed I had already made several trips to Turning Point, carrying what I could safely manage, but there was no stress involved, no urgency and no perspiration. Isabelle, the young woman I first encountered in the hospital, was always there and once I had deposited my belongings, we would head into the lounge and have a coffee together. After making my final trip I told her I'd be living there full-time within a couple of days. As I got up to leave she showed me to the door.

'I'll see you in a couple of days, then.'

'You can count on it.'

The time was mine now, or so I thought.

CHAPTER FIFTY

Crime (Sentences) Act 1997

The secretary of state hereby authorises the release on licence within fifteen days of the date hereof of **MICHAEL COOPER** who shall on release and during the period of this licence comply with the conditions or any other condition that may be substituted or added from time to time.

'I suggest you read carefully through that so that you understand it fully because should you breach any of the conditions, you risk being recalled.'

I was sat with my probation officer, trying to control the surge of anger that I felt at hearing the word recall.

When I was still learning to crawl.

I eventually picked it up, afraid that my reluctance might be viewed as insubordination and automatically put me at risk.

1. He shall place himself under the supervision of whichever probation officer is nominated for this purpose from time to time.

2. He shall on release report to the probation officer so nominated and shall keep in touch with that officer in accordance with that officer's instructions.

3. He shall, if his probation officer so requires, receive visits from that officer where the licence holder is living.

4. He shall reside only where approved by his probation officer.

5. He shall work only where approved by his probation officer and shall inform his probation officer at once if he loses his job.

6. He shall not travel outside Great Britain without the prior permission

of his probation officer.

7. He shall comply with the requirements of the psychiatric supervision of Dr Bloomberg or her nominee of successor.

Unless revoked this licence remains in force indefinitely.
November 2002.

'Is there anything in there that you don't understand?'

'What's not to understand? It's just a list of do's and don'ts, mostly don'ts.'

'You have to remember you're a lifer.'

'Like I could ever forget.'

* * * *

A couple of days after moving into the hostel I noticed that Isabelle was cooking a very simple meal of pasta and pesto. Enquiries revealed that this was her staple diet. I couldn't figure out why she was there, or why she needed to be, but if she wasn't I wouldn't have had the chance to care and that would have been my loss.

The following day I took a gamble and was surprised by how unconcerned I was at the possibility of rejection. Just wanting to ask stripped away layers of institutionalised thinking and switched off the survival instincts that had taken years to develop. I had heard that she was predominantly vegetarian and one of the dishes I really liked to cook was a spinach and potato curry. I didn't even know if she liked curry but like I said it was a gamble. It was hugely exciting, setting off for the shops to buy all the ingredients I needed for a meal I might have ended up eating alone, but it was a vibrant shopping trip as I ordinarily hate shopping. So later that evening, I went downstairs around thirty minutes before she would normally start to prepare her meal, took a sharp intake of breath then walked over to the table where she was sat reading the newspaper.

'Hi, Isabelle.'

'Hello, Mini.'

'Listen, I've made a spinach and potato curry but I've done too much so if you, erm… fancy a portion, you're more than welcome to join me.'

'That would be lovely, I'd really like that.'

She joined me in the flat, the first time in my life that I had effectively invited someone to dinner, even if there was a little subterfuge at work, but I was still learning. There was nothing instinctive in the way I prepared the table, nothing natural in my manner, I felt like an awkward teenager, wanting to impress the boss's daughter, an indication of how separated I felt. I bounced back and forth from the kitchen to the lounge, a bundle of nervous energy and forgetfulness, but it stopped me from having to sit close enough to feel her breath and perhaps lose my own. In the end I ran out of excuses and I guess she sensed my nervousness but of course she didn't understand why. She came for food so why not just eat?

'I hope it's okay.'

'Mini, it looks absolutely fine. Let's enjoy it before it gets cold.'

I was more tentative in approaching the food than she was, unable to relax until I was able to gauge her reaction to it. Naturally I wanted her to like it because I wanted her to enjoy a meal that wasn't merely functional. I was also proud of being self-reliant; I was an able, if not spectacular cook, I could launder my own clothes, clean my own living space and basically depended on no one for my basic needs. But I couldn't fit a plug to a kettle. If she enjoyed the food I hoped she would appreciate where it came from, that like her I was more than just the basic ingredients.

'Mini, this is gorgeous, it's like being in an Indian restaurant. Where did you learn to cook curry so authentically?'

So what should I tell her? That I spent a year in India during my university studies? Or that whilst serving a life sentence I got a job in the laundry and put in a few unpaid hours washing the clothes of our Asian population, who wanted them because they were visiting with their families the following day? In return, they would feed me curry, better still they taught me how to make it.

'It's a bit of a hobby, really, I never did see the point of building model aeroplanes. My old man and my brother were into that, spending hours sticking bits of plastic together and for what? You never get to fly it, but with a curry you get to be creative then you get to eat it, nothing's wasted.'

Indeed nothing was, for by the end of the evening there were two empty plates She stayed a while longer, playing a selection of her music. She had an eclectic taste whereas I had given all mine away apart from a few ABBA CD's. They remained hidden away.

I didn't see her around for a couple of days after that. I wasn't deliberately avoiding her, I had my own commitments and of course the running kept me grounded. One afternoon I walked in during a political discussion between Isabelle and a member of staff, not so much a debate, as they both clearly shared the same beliefs, which were similar to my own. I listened for a while and without wanting to hijack their discussion, I joined in and offered a few opinions of my own, which seemed to please rather than annoy her, giving me the confidence to carry on.

'I never knew you were a Lefty,' she smiled.

The discussion carried on for a while, and it was exciting. Sure, I stumbled a couple of times but I never felt the lion's bite.

'Mini, would you like to go for a drink sometime?'

'I don't drink.'

The words flew out of my mouth in a semi-aggressive tone before I had chance to catch them. Her disappointment was palpable, her face having changed in an instant, and I wanted mine to belong to someone else.

'Oh, right, okay.'

The next few minutes were torture as I sat lamenting a lost opportunity, the only one I might get. I sat there, silently imploring the staff member to go and find some work to do so that I could speak to Isabelle alone, before my words became redundant, and my hopes bankrupt. When he did eventually leave I wasted no time in crossing the room and sitting conspiratorially next to her.

'Listen, Isabelle, I had to say that with him in the room. I'm not really supposed to drink but if you still fancy going out, I'd love to.'

'Oh, right, when you said you didn't drink I thought you might be one of those evangelical Christians!'

I broke into a fit of giggles that wasn't borne of nervousness or embarrassment and certainly wasn't intended to mock her.

'So would you like to go out for a drink with me, then?'

'Yeah, I would.'

It wasn't a particularly well thought-out decision, in fact I doubt any real thought had gone into it. I was putting desire before consideration, but a part of me resented the fact that I was expected to think differently.

We went to a local boozer where the alcohol was cheap but so was life and all its interpretations, and I still valued mine so without making a big play I took up a position near the door where there was no one sat behind me, experience being the only teacher I ever really listened to. I bought bottles of alcohol mixed with fruit juice that I then poured into a glass, a type of drink very popular amongst young people at the time, but for me they simply hid the truth. Isabelle drank gin and tonic like it was going to kill her not to, but she seemed to have hollow legs which was just my luck really, as I like to keep up with the person I'm drinking with, but it had been a while and I wasn't ready to push things too far. For tonight at least, her company was far more important than being able to prove that I knew no restraint, through fear that it would define me. We talked and drank for a couple of hours and although I noticed that at times she appeared preoccupied and distracted, there was a smoothness to the way she spoke, an unrestrained fluidity to her conversation and she was extremely funny.

I never asked how she came to be in her current situation and she never asked me the same, but we never stopped talking the whole time we were there and by the time we returned to our temporary lodgings I had at least learned two things about her: she hated football and for someone as articulate and as eloquent as she clearly was, she swore like a fucking miner!

Perfect!

From that moment on, we became virtually inseparable. The conditions for once proved fortuitous as stimulation was in short supply. The building's interior was in greater need of rehabilitation than most of the residents and even the television kept changing colour halfway through a programme. I would generally rise before she did and go for a run then after bathing, dressing and a light breakfast I would take a leisurely stroll through town and buy the newspaper, which I would read over a couple of cups of strong coffee, then wait impatiently for her to arrive.

I picked through my clothes, deciding what to wear, only to change my mind again and again and again.

I had finally reached puberty, aged thirty-eight and a half.

CHAPTER FIFTY-ONE

'Listen, Isabelle, I've really enjoyed your company these past few weeks, I really look forward to you coming through to the flat in the mornings.'

Okay, so it was hardly masterful but give me a fucking break, my arse was twitching like a budgie's beak and my perspiration was adding a little unwanted seasoning to the food!

'That's really sweet and I enjoy your company too.'

'It's just that, well, over the last couple of weeks I've developed really strong feelings towards you,'

She wasted no time in replying. I had expected her to pause for thought but she didn't hesitate.

'I don't want a relationship with you, Min. I'll be your mate but I don't want to be your lover or anyone else's.'

Thank God for the fucking plate! I stared silently into it, hoping that if I fixed my gaze long enough, I would become as inanimate and as easy to ignore as the half-eaten meal that stared back at me.

'Have I offended you?'

'No, no, of course you haven't, you're just being honest.'

Whilst gutted, I appreciated her honesty and figured I, too, owed her the truth.

I had always known that this day would come, when I would have to sit down and explain who I was or what I had been and lay everything on the line, just as she had. I had first considered this when I was fifteen or sixteen years old, and it scared me then but the scrapbook was a whole lot fuller now.

'Isabelle, there's something I really need to tell you.'

I could barely get the words out but thankfully she was looking down at her plate, loading up her next mouthful of food. Had she been able to offer direct eye contact I feel sure I would have crumbled.

'Oh yeah, what's that, then?'

She continued to enjoy her food, seemingly unaware that I could possibly have anything to say that might disrupt it.

'I'm not who you think I am.'

The words just tumbled out. Grateful that the pretence was finally over, I no longer had the will to try to stop them, perhaps not even the strength.

'Oh yeah? So who are you, then?'

She laughed, forcing me to smile, but I was still unable to look her in the eye until I had delivered the headline news.

'I'm a lifer. I served almost twelve years of a life sentence.'

I looked up at her instantly but she wasn't looking at me, she was staring down at her own plate, even though her fork was loaded and ready to be delivered. I was far more interested in what would come out of her mouth, I sat there, silently imploring her to say something.

Anything.

Quite predictably she wanted to know if I'd killed someone. When I assured her that I hadn't she seemed surprised, a little sceptical, even. Not entirely unexpected, given the huge number of people who are still unaware that a life sentence can be imposed for crimes other than murder. She wasn't quite done, and asked, not unreasonably, if my crime had been an attack on a woman. This temporarily unsettled me as I had to decide whether she believed me capable; if she did, the door had already closed.

'No, I didn't attack a woman or anybody else, I attacked a pile of fucking rotten wood!'

She immediately burst into a fit of the giggles, then seeing that I hadn't, stopped and apologised.

'So, how come they gave you life?'

I briefly outlined the facts of the case, including providing her with some background information but not much, I didn't really go further back than the crime itself; she already had enough to digest for a first instalment.

'And you think I won't want to know you anymore, don't you?'

'It crossed my mind.'

'I'm a revolutionary socialist, mate, I don't go in for all that petty bourgeois morality shit.'

* * * *

I had for some months been sharing the flat with a quiet, unobtrusive young guy who mostly kept out of the way. In fairness, we didn't really make it easy for him as Isabelle and I were together most of the time and I think he felt like he was intruding. However there was no agenda on my part to push him out, no concerted effort to make life unbearable for him, but in the end he came to me and offered to move out, should Isabelle want to move in. This idea had already occurred to me, I felt by sharing a small intimate space it might help bring us closer together. Perhaps it was just arrogance on my part but I believed her earlier comments were borne out of fear and so I wanted to show her I was worthy and prove to myself that I hadn't misread the signals that were still coming my way, it was no longer a question of winning, it was about knowing, whichever way that might throw me.

Not knowing, without trying, would have plagued me all of this life, whilst still searching for her in the next

I put it to Isabelle and she immediately agreed. The next step was to put it to the management and staff, where we experienced first hand how petty jealousies and resentments can sometimes manifest themselves, certainly the attitude of several members of staff changed towards us, as if they resented us having a chance of happiness, after all I was a lifer and she was a challenging client. In the end they agreed to contact head office and take instructions from them, which resulted in the manager being asked to interview us separately, the purpose of which was never explained. When I mentioned it to Isabelle her response was entirely predictable.

'They can fuck right off! This isn't a police station and we haven't committed a criminal offence. Tell them if they want to interview us, they'll have to interview us both at the same time.'

The eventual outcome was that having once again sought advice from head office, they did a complete u-turn; neither of us was interviewed and Isabelle duly moved into the flat, having her own room, of course. I felt buoyant, almost invincible, with her at my side during these disputes and it was also refreshing to use the system they had unquestioningly chained themselves to, in order to poke fun at them and expose their weaknesses. I was beginning to re-establish the art of intellectual revolt, rather than the physical, destructive model that had kept me in chains, if the price was their resentment then I was already liberated.

Although we were now sharing the apartment we were still only friends, something we were at pains to point out to staff, although judging from their reaction they clearly didn't believe us. Consequently they would invent all manner of excuses for turning up uninvited and without even knocking, on the pretext of being caring professionals. Had they succeeded in finding us compromised and embarrassed they would have had sufficient ammunition to contact the benefits agency to inform them that we were cohabiting, and therefore getting our money reduced. Given the continued hostility they were showing to both of us, I have no doubt in my mind that this was the real motivation behind their random appearances.

Despite her natural feistiness and strength, Isabelle also had moments of extreme fragility, rendering her at times, as vulnerable as a frightened child. It was hugely distressing for me, to see her like that, so alone, so tortured. During these periods she would often take to her bed for hours and sometimes days just lying there being punished, sometimes she would call out to me and I would go and sit on the edge of her bed and try to offer what little comfort I could. It was difficult having to absorb, rather than being able to change the conditions, but I would sit there talking to her, whilst gently stroking her hair and occasionally drying her tears. It wasn't entirely selfless because it allowed me to consider the needs of someone else and they weren't too dissimilar to my own, when I too, was a frightened child, with no one to tell.

We were living in a tiny space, almost tripping over one another and as the weeks rolled by we became increasingly close. We became more and more tactile, a situation I had never previously been at ease with, however I enjoyed every kiss, every hug, it felt like I'd finally been switched on. We also continued to share more of our life experiences, sometimes funny stories, sometimes recounting some minor victory over the authorities, which at the time seemed huge.

My frustration continued to bubble under the surface and my confusion was close to partnering insanity. Every time she touched me my senses danced like they had just been invented, the immense, mind-altering intensity of the feeling certainly had, in my case at least. I felt I was receiving mixed messages, although perhaps I wasn't getting any at all, I was working from a script written and devised by a novice so I resolved to seek counsel from those who may be able to advise me. I was desperate.

I first approached my psychiatric nurse whose advice was fairly measured and her approach both professional and unprovocative but I still felt unsure, perhaps because I was looking for an unequivocal green light. I therefore approached my social worker who began by suggesting that Isabelle struck her as the type of woman who might use sex as currency. She went on to describe Isabelle's highly manipulative behaviour whilst under the auspices of psychiatric services, including bullying the doctors into constantly changing her medication. She also revealed that Isabelle had once been found secreting medication. I wasn't deluded nor was I in denial, I accept it was possible for her to manipulate medical staff, they were doing the same to her on a daily basis without conscience, they fed the label but ignored the person, why complicate things? My own extensive experience had also taught me that some of these medications can have horrendous side effects and therefore it's perfectly normal for people to be resistant to them, choosing life instead. I decided some weeks later to take a massive gamble with Isabelle. I figured that in order to be able to live with myself I had to fail trying, rather than be ignominiously defeated through fear and cowardice. There was also an element of self-protection at work I needed to be able to walk away if that was to be the only outcome. We agreed to meet at a local pub and there I told her that I respected her feelings but if they did not reciprocate my own then I couldn't go on as we were, that I thought we should calm things down completely. She became angry and stormed out, without even touching her food or her drink. I guess she must have felt that I was trying to emotionally blackmail her. I may well have been clumsy in my approach but I certainly wasn't trying to coerce or bully her, I just didn't want to continue crucifying myself.

We pretty much carried on as normal without really mentioning it again. I had just begun to adjust when I was completely and unexpectedly blown away, by a kiss that wiped away the years, and the following day we were lovers. I reclaimed my youth.

Then as if by magic, I was offered my own apartment.

CHAPTER FIFTY-TWO

Just walking through the door to view an empty apartment was monumental, and I could barely contain my excitement, as the old journey was beginning to peter out with the new one already waiting in the wings. I felt like a child again when I owned the open spaces that I never quite left behind and the sun felt like it was shining just for me, until I was returned, beaten but not quite defeated. It was a place I could call home and I was ready to have one, it was spacious and light with a huge bay window looking out onto a street I had walked a hundred times or more. It was also next door to the police station but that made me smile more than frown, being so close yet invisible.

A two-bedroomed apartment in an excellent state of decoration, with carpets throughout; a simple signature and it was mine. So breathtakingly easy, so much for so little when previously I had only ever signed to be handed back what was already mine. So actually there a was a great deal more at stake than just writing my name, because for once it had real value in an ordinary world that had taken an awful long time to forgive.

The social worker was in attendance, along with a housing officer and I also invited Isabelle along for a private viewing as her opinion mattered to me. I had been seeing her for a couple of months already and it was my hope that she would end up spending a great deal of time with me and so I wanted her to have some input into the decision making process. I hadn't yet told her what the social worker had said but she didn't know that and I wanted the social worker to feel uncomfortable because she fucking deserved to.

'What do you think?'

The social worker and housing officer had gone into the kitchen to have a look around, so I seized the opportunity to have a private word with Isabelle. It was our decision to make, ours alone.

'I can't believe it, it's big, it's well decorated and it's got fitted carpets! I know one or two people who have flats in Worksop and they're nowhere near as good as this.'

She was absolutely right; it was sealed. I guess I just wanted to hear my thoughts bounce audibly off the walls. Once we had reached agreement we wandered through each room commenting on what we might do to each one. It was fun, exciting even, and I already began to feel like the tenant and no longer the borrower. When we returned to the lounge they were waiting, all smiles and teeth but it was superfluous and I enjoyed recognising that, just to feel that I had something they had to ask for.

'So what do you think?'

'Yeah, I'll take it, who wouldn't?'

I borrowed his pen to sign the agreement then it was all systems go. The first week's rent was waived and I'd already decided that although the décor was of a very high standard I wanted to make the lounge my own and that week would allow me to redecorate. An application was made for housing benefit, which would cover the rent until I no longer needed assistance, and a further application was made for a community care grant.

Isabelle and I pooled our immediate resources and bought the necessary in order to decorate the lounge, while the social worker provided the loan of a pair of stepladders. When the decorating was complete the place felt like it was ours and not just mine and I never thought I could ever feel good about that, like it was something that had been missing without being missed. We also began to plan for the future and discussed the possibility of us eventually living together. Whilst such a move wasn't imminent, it did require a certain amount of organisation and it entitled Isabelle to put forward some ideas of her own as to what kind of furniture we should buy, finances permitting. This is when we had our first row but nothing as trivial as what colour curtains we should buy or what type of toothpaste we should use, it more a question of history overwhelming me yet again.

I received a community care grant of a little over four hundred pounds and I had already begun to trawl second-hand stores and charity shops, when the Benefits Agency also agreed that I had been underpaid for the past twelve months and returned all the money I had missed. I now had a substantial amount of money which significantly transformed my circumstances in a way I had never imagined. For the very first time in my life I could afford to furnish my place with brand new goods which left me feeling a little overwhelmed and unable to make up my mind.

Isabelle also had savings and it was eventually agreed that I would buy a fridge-freezer, a cooker, a bed, a sofa and a television and stereo. She would supply most of the lounge furniture. As it was hoped that one day she would move in, it seemed the natural thing to do and when the time came, we would sit down and choose pots and pans and all the usual bits and pieces together. It was a hugely exciting time but I refused to allow myself to be carried away by it. Having spent the majority of my life stretching what little money I had, I found no reason to change my approach. I decided, therefore, that I wasn't going to splash my money around just to enjoy the novelty of it, I still wanted to feel I'd gotten real value, the best my money could provide, so I visited every single store and even managed to barter a little. There was a twenty pounds delivery and installation charge for the cooker, which I had purchased from a small independent store rather than a huge company lacking the personal touch. By paying cash I managed to have this charge waived, which paid for a set of non-stick pans. Whilst I was resourceful and able to negotiate, even to the point of recognising and eventually dismissing sales talk, there were other things I had no real practical knowledge of and my naivety was soon exposed. When the bed arrived it did not, as I had imagined, come complete, instead I had to assemble it myself. There were no plans and I didn't even own any tools, but more to the point, the excitement I'd felt when choosing and then handing over the money for it, quickly evaporated as I stood staring at a pile of timber that looked no different to any I'd previously set fire to.

But I still wasn't tempted.

A couple of people from the social work department came over and assembled it for me as I looked on impatiently, desperate to see it built and standing there in my bedroom, the one they were in, only because I had invited them. When the job was complete and the mattress went on, followed by the duvet and the pillows, I nearly wept. I was almost forty years old and I'd never owned a bed or slept in one that smelled clean, free from urine stains, semen stains and even the occasional puke stain. I thanked them for their labour and kindness but as soon as they were gone I did indeed weep, but I felt no shame or weakness, as I remembered those I had battled just to be here.

Isabelle busied herself sourcing the furniture for the lounge. I had allowed her a free hand, she was eager to show me what she had chosen and I have to say she had great taste. Once everything was assembled and finally in place I felt sure it would be a home I would never tire of coming back to, a place that would always welcome me, whatever mood I was in. She paid for the goods and we were issued with a date when we could expect delivery. It was all so painless I could barely believe it, but I wasn't complaining. Over the next few days, however, things took a different turn as the momentum swung away from me. I was trying to share the moment yet at the same time I didn't want to relinquish my claim to it.

Isabelle had been making lists of all the sundries that would be needed, everything from teaspoons to tea towels. Every time I walked into the lounge at the hostel, she would be at the table, hard at work. On seeing me enter the room she would ask what I thought of this item or that, a set of soup bowls, for example or a kettle. I just wished she had sought my opinion before they'd already been added to the list. On the face of it, it was a small matter, hardly worth falling out over and I certainly wasn't looking to turn it into a major drama, but I felt like I was being excluded and ignored. I wanted what was mine to feel like it was, and not another hijack that told me what I wanted.

'Listen, Isabelle, I thought we were supposed to be doing this together.'

I was angry and hadn't yet quite mastered the art of assertion without a hint of aggression.

'You should be fucking grateful that I've taken the trouble to do it, that I could even be bothered!'

She may have had a point, but these were the things I wanted to embrace because they were new to me.

'I am grateful that you can be bothered, I'm just pissed off that you didn't discuss any of it first. This isn't Red Bank or Aycliffe where they take control then tell you what you want only it isn't, we're talking about my home, where I decide what I want. At least allow me that.'

I grabbed the sheets of paper, crumpled them into a ball and threw them into the waste paper basket, not my most eloquent gesture or even my most mature.

'You can go fuck yourself! You get on with it, see if you can do a better job.'

'It's not a competition, Isabelle, it's more important than that. If we fuck this up then we'll fuck everything else up too!'

She fell silent for a moment. I'd hurt her and in turn had wounded myself but the pain would have been far greater and longer lasting if I'd ignored whose name was on the tenancy agreement. I wasn't willing to give it up before I'd had a chance to treat it as normal. She eventually got to her feet and moved towards the door. There was an awkward silence that seemed to last longer than it probably did. Before leaving, she stopped and paused.

'I wasn't trying to take over but like you, I've never had a decent home, either. I was excited, that's all, but I'm not allowed to be excited, am I?'

I stared down at the ground. I guess maybe I resented her a little for wanting it as much as I did. I guess her feeling like it was home already, robbed me of a moment that I wanted to own exclusively for a while, then set it free.

I eventually relented and retrieved the crumpled up paper from the waste bin, straightened it out as best I could and placed it back on the table. I didn't regret what I'd said, only the manner with which I said it, but I couldn't change that.

I never mentioned that list again, except to add to it.

A couple of weeks later, having packed the remainder of my belongings into a box, I moved into my new apartment.

It was important for me to spend the first night alone, not to mark my territory or any thing else equally primitive, I just wanted that bed all to myself just for a few dreamy hours. Isabelle remained at the hostel although she spent most weekends with me and sometimes she stayed over during the week. One morning I popped down to see her and she answered the door, looking absolutely terrified. We went into her room and she told me that she thought it was someone else at the door and that's what had scared her. After further probing she explained that she had knocked on the office door during the early hours of the morning, only to be verbally abused.

Members of staff at the hostel were required to sleep over in case any of the clients suffered some form of crisis and needed support. Isabelle had asked for a sedative, which had been prescribed on a 'prn' basis, meaning it was to be taken only when required. However, when she knocked on the door and asked for the medication, the worker in question had unnerved her by screaming and shouting. I had never liked this member of staff, he'd been my caseworker whilst I was there and, apart from anything else, always turned up for work looking like he'd been sleeping rough. On one unforgettable occasion I turned up for my case conference to find him sat there with his feet up on the table, before pulling out a crumpled piece of paper from his pocket on which he'd written his notes.

Later that afternoon I took her for a drink and she was incredibly subdued, just sitting, staring into her drink. I struggled to find a way of communicating with her. She had clearly fallen deep inside herself and I was naturally concerned and anxious about her having to return to the scene of the crime.

'Listen, why don't you stay at my place for a couple of days just to let things die down a bit?'

'Do you mind?'

I didn't want her to give it a minute's thought, I just wanted to get her out of the way for a while, knowing how vengeful and vicious these people can be.

'The sooner you leave that place the better, I was so desperate to get out of there I would have moved into a tent.'

She stayed with me for a couple of days then returned to the hostel, but within an hour or two she was on the phone to me, once again distressed.

'They've told me that I can't keep staying at yours, if I do they are going to report me to housing benefit and if I lose my benefit I'll have to go back to the hospital.'

'Well, there's only one thing for it, you'll just have to move in with me. That'll shut the bastards up.'

It was said without thinking, an impulsive trigger or maybe just a habitual memory, fresh out of hibernation.

'You want me to move in with you?'

'Why not?'

Within a few days Isabelle had moved in. It was all done according to the rule book which principally meant informing the benefits agency. Although this involved a deduction in our weekly allowance, it wasn't a concern. Money wasn't something I ever really fretted about but space was, and now I had it all, everything I had dreamed of during those dark years.

Besides, I wasn't looking to save myself, there's no adventure in that.

I didn't know what to expect but that was familiar, it was what I knew best and it kept everything open and waiting. The first few days were exciting, but I quickly found myself becoming increasingly agitated about things that ordinarily wouldn't have troubled me. Isabelle had a carefree approach to most things, whereas I tended to be more ordered. For example, she would leave the tops off shampoo bottles or the toothpaste, or she would forget to put the milk back in the refrigerator. It drove me crazy, as I could see no reason for it other than laziness, yet when I complained I was accused of being controlling, even though the place was beginning to resemble a council refuse tip. I'd never had the luxury of being able to just drop things on the floor and ignore them, never had a bedroom that had my signature on it, I had been trained in keeping everything neat and tidy without ever knowing why.

Or knowing how to be, like Isabelle.

Perhaps I resented her most fundamental freedoms, or maybe I just didn't recognise them anymore because I still had to keep the bathroom clean, except now I wanted to, because it was part of a home.

Another problem that quickly began to manifest itself was that we seemed to spend every waking hour together and I was afraid it might start to choke the life out of our relationship, by suffocating me. I had continued to attend the day centre and although I still resented it, I now began to look forward to the days when I would be in attendance just to have something different, something I had more control over, if only to make it there on my own.

I knew it wasn't working already.

Yet I felt unable to tell her, I just didn't have the heart because there was still the question of where she would go, so I did nothing.

We were both supported in the community by our various teams. In my case I was bound by the terms and conditions of my licence but her intervention was largely a voluntary arrangement. The authorities would only take control if she suffered a relapse and refused to be admitted to hospital, in which case she would be sectioned under the Mental Health Act and then forcibly detained. Isabelle's team was newly formed, with a remit to offer support to those who had a history of disengaging. They were provided with substantial resources, which allowed them to offer services most of the other teams couldn't. They would come to the apartment three or four times a week and take her out for lunch or to a country house. The intention, in part, was to provide us with some space and provide her with some counselling, should she require it, in a less formalized non-clinical environment.

The problem was that she wouldn't speak to them other than to make small talk. She felt constantly undermined as she disagreed with their analysis of her situation, and felt frustrated at their refusal to give. The net result was that I had to sit through an incessant dialogue on a daily basis and I wasn't equipped. Nor did I want to be a nurse, a social worker or a therapist, I just wanted to be her partner and I wasn't being allowed to.

Inevitably, we began to row, with one or two being pretty explosive and draining. I tried to persuade her to think differently about what was going on but she refused to deviate from her own hypothesis. She believed she knew her own mind best and that there was nothing wrong. Any attempt at trying to get her to yield would automatically be met with a verbal onslaught that left me feeling like I was under siege.

Five or six weeks after she had moved in, I was woken in the early hours of the morning.

'Min, I think I need to go to hospital.'

'Okay, well I can make the call but once the process starts, it can't be stopped.'

'That's okay.'

I wasn't bothered in the least about being woken up in such a manner, it was far more important to me that she was attempting to recognise her own situation, and take control of it.

I rang for an ambulance, which delivered us both to the accident and emergency department of the local hospital. Once there, we waited for the duty psychiatrist to assess her. It was quickly decided that she did indeed need to be in hospital so I accompanied her onto the ward and stayed with her throughout the admissions process.

Isabelle was prescribed a sedative and the nurses allowed me to sit, holding her hand until she fell asleep.

'Listen, thanks for that, she's asleep now.'

'Okay, Min, you take care now.'

'I'll try.'

I left the hospital to walk the two or three miles back to my apartment. It was a little past four am and just as it was when I arrived, it was still dark.

CHAPTER FIFTY-THREE

'Don't you want to go out with me anymore?

The words stung because she looked so desperately fragile and because I was still hopelessly in love with her, but I was confused and didn't quite know how to proceed, having already decided that we couldn't go on living together.

'I love you to bits, Isabelle, but if we go on living together we'll end up killing each other.'

We had already begun to hurt each other in the days leading up to her admission. The rows became increasingly intense with an element of cruelty on both sides. Certainly, some of the things I said were inexcusably spiteful.

'But we can still see each other, can't we?'

It was all just too perfect, and selfish, of course. I wanted to continue seeing her, I just wasn't convinced I could offer her what she needed, wasn't entirely satisfied I was being fair on her.

I lacked the courage to set her free.

'Whatever happens, I'm not going to walk away from you.'

I continued to visit her every day whilst she was there and when she was strong enough to venture out, we would occasionally go for lunch, or return to the apartment and listen to music. After several weeks she was well enough to be discharged, and was sent to Stepping Stones.

* * * *

One evening whilst listening to music and generally feeling pretty sorry for myself, the phone rang and it was Isabelle inviting me out for a drink. Every inch of me wanted to say yes, whilst heading for the door, but inexplicably I refused, because I still missed her in everything I did. Within a few minutes I had received a message stating that she had arranged to go out for a drink with a guy we both knew, who had a huge soft spot for her, and it bothered me.

I paced back and forth across my lounge floor, as my mind started throwing punches from all angles and I didn't even try to duck. In my increasingly small pocket of a mind, I was jealous. Despite imploring myself to take a step back I seemed completely unable to do anything except follow my impulses so I raced to the boozer and found Isabelle sitting alone. She smiled as I stepped through the door and it threw me. I expected her to be angry.

'So where is he?'

'He couldn't make it in the end.'

I sat down and tried to count my thoughts, anything just to buy a little time so I could try and figure out what the fuck was going on, but it didn't take long, her girlish demeanour gave it away.

'So was this just some pathetic attempt to get me here?'

'I'm not keeping you, go home if you want.'

I bought a couple of drinks and returned to the table but I was looking at her differently now. I was angry at her use of subterfuge, angry that she had successfully engineered this meeting, even angrier that I had so easily fallen for it, because my intellect and emotions were in opposition, one gave me power whilst the other tried to take it away.

I walked her back to Stepping Stones, but on the way I launched into a verbal assault, accusing her of making matters worse for herself, by being in a constant state of denial. I argued that she should start accepting she had a problem and learn to manage it. Her response was loud and vitriolic and extremely animated, almost making me dizzy. I had never seen this side of her before and it was ugly, and actually quite scary, because in that moment she was full of hate.

'I'm calling the police.'

'The police!'

I was both scared and confused, scared because any dealings with the cops whilst on life licence put me at serious risk of recall, confused because I didn't understand the need for their intervention.

'I'm going to tell them you're harassing a vulnerable woman.'

I made a grab for the phone and a wrestling match ensued. I was surprised at how strong she was and there was a lot of pushing and shoving before I finally rescued the phone, and hurled it down the street, watching as it broke into several pieces.

'You're not calling anyone now.'

I walked away without another word. I glanced over my shoulder and although Isabelle was no more than a ten minute walk from the hostel, I saw that she was trying to flag down a passing motorist. I had no wish to be set upon by a group of vigilantes nor did I believe I was being paranoid given the nature of the earlier exchange so I quickly broke into a jog, making sure to avoid the obvious and quickest route. I was breathing heavily but not from jogging, there was an element of fear and uncertainty and I just wanted to get home and bolt the doors, but I was unsure how to control my anger and make it work for me.

When I arrived home I screamed at myself, incensed that I had fallen for such a cheap trick yet still not quite knowing how, perhaps there was far more wrong with me than there was with her. I was also disturbed by my act of violence in hurling the phone, because in that moment I became everything I had fought against, everything I'd been forced to swallow but never quite digested, everything that was my father. I felt hopeless because I simply didn't understand and for once the silence didn't offer any clues, not even solace. I had lessened myself and not even my ego could argue against that. I sat alone in my apartment but didn't quite feel at home, because I had no way of knowing what was truly mine, a simple misplaced word was all it took to separate me from it

Then, in the dead of night, the militia came banging on my door.

'Michael Cooper?'

'Actually, it's Mini, but go on.'

I turned and made my way through the hallway, leaving them to secure the door; they were far better at it than I would ever want to be. On reaching the lounge I sat but didn't invite them to, their uniforms might have stained the fabric on my sofa.

'Do you know a Ms Isabelle Dempsey?'

'Yes.'

'When was the last time you saw her?'

'Tonight.'

'There's been a complaint made against you, that you assaulted her outside a pub.'

'That's ridiculous.'

'Michael Cooper, I'm arresting you on suspicion of assault.'

He performed the usual ritual of explaining my non-existent rights before placing me in handcuffs and leading me away with an unnecessarily firm grip on my arm.

'I've already told you, it's Mini.'

Outside in the car park I was stunned at seeing a huge police van just for me. They opened the back doors and inside was a metal cage that was locked. We could have walked to the station in a couple of minutes, and certainly without such a show of strength. I received better treatment when I was actually guilty of a crime. I was locked inside the cage and the enormity of the situation suddenly overwhelmed me, I was no ordinary prisoner and guilty or not I could be going back to jail. I struggled to digest that, but I couldn't ignore it.

By daybreak, having been awake all night because they hadn't provided me with a blanket and I didn't ask, the cell door swung open.

'The custody sergeant wants to see you.'

I walked with him to the reception area without exchanging a single word. Once there I stood in front of the desk and waited.

'Right, you're being released on bail, pending further enquiries. Do you understand what that means? You need to report here a week from now at six thirty pm, failure to do so will result in a warrant being issued for your arrest.'

'I better not book a holiday then.'

'Get him out of here.'

The laces had been removed from my shoes, along with the belt from my trousers. I sat down on a bench to sort myself out before hitting the street, I wanted to leave in the same manner that I had arrived.

Intact.

'Come on, fella, you can do that through there.'

He pointed towards the waiting area that members of the public access immediately upon their arrival. However, I rather enjoyed the fact that whilst I was still behind a locked door, I was no longer under arrest.

'I'm not a prisoner anymore, when I'm finished, then I'll leave.'

A few minutes later I hit the street. I broke open the plastic bag containing my personal effects and lit a cigarette, inhaling all the way down to my shoes. It was a great smoke. From where I was stood I could see my apartment yet curiously I seemed in no great hurry to be there, it was such a fragile piece of real estate that could just as easily belong to somebody else, as the cell could just as easily call me back. It was a delicately poised game of chance that reminded me of just how vulnerable I was, and I even began to question the value of such an existence and the validity in wanting it.

It wasn't enough to have laces in my shoes.

Angry but not vengeful, I returned to my apartment because for now at least it was still my home, I was still the holder of the key. I hadn't been there long when it suddenly occurred to me that there had been no mention of the damage to Isabelle's mobile phone. It seemed odd not to be questioned about something I was guilty of, instead they got twelve hours out of me for free. I still had a moral obligation, if not apparently, a legal one, towards the phone. So once I had washed their stench out of my hair and had something to eat and drink, I headed into town to buy a new phone and then made my way to Stepping Stones in order to deliver it.

It hadn't been inserted as a condition of my bail that I cease to have any contact with Isabelle until the investigation was complete, nevertheless I felt it would be safer, so I intended to hand the phone over to a member of staff and then just walk away. The guy who met me at the door was someone I'd known for a while and had enjoyed a good relationship with. He smiled warmly as I approached but I still felt a little awkward.

'I'm not stopping, I just brought this for Isabelle, just tell her I'm sorry the other one got damaged.'

I handed him the bag containing the phone and he looked inside it, pulling out the box, then he smiled again.

'An expensive mistake.'

'Yeah, it was, in more ways than one.'

It was glaringly obvious that I wasn't going to be able to keep my night in the cells away from the authorities, it's a small town and everybody talks to one another, constantly sharing information. If I had tried, I would have inevitably failed and held to be guilty through omission so I decided not to head straight home, but rather call in at the social worker's office first.

I was extremely anxious and resented it, I was also angry at having to justify myself separately from an ongoing investigation and all the time I was having to deal with it on my own. I didn't offer a verbatim account of the evening as it simply wasn't necessary but I did include all the relevant facts. I spoke of my stupidity at racing off to the pub when my instincts told me I might be heading straight into the lion's den. I explained how the phone came to be damaged but I did lie about how much we'd had to drink, as the mere mention of alcohol had everyone panicking, purely because it had been a feature many years ago, even though it no longer was. Finally, I admitted that I had been arrested on suspicion of assault and was currently on bail while they continued with their enquiries but I denied the allegations.

'I'll need to talk to the rest of the team, particularly probation, but I don't think you'll have anything to worry about. I suspect this will soon blow over but in the meantime I'd strongly recommend you have no contact with her.'

Well, I didn't need asking twice. I returned to my apartment and later in the day received a phone call. The probation service had decided to await the outcome of the police investigation before deciding on an appropriate course of action.

The clock was ticking.

It was all I could think of each day in between bouts of frustration and even desperation. Was it always going to be like this and would I ever have the tools to suffer it with equilibrium? I had survived many things in many different ways, but that's all, now I required a different kind of courage, the ability to accept with equanimity the conditions I couldn't change or ignore.

The following days were chaotic as I tried desperately to provide myself with sufficient resolve not to fold. It was too easy to fail and success was defined as simply staying out of jail. Instead I spent several hours and a great deal of money getting gloriously drunk in the company of strangers, most of whom I didn't even like, and still didn't long after I'd bought them a drink.

There was no question that I was going into meltdown, afraid of being returned to prison, yet playing the dumbest hand I could. Part of me was convinced I was going back so I figured there was little to lose in abandoning the maturity that had brought me this far. I was also consumed with rage and an undiluted sense of injustice that threatened to blow me off course. Nevertheless, it wasn't very smart to be saying, 'fuck you!' when I should have just waited quietly in the wings. Although I wasn't in breach of my licence I had once again shown a propensity towards recklessness. By the end of that week there was nothing I could do to affect the outcome except wait, but I was never very good at that. On the day that I was due to present myself to the police station I had pretty much made up my mind what I was going to do, but I decided to call Franc first in the hope that even without him knowing, he might persuade me to change my mind.

He was incredibly reassuring, I explained what had happened and outlined my fears but he constantly reiterated that I had done nothing wrong and therefore had nothing to fear. Despite his best efforts I wasn't to be persuaded, I didn't want to live like this anymore, didn't want freedom in name only and didn't want to wait for a knock on the door every time I had a row. I went to my local off licence and bought a bottle of Merlot, then returned to my apartment where I immediately opened a box of anti-depressant tablets and spilled them all over the surface of the coffee table. I was on automatic pilot, afraid that if I hesitated I might change my mind when it was simpler not to. I had only managed to swallow three or four pills, washed down with a large glass of wine, when there was a loud knock at the front door.

'Come on, Mini, open the door, I know you're in there.'

The order came from my social worker, her timing appalling and the echoes of her voice unwelcome but difficult to ignore. However, I failed to understand her conviction that I was home given the silence, so ignore her I did and grabbed another handful of pills.

'Mini, if you don't open this door right now we'll break it down!'

'Alright, alright, I'm coming, for fuck's sake!'

I opened the door and my social worker and her colleague brushed past me without being invited in. I was feeling pretty cranky, both at the ease with which they had gained entry, and the manner of my surrender.

'Don't sit down, you're not stopping.'

'Have you been drinking?'

Given that an open bottle of wine was sitting in the middle of the coffee table, I could hardly deny it. Indeed, her colleague picked it up and looked at it.

'Good choice.'

'Help yourself, I've only had one glass, there's plenty left, as you can see.'

'What are all these tablets doing here?'

'I was counting them.'

I wasn't doing myself any favours by being so obnoxious but I wasn't seeking to, I was losing the battle with myself yet still didn't want to be at their mercy.

'And if we hadn't turned up when we did, would you have taken them all?'

Despite the lethargy that was slowing my mind and diluting my will, I still had enough awareness to recognise the significance and indeed, the importance of my next answer.

'No.'

'We're all worried about you, you've not been yourself for a while and we know you've been drinking, we think you should go into hospital for a few days just to give yourself time.'

'I have to report to the police station in an hour.'

'Don't worry about the police, we'll speak to them and explain what's going on.'

I'd never been told not to fear the police before and the novelty almost made me laugh. Crucially the idea of having them off my back for a while longer was definitely an incentive so I followed them to the car. When we arrived the psychiatrist was busy so we were shown into an interview room where we waited. I felt increasingly uncomfortable, knowing that I neither wanted nor needed this.

'I need a cigarette.'

As I stepped into the corridor I felt more like a visitor for I would never fulfil the stereotype of the deranged psychotic, and I resented being made to try, angry at the part I had played.

'I'm not staying, I want to go home.'

'But we've only just got here, the doctor will be free soon.'

'I've nothing to say to her. Now you can either drive me or I'll walk.'

Without waiting for their reply I turned around and was gone, having finally rediscovered a genuine sense of purpose and belief. Nevertheless I didn't expect them to capitulate, fully expecting an army of nurses to surround me before returning me to be sectioned. To my utter astonishment and sheer disbelief, I was given a free passage out of the building and into the car park. My escort eventually caught up.

'Well, know that it's an option should you ever need it.'

What I really needed was a huge glass of the delightful Merlot she so ungraciously poured down the sink before we left.

'Yeah.'

When we pulled into the car park outside my apartment I spotted a cop pressing my buzzer. His presence had brought the neighbours out to witness their very own soap opera, but I was more angry than embarrassed. My social worker went over and spoke to the cop whilst I remained in the car. I was still a little anxious as I had no idea what was being said. I tried desperately to study their body language but it offered no real clues. After a couple of minutes she walked towards the car and he walked towards his. I got out and met her halfway across the car park.

'You're not going to be facing any charges, there's no case to answer. You're in the clear.'

CHAPTER FIFTY-FOUR

'Nobody's suggesting you've done anything wrong but surely you must know that if enough mud gets thrown, then eventually some of it will stick.'

'That's my concern.'

I was once again at the offices of the probation service, having just spent yet another night in the cells. Unlike the first time, however, I was released without charge the following morning. Isabelle had unexpectedly turned up at my flat and if I'd had any sense at all I wouldn't have let her in but I did, because I'd missed her and I still wasn't quite used to it. Once we'd started talking I instantly regretted my decision and I asked her to leave but she wouldn't, insisting that I hear what she had to say first which seriously pissed me off.

I was at home and if I couldn't control the conditions there, then what was the point to any of it? I grabbed her, marched her down the hallway and threw her out, slamming the door shut before locking it. I returned to my lounge actually feeling pretty shitty, the force with witch I'd used to eject her had both startled and frightened her, it was an image that continued to torment me long after the event itself. It was also quite late and although she hadn't far to go, it was getting dark which always made her nervous. I felt pretty mean but the alternative was to call the cops and have them remove her, but I just couldn't do it, civilian life could never extend that far.

Eventually I went to bed but unable to let go of my feelings, I struggled to sleep. An hour or so later I was disturbed by a loud banging on my front door. I assumed Isabelle had returned so I climbed out of bed, wearing only my boxers, and opened the door.

'Mr Cooper?'

Two cops were stood there, a man and a woman. It didn't take long for me to figure out what was going on, only this time it didn't unhinge me, it made me angry and belligerent.

'Yes.'

'I'm arresting you on suspicion of assault.'

'You're having a laugh.'

'Put your clothes on, you're coming to the station.'

'This is a joke, I'm going back to bed.'

Before I had the chance to turn around, she'd slapped a pair of handcuffs on my wrists with enough force to make me wince.

When we arrived at the station it was the usual pantomime of them insisting that I provide information that was already stored on their computer, courtesy of my first visit.

'You already know where I was born, when I was born, but thankfully not quite how I was born.'

Two male officers then escorted me to a cell to perform the ritual humiliation of a full strip search, the ultimate degradation.

'If it makes you feel any better, we don't enjoy this anymore than you do.'

'Yeah, well I don't see anyone shining a torch up your arse, you're just a bunch of fascists.'

'Yeah, yeah we've heard it all before. Here, put these on.'

He threw a tee shirt and a pair of jogging pants at me, then dropped a pair of plimsolls on the floor near the door. I put them on out of necessity and settled down, waiting for the inevitable interrogation. The door once again opened and a middle-aged cop, whose best days were clearly a distant memory, stood there looking like a sack of shit.

'Come on, son, let's get you photographed and finger printed.'

'You've already got my photograph and finger prints on record, you've even got my fucking DNA, what more do you want?'

'Look, I just do what I'm told and if you did the same you wouldn't be here now, would you?'

The following morning having slept very little the door swung open and I was released. I collected the sealed bag containing my damaged property and waited to be let through.

'If you want my advice, I'd stay away from her.'

'Yeah, well, if you want mine, you should try establishing the facts first before dragging someone from their bed.'

Wearing the same clothes they had provided, I went straight home, showered, changed and then returned them to the pigsty. There's no doubting I could have made life a whole lot easier during my period of detention, but it helped to pass the time instead of fearing it, It also relieved the boredom.

The entire experience however, had been extremely damaging, as it now seemed that I was on everybody's radar except my own. Of even greater concern to me was my own culpability in all of this. Both situations were avoidable but on each occasion my decision-making was seriously flawed. Whilst I was unwilling to call the cops, a decision I still stand by, I didn't have to let her into the property and my reasons for doing so were self-serving and pitiful. As were my reasons for racing halfway across town like a tortured adolescent because I hadn't the emotional capability to resist the immediate impulse, in preference to the safer, if more unattractive, option.

* * * *

A few weeks later I was invited to Isabelle's new apartment where she greeted me smiling and proud. She had some incense burning and the place looked and smelled wonderfully. The lounge walls had been decorated with photographs and political quotes, and she insisted on showing me each and every one. In the kitchen were her little knick-knacks, which wouldn't have been out of place in a country cottage, all of it in stark contrast to my place, which was more functional rather than an expression of ideas and creativity. There was no doubting her desire to build a home to live in and not just to occupy, whereas I delighted in just having the space to myself.

Dinner was fabulous, washed down with a fine bottle of red wine, the perfect accompaniment, along with the music and, of course, the company. I was invited to stay the night and I did.

The weeks that followed were spent between our respective places. She'd spend a couple of nights at mine, I'd spend a couple at hers and the rest of the time we were alone, which appeared to suit me more than it did her. It caused a few problems but not necessarily in the way you might think. I had begun to notice that when Isabelle was feeling fragile she would want me around for support. She could be extremely demanding, often wanting me to drop whatever I was doing and rush to her side, including during the night. There was no question of me not wanting to support her, I had continued in that role for the entirety of our time together, but I sometimes felt a little neglected. When Isabelle was extremely well she was full of energy and extremely independent, it's what I wanted for her but not at my expense. Often I would call her and she didn't want to speak to me because she was busy entertaining friends and could sometimes be rude. When I pointed this out to her she became angry and accused me of being bourgeois and jealous, even suggesting that I was trying to isolate her.

'You don't like it because I've got friends and you haven't.'

I chose not to have that many friends because I didn't want the demands that came with it. But I still needed to feel valued beyond my role of carer, wanted to share in her wellbeing, to experience her laughter, her joy and her unabridged personality. I wanted to experience her whole, to feel like a lover should, meeting each others' needs, but ultimately it became abundantly clear that mine weren't as important as hers.

'We need to resolve this, Isabelle.'

'I don't need to listen to this crap! It's over, Min.'

'It's over, just like that?'

'I'm sick of you picking me up and putting me down like a rag doll.'

'You always fucking do it! Refuse to listen to what you don't want to hear so nothing ever gets discussed!'

'Go fuck yourself!'

I headed for her place, not wanting a fight but accepting the possibility of it becoming one. I had to do it because I was always told it would be different once the locks had been changed, that I would always have a right to reply because I had crossed the meadow to the other side, but all I found were strangers with familiar faces. I arrived at her door, breathing a little heavier, and took a few seconds to compose myself then I knocked firmly. A guy wearing a baseball cap answered the door, grinning like an idiot.

'I'm here to see Isabelle.'

'No, mate, you're not coming in.'

'And who the fuck are you to tell me I can't come in?'

'Look, mate, you're not coming in, so just piss off home.'

'I don't think so and I'm not your fucking mate!'

I attempted to brush past him but he put one hand across my chest and slapped me with the other. It made me chuckle because guys generally punch so as well as being ineffectual, I couldn't help but think that she had hired muscle from a Morris Dancing class.

'Do you think that's funny? Do you? You fucking prick!'

Suddenly, this other guy appeared from nowhere and was snarling in my face. I pushed him away, purely as a reflex as I was drowning in his spittle and I certainly didn't want to kiss the fucker!

'Who are you calling a prick?'

Words were exchanged between all three of us, further inflaming an already volatile situation. Suddenly punches were coming at me from all angles and the speed and precision of them soon sent me crashing to the ground, helpless, bloodied and dazed. They kicked me around like a football and it was then I noticed that Isabelle had stepped out of the apartment to enjoy the entertainment. I was wounded more deeply than anyone had ever managed before and I lost the will to resist, I just lay there and looked at the stars. Eventually I was dragged down several concrete steps, my head bouncing against each one. At some point, I slipped into unconsciousness.

When I came round I was in a large room with lots of beds and it didn't take long to realise that I was on a hospital ward for the very first time in my life, apart from the farm, another piece I gave away. I pulled back the covers, unaware that I was completely naked, so I quickly grabbed a towel from the bedside locker and wrapped it around myself before heading down a corridor in search of my clothes. A nurse spotted me and asked if there was a problem, I told her I was looking for my clothes and an awful lot was resting on her answer because I wasn't asking simply out of curiosity.

'Are you the man who came in with the police last night?'

'Yes.'

'Then they're under your bed in a plastic bag.'

Perfect! When I hadn't seen them I was paranoid that they had been deliberately withheld and that could have only meant one thing. At least now I didn't have to expect visitors. Whilst talking I noticed that the left side of my head began to itch so I attempted to scratch it.

'What's this on the side of my head?'

'Glue, you suffered a head wound and we don't stitch head wounds anymore, we glue them.'

'Lovely.'

I returned to the ward and immediately retrieved my clothes before dressing and heading for the exit.

'Mr Cooper, I really don't think you should be leaving so early, you need bed rest and observation.'

'You've got my address, feel free to call round.'

I left a little after five in the morning and walked home, feeling a little groggy and in some pain, but happy to be returning to my own bed. I, too, had some observations to make once I'd had time to lick my wounds and had stopped feeling sorry for myself. I immediately ran a bath and encountered my first obstacle. There was some damage to my lower back which, when walking or lying, caused nothing more than some slight discomfort, but sitting or trying to climb over something was virtually impossible because the pain was nauseatingly intense.

Getting in and out of that bath brought tears to my eyes, and further dented my already fragile pride, but I refused to be disabled by it. In addition to my back I also had a black eye, some blemishes around my face, and my torso was covered in bruises. I eventually devised a method of sitting that required me to perch right on the edge of the chair leaning slightly to one side, with one leg stretched straight out in front of me and the other bent at the knee. This is how I managed to eat without having to stand up, which is what I was doing when the phone unexpectedly rang and interrupted my meditation.

'Hello, Mini, it's Isabelle.'

'What do you want?'

'How are you?'

Just hearing those words shut everything down for a moment or two because there was nothing in them that fitted any regular pattern, they just fell from her lips without restraint.

'Well, obviously I'm still alive, does that disappoint you?'

'No, why should it?'

Over the years I had had many conversations with a number of extraordinarily difficult people, but none that had me struggling and grasping for reason because the game kept reinventing itself.

'Look, Isabelle, why don't you just say what you want to say then fuck off, preferably to another country, or outer space, even!'

'I'm seeing somebody else now.'

We'd only been talking for around thirty seconds but every time I tried to maintain some level of control I'd be sent spinning by her sleight of mind. Her timing was impeccable, but on this occasion so was mine.

'Well, even by your standards that's pretty fast, I mean, we've only been separated three or four days. Just don't ring me when it all goes tits up.'

'Go fuck yourself!'

If only I'd been able to, I could have saved an awful lot of people from wasting their time.

CHAPTER FIFTY-FIVE

'We're concerned about your relationship with Isabelle, we think it has the potential for danger so we've written to the parole board asking them to consider adding an extra clause to your licence that you have no more contact with her.'

I was so angry I could have cried, the authorities had held a meeting in secret and only summoned me once they had arrived at their decision. Maybe they were trying to protect me, but I was unwilling to publicly acknowledge that.

'You can't legally enforce that, it breaches article eight of the Human Rights Act, my right to a private life.'

'Well it's going to be looked into but in the meantime, as your supervising officer, I'm instructing you to have no further contact with her. If you do, then you know the risks.'

Regardless of the risks I knew full well that I wouldn't comply because if I did, what would be next? When the initial impact of the blast had died away, I found myself stranded in a wilderness, not knowing which direction to take because they all looked the same and there were no signposts.

Just space.

Over the course of several weeks, through a combination of frustration, rage and unadulterated hatred, my mind was in danger of self-imploding. I lost my appetite, I couldn't sleep and I couldn't concentrate for more than a few minutes, I just ran every day on an empty tank, and walked through the night taking pride in each step and not succumbing to exhaustion. It became a competition, a rallying cry, a show of strength and heart, of which they had none. Inevitably I was summoned to see the psychiatrist and I was convinced they were up to their old tricks again.

'I've been asked to see you because there are some concerns about your mental health.'

'There's nothing wrong with my mental health.'

'Well I believe there are sufficient grounds to have you assessed under the Mental Health Act, but I'd rather you agreed to come in voluntarily.'

I had little option but to agree if I wanted to avoid virtual house arrest but I felt as powerless as a child again, and the dull lonely ache had returned with a vengeance. It was all too familiar, frighteningly so. I became subdued and disjointed as everything I looked at, every sound or smell confirmed my separation. By early evening I'd made up my mind.

I left the ward and went downstairs for a cigarette. There were one or two others milling around but I was so deeply immersed in my own thoughts that I hardly noticed them, once they were gone so was I. I raced across the hospital car park, looking once over my shoulder to make sure I wasn't being chased. I then ran across the main road and disappeared into a housing estate. All the old instincts were once again heightened, the familiar rush of adrenalin seemingly the only way I knew how to feel good about myself, and I needed that feeling again to stop the dehumanising effect and to rediscover how to measure it. I gave little consideration to the risks to my personal freedom as I had yet to acquire it. I was more concerned with having a right to reply that couldn't be edited or diminished, or falsely represented. Unless by me, using the methods they taught so well.

I reached my apartment, closed the living room curtains and sat in the dark, waiting for a knock on the door. Because I was an informal rather than detained patient, the police had no powers of arrest unless there was evidence that I was a risk to myself, or others. The procedure was that they would simply call on me to check that I was okay, but it still wouldn't be an invite. Within a couple of hours, there was indeed a firm knock on the door.

'Mr. Cooper, it's the police. We just want to talk to you, to make sure you're okay. If you're in there, would you come to the door, please?'

Better to pretend that I wasn't, although it was hugely tempting to stand toe to toe with a cop who was impotent, and to witness one being sensitive and compassionate was surely one for the cameras. They repeated their request several times, including one offer of simply showing them my wrists through the letterbox, to prove I hadn't hurt myself. I ignored them all but I knew they'd be back sooner or later.

Whilst the police weren't able to apprehend me, I was in breach of my licence conditions and I was pushing my luck. If I was mentally ill, it wasn't enough for it to be recognised only as an alternative. I wanted absolution, I wanted those responsible to own up and I was willing to pay just to witness it, no matter how backhanded.

The following day, after a restless night, I took the train to Mansfield, already beginning to feel that maybe it was over, that I hadn't really the heart for it anymore, just the same old contempt. My phone rang incessantly and I figured it was probably the hospital wanting news of my whereabouts or possibly the probation service, wanting the same along with pointing out the ubiquitous risks. I ignored them all without regret, all except one and that was from Franc, although I initially hesitated as I was enjoying the freedom of not knowing what to do next but equally not having to ask, or seek permission. In the end he was still a pipeline to humanity and common sense but ultimately he was my friend and I missed him most during the hunting season. I told him what I had done and angrily rejected any notion of wrongdoing on the basis that I was being held on a corrupt premise. He listened intently and his advice was calm and measured, but not what I wanted to hear.

'Listen, Mini, I understand your feelings about how they are treating you, but by running away you're helping them to promote this idea that you're unstable and unpredictable and it's going to make it easier for them to keep you in there for even longer.'

I hated it when he was right, hated it even more whenever he suggested that the only meaningful course of action was to tough it out. Maybe I wanted it all. I agreed to go back, I just didn't say when and in the meantime the pubs were open, everything else could wait. However when I returned to my apartment later that evening, everything seemed to change in an instant as I was catapulted without warning into a minefield of contradictions. I initially intended to honour my agreement with Franc and return myself to the hospital, but as I sat holding the phone in one hand and a cigarette in the other, despair once again snuggled up to me and nudged me encouragingly.

I had lost my way.

I once again poured my medication onto the coffee table, then began screaming angrily at myself for having even thought it, but I was being torn apart by two opposing needs. I swept my hand across the table, sending the tablets scurrying across the floor in shame then I dialled the number, almost in surrender. They sent an ambulance to pick me up and within minutes I was back on the ward.

* * * *

I had just been given a seventy-two hour section and whilst intended to last for that period, it actually extended to a couple of weeks thanks to the intervention of the probation service, and the feeble minded doctors.

Fuck you very much!

It was eventually lifted when I agreed that I would no longer attempt to do a runner, it was kind of a first in that when making the promise, I genuinely believed I would keep to it.

A few days earlier I had been unceremoniously hauled before the deputy director of Nottinghamshire probation service and effectively given a final warning, seemingly mental aberrations weren't part of the model. Shortly after being discharged from the hospital I was actually walking past a pub when I spotted Isabelle through the window, deep in conversation with two guys, one of whom was known to me. It concerned me deeply that she might be about to get involved with a highly manipulative psychopath who I felt sure would exploit her, so against all advice I rang her. She was hostile and accused me of trying to control her life, ending the call with a sting.

'You're not my boyfriend anymore, Min.'

Fairly quickly her mental health deteriorated as these omnipresent fuckers seriously got to work on a vulnerable woman who trusted anyone out of sheer desperation to be rid of her own demons. They'd already gotten her to dispense with her medication, persuading her that it was the Devil's.

I decided to stay close to her and so I effectively moved in, staying four days and four nights without a minute's sleep, because she didn't and I was too paranoid to leave her alone with them. She wandered from room to room, talking constantly, different voices, different accents and I struggled to keep up. On the fourth day I had to take temporary leave as my birthday was in a couple of days and my mother and eldest sister were coming over to visit me and bring birthday gifts, but I made it clear that I would return later that evening.

I had already decided to incur her wrath and become public enemy number one, by admitting her to hospital and hopefully ridding those parasites from her life for good. Back at my apartment, my mum and sister came visiting and my sister can recall how manic I appeared myself. I had offered to make them a cup of coffee but apparently took half an hour to complete such a basic task. She claims that I talked incessantly as I went to and fro from lounge to kitchen then back again more times than was required, and they found it hugely difficult to engage with me as I was constantly changing the subject. When the coffees finally arrived they were cold, I'd forgotten to switch the kettle on. When they eventually left I opened my cards. I was a little broke and knew there was money in them. I needed time on my own, needed rescuing myself, but enjoyed a glass of wine or two at a local hostelry instead.

Upon my return I was feeling hungry and in need of comfort so I placed a couple of burgers under the grill, peeled and chopped some potatoes, switched on the chip pan and sat down on the sofa. Due to my lack of sleep or any other form of respite, the wine acted as a sedative and I quickly went under.

The next thing I remember I was grappling with a number of masked men, I didn't know if I was suffering from some kind of terrifying nightmare or if I was indeed being burgled. One of them picked me up and carried me downstairs and I was apparently laughing all the way. He placed me down on a bench and a paramedic administered oxygen whilst I continued to laugh, ignoring his pleas to have me admitted to hospital.

Adjacent to my apartment, directly across the road, was a hostel for young homeless people who had been victim to various types of abuse and had developed alcohol or drug dependencies. A young inhabitant of this hostel had seen flames raging throughout my kitchen and a member of staff rang the fire brigade. It was they who wore the masks. I was out cold, effectively dead to the world, so they had to break down the door to gain entry, which apparently took five or six attempts, but I never heard a thing. The chief fire officer told me afterwards that had the kitchen door not been closed I would, in all likelihood, have died.

Once the fire brigade had finished I walked back into the apartment. The first thing to hit me was the smell, then how dark it was, the walls having been blackened by the smoke. The cooker stood condemned in the hallway and the lounge floor was covered in debris from the kitchen.

This was karma at its most taunting and cruel.

I was overwhelmed by the scale of the damage and was now experiencing first hand just how devastating fire could be, and whilst this was an accident, the one in my parents' house wasn't; this was what it must have looked and felt like. I stood there, almost catatonic and not knowing what to do, not even where to begin. I didn't possess even the most basic practical skills, I couldn't drill a hole in a wall without being afraid of collapsing it. I only knew how to decorate and even that task appeared daunting.

I couldn't bear to look at it anymore so I headed across town. Isabelle's situation still needed dealing with and rather selfishly I thought it would offer a distraction from my own. I arrived feeling pretty beat up and in no mood to be pissed around by a couple of low-life scumbags. I took a couple of deep breaths then tried the door. It was open, so I entered. I found Isabelle standing on her bed, pointing at the wall and ranting at who knows what, whilst the others were relaxing in the lounge, listening to music, seemingly oblivious to what was going on in the next room.

'Right, I've had enough of this fucking shit! I want you lot out, now!'

Within minutes they had gone. I immediately phoned the hospital and an ambulance was dispatched. She reluctantly went with the paramedics but on her way out screamed at me that I had once again let her down badly. I was impervious to the insult, satisfied that I had done the right thing. I secured her property, having first switched everything off, then handed the keys over to the paramedics. I returned to my own apartment equally reluctant. Despite it being August, the place felt incredibly cold, but at least the bedroom didn't smell of smoke.

The following afternoon, whilst sorting through the debris, I received an unexpected call from my psychiatric nurse.

'I'm calling to let you know that the parole board have decided not to insert the no contact clause into your licence regarding Isabelle. Now we've had reports that you've been over to her flat but her social worker has asked us to cut you a bit of slack because you got her away from those unsavoury characters and into hospital.'

I spent the next couple of days effectively living in my bedroom, which was kind of weird in that it was almost identical to occupying a prison cell, with the obvious exception being that I could let myself out of the building at will. It was kind of exciting knowing that. The housing association was very sensitive to the circumstances and arranged for a contractor to come out and repair the quite substantial damage to my kitchen. In the meantime I had called Franc and poured out my feelings in what must have sounded like an indecipherable rant. Nevertheless, he invited me to stay with him for a couple of days, so when the guy turned up I simply left my keys with a trusted neighbour and headed off to the metropolis for a much needed pep talk, and a little bit of love.

As per usual his support was immeasurable but a mature relationship allows your friends to challenge you, and whilst we both smiled at the irony of me almost perishing in a house fire, he was extremely concerned about my general wellbeing and began questioning my choices.

'I don't understand what the attraction is, Min. This is a woman who had you beaten up and then arrested more than once, yet you keep going back to her when she could get you locked up.'

'She needs me, Franc, I've never been needed before.'

Powerfully seductive, the need to be needed, despite the misshapen reality it weaves in and out of, and the cognitive dissonance it inspires; rescue her and I might just manage to rescue myself. That pretty much took care of the wait between courses and whilst he wasn't necessarily convinced he at least kept enough slack on the rope to prevent it from becoming fatal.

'You know, Mini, you really should write your book. I think it would be fascinating.'

In my early twenties I had attempted to write a memoir but didn't get beyond the second chapter. That's where I was in life, trying to move forward with leaden feet and no compass. Things were different now and it felt like the right time to open the vault and climb out without a safety harness.

After a couple of days, and having confirmed that I would give it a go, I left London for Worksop feeling both stimulated and inspired. I had shared a number of different ideas with Franc and was hugely excited. However, once I was back, I was once again summoned to the probation services' office as they had some information for me. I was concerned that as it couldn't wait, it couldn't be good.

'You know we had to inform the parole board about the recent fire in your flat? Well, they've issued you with this.'

I was handed a single sheet of paper and written across the top in bold letters was, 'Warning letter.' It went on to state that my behaviour was giving rise for concern and I was being warned about my future conduct.

'The fire was accidental, everyone accepted that! The police didn't even attend the scene, so what's this about?'

'Nobody's saying the fire wasn't an accident but there have been a number of concerns about your drinking.'

'I've told you, I only had a couple of glasses of wine. That's hardly excessive, by anyone's standards.'

'But it's not always just been a couple has it, Min? We've had reports in the past of you falling down in the street drunk, so the parole board have inserted a new clause in your licence, for you to abstain from alcohol.'

I was going to have to find another way to pass my time.

CHAPTER FIFTY-SIX

Franc's latest venture was to set up a publishing company and it was hoped that he would publish my book, providing, of course, that I could deliver a publishable manuscript. It was a healthy kind of pressure and for once I didn't shirk, because I was the narrator. I was hugely excited to be directing myself, but it also required discipline and concentration, two qualities that always seemed to be just out of reach. I had time and that's all I needed, enough time to think of nothing but writing. The moment had come at last and I was ready to embrace it, instead of wondering what to do next just for the sake of it.

A couple of weeks after starting I was heading for bed, having spent several hours working at an old laptop my brother had given me. It was late, a little after eleven-thirty pm, when my buzzer went.

'Yes, who is it?'

'It's Isabelle, I need to talk to you, it's really important.'

I should have told her to go home but I hadn't stopped caring altogether and I knew that voice, knew that it meant she was in some kind of trouble, perceived or otherwise. I was caught between two swords, not really wanting to invite her in, yet reluctant to leave her on her own.

'I'm coming down.'

When I reached the foot of the stairs I could see her through the glass-panelled door. She was pacing in a highly agitated state and any thoughts I may have had about quickly sending her on her way, were soon banished.

'What's going on, Isabelle?'

'Can I come in? I don't want to talk about it out here, some of the neighbours are watching.'

I took her upstairs and once inside the apartment, I made us both a hot drink and sat with her on the sofa as she explained what was troubling her. She had not long been discharged from hospital and had been spending time in the company of a group of people who attended the same church as her boyfriend. On this particular evening, however, and with the acquiescence of the boyfriend, they drove her to the accident and emergency department of the local hospital and having registered her, simply left.

I guess they thought they were doing their Christian duty in trying to get her some help, sadly as I wasn't around at the time, I wasn't able to intervene on her behalf and try to offer some reassurance. Now Isabelle was paranoid that they had some sinister motive for doing this and immediately fled in a state of terror, particularly given that she now believed that he was a willing participant in whatever conspiracy that was about to unfold. Too afraid to return home, she came to me. Some might argue that I myself should have persuaded her to go to the hospital but on this occasion I believed she needed reassurance and to be made to feel safe and she trusted me. She stayed for a couple of days before eventually returning home. Over the coming weeks we began seeing more and more of each other and she never mentioned the boyfriend, except to say she didn't trust him and never wanted to see him again.

It was back on.

I was for a while operating on two separate fronts, trying to find time and space to write whilst also finding time for her, a difficult and exhausting juggling act which left me feeling schizophrenic for a while.

Then we had a row and she went running back to him.

This became the pattern over the following eighteen months, where we basically shared her but never at the same time. I never really knew myself during that time because it abrogated every principle I held to be of value, and I gave them up to satisfy my ego whilst probably also satisfying hers. It became a competition in which I believed history was on my side, both in terms of what Isabelle and I had already shared and because of course, I already knew when to stick and when to twist. Everyone around me, including my closest confidantes, were pulling their hair out at this sorry state of affairs, but despite their wise counsel I continued to believe that to walk away would be to throw in the towel, when the evidence clearly suggested that the only way to lose was by staying in the relationship. Yet stay I did, I didn't have the tools to dismantle it. I was tunnel vision-ed, with only one objective, to win back her heart even though I was no longer sure I wanted it. I simply knew that I wanted her to need mine above his.

Eventually I got my wish. One evening, I was at her apartment whilst lover boy was at the pub; he didn't return and I stayed the night, and the next and the next. I wasn't proud nor did it feel like a victory, many things had changed, most of them disproportionate to their aim, and the truth was no longer burdened with the facts. I tried desperately to convince myself that I was utterly devoted to her, that the strength and depth of my feelings justified my methods because I was pursuing a greater end, but in the final analysis I just couldn't bear to be replaced by someone who'd already given up.

I gave him no more thought because I couldn't afford to, the stains were already stubbornly refusing to wash off and I walked with myself knowing something had changed that could never change back. I had fractured myself, deceived without meaning.

Miraculously, throughout this half-baked chess game, I had still managed to write and had almost completed the first draft by the time my relationship with Isabelle had resumed. Therefore the intensity of those first couple of weeks didn't provide too damaging a distraction, I had a routine that was important to maintain because I knew I could rely on it without explanation. I was in the middle of printing off the manuscript when my phone rang.

'Hi, Mini, it's Franc, how's the manuscript coming along?'

'I'm printing it off as we speak.'

'So when can you come to town?'

'Tomorrow, if you like.'

'Perfect.'

So the following day I stood on the platform of Retford station, leaning against a post, nonchalantly smoking a cigarette and trying to look slightly enigmatic, although in truth I didn't feel it, I felt sick with nerves. The manuscript had been a year in the making and over forty years in development. I believed in what I was doing but felt that if I meekly handed it over whilst staring down at my shoes, it may not encourage Franc so I needed to present as confident. And I needed a drink … so I had a few.

Franc greeted me at the door where I stood looking pretty sorry for myself and somewhat the worse for wear. My pride had taken a knock, along with the obvious embarrassment. I was drunk.

'Hey, Mini, looks like you've had a pretty rough trip.'

I quickly explained what had happened as I dragged my suitcase behind me. We went inside where he made coffee before getting down to business. The book had reached a critical stage in the process so this was an important meeting. I struggled to concentrate on what I did have a say, limiting my contribution to taking a few notes. I could sense Franc wasn't impressed. After all these years I'd never seen such abject disappointment written all over his face and I was terrified that he might have been thinking that he had been wrong. It was perhaps the first time I had fully experienced the deeply debilitating impact of having hurt someone you love. I had let him down badly but I also needed to understand how badly I'd let myself down.

The transition from child to man had been difficult, often fluctuating between what I had already achieved as a boy and the sometimes tedious expectations of adulthood with its emphasis on responsibility. I wasn't cute anymore, I just sometimes acted as if I was, believing that I could still get away with it, but mostly I was pathetic and that often confused me, always an outsider, even when amongst outsiders.

I didn't know what else to be.

Franc brought the meeting to a premature close and all things considered I could count myself lucky that he hadn't given up on both myself, and the book. Instead he took me for lunch with a little pep talk thrown in. I didn't mind, as it was more advisory than a strict bollocking.

'You know, Mini, I don't think alcohol agrees with you. You could be about to enter professional life so you don't want to be getting involved in that northern drinking culture.'

'Yeah, you're right.'

No real decisions were taken on the day, it was more a sharing of ideas and energy, clearly Franc had to go away and read the manuscript, after which further discussions would take place.

Shortly after returning home Isabelle mentioned that she wanted a carpet for her lounge. I had a little money saved and her lounge was small so I figured I could probably fund it, then ten days after it was fitted, she announced unexpectedly that she had organised a move to Sheffield and wouldn't be taking it with her.

It was a punch, rather than a slap in the face, a punch that I had paid for.

I had been taken completely by surprise by Isabelle choosing to move and needed to work through my feelings but I wasn't given the chance for no sooner had the announcement been made public, when I received a formal instruction to admit myself. Had I been in the throes of a manic episode or showing the obvious signs of suffering some other form of mental collapse then the decision would have been justified, but I wasn't. My health was good I spoke coherently and was generally feeling positive as I awaited feedback from Franc.

None of which seemed to matter.

Instead the probation service, in collusion with psychiatric services, decided to launch a rather crude and clumsy pre-emptive strike. Fearing that I was about to fall apart due to her moving, they effectively held me under house arrest until she had gone, even to the surprise of some of the nursing staff. Of even greater concern to me was the fact that the clinicians weren't making the decisions, the probation service were, so although I was an informal patient I was being treated as if detained under section, only being allowed off the ward if given permission, which came from probation via the doctor. Yet on the face of it nothing had changed, I remained stable and there was absolutely nothing in my treatment regime that was any different to that which I received whilst living in the community. They had flexed their muscles yet again and just like before I was powerless. I was consumed by anger and a sense of foul play and whilst I wasn't about to become reckless, neither was I willing to join the knitting club. I became deliberately problematic which helped me through the tedium of the day and reminded me of my identity, which wasn't tied to a bed in a dormitory, or the fuckers who allocated it. I questioned every instruction, no matter how small or insignificant, and challenged issues I already knew the answers to. It became sport, helping me to concentrate my mind and occasionally forget, just long enough to feel something close to a satisfying taste.

After a few days of concentrated rebellion, a nurse invited me into the office for a quiet word. He had been appointed my key worker for the duration of my stay and whilst not an unreasonable man, he still wore a coat of arms.

'Listen, Min, I understand that you're unhappy about being here but you're not doing yourself any favours by getting everyone's back up. The best way to prove them wrong is to keep your head down and get out of here.'

'I've proved them wrong every day I've been here, this fucking conversation proves them wrong. You know I'm not nuts yet you help them to wield their stick. They never gave me a chance, that's what's pissing me off.'

'How do you mean?'

'They just assumed that because she was leaving I was going to collapse. They never even talked to me, I was simply ordered to come up here. Why should I care whose back I get up when mine's almost touching the fucking ceiling!'

My anger was duly recorded but it didn't change anything except for the staff only approaching me when it was absolutely necessary, which thankfully wasn't very often.

Within a few days, Isabelle completed her move to Sheffield and I was discharged, just like that. Shortly afterwards Franc called, having read the draft copy. He shared some initial thoughts with me and I countered with a few of my own. In the meantime we agreed to meet in London to discuss it in greater detail. I couldn't wait. I travelled down there, armed with a copy of the manuscript and my notebook, in which I had already scribbled some notes. I was massively excited and felt there was a real purpose to my journey and as I looked around the carriage, I no longer felt out of place, I even had a seat reservation.

Franc greeted me in his usual way, made some fresh coffee and we set down to work. His editor was also present, adding to the overall splendour of the occasion. We were there to discuss **my** work; my dreams.

I was naturally reticent at first, listening more than talking. Franc offered an overview of the work picking out several passages that he was particularly pleased with and then some areas of the work that he felt needed improvement. Having listened intently for several minutes it seemed an appropriate time to offer some thoughts of my own. I had been scribbling fervently during his presentation and now referred to those notes. This was where the process really began and I picked up on some of the issues he'd raised and attempted to explain what I wanted to portray by writing those passages the way I had. In doing so I was effectively challenging his analysis, but crucially without being argumentative or obnoxious.

Franc, in turn, would counter my arguments by refining his own. One thing was immediately evident: the special nature of our friendship bought me no favours. He wanted to publish the book, he just didn't want to publish any book.

Thankfully, nor did I.

The meeting lasted several hours and by the end of it I was mentally and physically drained, but otherwise unscathed. Franc and I took a walk through Notting Hill before I departed for home. I had spent years on those pavements, sometimes wishing they were part of my daily landscape, sometimes enjoying the distraction, but mostly I was just a penniless kid in a toyshop full of dreams. This was the first time it was real enough not to want it to be different, I only wanted what I already had, because it was mine by right. Who knows what the children of Notting Hill dream of?

Franc had clearly enjoyed our meeting and was full of energy. He complimented me on the mature way with which I'd handled the process and also the way I had presented my arguments. It was a defining moment that had brought me home. It was, of course, a huge learning curve, but for now at least, I had learned to defend my corner when my creative and intellectual instincts told me I should. Equally, I had learned not to if there was nothing credible to defend.

It was the closest I had ever come to equilibrium.

Before parting, Franc gave me a little money to help cover my expenses and a huge hug to cover what money couldn't. As I walked away the sadness, for once, didn't follow me; my mind was so busy as I walked the short distance to the underground, providing an entirely different kind of torment. Problems that excited, difficulties that provided challenges that I hoped would help me to excel creatively, and give me the kind of concentrated day that sleep could only disturb.

Although it only took twenty-minutes to reach Kings Cross it was a complete nightmare. The tube was packed to the rafters and had there been a luggage rack, I would have been sorely tempted to crawl into it. I was fucking trapped and I panicked!

The need for escape has been a recurring theme throughout my life, without it the fear overwhelms me. It was standing room only, shoulder to shoulder, and had it come off the tracks, the impact wouldn't have killed us, we would have just suffocated.

When I finally disembarked it was as if I had been holding my breath. I stood on the platform, drawing in huge gulps of air; for twenty minutes I'd had nothing but second hand oxygen and it felt contaminated.

I had roughly an hour to kill before my train headed north and my first priority was to get above ground and see the sky, my second was to head for the pub. I ordered a pint, believing that the probation service's reach surely couldn't be that long, and it would be unbelievably bad luck if it was. I sat down and tried to study my notes in a desperate attempt to remind myself of why I was there, but the stress and anxiety I had suffered earlier hadn't quite dissipated, nor had the trembling. I felt increasingly daunted at the prospect of making the long journey home when only a few years ago it wouldn't have mattered, but here I felt diminished, even weak, because I was now scared of the very things that had once delivered me. Perhaps not having a ticket and the risks it posed provided the necessary adrenalin. Without that, travel was dull and ordinary.

The station was only a few minutes from the pub and eventually I made my way there and took my place in a monstrously long queue and waited impatiently to be allowed through the gate and onto the platform. Once we got the nod it was a free-for-all, with people pushing and shoving and generally using whatever method they could to gain some slight advantage over their fellow passengers. I once again had a reserved seat so I strolled. My seat was at a table, which was perfect because I was eager to make some fresh notes whilst I was still clear about what needed doing. There were three other spaces around my table, but I wasn't overly concerned, it was a weekday and the holiday season was still several weeks away so I didn't expect the train to be busy. Within minutes, however, the panic once again engulfed me and this time it was relentless as firstly a rather large woman sat next to me and seemed to need my air as well as her own, then a couple sat in the seats directly opposite, cutting off leg space and taking up two thirds of the table with magazines and snacks.

It was impossible. I couldn't work, I couldn't breathe and I couldn't fucking move, on top of which sweat had begun to drip off my brow; I had to get away, otherwise I wouldn't make it. My mind was racing and I couldn't keep pace with it. Every time I tried to cling to a thought several more would be unleashed until I felt like I was being driven to the edge of insanity. The doors to the train were still open and the platform awaited. I was almost in tears due to the sheer frustration I was experiencing, I was desperate to get off that train but my ticket was only valid for the train I was on and I couldn't really afford to buy another one.

As I stared longingly at that slab of concrete, pale and grey, I knew the ten-year-old wouldn't have hesitated for a second, but the adult was expected to behave like one. I've never been at all comfortable, trying to embrace this adult world with its nefarious hypocrisies and corrupt themes, I just stumble my way through, trying to preserve as much as I can, but it's never enough. If it was, I wouldn't have been standing there, sweating. I shouldn't have been standing there at all but I had hesitated for so long, unable to reach a decision, when the doors closed and wouldn't open, for me at least, until I reached Retford. In that exact moment the sound was more deafening and mind-numbing than a cell door slamming shut, for as one provided solitude from the chaos, this created it.

I made my way to the buffet carriage and bought a couple of those small bottles of wine, each one holding a fraction more than a glass. By the time I disembarked I was pretty drunk and highly relieved to be free of my high-speed coffin. I celebrated this escape by visiting a local pub, preferring it to a cold, dark, isolated platform. I bought and drank half a pint of lager then I made my way back and caught the train home.

The following day, I had my usual appointment at the offices of the probation services. It followed the regular pattern, the same old questions that invariably provided the same old answers; very little changes in a town like Worksop. So having told them I was fine and that I had pretty much done the same as I'd reported during my previous meeting, my probation officer unexpectedly and even somewhat casually enquired:

'How's the drinking?'

I'm sure the colour must have instantly drained from my face as I tried to stare into her mind to see what she was thinking. I refused to believe that she could know from such a distant vantage point.

'I've not had any.'

CHAPTER FIFTY-SEVEN

Despite Isabelle moving to Sheffield, I continued to see her from time to time and a couple of days later she came over and stayed a while. On the Tuesday of the following week I popped out to buy some beers. On my return a couple of cops were knocking on my front door, yet it still didn't occur that they might be looking for me.

'I live here, is there some kind of a problem?'

'Michael Cooper?'

'Actually it's Mini, but go on.'

'Could we talk inside?'

'Why what's up?

'I'd rather discuss it inside.'

It was pretty obvious they weren't going to talk to me unless I invited them in, so naturally I did.

'We're here to inform you that your licence has been revoked, we've got to take you to the station.'

'So what have I done that requires me to be sent back to prison indefinitely?'

'I don't know, you'll have to talk to the relevant authorities about that, our job is just to arrest you and take you in.'

'Oh my God, oh my God!'

Isabelle was panic-stricken and her expression along with her tone suggested she was in danger of going into meltdown.

'Isabelle, I have to go. Take my phone and this tenner and put some credit on it, then ring every number and let everyone know what's happened. I'll contact you as soon as I can. Don't worry, we'll be fine.'

I hugged her and was close to tears, but I had to remain strong as I was about to enter the coliseum ten years after my last engagement, which I had hoped would be my last. One of the cops came forward with a pair of handcuffs and I raised my hands slowly in a gesture of conciliation.

'I can assure you, you don't need those. I'm not going anywhere, other than where you're taking me.'

She quickly placed them back in her belt and I liked to think that the calm gentle tone I had adopted, along with my acceptance of the situation, persuaded her that I didn't pose a threat. As we left my apartment I suddenly had a deep craving for a cigarette and remembered that the pigsty was a smoke free zone.

'Listen, do you mind if I have a fag before we get in the car? I don't mind if you handcuff me, if it makes you feel any better.'

'Yeah, it's not a problem.'

I had my fag free of restraints. It was almost surreal, standing there, chit-chatting with a couple of easy-going cops who were there to lock me up. Once we arrived at the station the preliminaries were taken care of and I was thrown in a cell.

I don't know whether it was shock or denial but I had arrived there with only the clothes on my back when I should have gathered together a few essential items such as my reading glasses. I wasn't able to read or write without them, and I would need to do plenty of both. Being alone in that cell had a comforting normality about it, a familiar reality that was easier to comprehend than the labyrinth of abnormalities that had experimented with truth, their truth, their, conversion. I wanted it to faze me, to disturb my senses but it didn't. Maybe I was numb or maybe I had crawled inside myself for sanctuary, an escape of sorts, a silent dismissal of their dislocated morality.

I still didn't know why I was there.

The cell was too warm and with the light constantly beaming its intrusion, it would be impossible to sleep. I removed my winter coat, a present from Franc a couple of years earlier, and paced. Sometimes I would go clockwise, sometimes anti-clockwise, other times I walked corner to corner, then the width, then the length, but never in circles.

In the morning a cop came to my door and offered me breakfast and a cup of tea. He seemed genuinely surprised that I refused, asking only for a glass of water. He then explained the situation. As the prisons were at that time vastly overcrowded, they had to call some kind of central office who would allocate a place, then the private security firm who transported prisoners would also be contacted. In essence this meant that whilst ordinarily you would be sent to the prison nearest your locale, under this system it could be anywhere in the country, making it harder for family and friends to visit. Without that, you really are on your own.

Just before lunchtime the door opened once again and I was given the news I had been hoping for; they had allocated me to Lincoln, which was approximately forty minutes away. There was also the added advantage of having already been there and knowing the routine. I was escorted from the cell to the custody suite, where the desk sergeant was handing a small, sealed bag to a glorified security guard.

'Your missus came in earlier and brought you some fags and fifty pounds in cash, it's in that bag.'

'Thanks.'

It was thoughtful and sweet and I silently blessed her for it whilst at the same time being mildly amused at her naivety. The money would be hugely welcome but I had no doubt the cigarettes would be confiscated.

I was handcuffed to the bag carrier and walked out to the waiting van. Once inside my tiny cubicle the reality hit me with such severe intensity, it really did disturb my senses. I didn't want to go back to jail just when I was beginning to forget what it had been like a decade earlier. I was learning to finally walk on the right side of the road, and now I had to learn the opposite again.

It was February and a sprinkling of snow dropped from the skies as the van pulled out of the police station but I doubt it could have been any colder. As we slowly passed by my apartment block, I stared up at my window, wondering if I would ever see the place again. The prospect of losing the only decent home I'd ever had, the only one that wasn't just a dwelling, became a stark reality. As we trundled along in the snow, my future as uncertain and as unpredictable as the weather, it already began to feel like the keys belonged to somebody else.

I began asking some pretty searching questions of myself as I sank deeper and deeper, struggling to function under the extreme weight of helplessness and frustration at what I perceived to be an arbitrary and criminal act. I had lived in the community for several years and whilst it wasn't without its problems, there had been no criminal activity or any suggestion of a return to previous methods of problem solving. On the contrary, I had made every effort to build a life I could live with, under a regime thick with camouflage.

Yet there I was, on my way to prison.

As I had never before been subject to recall I had no understanding of the process or how long I could expect to remain in prison. I only understood how quickly everything could unravel, and how I would be expected to put it all back together again without complaint. That's what stuck in my throat and wouldn't budge, the thought of spending two or three years in jail, only to start from the beginning again. The prospect of being housed in a bail hostel, where teenage junkies would steal your underpants if they thought they could sell them, made me instantly decide. If I lost my home and everything in it, then Her Majesty could pick up the tab for the next twenty years. By then I might just have forgotten. When we eventually pulled up outside the prison gates, the process was no different than before. The van was escorted to reception where I was removed and placed in a holding cell with several other prisoners.

It had started.

I stared at the floor as I was in no mood to talk. Prisoners loved to talk, particularly about their crimes, but I'd heard it all before and wanted no part of it. No one likes the silent one, he's more of a threat than the talker because the talker reveals everything.

'What's up, mate, you look like you've seen a fucking ghost?'

'Maybe I have, maybe you have.'

'You'll be alright, prison's a piece of piss once you learn the ropes. So how long you doin'?'

'Life.'

Silence, followed by a few curious but not necessarily threatening stares, and then worse, the warped admiration, followed by a barrage of questions I thought I would never have to answer again. Reprieve came in the form of an instruction to step outside in order to be formally processed.

'Right, take a seat in the corridor, there, the nurse wants to see you.'

I sat watching a constant flow of human traffic, trying to discern who the real criminals were. Mostly it was difficult to tell.

'Are you Cooper?'

'Yes, Mini Cooper.'

'Follow me, please.'

She was small, Scottish and it was hard not to visualise her goose-stepping her way down the corridor and into the nurse's station.

'We've had a phone call from your community psychiatric nurse expressing concerns about your mental health and asking us to ensure that you receive your prescribed medication.'

I stared at her in utter disbelief, thinking I must already have gone fucking nuts and it was scary that I was the only one still breathing.

'I believe you suffer from bi-polar, is that correct?'

Eventually, I was relieved of my personal clothing and provided with a jogging suit, although I was allowed to keep my footwear. I was then photographed and within a couple of minutes was issued with an identity card bearing the very same picture and my prison number.

'Do you smoke?'

Given that I was standing there holding one hundred cigarettes in a transparent plastic bag, I was taken aback by the question and wasn't even sure I wanted to answer, but I did.

'Yes.'

'Do you want a smoker's pack?'

I was struggling to keep up: prison uniforms replaced with jogging suits, non-confiscation of what had once been deemed contraband and now the offer of more? Maybe I should never have left.

'Yeah, okay.'

I was handed another clear plastic bag, which of course required the obligatory signature. The pack contained a twelve point five gram pouch of rolling tobacco, a packet of cigarette papers and a box of matches, which was a cause of great relief and ended the torture of cigarettes without ignition.

The unit I was heading to had been adapted from the former reception area and had no facilities, not even showers, and certainly no opportunity for any out-of-cell association. That suited me as I was in no mood to socialise and was already bored with the inane line of questioning where even the voices sounded the same.

The cell was empty except for yours truly and provided a much-needed respite, although I suspected it wouldn't last very long, as there were two bunks. I sat on the lower bunk, knowing that sooner or later I would have to make the bed but I lacked any real motivation, not wanting to acknowledge or recognise that this was my home. If it was, I would have bought a better mattress and a softer pillow. Along the far wall, two small tables had been placed together and provided further evidence of the changing face of prisons, for sitting there, almost defying me to touch it just to prove it was real, was a portable television set, and it was colour, and next to that was a small kettle. Comfort to while away the hours and dull your mind into thinking it's where it belongs, until the gates open and the pub beckons and no one notices the voice behind the glass.

Some things never change, however, and it didn't take me long to seize the moment before it was too late. First in, first choice, so I chose the bottom bunk, not particularly symbolic but it was easier to get in and out, and should you roll out during a difficult night, it wasn't so far to fall. I quickly made the bed then approached the tables where there were two sets of toiletries, soap, shampoo, toothpaste, a razor and some shaving gel. These were the only freebies on offer, when they ran out you had to pay and if you couldn't afford to, you stank. I wouldn't be needing the razor as I had a strict rule whilst in prison, I never shaved, nor did I have a haircut. It was my prison mask and protected my real features from further contamination. I unpacked my plastic crockery and cutlery, and organised them in similar fashion; next one in could have whatever space was left. I lay on my bunk, smoking a cigarette as I always do in such moments, when the door unexpectedly opened.

'Grub up.'

I grabbed my plate and headed for the smell, not exactly alluring, just a guide and I don't remember what I was given or how it tasted, just that it wouldn't have tasted any better if I had. An hour or so later, just as I was beginning to lay claim to the space, the door opened once again and in stepped a grey-haired man. I was almost grateful that it wasn't some snotty-nosed kid, but it still altered the dynamics.

'Listen, mate, I'm not being funny, but do you mind taking the top bunk? I've got a problem with my back and there's no fucking way I'm going to be able to climb up and down that fucker all day long!'

He was a Londoner, fresh in from a prison down south. He only had three weeks to go yet they still moved him at considerable expense, both for them and for me. I didn't want to be part of the fucking countdown. His manner wasn't aggressive in tone and whilst I was aware that he may have been conning me, I agreed to his request and moved my bedding to the top bunk, but I couldn't be arsed to make the bed again just yet.

While he began sorting himself out before bedding down in front of the television, I decided to write to Isabelle. I had been so wrapped up in my own self-absorbed view of the world, I'd hardly had time to think about her. Now as I began to write, aware that she herself was probably feeling just as helpless, just as lost, it was an emotional time and I began to feel pretty sorry for myself. It was a dangerous place to be, with hunting packs of hyenas and coyotes searching for anyone too weak to resist. Well, the bastards weren't having me! Some things were instinctive and didn't need to be taught, private and public, a face for all occasions, it was like going back to school having already passed the exams.

Letters weren't allowed to be sealed, and of course were read by prurient mother-fuckers who were unseen. I took comfort in knowing that their life was nothing without mine. When I finished writing I lay on my bunk, tangled in a mess of blankets and sheets, but it didn't matter. In a few days' time they would be somebody else's mess, as they wrote home.

'Cooper, the nurse wants to see you.'

I didn't even hear the door open, nor did I welcome it, nor the news that an unnamed uniform demanded even more of my time, whilst insisting it was theirs not being put to better use.

'Cooper, you want to think yourself lucky that a member of your community team provided us with the information we needed so we've been able to order your medication.'

'Well, I guess that's me all over, I'm just a lucky guy.'

I took the medication from her cold iron fist and without another word returned to my cell, ignoring the monosyllable mutterings of my guard as he found the lock with his key. That night I slept on top of the bed without undressing, except for having removed my shoes.

* * * *

'Cooper, I'm the lifer liaison officer, can I have a word?'

I climbed down from my bunk but was in no great hurry.

'I take it you know why you've been recalled?'

'Actually, I don't.'

'Well, these are the official reasons in writing. Take a minute to read them and let me know if you agree with them.'

She handed me the document in the full expectation that I would read it with her standing next to me.

'Whether I agree or not makes no material difference, it simply allows you to record my response.'

'Well, if you have any questions, just put in an application to see me.'

Oh, yes, the obligatory applications, without which the system would collapse. If you needed a doctor, put in an application; if you wanted to grow a beard and therefore change your appearance, put in an application, likewise if you want to shave one off. You even needed one to access God; I guess the penal system kept him busy.

I returned to my cell, eager to study the reason for my being there. I had been given two documents, one outlined the process involving a recalled prisoner and the options available, a legal document that obviously required my full attention, so I put it to one side for further reading. I would need a coffee and a fag for that one.

Within seconds of reading the probation service's crooked justification for their action, I was shaking my head in disbelief and already reaching for my cigarettes, inhaling all the way down to my shoes. I never considered being spied upon in Retford, some nine or ten miles from where I lived. Apparently, I was seen by a member of the probation staff who, according to the script, was known to me, entering the pub in an already intoxicated state. Having witnessed me purchase half a pint of lager, this unnamed person sought confirmation from the bar staff that I had in fact bought alcohol, thus placing me in breach of my licence. Although I found an unoccupied table and quietly drank my beer alone and without causing a nuisance, I did, upon leaving, accidentally knock my chair over, but I simply stood it up and placed it neatly back under the table. On my way out I also apparently walked into a parked car, without causing damage either to the vehicle or myself, nevertheless for this to have been witnessed clearly suggested I was being followed. Despite these difficulties in coordinating my movements, I successfully negotiated the fifteen-minute walk to the station, boarded the train and made it back to my apartment without further incident. Had I been threatening or abusive and therefore liable to be arrested and risk being charged with a criminal offence, then I would have felt there was some justification in taking this action, but I wasn't.

I was just pissed.

Nevertheless, the bar staff were happy to serve me and clearly wouldn't have done if they'd felt that I was so wasted as I might have posed a problem either to them or the other customers. Indeed, had I been arrested for being drunk and disorderly, the maximum penalty I would have incurred would have been an eighty pound, on-the-spot fine. The implicit suggestion was that because alcohol had been a factor in an offence committed almost twenty years earlier, they had a duty to act swiftly for the protection of the public, an argument I found seriously flawed. Firstly, alcohol was only one of several factors. Some self-proclaimed experts believe that the breakdown in my relationship with Marilyn was a key ingredient in the build up to the fire, therefore why wasn't I recalled every time my relationship with Isabelle collapsed? More significantly, yet conveniently omitted from the current document, was the fact that the authorities had known for a couple of years that I had been drunk on many occasions, yet similar action was never taken. The document concluded that not only had I breached my licence, I denied when questioned, having had a drink, so I was being locked up for lying.

Even more curious, having outlined their reasons they deemed the risk sufficiently serious to request an emergency recall within two hours, yet it was several days before I was picked up and detained.

All this had me reeling as I grappled with the vagaries and inconsistencies of a justice system with an identity failure, and questionable ethics, the impact of which was aggravated by their remorseless condemnation without trial.

I lay on my bunk, smoking cigarette after cigarette and spent several moments questioning the purpose of challenging the recall. If successful, I would only be making myself vulnerable once again to the piece of elastic that could bounce me straight back; it was all too easy. Ultimately I'm just a sore loser, particularly when I have little respect for the opposition, so aided by a little caffeine injection and yet more nicotine I began to readjust my thinking. As a wise man once said, when injustice becomes law, resistance becomes duty.

I picked up the second document and studied it carefully. There were two options available should I choose to launch a challenge. I could allow the parole board to study the evidence, including my own written representations, behind closed doors, or I could request an oral hearing in front of a panel, whereby I could be legally represented. I was initially reluctant to face the panel, not out of any fear of being unnerved by them, or potentially destroyed, it was much simpler: I resented going cap in hand and begging to be set free by offering a series of explanations that were no more relevant than the process that necessitated them.

I had a couple of weeks before I needed to sign and return the form and in the meantime, sleep came easy.

Within a couple of days a steady flow of mail began to arrive. Isabelle had contacted every number in my phone and informed them of my situation and they in turn discovered my whereabouts. The only obstacle arose when she contacted my brother. His partner answered the phone and after being informed of my detention, told Isabelle not to ring again. My other correspondence came from Franc who enclosed a little money, as did members of my family and of course, Isabelle, who had little money to spare but generously gave what she could. This enabled me to live reasonably comfortably by prison standards. For example, I have a partial denture and without the financial assistance on offer, I couldn't have afforded the tablets needed to clean it, nor would I have been able to purchase toiletry products in order to maintain some basic standard of human cleanliness. As for sheer luxury, I could afford a Sunday newspaper, which gave me enough to read for several days.

The only formal letter came from my lawyer and was stamped, 'Rule 39', meaning that the prison authorities couldn't open it in secret and read it as they did with all private correspondence. It was the first time a solicitor had ever used this rule when writing to me. On delivery the screw handed me the envelope for me to open in his presence.

'London lawyers, you must be guilty.'

Bindman's of London were a human rights firm who also had a large mental health department. I had initially approached them after rather clumsily stumbling upon some fresh medical reports, in which it was being suggested that my offence was a result of undiagnosed mental health issues. I wondered if it would be possible to launch a fresh legal challenge with regards to the original sentence, I certainly felt it was worth investigating and so I contacted them. A young trainee solicitor called Emma Norton agreed to take on the case and whilst pointing out the inherent difficulties due to the passage of time, she agreed that it was indeed worth investigating.

Little did I realise I would be needing her so soon and as I lay on my bunk, reading her current letter. I decided to accept her advice unequivocally and immediately demanded an oral hearing. Not only was I convinced that I finally had an excellent advocate, I was also reassured in knowing I had a dogged ally.

CHAPTER FIFTY-EIGHT

'Cooper, get your things together, you're being transferred to the main wing.'

Having spent almost a week being closeted from the rest of the prison population, the moment I had been dreading had finally arrived. The unit held a small number of prisoners but now I was being thrown unceremoniously into the smelting pot, and there was no way of turning down the heat. I was shown to a cell that already housed a young guy who was lying on his bunk watching television. I threw my stuff onto the top bunk, climbed up after it and rolled an habitual cigarette.

'Where you from?'

'Worksop.'

'Fucking hell, me too! I've lived there all my life. So how long you doin'?'

'Life, what about you?'

'Oh, I've only got five days left.'

I was pretty stunned and tried unsuccessfully to establish some form of rationale or even a basic understanding of the situation. It seemed clear to me that it simply wasn't enough that I was there, they had to twist the fucking knife even further, by thoughtless actions, casually administered. A few years ago it would have been inconceivable for a lifer to be housed with someone who only had a few days left, but things had changed, radically, with prisons so over-crowed that some guys were spending weeks at a time holed up in police stations, living off takeaways.

Early one morning the cell door opened before I'd had chance to get my bearings.

'Cooper, you've got a legal visit, make your way down to the ground floor and join the other lads.'

A legal visit could be anything from an interview with the cops, a visit from your lawyer, or the probation service. I joined the rest of the herd as instructed and we were ushered onto 'B' wing where we collected a few more.

As I stood impatiently waiting, just wanting to get it over with so I could return to my lair, I stared up at the cell I had occupied when I was first convicted, but it held no memories, just somebody else's time, spelt differently.

After being given a virtual guided tour of the entire nick, we finally arrived at the visitors' centre, where we were squashed into a holding cell, waiting to be called forward.

'Cooper, probation.'

I stepped onto the wooden box for the obligatory pat down search then grabbed a yellow bib, lest we forget who's leaving and who's staying. After giving my name and number, I was instructed to make my way towards my allocated table. I had no idea where this table was located but I didn't need to know, a quick scan of the room revealed where I needed to be. She sat there like it was just another day at the office, even smiling as I approached. I had hoped it was going to be Emma, my lawyer, but instead it was my probation officer, all the way from Worksop. I could think of better places to visit.

'So how are you coping?'

'I'm coping alright, it's what I do best, probably because I've had more practise at it than anything else.'

'I've brought your glasses, you'll probably get them when you get back on the wing.'

'Thanks, I've been lost without them.'

I had indeed. It's one thing to write in block capitals but you can't really expect journalists and editors to do the same. Without the television I wouldn't have known what was going on in the world, and there was still a considerable amount of personal correspondence still waiting to be read. All because my house keys were locked in a safe and the administrative rigmarole of removing them, and sufficient funds taken from my account to cover the postage, were tasks sadly unwilling to be undertaken by most.

'Your solicitor has informed us that you have requested an oral hearing.'

'Yes.'

'Well, no doubt you will want to call witnesses of your own, but it's standard practice for the panel to call the supervising probation officer to give evidence.'

'And what do you intend to say, or am I not allowed to be privy to that kind of information?'

'The probation service are currently happy to recommend to the panel that you once again be released on life licence.'

I stared at her in disbelief, struggling even more to understand the purpose of this break in the tide. I searched for the tiniest hint of self-consciousness, embarrassment even, but she never broke eye contact. It was me who, in the end, had to look away, for had I not, her matter of fact delivery and indoctrinated state of denial might well have consumed me and posed a serious threat to my chances of being released.

I returned to my cell where shortly afterwards my glasses arrived. Those, and my decision to remain silent in the face of an open invitation to self-combust, had now empowered me. I figured if the probation service were willing to recommend my release then the others would surely follow suit. Having put a dampener on my earlier feelings, having silenced the rage in pursuit of winning, rather than being handed my release, I was feeling pretty good, confident I would be home soon.

Then came the letter.

Emma had written regularly during my detention, keeping me fully updated regarding all developments, no matter how small. It was deeply encouraging and filled me with confidence. I read the letter but quickly felt their punch rip through my internal organs. The parole board had set a date for my hearing but it was several months away and I could feel myself sinking into the cell below me. Emma was equally disappointed by the news and also concerned that my mental health may deteriorate, both due to the length of time involved and my own struggle with it. I was certainly pretty low and in danger of sinking even further, but the parole board cited a lack of resources as the reason for arriving at their decision, although it was my time being resourced, my time that was filed under wait and see. Emma outlined her plan to me. She was unwilling to accept their initial decision and believed it might be possible to challenge it. She wrote to each member of the clinical support team, asking them to submit letters, should they agree, supporting her contention that such a delay could be detrimental to my mental health. If they agreed, thus making the whole situation a human rights issue, she hoped to demonstrate that the issue of resources was something that the parole board needed to address with their quartermasters, and could not be excused at the expense of someone's human rights.

She submitted the material to the parole board, fairly confident that they would acquiesce to her submissions on the grounds that there was nowhere for them to run, no more excuses for them to hide behind, but they proved to be stubborn, obstinate and at times obnoxious as they continued to refute her submissions, this time claiming that should my mental health deteriorate sufficiently, it was possible for the prison authorities to have me transferred to hospital.

But it had to happen first.

Emma continued to press and during a visit to the prison where she took further instructions and outlined her proposed strategy, she suggested that we apply to the High Court in London for a judicial review. These proceedings would look at the parole board's decision legalistically and decide whether or not the reasons for them coming to such a decision in the manner that they had was manifestly flawed.

The court could then decide to either compel them to look at it again or order them to change it.

I agreed in principle but also supported Emma's decision to launch one final roll of the dice, whereby she planned to contact the parole board directly, outlining our plan in the hope that they would finally capitulate. They knew, of course, that a hearing in the High Court can take time, perhaps that's why they were so bullish in their refusal to listen to her submissions.

By now, Emma had instructed a barrister and an application was submitted, which was summarily rejected by the court. An appeal was immediately launched and much to my surprise, we were granted a full hearing. I immediately dispatched a letter to Emma, thanking her for her persistence and refusal to be bullied, then continued with the business of waiting and hoping. I now had a routine in place that didn't make the days any fuller or more meaningful, but they did chalk themselves off the calendar a little quicker.

Isabelle would visit every week and family members, too, when they could arrange it outside of their own commitments. Isabelle always made me feel proud, she dressed fabulously and the way she wore her hair and her make-up, with an understated touch of class, spared me the ugliness and helped to keep my spirit alive, which was crucial, for I had also found employment in a sweatshop that sadly wasn't media sexy. I would stand all day at a large wooden table, hidden behind a huge pile of tee shirts which I would split into two manageable piles, then get to work. The shirts had been delivered from the over-locking machine and my job was to snip off all the loose threads for a weekly wage of eight pounds.

When I wasn't making up the numbers in this legalised slave trade, I would largely remain in my cell writing letters. I never took up the daily option of exercise, as I had no wish to circle a cage. I only ever went on association to take a shower or to call Isabelle.

One evening, whilst waiting excitedly to hear her voice, I finally made it to the front of the queue for the phone, but she was the one full of excitement.

'Guess what?'

'What?'

'You fucking did it! You've won.'

The rest of the conversation was largely subdued as the shock of what had happened struggled to sink in. I had won my judicial review, the court had found in my favour and ordered the parole board to expedite the hearing.

CHAPTER FIFTY-NINE

A little after seven thirty am my cell door opened and within an hour I was in the visitors' centre, in conference with both my solicitor and my barrister, who took a few last minute instructions from me.

Eventually we were escorted to a small room in the administration block, where the hearing was due to be heard. As I entered the room and saw the panel sitting there, I was sick with nerves and just hoped it wouldn't restrict my ability to think. I sat to the left of the barrister, Emma to his right and to the left of me, a solicitor representing the Home Office. With five people all entitled to cross-examine witnesses, it was obviously going to take some time.

The judge wasted no time in introducing the panel and explaining the legal requirements. He smiled his way through it and I began to relax, having imagined a much sterner affair, but I wasn't about to become complacent. My barrister then outlined our case and why the panel should consider releasing me. It was my intention to be completely honest with them, to show them myself rather than what the file said I was.

First into the hot seat was my consultant psychiatrist. My barrister immediately asked him if he agreed with the decision to recall me, he said that he didn't, and the judge intervened.

'Obviously, it's the responsibility of the probation service to revoke the licence if deemed necessary. What would you have done differently to deal safely with any concerns?'

'Whilst Mr Cooper has been under the supervision of the Community Forensic team there have been occasions when his mental health raised concerns and the probation service did consider recalling him, however after discussions with the team we were able to bring him into hospital.'

'And did he comply with his treatment?'

'Yes he did. Mr Cooper has always been medication compliant, both in hospital and in the community, so there were never any issues regarding that, but when he came into hospital there were a number of restrictions put in place that prevented him from leaving the ward and although he was unhappy about it, he accepted them and understood the risks should he not have done.'

The judge scribbled furiously on his notepad and it was strange, seeing everyone sit in silence until he had finished, when the Home Office lawyer chipped in; I'd almost forgotten that she was there.

'Doctor, is your hospital secure?'

'No, there are no locked doors and no bars on the windows.'

'So presumably, there was nothing to stop Mr Cooper just taking off if he'd wished to?'

'No, but he didn't, he understood that if he had, he would in all likelihood have been recalled. It was his decision to stay and comply with his treatment regime.'

By the time my probation officer took her place, the proceedings had already lasted well over an hour and I was comfortable with it. The doctor had offered strong evidence as to why recall wasn't necessary and I was confident she wouldn't be able to offer a more balanced rationale, besides the service were supporting my release. My barrister immediately sought to undermine the process and the handling of the recall. My probation officer agreed, when questioned, that she had requested an emergency recall within two hours and also acknowledged that I had indeed been allowed to remain at large for an entire weekend. The judge once again interjected, observing that if I was deemed to be such a high risk of re-offending, why was I allowed to remain at home for a further seventy-two hours? She was unable to offer a satisfactory explanation, other than outlining some procedural difficulties.

'Can you help me out because I'm a little confused? Was the decision to recall Mr Cooper taken because he had breached his licence, or was it because he had lied about drinking?'

'Any breach of licence can result in a person being recalled, but we have spoken to Mr Cooper a couple of times already about the need for openness and honesty.'

'So he's been recalled because he lied?'

'He needs to understand that such behaviours will be punished, yes.'

Finally it was yours truly, except the judge generously allowed me to remain where I was sitting. Being in the hot seat makes you acutely aware that the focus is on you, for even those who aren't asking the questions stare impassively. I took comfort from being allowed to remain sitting alongside my legal team and because of our position I was able to look directly at the questioner without feeling everyone else's eyes boring into my psyche.

My barrister began by asking me a few straightforward questions. Did I agree that I'd been drinking, did I now accept the need for an open and honest relationship with the probation service? I answered yes to them both. After a few more standard questions he then asked if I agreed, should I be released, to the probation service's recommendation of spending a couple of weeks in hospital? I once again answered positively; to have said no, would have brought the whole thing to a close, and my life with it.

The independent psychiatrist then began questioning me about the events on the train. He specifically wanted to know how the attack had manifested itself, what were the symptoms. He probed in a very gentle, sensitive way, but all the time his expression remained deadpan and his body language neutral. Everyone else then had an opportunity to interrogate me further but it didn't really feel that way. There were a couple of questions about my drinking habits but nothing that prevented me from offering a satisfactory reply. I mentioned that after discussions with my probation officer it had been decided to refer me to the dual diagnosis team should I be successful in securing my release. This team specialised in drug and alcohol problems.

I was proud of myself for all the wrong reasons, satisfied that I had bitten the bullet and played by their rules. I had shown myself to be insightful and in not seeking to blame, reasonable.

But I was still seething inside.

When it was over the lifer liaison officer escorted the Home Office representative, along with my legal team, to the prison gatehouse whilst I was returned to my cell. The hearing had lasted approximately four hours and everyone had already left for the workshops.

It was a huge relief as I was so distracted I may well have cut my fingers off. Instead I spent the entire afternoon locked in my cell, pacing back and forth constantly, as I tried to keep pace with my mind. I'd been ambushed once without openness or honesty, if I was going to be shafted again I at least wanted to see it coming, even though I couldn't duck. After several hours of pacing, even drinking my coffee on the move, I settled down for the night, still unsure. I would be informed of the decision within seven days and I had a feeling that time was about to show its cruel hand by slowing everything down, just for its own personal amusement. I became grateful for the job and the routine that came with it. By the fourth day, I still hadn't heard anything and I began to feel edgy. After lunchtime lockdown I was expecting to be unlocked and taken to my workplace. I heard the screws marauding the landings, unlocking everyone, but they bypassed my cell. I was confused, wondering why they had forgotten me, but then my mind went into overdrive; screws never forget shit because they are programmed to remember without even realising it.

I became giddy with excitement, believing that this was the moment already decided and nothing could get in the way of that, they would have to release me because the paymaster general had instructed them to. So important was it ,that I wasn't willing to take any chances, so I pressed the buzzer, waiting and hoping for confirmation.

'What's up, fella?'

'I haven't been unlocked for labour, how come?'

'I'll find out for you.'

I paced back and forth furiously, almost jumping up and down with glee and already planning my exit.

But he never came back.

Instead, a couple of hours later the cell door opened and a couple of screws walked in wearing latex gloves.

I was gutted.

'Listen, Coops, we're here to search your cell but you've kept your head down and you've not given us any real shit, so we don't want to cause any problems for you. Have you got anything in here that you shouldn't have?'

I hesitated for a second, not because I had anything to hide but because I wasn't familiar with the current rules.

'You don't seem so sure.'

'Come on, guys, it's been ten years since I was in a prison cell, I don't know what's considered contraband anymore, but feel free to search the place.'

'No, you're alright but if anyone asks, we did.'

'Sure.'

When they left I felt totally desolate, having just experienced both extremes of emotion within a few minutes of each other. I became convinced that it was an omen and the hope I'd previously felt, evaporated. The weekend came and went, followed by the start of a new working week. More significantly, the seven-day period had now expired and I still hadn't received the panel's decision.

I trudged off to the workshop with leaden feet and spent the morning quietly going about my work, but with no real commitment or satisfaction. Just before exercise was due to be called, a screw appeared, but as they often did for a variety of reasons, I paid him no heed. I just carried on snipping away, lost in my own battle and trying not to sink deep into the abyss, or allow it to stare me out.

'Coop, I need you a minute and bring your scissors.'

I turned around to see the instructor beckoning me towards him and began to feel irritated at yet another interruption.

'What's up?'

He took the scissors off me and passed them to his junior. He then shook my hand, gripping it firmly and sincerely.

'Well done, mate, you're going home.'

* * * *

It was a beautiful June morning and the sun was blazing down on me as I stood there, basking in a brand new experience. I had never walked through prison gates before and taken my first tentative steps as a liberated man, it was almost orgasmic in its natural seduction.

And the gates behind me couldn't withhold it, or lose it.

After several minutes soaking up every visual image and every sound that drifted past me with a gentle caress, I sat down on a nearby wall and rolled a cigarette to mark the moment. As reality replaced delirium, I began to feel confused. Because I had agreed to go into hospital, I assumed my psychiatric nurse would pick me up and take me there, despite having been issued with the statutory travel warrant. However, he was nowhere to be seen and I didn't know my way into town, or to the train station. I would once again have to rely on my old instincts, or suffer a serious loss of pride should I get lost.

Left or right, those were the only to options. When I arrived from Mansfield all those years ago I remembered we came in from the left and there had been no sign of city life, so it had to be right and so was I.

It took approximately twenty minutes to reach the city centre, and once there I walked into a bar and ordered a pint. I took a mouthful and suddenly remembered my licence and I was already in breach of it. I took the offending document out of my pocket and read it. I couldn't believe my eyes: the 'no alcohol' clause had been replaced with another stating that I should abstain from alcohol if directed to do so by my probation officer. Well, they weren't there, so I sat back and enjoyed it, followed by another, before boarding the train back to Worksop.

As soon as I arrived, I headed straight for my apartment. It may well have been that I was expected to go immediately to the hospital but I considered that if my mental health really was suspect, then I should have been admitted formally in the company of a healthcare professional. Besides, I wanted to enjoy my release for a little while longer and not have it stifled or squashed just to satisfy the militia. When I arrived home there was a mountain of mail and I put it to one side as I began to feel overwhelmed. There was a lot to sort out, much to organise, bills that hadn't been paid, benefits that needed reinstating and the rent on the apartment which hadn't been paid for the duration of my imprisonment, could still result in eviction. It was a heavy load to carry just after being released and it made the recall all the more real.

Despite feeling like a precious moment had been stolen from me, there's no doubting that it was a huge relief to be out of prison, but it didn't quite feel like I was at home either. Being able to sleep in my own bed, wrapped in quality, unstained linen and without disturbance, was priceless, as was waking up to nothing more than the sound of a blackbird or a passing vehicle marking the start of my day. Sometimes I would stay up into the early hours, just sitting in the silence because I could without someone trying to hurry me to my bed. Prisons and hospitals are noisy, chaotic places without manners or consideration.

I just wanted to hear myself.

I was battling with the benefits agency who were becoming increasingly difficult to deal with and not knowing when I would receive a payment or how to structure my finances with regards to paying bills and generally running my home, created a period of immense stress. Once again I was forced to rely on the generosity of others, Franc in particular, to at least put some food on the table, and whilst he and members of my family were willing to contribute, it still created uncertainty.

Despite the stress and instability this caused, I was determined to crack on with the book, for whenever I sat typing I felt free of all the external bullshit designed to crush our spirit, every written page being a testament to that. But it just wasn't happening and caused much frustration as my concentration wandered every few minutes. The problem was, I felt sitting at my desk all day long when I had a choice to leave was no better than being stuck in the cell I had recently vacated.

I had lost my sense of balance and perspective.

I took to wandering the streets again, relishing the fact that the clock had lost its hands. I could return whenever I liked or whenever tiredness dictated that I should; I didn't know where I was going and I didn't care.

Another needless distraction that added to my sense of containment was that having been recalled, I was now required to report to the probation service weekly as opposed to fortnightly, for a minimum of sixteen weeks, along with increased intervention from the clinical support team. In addition, I was also required to see a member of the dual diagnosis team once a fortnight where I was subject to random breathalysing. Although I had agreed to this measure in an attempt to turn down the heat, it was never really a choice, it just looked like one on the report.

Then there was my relationship with Isabelle. We hadn't spoken for a while, having once again allowed a fairly trivial dispute to descend into a full-scale war of words that neither of us could profit from, although eventually we did start speaking again.

Finally, after several weeks, my excuses ran out and there was no one left to blame for my inactivity apart from myself. The recall had been a severe blow but I wasn't there anymore and I couldn't afford to bring it home and create a self-imposed prison without leave to appeal. There were enough reminders already, without me succumbing meekly after all this time. My lounge had a big bay window that looked out onto a busy road and this was where my desk was situated. The road in question formed part of the route to Lincoln and, of course, the prison. Several times a week I would observe the prison van with its valueless cargo, slowly making its way and it once again reminded me of snow. It became the major catalyst in refocusing my attention towards the book, for every time I saw the van I saw myself once more being transported, the distance being too short to measure, even though a window separated us.

The uncertainty never quite went away. Whenever my buzzer went unexpectedly, my heart would miss a beat, assuming that the cops were here again. I would rush around switching everything off, then sit in silence until it was clear there was no threat to my personal security. It was like living under a totalitarian regime; without the rhetoric and fancy dress, that's probably what it was.

I figured the only way of effectively managing my time that allowed me to have more control over it, and more purpose in its execution, was to resume work on the book. It helped to restore my self-belief. I didn't need their sanction, and they wouldn't get my apology.

I quickly began to find some rhythm and the confidence that helped to promote impacted positively on my daily life. I had more bounce and energy, I looked forward to the start of each day, and on a really good one I didn't want to go to bed, afraid that I might miss something.

CHAPTER SIXTY

As Christmas once again loomed, and Isabelle and I had managed to get through the best part of the year without killing each other, she suggested we spend it in Sunderland where she had friends. They only had a small, one-bedroom apartment so the plan was to book into a hotel for a couple of days as it was all we could afford. Isabelle checked out which hotels were offering festive packages, I had a little money and all she had to do was find the money for her rail fare and whatever she would need to cover additional expenses. The hotel costs were approximately five hundred pounds and because I didn't want to carry such a large sum of money on me, I gave it to Isabelle and she paid for it on her card.

As soon as the letter arrived confirming our booking, we went to the station and obtained a couple of advance purchase tickets. We were due to depart lunchtime on Christmas Eve and return on Boxing Day. Our tickets meant we could only travel on the services stipulated. Should we mistakenly get on the wrong one then our tickets would become invalid and we'd have to purchase new ones at the full asking price.

We were travelling from Sheffield so I stayed at her place the night before. I had never gone away for Christmas before and although I felt quite excited by it, this was coupled with one or two reservations. It was a long way to go at such a frantic time of year, when normally I would avoid crowds. I had never been particularly good at celebrating what was, of course, supposedly the birth of Christ so part of me still wished I could spend the time quietly at home. I was also uncomfortable about travelling on Christmas Eve, figuring it would be total madness. I should have had the courage to kill off this idea whilst it was still in its infancy, but I didn't. In a little over twelve hours we would be boarding the train. It would have been unbelievably cruel to change my mind when she was so excited by it.

We arrived at the station in good time but then disaster struck. We heard via a tannoy announcement that an earlier train had been cancelled, so as well as all those waiting to board ours, there was the traffic from the cancellation.

At that moment in time I didn't want to be anywhere near that train.

Although we both had seat reservations it took twenty minutes to find them as we battled through crowds of people standing in the aisles and unwilling to move out of the way. By the time we finally reached our seats, I was already sweating quite heavily and once again feeling claustrophobic. When we finally made it to the hotel all I really wanted to do was take a shower, change my shirt and have a refreshingly cold beer, preferably in that order, just as soon as we were given the key to our room. I imagined it would be a straightforward process of confirming the booking then getting on with what still remained of our holiday, but we just weren't having that kind of a day.

'When was the booking made? There's nothing on the computer under that name.'

'Several weeks ago, I booked it on my debit card for the special Christmas package for myself and my partner, show her the letter, Min.'

I fumbled around frantically in the bag, searching for the letter, becoming increasingly agitated. Eventually I found it and handed it to Isabelle without a word. I was confident she would deal with it, whereas I would have been tempted to make the receptionist eat it.

'I'm not sure that we're doing the Christmas packages anymore.'

'Well, you were at the time that letter was written and it's proof not only of our booking but also that it's been paid for. That letter represents a contract and I expect you to honour it.'

'Well, I'll need to check if we still have any rooms available.'

At that point I stepped away from the reception desk as I was ready to explode. Santa Claus obviously didn't have us on his mailing list and his elves took their instructions from a machine. I wandered aimlessly around the foyer for a few minutes before returning, believing it to be unfair to leave Isabelle to deal with this on her own. As I approached the desk once more I saw her handing over her bank card in exchange for a key.

'Have you sorted it?'

'Not entirely, they're going to check to see if they can find a record of my bank details. In the meantime they've let us have this room until something gets sorted. They're going to ring us in an hour or so.'

I was done with carrying the bag, it was heavy, so Isabelle took it into the lift whilst I took the stairs. The hotel corridors were like a rabbit warren and after taking several wrong turns I eventually found our room. I sat by the window and lit a cigarette.

'Min, you can't smoke in here.'

'So why is there an ashtray?'

'If you set the smoke detector off we're guaranteed to be thrown out.'

I opened the window in order to appease her, but I certainly wasn't in a conciliatory mood, I was ready to go to war with the hotel staff.

'This is just ridiculous, I've never known such piss poor organisation in all my fucking life!'

'Calm down, Min, it'll get sorted.'

'Well, if it doesn't, I want my money back because we'll have to book new train tickets and imagine travelling late Christmas Eve, it'll be an absolute fucking nightmare!'

I finished my cigarette but left the window open. There was a stiff breeze coming in off the North Sea, which should take care of the smell, besides the room was far too warm for it to be comfortable. I then began unpacking the bag, placing our toiletries in the bathroom and the gifts on a small table. It was kind of surreal, seeing them sat there all wrapped up in a borrowed room.

I took a long leisurely shower and when I emerged, Isabelle's friends had arrived. I knew they were due at some point but I would have preferred them to have come after I had dressed. I would also have preferred them to have waited for me, before opening the bottle of wine we had brought with us. It certainly didn't help improve my mood or my appetite and we were due at the restaurant in an hour.

'Min, the receptionist rang while you were in the shower. Everything's sorted, they've found our booking and they've got a receipt for us, we can pick it up when we head to the restaurant.'

'No, you're alright, I'll go down and pick it up now before they lose that fucker as well!'

I'd already met her friends once before so formal introductions weren't necessary. It was an excuse to get out of the room, which wasn't really big enough to house four people and throwing one out of the window wasn't an option.

So I got lost again.

I made sure I found my way back with a little time to spare in order to make the restaurant on time. Isabelle was in animated conversation with her friends as we walked along the sea front. Prior to arriving she had researched local restaurants on the Internet and had found a small Italian place at the entrance to a marina. I had no idea what the food would taste like but the surroundings looked stunning on the photographs. Now, as we walked and they talked, I spent a little time taking in the landscape, feeling no pressure to invite myself into their private reminiscences. I didn't know them that well and simply used the time for some quiet reflection. I've always loved the sea at night, its power of seduction, the secrets it holds and the enchanting flickers of light that shimmer nervously across its eyelids, keeping to the blind side.

It was a fifteen-minute walk to the restaurant and a table had been booked in advance so there was no fear of being turned away. However, in keeping with the pattern of the day, when we arrived the table wasn't ready and we were told to expect a half-hour wait. Isabelle shot me a look that basically said, it's Christmas Eve, I'm with my friends, please don't cause a scene. The truth was, I didn't have the energy, I was all beat up so I just went outside, had a cigarette and stared across the marina. Within a few minutes she joined me, carrying two glasses of wine, one of which she gave to me.

'Look, I know it's not perfect but it's Christmas, they're bound to be busy.'

'It's okay, it's just been that kind of day. To tell you the truth I'd almost forgotten that it was Christmas tomorrow.'

'Well, look, I'm going back inside, it's not fair to ignore them.'

'Of course not, I'll come and join you in a second.'

I finished my cigarette and returned to our guests. Once we were seated at our table I began to relax almost immediately helped in part, no doubt, by the glass of wine I had already finished off. We ordered a bottle of Merlot to share, which basically amounted to a glass each, hardly excessive, and when it came to the food I opted for the safe, lazy option and ordered a Bolognese. As the evening drew to a close and our guests were ready to leave, I pulled a twenty-pound note from my wallet and slid it across the table.

'What's this for?'

'Get yourself a cab, it's Christmas Eve, and it's getting late, you don't want to have to run the gauntlet of boisterous young men spilling out of the pubs, pissed out of their minds and looking for a fight.'

Their place was some distance from where we had eaten and the route took them past several of the town's pubs, whereas we had a straightforward walk along the promenade.

'Well, look, we really appreciate this, thanks.'

'Merry Christmas.'

'Yeah, Merry Christmas.'

We waited for their cab to arrive and as soon as they departed we took a slow walk back to our hotel. Although there was an absence of snow, the fresh clear air coming off the sea, coupled with the winter chill and a spectacular array of lights, really did make me feel like it was Christmas.

I wanted to immerse myself in the moment and stay with it a while. I had spent the vast part of the day battling various forces, some of them self-imposed, and I needed a little time to re-establish my own thought patterns. I am principally a very private person and whilst I occasionally enjoyed company, it wasn't something I particularly yearned for, or missed. I needed time alone in order to replenish myself. So when we arrived back at the hotel I decided to find a quiet corner of the bar and just sit inside my own mind, without disturbance.

'You can if you want, but I'm going up to the room.'

'You don't mind?'

'No, but don't get pissed.'

I ordered another glass of wine and managed to find a corner table that was unoccupied. The bar was bustling as you would expect, but I was able to find what I came for. I guess you must stand out a little when you're sitting there alone, neither speaking or being spoken to, but I didn't care about any of that, I just wanted to hear myself and once I had, I returned to our room.

As soon as I walked in I could sense tension. Isabelle was sat by the window, smoking, and hardly acknowledged my presence, when normally she would have greeted my return warmly.

'What's wrong?'

'I don't know why you bothered to come up here, Min, because you've been a pain in the arse ever since we got here.'

'What the fuck are you talking about?'

'I'm talking about you not being willing to make the effort. On the way to the restaurant you walked behind us, then when we got there you went outside and just left me to deal with them on my own.'

'They're your friends, Isabelle, not mine, and what would you have preferred, that I made a scene and embarrassed them and we got asked to leave?'

It had already begun to form part of the usual pattern and I was a long way from home but it didn't matter, I was unwilling to capitulate and accept a wrong that wasn't mine, I didn't want to be part of these mental gymnastics, yet didn't quite know how to extricate myself.

I just regretted being there.

'You're just jealous because I've got friends and you haven't.'

'According to you, half the fucking world is jealous of you, including people you don't even know!'

'I think you should go, Min, this isn't working and I want you to leave. If you don't, I'll call the police.'

At that precise moment I positively despised her, and wasn't particularly fond of myself for having been there when I could have been alone in my apartment, with no thoughts other than what the television allowed me. I had breached everything I thought I stood for, confused love with need, and just wanted to return to my island, where I was king.

'You seem to be forgetting something, I've paid for all this. If anyone leaves it'll be you! You can stay at your friends', whereas I've got nowhere to go and it's Christmas Eve.'

'Yeah, but it's my name on the receipt.'

'And my fucking money that paid for the ink!'

'You can't prove that, if I show it to the police you're the one that'll have to fuck off or they'll arrest you and you're on life licence, remember!'

Red rag to a bull and I feel sure that had I gathered her up in my arms and dropped her out of the window to an almost certain death, I probably could have learned to live with myself. But I didn't have to, instead I walked straight past her without looking and opened the door to our room.

'Get your things, then, get out.'

I walked back into the room again without looking at her and sat by the window where I lit a cigarette. I heard the door slam shut and couldn't believe she would have stormed off without first collecting her belongings.

I instantly looked up and saw her standing by the door almost hopping from foot to foot.

'You just don't get it do you, Min? I want you to leave and I want you to leave right now!'

She gathered up the holdall and started brutally stuffing my belongings into it, along with the gifts I had received from my family. I launched myself across the room and grabbed hold of her.

'Stop it! Stop it now, have you gone completely fucking nuts?'

'Let go of me, Min, or I'll scream the fucking place down and you'll get locked up! Now just walk away and you'll be fine!'

'You can scream all you fucking want just as soon as you're through that door!'

There was an almighty struggle with me trying to push her towards the door and her trying to push herself into the middle of the room. I knew I had to get her out of there to have any chance of survival. With one hand on her arm and the other trying to unlock the door, I frantically managed to shove her out into the corridor and quickly slam the door shut behind me, hoping that would be the end of it. But it wasn't, she began knocking on the door and pleading with me to let her in so she could collect her things but I refused, not out of meanness or spite, but because I was afraid that one of us might just end up going out of that window.

Eventually the noise subsided and I was grateful that the scene had ended without official intervention. I began to once again rearrange my gifts on the table, including those I had bought for her, but it all seemed such an empty gesture. Even if she came back for them she would only have taken them away with a few disparaging remarks. Her friends would have looked on, embarrassed in their roles as enforcers, and I would have sat there smoking a cigarette, wishing I was somewhere else. I suddenly became acutely aware that she was no longer in the room and I was already doubting my handling of the situation. I was desperate to find her before she found me accompanied by the local plod. I frantically searched the hotel but if she was there she was doing a good job of making herself invisible. I returned to the bar, satisfied that she had simply slipped out and gone to stay with her friends, no doubt giving them chapter and verse as to what a complete bastard I was. I ordered a glass of wine but it never touched my lips.

No sooner had I found a place to sit when a couple of cops appeared at the entrance accompanied by a receptionist who pointed directly at me

'Mr Cooper?'

'Yes.'

'Mr Cooper, I'm arresting you on suspicion of assault, you don't have to say anything but....'

He read me the usual rights. I swear to God, if any of those fuckers talked in their sleep, that's what they'd say.

'This is absolute nonsense.'

A female officer stepped forward and slapped the cuffs on me. Well, I certainly stood out now as I was marched through the bar and out the back to a waiting patrol car. The cells at Sunderland police station were being refurbished, so I was driven to Washington, just a few miles away.

CHAPTER SIXTY-ONE

I lay on the bunk feeling a combination of outrage, sadness and sheer stupidity, but I felt no wrong. None of this would ultimately matter because only my actions were under the microscope. After a couple of hours, the cell door opened and the two arresting officers stood there.

'Come on, fella, we need to interview you'

I followed them down a corridor to a small interview room. After the usual preliminaries they got on with it.

'So do you want to tell me what happened tonight?'

'Do you want to tell me why I'm here?'

'You're here because your partner has accused you of launching a brutal and sustained attack against her.'

This was the voice of the female cop who had clearly already decided that I was guilty and therefore the ultimate scumbag. I turned back to the guy.

'What am I supposed to have done?'

'She claims you punched her several times around the face and head, that you tried strangling her and that whilst she was lying on the floor, you jumped up and down on top of her.'

'Well, presumably if I had launched such a ferocious attack she'd have some marks to show for it?'

'She's got a couple of scratches on her neck.'

'You've got to be fucking shitting me! A couple of scratches? She could have gotten those in her sleep.'

I was almost manic with rage, unable to keep still as I was in the ridiculous position of fighting for my liberty by pointing out the glaringly obvious.

'What about finger marks on her neck where I'm supposed to have tried to strangle her? Or a footprint from having jumped up and down on her several times? I mean, come on!'

'Well, why would she make it up?'

When all else fails, when everything is lost rather than go back and reinvestigate, they offer that old chestnut.

'Well, it wouldn't be the first time. Why don't you contact Worksop police?'

'So are you denying her allegations?'

'Absolutely.'

I didn't for a minute consider that they would contact Worksop, the way he casually deflected it convinced me of that. I was also convinced that it would be ludicrous to pursue a prosecution when there were no injuries to support her claims. So when I was returned to my cell I wasn't unduly concerned or anxious, I climbed on my bunk and fell asleep.

'Cooper, come on, marra, the custody sergeant wants to speak to you.'

'What time is it?'

'Seven thirty.'

I must have been asleep for several hours but it certainly didn't feel like it as I got to my feet. I followed him out with the blanket still draped over my shoulders but was told to leave it in the cell.

'Mr Cooper, you were brought in last night on suspicion of assault, is that correct?'

'Yes.'

'The Crown Prosecution Service have looked at the evidence and their decision is to charge you with common assault.'

I was stunned, barely able to move or think. I just stared at the piece of paper he was holding, still waiting for him to announce I was being released without charge. It was Christmas Day but it might just as well have been any other day.

'Now, you're being bailed to appear at Sunderland Magistrates on January the seventeenth at ten am. Is there anywhere you can stay for a day or two as you obviously can't go back to the hotel?'

I was struggling to keep a lid on things. It never occurred to me that they would release me on Christmas Day when they knew I was a long way from home, without any available transport. I explained to them that I couldn't afford to book into another hotel as I'd already paid five hundred pounds for the one I'd yet to sleep in and what little money remained had to last me another week, but my pleas were met with a yawning apathy and it seemed incredulous that there was no organisation or planning involved.

'In that case all we can do is drive you to the motorway. There's a service station and you can thumb a lift from there.'

As difficult as this is to admit, I would have preferred to remain where I was for another twenty-four hours, it was warm and I would be guaranteed a meal then in the morning assured of my seat on the train.

Twenty-four hours. In the grand scheme of things just a tiny droplet of time, no more significant than a bad dream, that's just as easily forgotten. But I'd have to plead and I just couldn't do it.

It had already been an expensive mistake.

'I suppose it'll just have to do, then.'

The custody sergeant handed my holdall to the constable and I followed him out into the compound. As soon as we stepped outside the cold air hit me and visibility was poor due to the freezing fog. When we arrived at the service station the cop dropped my bag by the side of the road and was gone. It was still dark but that made little difference, it was extremely cold and I needed a plan.

I basically didn't know where the fuck I was except that I was somewhere in Tyne and Wear. Ordinarily, I would have quickly scanned the surrounding area to see if anywhere offered shelter should I need it, however visibility was poor and even when the light came up I didn't expect it to improve. It did occur to me that should I still be standing there come nightfall, it might be a good idea to pop into the nearest town and find a pub that offered cheap rooms. The problem was, of course, that I had no real idea as to how far it was to the nearest town and the bag was so heavy I probably wouldn't have made it anyway. I had no choice but to remain there until I was either lucky enough to be offered a lift, or the clock pointed me in the direction of the train station.

The service station was naturally closed except for the little kiosk that sold cigarettes and confectionary and where motorists paid for their petrol. I was solely reliant on these motorists as they passed through, hoping they would take a little pity as they saw me hopping from foot to foot trying to keep warm.

It's much more difficult these days to obtain a lift and impossible if a woman is driving alone, and there wasn't that much traffic, reducing the odds considerably, but every passing car still offered hope. Within an hour the light came up but I could barely feel my feet. I reached into my bag and pulled out a spare pair of socks, which quickly went over those I was already wearing. My fingertips were also starting to feel numb despite the fact that I was wearing gloves, and my nose had begun to run and I didn't have a tissue. I had no choice but to brave the kiosk, which I had so far deliberately avoided, even standing with my back to it. I was mindful that whoever was working inside would have seen me being dropped off by the police and I was in no mood for an inquisition, but I didn't want to have to wipe my nose on the back of my gloves, either.

I left my bag by the side of the road still containing my presents, which remained unopened. I was tempted to randomly select one and unwrap it just to remind myself that it was still Christmas.

It just seemed out of context, yet strangely fitting.

I ventured into the kiosk and was immediately struck by the warmth and it almost took my breath away. I searched the shelves looking for tissues and quickly became aware that his eyes were following me.

'Do you sell those little travel packs of tissues?'

'No, but I can let you have some of this if you like?'

Behind his counter stood a huge roll of tissue and he pulled of a generous amount before handing it to me.

'Do you want a cup of coffee? You must be freezing out there.'

'It's not too bad as long as I keep moving, but I will have a coffee, black and strong, no sugar.'

He stuck a paper cup under the nozzle of his machine and filled it up. Even the smell had me salivating.

'What do I owe you?'

'It's on the house.'

'Thanks, I appreciate it.'

I really did, an unconditional act of kindness in keeping with the true spirit of Christmas and the true value of humanity.

Once outside, things somehow didn't feel quite so bleak. I even managed to forget about the cold for a while and didn't curse the motorists who didn't stop. Within a couple of hours, one battered old car did. I wasn't sure if it was roadworthy but I wasn't about to ask.

'Where are you heading?'

'Worksop in Nottinghamshire.'

'I'm going to Derbyshire.'

'Perfect, my turn off is before yours.'

I dropped my bag on the back seat then climbed in the front, grateful to finally be on the move and relieved to once again be able to feel my fingers and toes. Gratitude, however, quickly turned to irritation. I felt under siege as he bombarded me with a non-stop barrage involving his sexual conquests. Almost every major town we passed along the way evoked a memory of some woman he once 'knocked off' or some blowjob administered on the back seat of his car, in a pub car park. I was seriously relieved to get out of that car, especially when he informed me that it had once been a police car. I still had another seven miles before I reached town so I stuck my thumb out again. All I got was a few hand gestures and a string of verbal abuse. I knew then that I was back home.

Once it became pretty obvious that no one was going to stop, I started walking but the bag was so heavy I had to stop every few yards. After approximately an hour, in which time I probably hadn't travelled more than a mile, I came upon a hotel and it was open. I wandered around inside searching for a phonebook so I could phone a cab. It would be expensive but I had no choice, I was close to home and now all I wanted was to get there as soon as possible. The taxi fare came to twenty pounds, which I could ill afford but at least I was home. More significantly I was alone and I could have bathed in the silence, that is, until reality kicked in. I had no provisions and of course the supermarkets were closed until Boxing Day. My local shop was open but it was small and offered very little, but I managed to buy sufficient ingredients for a nutritious if non-traditional meal.

Washed down with a bottle of cheap plonk.

As the alcohol began to take hold I found myself ruminating on the events of the previous twenty-four hours and in particular the charge of common assault. Slapping someone across the face or shoving them is a common assault. I became increasingly angry, believing that if they genuinely felt there was a case to answer in accordance with what she had alleged, then the charge should have been a more serious one. I was in limbo. As yet I hadn't received any legal advice, my lawyer was on holiday and I declined to see the duty solicitor on the basis that they are often no more than police puppets. I was due to see my psychiatric nurse in a couple of days and I stayed up long into the night, swinging backwards and forwards; should I tell him or shouldn't I? If I did, I felt sure I would be recalled and if I didn't and they found out, it would be a nailed-on certainty. Naturally, I didn't want to have to tell them if it could be avoided so I spent several hours trying to figure out each possible scenario. It was difficult because I kept coming back to the licence. I imagined that the Magistrates' Court, and in particular the Crown Prosecution Service, would be aware of it, so it seemed inevitable that sooner or later someone would contact the probation service.

Nevertheless, I decided not to tell him because ultimately I was entitled to legal advice and once I'd received it I would act accordingly.

But I still didn't sleep for a couple of days.

＊＊＊＊

I sat in his office, gripped by paranoia, convinced that he already knew and was waiting for me to reveal all. I almost did, terrified that if I didn't I would be receiving a knock at the door. I felt trapped, backed into a corner, but all the time I was unwilling to capitulate under those circumstances because it was wrong. There was a massive power imbalance and I was entitled to some form of representation.

Some form of justice.

I left his office still feeling paranoid and still expecting a visit from the boys in blue but it never came. I spent the rest of the week still believing I was on borrowed time and couldn't wait to get the New Year celebrations out of the way so that I could call my lawyer. And hopefully put this thing to bed.

I stayed in on New Year's Eve, I wasn't in a party mood nor was I feeling particularly gregarious, not that I ever was. I sent a text message to Franc who normally spends the holiday overseas, it simply read:

'I think I'm in the shit.'

Within minutes he rang me and I explained the situation to him, whilst also expressing my fears. For once he was unable to reassure me as I understood the terms and conditions. As midnight struck I received the usual messages from family, then came a call from Isabelle which I refused to answer, not only for legal reasons but because I was afraid of what I might say to her. Predictably, she left a message.

'Me and my friends think you're a complete wanker, you left me on my own in a hotel on Christmas Day, now fuck off! I never want to see you again.'

Unbelievable! I took it to the police, explaining the criminal case pending and they rang her and told her if she persisted, the case against me would collapse. I hoped she would.

By Monday of the following week, I rang my solicitor's office only to be told she was on leave for another week. The situation was becoming intolerable, I decided it couldn't wait another week so I rang my psychiatrist, who informed me he would have to contact probation. By the end of the week an appointment was arranged. Half an hour before leaving my apartment, I was standing by my lounge window when I saw a police car pull into the street. There were two of them; there's always two when they come to arrest you. One of them was holding up a piece of paper, which I assumed was a warrant.

My buzzer went and I froze with fear but I didn't answer. I wasn't sure what I hoped to achieve by my silence but my rationale had been scrambled through panic. Surprisingly, they didn't pursue it by coming to the door but I was left in no doubt that an order to recall had been issued.

I wrestled with thoughts of doing a runner, my natural inclination, but I resisted because I felt I had right on my side and as depressing as prison is, I had to face it to come out of this clean. I put on my jacket and made the short walk, I wanted them to look me in the eye and tell me why, instead:

'I'm sorry, Min, you're being recalled.'

CHAPTER SIXTY-TWO

I was taken in handcuffs back to my apartment so that I could switch off the heating. Whilst there, I remembered to collect my reading glasses and the address of my solicitors. Once outside I was confronted by a small group of neighbours who had turned out to watch the show. I initially assumed they were being voyeuristic, preferring to be an audience in my life rather than concentrating on their own, but in fact they were there to offer messages of support, but I was too preoccupied to acknowledge them.

It was almost a relief to get to the station, as I desperately needed some quiet, uninterrupted thinking time. My mind was racing as feelings of anger and resentment threatened to engulf me. I was almost tearful through sheer helplessness. Whilst I partially understood the decision to recall me, they could not have genuinely viewed me as an immediate danger to the public, as it took them a week to arrive at their decision. I guess they were more afraid of the process than they were of me, scared of tabloid exposure. In any event, I felt it might have been more appropriate to have waited for the outcome of the criminal proceedings to be decided. After being processed I was again subjected to a full strip search. I ought to have been a prostitute given the amount of times strangers have seen me naked. At least then I would have been paid for the privilege. Once the indignities were completed the cell door slammed shut and I felt utterly despondent, believing that as it was approaching early evening on a Friday, I would probably be stuck in that cell all weekend.

Without a fucking cigarette when I most needed one!

Within a few minutes of being banged up the cell door opened and the custody sergeant stood there, holding a newspaper.

'I can't read that without my glasses.'

'Well, I can't let you have them, they're in a sealed property bag.'

Go fuck yourself, I muttered under my breath as the door again slammed shut.

I spent the next hour or so pacing the cell and having an imaginary and at times almost self-pitying conversation with Isabelle. Strangely enough, whilst I held her responsible for my current incarceration, I wished her no harm. I just felt she was being allowed to act freely and whenever she did I became the fall guy. Perhaps if she had been held accountable she might have thought twice about lying to the police. Mental illness may explain some things, but it doesn't necessarily excuse them. Ultimately I believed that her attacks on me had nothing to do with her illness, they were personality traits.

I had played a very dangerous game and now looked to be on the losing side. In fact, I hadn't yet managed to play a draw. Ordinarily I should have ended this relationship whilst it was still in its infancy, but I guess in my fucked up little world I didn't like to be proved wrong and therefore didn't listen to whatever advice was being offered. I tried to make it work in order to show my quality and perseverance, to prove my resilience and strength, my life's blood, which I refused to relinquish and have them patronise me, caressing my failure with words of discomfort. None of this was of any use to me now as anger and frustration were replaced by self-loathing. All I could do was to try and survive, relying more on instinct than on intellect, my enemy and friend.

Whilst locked in such thoughts and not wanting to escape from them, the cell door once again swung open without invitation.

'Grab your coat, we're taking you to Lincoln.'

Now I had a fresh set of ideas to deal with, a fresh set of problems as prison loomed and the reality bit like a rabid dog. Within seconds I was forced into the quiet, subdued acceptance of my fate.

There was nothing else.

Once again I was handcuffed before being ushered into the back of the car, a criminal before being tried, yet equally condemned. My only joy, temporary as it was, came when we arrived in the city of Lincoln, as the cops got lost. If they were expecting me to be their guide, they were sadly mistaken. I wouldn't run but the onus was still on them to deliver me and not myself. After taking instructions from a passer-by we did in fact reach the prison and I never really doubted that we would, but it was a nice thought for a while.

I had learned a thing or two from my previous recall and there was no way I was sharing.

'Do you have a problem sharing a cell?'

'Actually I do, I have mental health problems and in the past I've been beaten up by various cellmates.'

I was given a single cell without further investigation, such was their paranoia and fear of litigation.

Inside my cell, away from the madding crowd, I managed to find some relief, until I noticed something high up on the ceiling that I thought might be a camera. A couple of days later I spoke to a screw about it and it was indeed a camera, installed in an attempt to prevent self-harm and suicides. I figured it would probably prevent masturbation too.

Obviously I was due at Sunderland Magistrates' in a couple of weeks time so the prison authorities saw no point in moving me to the main wing, which suited me perfectly, even if it was only temporary.

On the day of my move I left everything behind, believing I would return at the end of the day. I climbed aboard the prison van expecting nothing more than a day out, an escape from the tedium.

I couldn't believe I could have been so naïve, so out of touch. Experience obviously counts for nothing when you want more than it allows.

There were a couple of other lads on the van who were required at Mansfield Magistrates and who at worst would receive sentences totalling just a few months. My solicitor had informed me that she couldn't represent me in this case, as she wasn't a criminal lawyer, but had found one who could and had provided them with all the background information. However, Emma would be representing me at the parole hearing, which was a huge relief.

Sunderland Magistrates' Court was very old and like most courts the cells were deep in the bowels, a miniature fortress. I hadn't been there long when I was called out to meet my lawyer. He introduced himself and quite honestly looked like he'd been sleeping rough, but I trusted Emma's judgment and therefore trusted him. He read out Isabelle's statement in full, the first time I had heard it verbatim.

'Well, obviously, you've got to plead not guilty to this.'

'I fully intend to.'

Within an hour or so I was handcuffed and taken into court where I stood as the clerk asked me to confirm my name before reading out the charge. Finally, I was asked to enter a plea.

'Not guilty.'

I spoke the words firmly and with certainty. I wanted everybody in that courtroom to be in no doubt as to how strongly I opposed this entire fiasco. The lawyers haggled over dates and eventually the trial was set for mid-February.

Over many years and numerous court appearances, I had never pleaded 'not guilty' and never experienced a trial, but I was ready for it. I wasn't however ready for the news that came next and it threw me. I wasn't being returned to Lincoln, I was going to Durham. I hadn't expected this, didn't imagine I would be held so far from home; it was like a punch in the stomach, like having to start all over again.

Prisons are severe places with an undercurrent of tension that can quickly and inexplicably erupt into violence. Familiarity is hugely important in helping to maintain a sense of calm, to be where you know and are known is a massive psychological advantage. The opposite being true when you don't.

I was severely unnerved and a little scared. I've never adapted that well to change when it's enforced, I prefer self-discovery with its magnitude of riches, not the poverty of limitation. I was also concerned about my stuff, which I had left behind. Whilst I fully expected the cleaners to clear out my cell and in the process commandeer my coffee, tobacco and toiletries, I desperately needed my legal papers, not for trial but to fully prepare for the parole hearing. All in all, it was a bucket of shit.

Travelling through the streets of Durham in the back of a prison van was a nauseating experience. I knew those streets better than the driver as I had walked them so many times, mostly when I should have been somewhere else. During my time spent living in County Durham as a child, I was aware that there was a prison, but despite it being a relatively small city I had never walked past it, I didn't even know where it was located.

I fucking well did now.

The van pulled in through the large, electronic gates and we were ushered into the reception area to be processed. I was once again asked if I had a problem with sharing a cell and I simply reiterated what I had said upon my arrival at Lincoln. Eventually I was transferred to the induction wing and a cell all on my own.

It was a total shit pit.

I spent the first couple of hours scrubbing the place just to make it habitable. I piled all the rubbish into the corner where it would have to remain until the following morning.

By the end of the week, whilst still struggling with my new regime, I was handed a document once again outlining the reasons for my recall. I stared at it in total amazement, wanting to make the governor who handed it to me, eat it. I was acutely aware that he was there to monitor and record my response, well, that's the one that would have given me the most satisfaction, but instead I just turned away from him and stepped back into my cell.

'Any comment you'd like to make?'

I pushed the door shut and sat on my bunk, almost trembling with rage. It seems the criminal case against me was an irrelevance as far as the authorities were concerned, they were far more interested in the fact I didn't mention it at the first available opportunity, despite informing my psychiatrist only a few days later. Which they themselves omitted from that soiled document. As far as I was concerned the whole thing was an absolute fucking nonsense and I stared down at my worn out shoes, wondering if I had just been pissing into the wind all these years. I certainly struggled to cling to anything I could still believe in, except myself, but in that moment I wasn't sure if it was enough, wasn't convinced that I could persuade myself that it was worth it.

I felt listless.

Part of a lyric from a Leonard Cohen song kept reverberating around my mind looking for a way of occupying it.

'You're living for nothing now, I hope you're keeping some kind of record.'

I spent a couple of days walking around the prison in a daze and although I was aware of the attention I was attracting from other prisoners, I refused to bow to it. Most of them saw it as a way of life, but for me it was an unwelcome and unnecessary interruption.

I wasn't a tourist.

By now Franc had returned from his overseas trip so I was able to write to him. Within a few days he had written back, once again enclosing a hugely welcome sum of money.

I spent a couple of weeks on the induction wing not even killing time, just watching it drift by mockingly. One day the cell door opened and a burly screw, with more waist than I had years, spoke into his clipboard.

'Grab your stuff, you're moving to 'c' wing.'

I was shown to a cell and quickly made the bed before arranging my stuff, the nearest I came to making it habitable. I looked out of the window and there it was towering over me, the cathedral, one of my favourite landmarks. I hadn't seen that many but that one was full of magical splendour, enigmatic uncertainty. It was the eyes of the city. As I stood there, slightly bewildered, viewing it from behind bars, my need to touch it was even greater because it had always been accessible until now; never out of reach, until now. I guess some inmates feel the same about their cars or their dogs, occasionally even their children, or the women who bore them.

I had different memories.

I figured some kind of optical illusion might be at work. Many years earlier, whilst still a child, I had climbed to the top of the cathedral tower and observed a number of prisoners walking around the exercise yard but the distance between the two seemed far greater.

Little did I know that there was a cell with my name on it.

Within a few days, and having aborted any attempt at settling in, the cell door was thrown open.

'Now then, young man, according to my records you've refused to do the induction course, am I right?'

Soon after arriving in this flea pit, I had been ordered to do the course, but refused on the grounds that I did it when I arrived in Lincoln only a couple of weeks earlier. I was unwillingly to comply just so they could tick me off their list, fucking robots, unable to function unless programmed! It takes away the thinking and the responsibility.

'I've already done it.'

'Well, it's fairly simple, if you won't do it, the television will be confiscated.'

He wasn't unpleasant in his threat but it was nevertheless a threat and one I couldn't defend against. I could either stand my ground and tell him to fuck off, or silently despise him and his fucking impotence outside of uniform.

'Alright, I'll do it.'

* * * *

As my trial date grew ever closer I found myself in a difficult position as I paced up and down my cell considering all the options. I had no real desire to put Isabelle on the stand and have her face a fairly robust cross-examination and if I could have avoided it I would have, but I was fighting for my liberty and my reputation and therefore decided to offer her the same consideration she had shown towards me.

The lack of any injuries, despite the ferocity of the alleged attack, should in my view have been enough to have had this case dismissed already but as it hadn't been, there was no room for complacency. I sat down and carefully compiled a list of all the unproven allegations she had made against various people over the years. Almost all were against men and I was determined to have each allegation put to her and for her to inform the court as to the outcome of each complaint.

It wasn't enough just to be acquitted.

On the day of the trial I was up and ready to go long before they came for me. I was full of nervous energy, as I wasn't particularly looking forward to staring across a courtroom at Isabelle.

So I decided I wouldn't.

I arrived at the Magistrates' in plenty of time for the hearing. Within twenty minutes I was called out to see my lawyer. I took a couple of deep breaths, then armed with my document, I strode purposefully into the interview room.

'Right, I've spent the weekend drawing up a list of allegations that she's made in the past. All were dismissed.'

Manic energy poured out of me like water from a burst pipe. I was almost bouncing up and down in my chair but before I could get fully into my stride he held up his hand. The interruption nearly choked me.

'Haven't you heard?'

'Heard what?'

'She's withdrawn her statement, the Crown Prosecution Service have decided not to proceed. You weren't meant to be here today, they were supposed to have written to you to tell you the charges have been dropped and the case dismissed.'

CHAPTER SIXTY-THREE

Back at Lincoln I was quickly processed and once again went through the induction nonsense before finally being awarded a single cell on the main wing. I was to be housed on the very top landing and I was actually quite excited by this. The top landings offered views over the prison wall of the surrounding fields and countryside. When I entered the cell I immediately went to the window and couldn't believe my luck; I was directly adjacent to another wing and all I could see was a wall, much closer than the one I was hoping to see beyond.

I had a little over six weeks before I once again had to face the panel and it didn't take long for the machine to roll into town. Doctors, nurses and of course probation, all with their pens at the ready, along with their smiles. Probation, not unexpectedly, once again recommended my release, and I wasn't surprised that my psychiatric team supported it. What was surprising, however, was that despite concerns being once again expressed regarding my mental state, there was no recommendation for me to have a spell in hospital.

Thank you.

I basically muddled along killing time as best I could. My mind was already out there, I just needed my body to meet up with it.

I met my lawyer, who looked like she might have had a rougher night than me. Not surprising, really, she was dealing with a number of complex cases and cared about them all. We discussed the case and both understood there weren't likely to be any surprises, however Emma felt the issue of openness and honesty might feature significantly. I agreed to compromise and accept that I made a mistake in not telling them immediately, but that it was an honest mistake, not designed to deliberately deceive or mislead. I was still pretty hung up on the idea that I was entitled to seek legal advice and when that was delayed I did in fact inform the relevant authorities. Emma agreed but warned against making it too contentious an issue.

Although we weren't expecting surprises we got one as soon as we entered the arena and sat down. The Home Office had declined to send their own lawyer and were therefore not represented. Naturally, I was encouraged by this as it clearly suggested that they believed they couldn't win. I only hoped that the judge, who himself looked and sounded like he didn't want to be there, didn't adjourn the hearing.

He didn't, but it was clear from the outset that this was going to be a far more fractious hearing than the previous one. The judge seemed to take an instant dislike to both myself and my lawyer before we'd uttered a single word, the lay person looked like he wanted to be chairing the proceedings, and the independent psychiatrist whose first language wasn't English, spoke so fast I needed a decoder.

All three had hearts of stone and complexions to match.

Once again the only witnesses were my probation officer and my psychiatrist who, as expected, supported my release, whilst refusing to support the decision to recall me, which enraged the judge.

'The decision to recall is the sole responsibility of the probation service. If you had him placed in hospital and he set fire to it, it would be the probation service that got it in the neck, not the health service.'

I was livid that he so readily introduced arson into the equation when nobody else had, before or during the hearing but he continued to give his evidence and the judge continued to interrupt it. I didn't know whether it was because he hoped to spoil Emma's concentration and rhythm or whether he was just old school and didn't approve of female lawyers. Whatever his motive, it didn't work. After each interruption she would simply repeat the question, calmly and evenly. She was also right about openness and honesty, it did feature largely in my probation officer's evidence, it was about the only thing that did.

My own performance was very brief. I did, in fact, concede that I had made a mistake but reiterated that it was an honest one. The judge appeared completely disinterested and it threw me slightly. He was asked if he had any questions and he said no. I then took a couple of standard questions from the other two panel members before we were finally dismissed with a cursory wave of the hand.

Outside, Emma seemed downbeat, and for a minute or two the mood was sombre. It certainly hadn't gone the way I had hoped or even expected but I still refused to be swayed from my earlier belief and conviction.

'What do you think?'

'I don't know, I just get the feeling he knows he's got to let me go but for reasons only he can explain, he doesn't want to.'

'Let's hope you're right but don't get your hopes up too high, we need to just wait and see.'

Emma was escorted to the gatehouse and I was returned to the wing. The hearing was much shorter than the first so I was back in time for lunch. I then went back to work and spent the rest of the week doing what I normally did.

As the working week drew to a close and my broom got to rest for a couple of days, I made my way back to the wing in time for my evening meal. As I climbed the metal stairs a screw shouted out to me that the lifer liaison officer had a letter for me and was waiting for me at the gate. I wasted no time in doing an about turn. She smiled, then handed me a sealed brown envelope, all very official and certainly more efficient than first time around when the right hand didn't know what the right hand was doing and the left was redundant.

'Aren't you going to open it? I already know what's in it.'

'Well, I've known you for a while now and you're smiling. I don't believe you would be that mean.'

I walked off without opening it, her smile told me everything I needed to know. The details could wait until I was alone with them.

* * * *

Five days later, I was back in my apartment but it didn't feel like a homecoming just yet. There was a pile of mail on the carpet, which I ignored, as I headed straight for the lounge to check on the health of Tolstoy. He was one of my plants (all of my plants were named after Russian writers), a cactus with an incredibly strong root. When I saw him looking a little worse for wear I stroked his leaves before giving him a well-earned drink. He had miraculously survived his second recall, but sadly Dostoyevsky didn't make it through his first.

I threw the corpse in the bin then took a shower. I stood for ages under that shower, wanting to feel every single drop and know that I could, without interruption. I dried myself off then changed into clean clothes. I still needed a haircut and my beard removing but it could wait until the following day, it was important to do it on my own time and not just use it to hurry things along and lose the real sense of it. I stuck my mobile on charge, then I picked up a shopping bag and headed for the supermarket, all very mechanical and all designed to keep me from feeling.

Because I was afraid, too afraid of breaking up.

After more than four months of prison food I needed a mixture of nutrition and comfort so I bought plenty of fruit and fresh vegetables along with a stack of chocolate and some ice cream. I realised that supermarkets aren't that far removed from prisons. They're loud and busy and extremely consumptive, hoards of stressed out shoppers, merciless in their intent, brutal in their disregard for anyone who stands in the way of frozen fish fingers. After putting my goods away and attempting to sort through some of the mail, it was time to go.

The meeting with probation didn't last long. Ideally I could have done without having to see anyone on my first day back but it was procedure. I gave a few perfunctory answers to the usual questions and was allowed to go and I did, straight to the pub. As I hadn't had a drink for a while I wasn't able to celebrate in the way I would have liked, prostrate. Instead, I just had a couple of beers before returning to my apartment where I prepared dinner before settling down to watch television in the company of ice cream, chocolate and a pack of Marlboro lights.

Eventually I climbed into bed and cried myself to sleep, because if I hadn't I might not have bothered climbing out again.

CHAPTER SIXTY-FOUR

'I just thought I'd give you a quick call to see how you are.'

'I'm fine.'

'I've tried ringing you a couple of times but there's been no answer.'

'I got recalled.'

'I thought you had.'

Isabelle's voice rose a pitch or two and I couldn't quite decide whether she was exclaiming or rejoicing, but she didn't return to the theme, she simply carried on as if we'd only spoken a few hours ago.

'I thought you might like to come over this evening and have your dinner here.'

Just like that.

I knew I shouldn't go, I knew I couldn't reason with myself and come up with one single, credible explanation as to why I should.

Except, I was lonely.

Not lonely from being alone, lonely inside, empty. I no longer believed in any of the things I said, just words, living and dying in a single breath. I scare more easily, too; I just don't run away from it anymore.

I was never certain enough.

'Yeah, alright, I'll come.'

I had a couple of hours before I needed to catch my train so there was still time to change my mind and I nearly did several times. I paced back and forth, berating myself for being so fucking feeble-minded. I was unhappy that she had glided so effortlessly across our torn and broken landscape without stopping to pick at the debris, and I was angry with myself for allowing her to do it. I had put need at the heart of my wellbeing, betraying all those years of struggle and relinquishing the strength and power that became trademarks, but I hadn't experienced any human warmth in over four months. Barked instructions and macho dynamics were all I'd had, I wanted to feel like I really was out of there, and so I took the train to Sheffield.

When I arrived at her apartment the table was already set. Place mats, cutlery and a bowl of garlic bread, either side of which stood two empty wine glasses that she began to fill with red wine. She picked up both glasses, handed one to me, then raised hers towards the ceiling, beaming her trademark smile.

'Cheers.'

I had absolutely no idea what we were celebrating and I definitely hadn't come prepared, but I wasn't sleeping either; when she was in this mood, I could either sit and let her pat me on the head, or resist and get caught in the avalanche.

'Cheers.'

I took a sip of my wine then sat the glass back down on the table. She had prepared a simple meal of chicken, some leafy salad, pasta salad and a little brown rice. She even made her own dressing and it looked and tasted absolutely fabulous. All of it washed down with a decent bottle of red, to the well-planned accompaniment of music, which had been carefully selected to remind me of our initial coming together.

It was all very seductive.

As the evening wore on and the wine began to take hold I edged more and more towards the wild side, watching her every move as she danced her way out of isolation. It was a dangerous place to inhabit because I still desired her physically, dangerous because it stopped the clock and then forgot. I kept checking the time, knowing I should be making a move before the last train left Sheffield but it became a pointless exercise when she produced a second bottle of wine.

I knew I wouldn't be leaving.

In fact, I stayed a couple of days, feeling pretty much how I might have felt if it had been a one night stand that I'd then regretted. I guess in a way I was desperate to try to show a softer, more sensitive side to my nature, more giving.

Eventually, I did return home and was still waiting to hear from Franc but I was in no hurry. I was anxious as to how he was going to view the manuscript and as I was still feeling a little raw, a little more time gave me more time. I continued to see Isabelle, sometimes at her place and occasionally she stopped at mine. It wasn't long, however, before I once again became concerned about her mental wellbeing.

She appeared to be deteriorating quite rapidly and as well as her paranoia intensifying regarding her conspiracy theories, she had also been putting herself at risk by travelling all over the country seeking, amongst other things, an exorcism. Her speech was also disjointed and lacked a little coherence she was absolutely terrified. I tried in vain to persuade her to speak to mental health services in Sheffield. Instead she turned up at my place late at night, after the last train had gone so I had no choice but to let her in. She seemed pretty strung out and whatever my personal feelings were at the time, it would have been unthinkable to leave her on the street.

Almost immediately, she launched into a conspiracy theory of epic proportions, claiming that the people who were talking to her inside her head were planting people on trains, buses, in shops and even on the psychiatric ward. I tried to suggest to her that it would require a huge amount of organisation, not to mention manpower, and not even the security services would have the resources to mount that kind of operation, and that ultimately she just wasn't that important, but there was a narcissistic element to her delusion, which was sadly extremely real to her, as was the fear as she sat there trembling.

I tried to comfort her as best I could but she was in a really dark place. Finally, in the early hours we went to bed but I didn't get much sleep. I was convinced that she had stopped taking her medication, as she sometimes did. I also knew that I would have to challenge her but it was a very sensitive issue and she was prone to angry outbursts at the mere mention of it. She spent most of the following day in bed, only putting in a brief appearance mid-way through the evening. She was incredibly fragile and I'm afraid I exploited it, seizing the moment when she didn't have the strength to resist. I didn't directly accuse her of not taking the medication, instead I spoke about the possibility of there being something in the tablets that helps form a barrier in the mind, therefore making it harder for these people to control her.

'I've left it in Sheffield, I'll fetch it tomorrow.'

'I'll go with you.'

The following day started off like any other but the speed with which it turned upside down was frightening. Around mid-morning I went into the bedroom to check on Isabelle, hoping she would be ready to make the trip.

'I've got to go to Sheffield, Min.'

'I know, we're going together, remember?'

'No, Min, you can't come. If I don't do what they tell me, your life will be in danger.'

'Listen, Isabelle, I'm not scared of those fuckers, get your bag and we'll get going.'

Suddenly she cried out in pain then began twisting her neck and shoulders left and right, doing the same with her arms, then in a voice I didn't recognise, she calmly announced.

'I am a crone.'

I had no idea what a fucking crone was, but that display was like something out of 'The Exorcist'! I had never seen her like that before and had no real experience of how to deal with it, but it didn't take a lot of figuring out.

'I'm really sorry, Isabelle, but I think this is a hospital situation.'

She followed me into the lounge and stretched herself out on the sofa whilst

I rang my social worker to get the number of the crisis intervention team. I spoke to a guy on the team who was known to me, having formerly worked as a nurse on the ward. I never liked him but I explained the situation to him, leaving nothing out. He flatly refused to help, stating in his usual, high-handed manner that as she lived in Sheffield, it was their responsibility.

'Well, what am I supposed to do? She needs proper care and I can't give it to her.'

'All I can suggest is that you take her up to A&E.'

There was no way I was going to be able to get her up there, I couldn't risk getting her on a bus and in her current state a taxi was also out of the question as no driver would have taken her.

Whilst I was on the phone, Isabelle's personality kept changing every few seconds, punctuated by anguished outbursts in which she became convinced that she had killed her mother. Her mother had died two or three years earlier of natural causes having suffered a brain haemorrhage, but my attempts to persuade her of this were utterly in vain, she was only listening to the voices. I dug out the number of her team in Sheffield and gave them a ring. Her care coordinator was on leave and her replacement was in a meeting but would call me as soon as he was free.

Then Isabelle upped the ante.

'I've got to kill you, Min, you made me kill my mother so now I have to kill you.'

'Nobody's going to die, we're going to get you into hospital and sort this shit out.'

She evidently had other ideas for over the course of the next half hour or so she made several attempts to dash into the kitchen in order to get her hands on a knife. Luckily I was able to block each attempt but I desperately needed to receive that call. All I wanted was for someone to remove her from my apartment. As soon as they saw her, there would be no doubting that she needed to be admitted into hospital.

As the minutes ticked by and I was beginning to feel more and more like I'd been abandoned, Isabelle made yet another attempt to get into the kitchen. It was starting to seriously piss me off, so I grabbed a chair, set it down in front of the kitchen door and sat on it.

'Mini, I have to kill you, so would you please move out of the way so I can get into the kitchen?'

Only she could have been polite whilst intent on killing someone.

'No.'

'Mini, I'm warning you!'

'And I'm telling you, you're not going in there, so sit your arse back down on that sofa.'

Suddenly and without warning she lunged at me, taking me completely by surprise and I had no defence as she put both hands around my throat. She had strength I didn't know she possessed, as she took a firm grip on me, and it took all of mine to free myself and push her onto the sofa. Even though her stranglehold had only lasted a few seconds, I was already finding it painful to swallow. After a couple of minutes it suddenly hit me; if I go to the cops and report this incident, they'll have her assessed.

I left her in the apartment and jogged the short distance to the police station, as I didn't want to leave her alone for too long. I was just about to walk in when my phone rang and it was her people from Sheffield. I explained everything, including the apathetic approach from the crisis team. I also added that her condition was deteriorating rapidly and whilst she remained with me I was at risk. This one was as ineffectual as the first guy. He wasn't willing to send someone over to collect her. He even asked me not to go to the cops and when I in turn asked what I should do instead, he suggested I take her to A&E. To this day, I still can't believe that I actually turned around and trudged back to the apartment instead of following my instincts, which rarely let me down.

'Fucking hell! What have you done, you idiot?'

I had returned to the apartment not knowing what I would find, but I was certainly unprepared for what I did. Isabelle was lying on the sofa, clearly in a different world, bleeding heavily from both wrists.

A knife with a serrated edge lay on the coffee table.

I rushed out of the apartment, taking the stairs two and three at a time. One of my neighbours let me have a couple of bandages and I asked him to call an ambulance whilst I attempted to dress her wounds. He arrived in my apartment sometime later and helped me to apply the bandages. Once done, I rang my social worker to tell him what had happened. While I was on the phone I had my back to Isabelle who was lying on the sofa, or so I thought. When I turned around she was standing with her arm raised above her head, holding the knife.

'Oh my God, she's trying to stab me!'

'I have to kill you, Min, I have to kill you ...'

I dropped the phone and immediately grabbed her wrist. There was no fucking way I was going to let go!

'Drop the fucking knife now! I'm serious, Isabelle, drop it!'

She looked straight through me. I was convinced she no longer knew who I was and she wasn't willing to give up the knife.

She continued with her tug of war and I was left with little choice but to apply pressure to her wrist using my thumb, gradually increasing it, until finally she let go of the knife, which fell back onto the coffee table. I then pushed her back onto the sofa.

'Now, stay there and don't fucking move!'

I picked up the knife and did what I should have done in the first instance. I dropped it into the kitchen sink before returning to the lounge.

'Mini, Mini, Mini! Speak to me, please!'

I had assumed that the phone had switched itself off when I dropped it but clearly it hadn't and, more significantly, my social worker had heard everything.

CHAPTER SIXTY-FIVE

'It's okay, I got the knife off her.'

'Well listen, it's important that you make yourself safe, you need to go outside right now.'

'I can't leave her here on her own, there's no telling what she might do. If I go outside she'll have to come with me and I don't want the neighbours seeing her in this condition. I'm staying put until the paramedics arrive.'

A few minutes after finishing the call a couple of paramedics arrived along with four cops. They took her away and one of the cops asked to see the knife. I showed him into the kitchen and having examined it, he wrote something in his pocket notebook. He then asked me how I spelt my name and where I was born, as if any of that was relevant.

Except to check up on me.

After he left I sat on the sofa holding my head in my hands. It was eerily quiet and I was tempted to shout, just to hear something. There was also a lot of blood spattered around, she must have wandered around the lounge dripping blood. I struggled to understand how anyone could spill that much claret and survive.

I didn't want the cops returning to my apartment so I went downstairs. I figured they'd still be in the car park as the paramedics generally liked to administer first aid before making their way to the hospital.

When I got outside there were two cops and the ambulance. I walked towards them and one of the cops held up his hand.

'I wouldn't go talking to her, she's still pretty wound up.'

'It's not her I want to talk to, it's you.'

'What can I do for you?'

'If you're expecting me to make a statement against her you can forget it. She needs help, not punishment.'

I turned to the female cop who had emptied the contents of Isabelle's handbag onto the lid of a dustbin and was searching through them, presumably to check if she had concealed a knife.

'You could have done that in the car, you know, instead of a dustbin. Those are her personal effects, respect them.'

I immediately turned around and headed back towards my apartment. I didn't want a conversation with those fuckers I just wanted to mark their card.

I didn't sleep well that night, not because I was stressed or anxious but because I was upset. I was upset at what she was doing to herself. There was no denying that there was a self-inflicted element to her situation. Because she steadfastly refused to accept that she had an illness she would often refuse to take her medication, the consequence being that she regularly lived in a climate of fear and paranoia.

But she had never been dangerous with it, until now.

I was also upset with myself and as is always the case when I think about her, my feelings were confused and contradictory. There was a time in our relationship when I would have walked barefoot over broken glass just to get to her. Now I fought back the tears as I realised that I wasn't sure if I'd ever really known who she was. I was angry, too, that I hadn't shown the strength to have walked away earlier. Instead I arrogantly persisted in my attempts to fix her problems and in the process, perhaps even made them worse.

The following morning I was walking around my apartment feeling hopelessly lost when I suddenly thought about the way she had been admitted to hospital. Because of the haste I figured she wouldn't have any of the basic items she would need to feel human. I hesitated for a while, unsure whether I wanted to face her but in the end I felt uncomfortable leaving her in a position where she couldn't wash her hair or brush her teeth. There was a supermarket not far from the unit but as I imagined she had been sectioned I knew she wouldn't be able to get to it so I jumped on a train and went over there. I bought her a hairbrush and a selection of toiletries as well as a couple of packets of cigarettes. The staff were all from the ward in Worksop as their unit was currently being refurbished and were obviously known to me, and the looks I got clearly suggested they were shocked at seeing me. I was enjoying it already. We were shown into a small interview room and the nurse who let us in hesitated for a while.

'It's okay, I don't need a bodyguard.'

He left but his body language suggested he would have preferred to have been allowed to stay. There was a glass panel in the door and every few minutes a nurse would appear to check that I was still alive.

'I'm really sorry, Min, I really am.'

'Listen, Isabelle, we do need to talk about this but not today.'

'They haven't sectioned me.'

It was difficult, sitting in that room with her, not because she had taken a knife to me twenty-four hours earlier, but because she looked so fragile and there was nothing I could do.

Except hug her.

'Am I going to see you again, Mini?'

'I don't know. I think we both need some space to think about all of this.'

Eventually she was transferred back to Sheffield and I went over a couple of times to meet with her socially. After a while she asked if she could come over and stay for a couple of days. I was a little reticent but in the end I missed her hugs so I agreed. Early that evening she announced that she was feeling a little depressed, which ordinarily wouldn't have set the alarm bells ringing, but on this occasion it did. As soon as she went to bed I raced around the apartment, gathering up knives, forks, utensils, in fact anything that could be used as a weapon, and hid them as best I could, before joining her. But I didn't sleep.

That's when I knew it was over.

The following morning she discovered the cutlery was missing when she made some toast. I came clean and told her I'd hidden them and we both agreed that we couldn't go on like this. She gathered her things together and I saw her to the front door, where we had a very emotional farewell.

Then she was gone and it hurt like hell.

* * * *

I don't know how long I'd been sitting on the sofa for I'd lost track of time as I went through a schizophrenic scale of emotions. Part of me ached for her to come back, part of me was angry with her. A few days later, when I was still in a place I hardly recognised and couldn't put a name to, Franc called.

We discussed the book and after again exchanging ideas we both decided that in its current form the power of the real story had been weakened by my attempt at fictionalising it. I agreed to write it as it deserved to be, a memoir. I had been asked by a number of people over a great many years to write my story and had always steadfastly refused but now I had agreed, not to appease him, it was far simpler than that.

I was ready.

I arranged to meet with him in London and stay a couple of days, a timely intervention, as the busy streets of the metropolis would distract me from the hurt I was feeling. I just wanted to forget for a while and let time do the rest.

Franc and I talked non-stop for a couple of days, exchanging a number of ideas as to how to approach the writing of the book. We were locked into it and at times became increasingly animated. It was a wonderfully creative and inspiring sharing of ideas that had me thinking faster than I could speak, and though at times exhausting it had me thinking in the way I wanted to, productive and concentrated.

As soon as I returned home I got to work immediately. Within a month, having worked without interruption, I had written the prologue along with the opening two chapters and immediately mailed them to Franc to give him a flavour of what was to come. He was extremely upbeat in his assessment and this provided the impetus to fully commit to a project that I knew from the outset would involve more work than I'd previously managed.

The only minor interruption came in the form of a case conference a couple of months after returning from London, where I was unanimously praised for the skilful way I'd dealt with Isabelle's knife-wielding theatrics. I didn't bask in the praise, nor did I welcome it, reiterating that I shouldn't have had to deal with it, and in any event what I did was purely instinctive and there certainly weren't any winners. More significantly, I knew only too well that it would have been a far different story if that phone had switched itself off and my social worker hadn't managed to hear what went on.

The one thing that did significantly change were the general attitudes towards me, they finally believed me. *They finally believed me.*

What a fucking epitaph!

PART FIVE

(45-)

EPILOGUE

It's now been many months since I closed the chapter on both this work and a long and eventful career. Writing has taught me a great many things, for example there is no licence condition to prohibit it, no diagnostic tool to discredit it and no monitoring device to control it. I'm at the controls now and the possibilities are limited only by my own desires and needs. The need to be productive in my own space, in my own time and on my own terms being the most dominant, not conflicting with the pressure to assimilate into society because that's the common expectation.

I'm too old to give in to such feeble aspirations and unwilling to allow history to keep on repeating itself. I have no peers because I never surrendered to them, never understood their need to keep things small and never finding a way of explaining that in a way that might help to explain me. Therefore I am alone, but still intact.

After forty years of locking horns with the authorities I am nevertheless still attached to the state-sponsored umbilical cord and it has an awfully long reach. However, my relationship with both probation and psychiatric services is now the best it's ever been.

I still have a number of legal obligations to fulfil which I do with equanimity because the rest of the time I'm largely left alone and I value that. It's particularly significant now because a couple of years ago my lawyers lodged an appeal against sentence with the European Court of Human Rights, which was recently dismissed.

Therefore now that the legal process has been exhausted, the licence will remain until I no longer do.

Myself and Isabelle seem to have finally and irrevocably managed to extricate ourselves from one another. Strange how, after all the high-octane disputes and intense psychological warfare, we bowed out with a whimper.

My life is currently so quiet and uncomplicated it's hard to imagine it actually belongs to me, harder still to imagine I would swap it.

Finally, I have been asked many times over the years whether I felt I was let down by the system. A two-year old child stewing in its own piss and shit whilst nobody notices, that's a genuine victim.

I, on the other hand, whilst perhaps not consciously choosing this path, nevertheless refused to bend, buckle or allow my nature to become subverted or corrupted. Instead I chose passion over order and whilst it often created chaos, it nevertheless sustained me in ways a counterfeit normality could only stifle. In the process I occasionally got to rock the status quo and question the health of its purpose.

For that alone I am completely without regret.

Not forgetting that should those pompous, arrogant executioners of truth, continue to support and maintain their earlier assessments of me, then I am also unashamedly proud.

*I would like to thank Samantha Hill, Dotti Irving,
Sarah Watson, Alan Yentob, Philippa Walker, Emma Norton,
Dave Wardle, Geoff Turner, Jim Garden
and of course, Franc Roddam.*

They came on board and never flinched.

I would also like to thank Ithaka Roddam for the cover photograph.